How to Kill a Lawsuit

BRIAN TURNER

How to Kill a Lawsuit

Stop A Lawsuit Dead In Its Tracks

How to Kill a Lawsuit

Published in the United States of America

ISBN: 978-1-62902-055-6
1. Law / General
2. Law / Litigation
13.12.11

DEDICATION

This book is dedicated to

David, Daniel, Deborah, and Lynne

DOUBLE BONUS!

- Free $10,000 protection policy with the purchase of this book. (See details inside.)
- This book may be tax deductible. (See details inside.)

Do you know the simplest, easiest, and one of the best ways to protect against lawsuits?

(The answer may surprise you.)

The first ever complete guidebook that teaches you how to beat lawsuits, judgments, creditors, and much more.

Learn a little-known way how to pay no taxes on stock profits—100 percent legal!

How to Kill a Lawsuit will teach you how to turn a potential tragedy into triumph. This easy-to-understand guidebook does not require any legal knowledge. It provides easy steps for complete lawsuit and asset protection.

- What is the simplest and best way to protect against lawsuits? (The answer may surprise you.)
- Learn the latest information on offshore trusts and why you could go to jail for having one.
- Learn how a simple child's trust can save you thousands of dollars each year in taxes.
- Learn how the courts use a special trust to take away your property that most experts don't know about and what you can do to prevent it!
- Learn why sole proprietorships are dangerous.
- Learn why you should never form a general partnership.
- Learn why a one-owner limited liability company will no longer protect you.
- Learn how a creditor can foreclose on your corporation.

- Learn why community property states (like California) are hazardous.
- Learn the secrets that lawyers charge thousands of dollars for.
- This is the most up-to-date and easy-to-understand comprehensive guidebook explaining simple ways to protect against lawsuits and to protect your assets, which requires no legal experience.
- Learn why you should always keep your personal assets separate from your business assets.
- Learn how to protect your home from foreclosure.
- Learn how to protect your home from creditors.
- Learn what types of businesses protect you against lawsuits.
- Learn what types of legal entities discourage lawsuits.
- Learn easy ways to make yourself judgment proof.
- Learn how a "friendly" divorce can protect you from creditors.
- Plus, learn many more lawsuit and asset-protection secrets.
- America has more than fifteen million lawsuits each year, and someday you too will probably be involved in a lawsuit. More people get sued than go to the hospital. This book will help you prepare against a lawsuit.
- Learn how a simple legal agreement in community property states (like California) can save your house in a lawsuit.
- Learn how to secretly and legally hide your money.
- The first ever complete guidebook that teaches you how to defeat lawsuits, judgments, creditors, and more.
- Learn about the lawsuit war that's destroying America and what you need to do to protect yourself.

This is the most complete up-to-date book available in lawsuit and asset protection written for the layperson. No legal experience is needed to use this book. It's simple and easy to use.

Learn the secret, special wording you must have in your legal documents to make them absolutely "bulletproof." There are just a few states in the USA where creditors can't take your home away. Can you name just one of these states? Learn how easy it is to dispose of judgments and how to improve your credit reports and credit scores. Every year one out of six Americans gets sued! Learn how to use foreclosure against your creditors when all else fails.

The first ever complete guidebook that clearly explains how to protect against lawsuits, how to protect your assets, and much more useful information.

$10,000 Maximum Protection Policy Terms and Conditions

The requirements for your $10,000 *maximum* protection policy that applies *only* to a fraudulent conveyance cause of action are as follows:

1. Applies only to a legal transfer and shall not apply to any preexisting lawsuits nor threat of any impending litigation
2. No fraud was involved with your transfer
3. Your transfer created *no* constructive trust
4. Your transfer created *no* resulting trust
5. Statute of limitations for a fraudulent conveyance has run (expired) either by statute or tolled by a court of law whichever is longer
6. You are the original owner (subject to no more than one claim) and have proof of purchase for this book
7. Expiration date (last day to file a claim) is December 31, 2025.

If all of the above conditions are met, then American Lawsuit Protection Services will pay up to $10,000 in legal fees to defend you in the event you are sued for a fraudulent transfer/ conveyance *after* the statute of limitations has run (expired).

The Double Guarantee

- A first of its kind! You get a free $10,000 maximum protection policy with the purchase of this book! (See full details above.)
- The purchase price of this book may be tax deductible. (See details inside.)

If you want to win, you must do it from a position of strength. Lawsuit and asset protection is what you need to win, and this book will give you the tools to win.

DISCLAIMER

Legal information is not legal advice.

This book is designed to inform users about the law, lawsuit protection, and asset protection. It should be noted that legal information is not the same as legal advice. Application of the law to an individual's specific circumstances should always be in consultation with a licensed attorney-at-law. Although the author has gone to great lengths to make sure the information contained in this book is accurate, it is strongly recommended that you consult a licensed and competent attorney if you want professional assurance that this book's information and its application to your particular situation is appropriate. The author and the publisher make no warranties regarding the accuracy of the information in this book. Moreover, the law is rapidly changing in the area of lawsuit and asset protection, and you are strongly encouraged to seek professional advice for current legal information, especially as it applies to your specific circumstances. Please note: legal documents that are filled out incorrectly can invalidate your lawsuit and asset protection plan. You are therefore strongly advised to have a qualified attorney review your legal documents. To locate a lawyer specializing in asset protection, contact the American Bar Association where their service lists over two hundred asset-protection attorneys.

TABLE OF CONTENTS

PREFACE

The primary purpose of this book really boils down to simple altruism: to help you avoid the pain I experienced of losing a home. I learned my lessons in the "school of hard knocks." However, there is a much better way to learn—it's called the school of easy learning—and it begins by reading this book. This book will teach you simple steps you can take right now to protect yourself against lawsuits. I have no ulterior motive behind this book. After you finish reading this book, I will not sell you a legal plan because I am not an attorney. In addition, I will not sell you an insurance policy either because I am not an insurance agent. In fact, I will not sell you anything. My desire is very simple: to help you avoid the problems I once faced with lawsuits and to help you protect your home and other valuable assets from creditors. I also want to teach you how to do this correctly so your protection plan will work. It makes no sense to set up an incorrect plan because this amounts to a "house of cards" in our legal system, and it won't protect you one bit. You need to set up a correct protection plan that will work when you need it most.

Think of this book as a combination reference guide and guidebook, which will guide you along the correct path toward successful lawsuit and asset protection. When reading this guidebook, think of me as your private tutor giving you personalized lessons. Imagine I am talking directly to you, one on one, carefully explaining the concepts of lawsuit protection and asset protection. My expertise comes from over fifteen years of extensive study and personal experience. I will teach you everything I have learned, including the "tricks of the trade" and, of course, the "ropes." I really would prefer to be giving each one of you personalized and undivided attention, but since that is not possible, then this is the next best thing. My sincere hope and desire is that this guidebook will do exactly what it is supposed to do—protect you against lawsuits and, if you are being sued, to protect you from ever losing your home and other valuable assets to creditors. I'm quite certain that if you follow the information contained in this guidebook, then in all likelihood you will achieve a level of protection that for all practical purposes can be considered nearly "judgment proof" or, as I would like to say, "judgment protected." When it comes to lawsuits, no one, not even the best attorneys can give you an absolute 100 percent guarantee. If they do give you a guarantee, then they are not being honest with you, and you should stay clear of them. Realistically, the best anyone can hope for is providing you with a very high degree of certainty that your protection plan will work, which this guidebook seeks to accomplish. Furthermore, I occasionally repeat material, because repetition is one of the best ways to learn.

I have tried to simply explain legal terms and concepts. I confess that some of this material may be difficult to understand. For most readers (who are only interested in general information), you can largely ignore the endnotes in this book. For other readers who may be attorneys or financial professionals, I have generously used endnotes throughout this book citing source information to support the myriad facts and statements contained in this book. For example, I have used many California and Federal statutes, not so much for specifics but to stress legal principles.

Knowledge is power. This guidebook will provide the knowledge and power to protect you against future lawsuits. While there are few guarantees in life, I am quite certain that implementing the recommendations made in this guidebook will provide invaluable and outlasting protection against future lawsuits and will protect you from losing your hard-earned assets to creditors. I have your best interest at heart, and I sincerely endeavor to help you in any way I can. So with that said, let us begin our journey toward lawsuit and asset protection that can be accomplished with surprising ease.

INTRODUCTION

The key question is, when should I begin asset protection? The sooner the better because it is never too late. However, the sad fact is that most people start their asset protection when they get sued. This is a major problem because, by law, you are not permitted to transfer your assets as part of an asset protection plan when you have been sued. Folks, the clear message here is that procrastination could literally cost you your home. You do not even need a lot of net worth to begin your protection plan. Just owning a home, even with little or no equity, is enough to get started with an asset protection plan. The next question is, how much net worth should I have before I start a family limited partnership or even an offshore trust? For a family limited partnership, perhaps as little as $50,000, and for an offshore trust, perhaps $100,000 or more. The expenses for a family limited partnership are relatively small. On the other hand, with regard to offshore planning, if you just want to establish an offshore bank account in your name only, this is very inexpensive and surprisingly easy to do yourself. If you wish to establish an offshore irrevocable trust, the expenses can be as little as $800 per year to several thousand dollars a year. In my opinion, you should probably have liquid assets (money, stocks, bonds, etc.) of at least $100,000 to seriously consider establishing an offshore trust. Based on recent court decisions, I now firmly believe that an offshore trust for your home is significantly better than a family limited partnership although the expenses are substantially more.

To properly prepare for a lawsuit, you need to attain a position of power and strength. This requires proper preparation *before* you are sued. Do not wait until you actually are sued. By then, it is already too late. (It's just like getting a flu shot *after* you get the flu—by then it's already too late.) This guidebook will give you all the necessary information and instructions that you will need to properly prepare against any future lawsuits. When your lawsuit protection plan is fully implemented, then you are in charge. (No pun intended.) Moreover, the emotional stress of a lawsuit is dramatically diminished or even possibly eliminated.

Being hit with a lawsuit is like coming down with a terrible disease. You are going to feel miserable, you are going to lose sleep, and you just might actually get sick. This book is going to help protect you against lawsuits, and metaphorically speaking, it works much like a vaccine to protect you against lawsuits; it's called the "lawsuit vaccine." If you carefully follow the recommendations in this guidebook, it will "immunize" you against lawsuits. For example, let us suppose your doctor gives you a tetanus shot. A few months later, you get a cut on your finger with the germs that cause tetanus. However, thanks to your vaccination, you will not come down with the disease. Even though you may be infected, you will not ever develop the disease. That is truly amazing. Asset protection works much like a vaccine. While you may be sued (which is like being infected), you will not lose your assets (which is like coming down with the disease).

Isn't it about time America wakes up and gets their "lawsuit vaccine"?

Lawsuit and asset protection can be relatively simple and inexpensive. On the other hand, you can also make it complicated and expensive. It's up to you and your advisors to decide. In my opinion, I believe that a good simple plan can work as well as an expensive complicated one. The benefit of a simple plan is that it's easier for the judge to understand it and less likely to perceived as a sham. While the area of asset protection is undergoing rapid change, I have tried to present the latest and most up-to-date information. One further note is that your property transfers can be challenged for several years after they have been made under the fraudulent transfer laws. Finally, to show my appreciation for giving me an opportunity to help you with asset protection planning, I am providing all purchasers of my book with a free $10,000 maximum protection policy. (Please see the applicable terms and conditions stated herein.) That is how confident I am that my guidebook will work for you. Remember, you need to win! Moreover, this book will help you to win.

If it can happen to me, I guarantee it can happen to you. Do you want to lose a lawsuit? Do you want to lose everything you worked so hard for during your lifetime? Do you want to lose your home? Do you want to gamble with unpredictable juries? Do you want to gamble with an unpredictable judge? You have a strong case, but you could lose on a small technicality. Lawsuit protection and asset protection *levels* the playing field!

Now let us look at this from another angle. If you are fully protected, you "win" every time! How can that be? What if I lose the lawsuit? Even if you lose the lawsuit, your opponents cannot collect on their judgment against you. That makes you a "winner." Remember, lawsuits are all about money! The real winner is determined by who gets or keeps the money—either you who keeps the money or your opponents who get your money. When you keep your money and assets that your opponents are unable to get, that actually makes you a "winner" every time. Just think of the tremendous benefits here. First, unlike people who are not fully protected, you will be able to sleep at night, you will not be anxious, and you will not feel insecure. A lawsuit for you will just be a little bump in the road. Oh sure, you will probably be upset. I would be too. However, I certainly would not lose any sleep over it.

When hit with a lawsuit, the very first thing you should do is contact your insurance company. In most cases, your insurance company will handle the lawsuit, and they will tell you not to worry about it. In the few cases where your insurance company won't handle the lawsuit is where asset protection planning comes in. You will either have to retain an attorney or represent yourself. If you retain an attorney, be sure to tell your attorney that you're fully protected against judgments and thatit would be extremely difficult for your opponents to collect on a judgment against you. If you represent yourself, be sure to inform your opponents that they will have a nearly insurmountable task in collecting on a possible future judgment. This information just might stop the lawsuit dead in its tracks. You may have to offer some sort of proof for this. However, once the opposing attorney sees that you are fully protected, I will bet that he or she will get "cold feet," and one way or another the lawsuit against you is somehow going to disappear. This is the main principle of "how to kill a lawsuit."

Whenever you are hit with a lawsuit, your first concern is, am I going to get wiped out by this lawsuit? That is a legitimate concern. In the author's particular case, his attorney assured him, "You won't get wiped out because this case is in limited jurisdiction, and any damages are limited to $25,000." The original arbitration award was $20,000. Nevertheless, the author appealed and went to trial. To make a long story short, the author's lawsuit was eventually transferred to unlimited jurisdiction where there are no limits on damages. The original judgment against him topped $1,000,000! Just ten years later, with accrued interest, the final judgment exceeded $2,000,000! Our legal system is like a crapshoot. Some call it the "lawsuit lottery." Jury verdicts are a "roll of the dice" and are often unpredictable. Some "strong cases" unpredictably get dismissed or settled for pennies on the dollar while some "weak cases" are awarded millions of dollars in damages. Therefore, with lawsuits, there is no way to predict the outcome. In addition, for most people, and I am sure you will agree, that is an unacceptable risk. One of the most laudable goals that everyone should strive for in life is to minimize risk. Wherever possible, regardless of what you do, it is important to minimize risk. For example, when you drive, you should always wear your seat belt and hopefully your car comes equipped with air bags too. These safety devices, in the event of an accident, will help minimize serious injury or death. Metaphorically speaking, your liability insurance is like wearing a seat belt and your asset protection plan is like an automobile air bag. The combination of liability insurance and a good asset protection plan is a formidable barrier against the myriad risks associated with lawsuits. You must have this protection today because the United States is the "lawsuit capital" of the world. Think smart. Act smart. And do the right thing. Use the tools provided in this guidebook for *maximum* protection.

To win, you have to bargain from a position of strength and power, not feigning strength and power, but *real* strength and power. This guidebook is guaranteed to give you the real power and strength to win a lawsuit, and no longer will lawsuits frighten you. They may certainly challenge you. But please do not forget, if you have nothing to lose, that by itself is a victory. It may be a different kind of victory, but by not losing anything of value, you have succeeded in winning. Not protecting yourself against lawsuits is wrong thinking. Implementing a *maximum* protection plan to protect against lawsuits is smart thinking. Military generals will tell you the same thing I am telling you. They inspire their troops in order to boost morale and they do so from a position of power and strength.

"I'm going to sue you!" Then one day the process server hands you a lawsuit, and that is when you have a bad day, probably a real bad day! You will probably be anxious, worried, and depressed because you really could get wiped out by this lawsuit. Well, all of this happened to me plus a lot more. I'm a survivor, and I graduated from the "school of hard knocks," having spent over a decade fighting some of the most ferocious creditors and collections attorneys in the United States and spent well over ten years studying every aspect of the law and spent hundreds of thousands of dollars working with many attorneys to assist with my case. Everything I have learned is contained in this guidebook. My recommendations will help you to fully prepare and handle any future lawsuit and will protect your valuable assets against creditors. I will show you the "ropes," and I will teach you the secrets that creditors do not want you to know.

Your liability insurance provides essential lawsuit protection in most cases. Perhaps about 90 percent of all lawsuits are covered by liability insurance. But that still leaves you vulnerable to the remaining 10 percent. It would be like having a home alarm system hooked up to your house with two doors and eight windows and one of the windows was incorrectly wired to the alarm system. You would be 90 percent protected. But that would leave the other 10 percent unprotected. Would you accept that for your home alarm system? Absolutely not. Then why settle for 90 percent asset protection? You need full and complete protection. Do not settle for less. You need to win. You need to fight a lawsuit from a position of strength. That strength only comes from full and complete protection. Coming in second place is not an option. You need to be the first to cross the finish line. This guidebook will give you all the tools for *maximum* protection. Easy-to-understand recommendations are provided throughout this guidebook. It is simple. It is inexpensive. It is perfectly legal. It makes sense. And it works. Isn't it about time you become a winner? Coming in second place is for the other side. It's not for you. You will never have to fear a lawsuit again. Even if the other side gets a judgment against you, they will never be able to collect on their judgment. That's not winning a lawsuit. It's losing a lawsuit! How can you win a lawsuit without collecting money? The answer is you can't! That makes you a winner every time—even if the other side gets a judgment against you. You actually win every time. Most lawsuits will eventually "dry up" when the other side quickly learns that you are maximally protected. This is one of the best ways to "kill a lawsuit"—become maximally protected! Please explain how getting a judgment against you and not collecting on the judgment is winning a lawsuit? It's not—it's losing a lawsuit!

If this guidebook is used for financial planning, it is probably tax deductible. But be sure to check with your tax advisor or the IRS for an opinion.

This guidebook is the unvarnished, naked truth. I know that some attorneys and asset protection specialists will not like what I have to say, and the US government may also take an exception to what I describe, but nonetheless, I document the truth. What is also known and often hidden is that it is not uncommon for lawyers and government officials to fabricate the truth. Why? Because sometimes the truth is uncomfortable. I am neither an attorney nor a government official. Therefore, there is no conflict of interest regarding any of the material I present in this guidebook. My job is to tell you the facts and the truth. I must also disclose that I have no financial interest at all in any of my recommendations. This is especially the case where I recommend the purchase of plenty of liability insurance. I do not have any financial interest in any insurance company nor do I own any public or private stock in any insurance company. A primary goal of this guidebook is also my unabashed desire for complete objectivity and to provide you with the "straight scoop." One further note, I neither condone nor encourage any criminal activity. There certainly is the potential to use the information here to engage in criminal activity. I strongly recommend that all readers of this guidebook follow and obey all laws, regulations, and rules. I specifically disclaim any responsibility at all for anyone who abuses the information contained in this guidebook and/or commits illegal acts based on the information in this guidebook. I also recommend that before a lawsuit and asset protection plan is initiated that you have it thoroughly reviewed by an attorney, preferably with expertise in asset protection.

Most free asset protection seminars ("road shows") that come to your city have an ulterior motive. It seems the promoters (otherwise known as salesmen or saleswomen) always want to sell you something and usually it is their legal services—a family limited partnership, an offshore trust, or some other legal plan. Moreover, their services are extremely expensive—hundreds of dollars per hour. And don't forget, they always throw in some free gift, like a one-hour free legal consultation or 10 percent off their usual setup fee for some special trust or you can buy a "do-it-yourself" family limited partnership for $1,500 that other lawyers typically charge $5,000 or more. These road shows are really a disguise for self-serving interests and represent a gross conflict of interest. I assure the readers that there is absolutely no conflict of interest in this guidebook. This is a comprehensive guidebook that covers most areas of lawsuit and asset protection and has application to most situations anyone will ever encounter. It is written in simple easy-to-understand language with clear explanations. Legal words are clearly defined, and numerous examples are presented throughout this guidebook to help the reader understand important concepts. No legal experience is required to understand the information in this guidebook.

There are many books on asset protection but few on lawsuit protection. While asset protection is essential to lawsuit protection, more emphasis should be placed on lawsuit prevention because lawsuit-protection planning will prevent many lawsuits. Just like the old saying, an "ounce of prevention is worth a pound of cure." Lawsuit protection is the "ounce of prevention" while asset protection is the "pound of cure." Most asset protection seminars will seldom give you any information about lawsuit protection. Their emphasis is on asset protection, which leads you down the path to their law offices. That's how they make their money. What is not so obvious is that the best and simplest way to protect against lawsuits is rarely if ever discussed at these asset-protection seminars. Why? Because they cannot make any money if they discuss the "best and simplest way" to protect against lawsuits. This guidebook will tell you the secrets—the best and simplest ways to protect against lawsuits—that you will seldom hear at asset-protection seminars.

Many asset-protection seminars advocate plans that are built on a "house of cards," and in due course, your protection plan will quickly unravel. Caveat emptor is apropos for these seminars. The information in this guidebook comes from statutory and decisional law, and it will withstand creditor challenges in the courts, assuming you follow the letter of the law. This is the real thing, folks! The information in this guidebook will give you the protection and peace of mind that you need in today's litigious society.

The protection plans espoused in this guidebook are predicated on having multiple layers of protection and using multiple methods to spread income, shift income, using Family Limited Partnerships (FLPs), using trusts, using Limited Liability Companies (LLCs), using corporations, and having plenty of insurance to protect against lawsuits. When all of these methods are integrated and used appropriately, you will have reached the pinnacle of lawsuit protection and asset protection. You will be judgment protected or, as some would say, "judgment proof." Believe me, you will not be able to do better than this. And what happens if you do get sued? By all means, do not panic! Remember, you hold the cards (not the "house of cards"), and you control the lawsuit. The plaintiffs will eventually learn this the hard way when they discover their judgment is only worth the piece of paper it is printed on.

All the asset protection seminars I have been to (and that's been quite a lot), have never once mentioned the little-known resulting trust. This guidebook is the first to clearly and fully explain to the public what a resulting trust is and how it can financially cripple you.

Most asset protection books state that "secrecy is not asset protection." I disagree and here's why: there's an old adage "loose lips, sink ships" so take heed. It applies equally as well here. For example, if you had a stash of money in your home and told others about it, I guarantee that eventually you would be a victim of a home-invasion robbery. If you did not give up your cash, you could get yourself killed. Obviously then, the best thing to do is to keep your mouth shut and keep it a secret. (If you do have a lot of cash in your home, there's a better place for it, like the bank, especially an offshore bank.)

In my opinion, all states should follow the lead of Florida and Texas by extending their homestead exemptions for unlimited protection so people won't be forced to lose their homes to creditors because of honest mistakes that they may have made. Personal exempt property limits have not kept up with inflation for decades and are obsolete. Most wage earners are barely able to provide for their families. A 25 percent wage garnishment could literally starve some families. Is it fair to starve children who aren't responsible for their parents' mistakes? Why penalize children for a verdict that one of their parents is responsible for? Wage garnishments can often be reduced or eliminated by obtaining a "friendly" divorce with court-ordered family support payments or alimony, which under federal law preempts wage garnishments. What happens if the debtor gets an unsympathetic judge who also happens to be a creditor? Our laws are antiquated and a spillover from nineteenth-century England where Charles Dickens was once put in prison for his debts! Only recently did the US Supreme Court rule that debtor's prisons are unconstitutional. And that ruling was made just recently! Here is my major life philosophy: Think smart! Act smart! And do the right thing! The right thing to do now is for you to take proactive steps to protect yourself against lawsuits!

Some experts say there are no cookbook instructions for asset protection and each case must be individualized. I beg to differ. I believe most people can benefit from the "boilerplate" instructions set forth in this guidebook with perhaps some minor variations. Most people using this guidebook will be just fine following my recommendations. The boilerplate or cookie-cutter approach really does work for most people despite arguments to the contrary. There's no need to reinvent the wheel. The use of a system that works and works well and has survived numerous court challenges is a system you definitely want and need to use. It will provide peace of mind, and just as importantly, it will work the way it was designed—to protect you against lawsuits and to protect your hard-earned valuable assets.

Emotions often interfere with sound decision making. That's why it's a good idea to start your asset-protection planning well before you're hit with a lawsuit. Your decision-making skills will be much better as you'll be more relaxed and not fighting a lawsuit. Moreover, during a lawsuit, most transfers you make will be construed as a fraudulent conveyance.

Little mistakes can have disastrous consequences in your life. Take for example a true incident that occurred many years ago to a young woman driver who happened to look down momentarily when a tape cassette slipped out of her hand and fell onto her car floor. In just a matter of seconds without noticing, her car veered off the road and she ended up killing a bystander. Similarly, a little mistake can "kill" your protection plan. The law is strict and most judges are always on the lookout and ever suspicious of fraud against creditors. Many judges will try to find ways to unravel your protection plan. It's therefore critical that you strictly follow the law when you set up your protection plan. That's why a licensed attorney with expertise in asset protection, business law, or real estate should review your asset protection plan. Please don't overlook this critical step.

Liability insurance is not foolproof. There are certain exclusions in every policy. Just read the fine print. Therefore, liability insurance needs to be supplemented with a lawsuit protection plan to give you *maximum* protection. The supplementation is where asset protection comes in. It fills the void left behind in situations where liability insurance doesn't cover a claim. Good liability insurance with a strong asset protection plan is a formidable fortress that will give you nearly *full and complete* protection against lawsuits. Remember, a judgment that can't be collected or satisfied in any way is really a lawsuit that has been lost. Many good attorneys know this. By being fully protected, you'll be able to stop most lawsuits dead in their tracks. That's the whole idea on "how to kill a lawsuit."

You'll learn important and critical information in my guidebook that's very difficult to find elsewhere, which even most experts don't know! For example, suppose your asset protection plan has transferred your home to a limited liability company but naturally you continue to make the mortgage payments. Guess what? A court can use a little-known trust to take away your home!

Beginning asset-protection planning during a lawsuit is tricky, and it's the last thing you want to be doing. You might even feel like you're being chased by the plaintiffs, always trying to stay one step in front of them. Then there's the worry that all of your plans may be undone by a court for a fraudulent conveyance. Folks, please heed my strong advice. Begin your asset-protection planning well before your hit with a lawsuit. In addition, the new bankruptcy laws now make it more difficult to get a discharge of all of your debts. Bankruptcy is no longer the panacea that it used to be. You can no longer expect bankruptcy to come to your rescue. You must take immediate steps now to begin your protection planning, especially if you want full protection. You can begin this protection plan so long as (1) you have not been threatened with a lawsuit, (2) you don't have a pending lawsuit against you, and (3) you don't have any existing creditors. If all three of these conditions apply to you, then you must start now. There's no need to rush but neither should you procrastinate. You can implement your protection plan while you're relaxed and not under any pressure or threat of litigation. It's the best time to start, and best of all you won't be committing a fraudulent conveyance and your protection plan will withstand any legal challenges. Trust me, it's one of the best pieces of advice you'll ever get in life.

Begin your protection plan during a quiescent period. Once you've been threatened with a lawsuit or have a pending lawsuit or current creditors, any transfers you make are fraudulent transfers which could (1) be unwound by the court, (2) face you with criminal charges, (3) subject you to monetary damages including punitive damages, (4) make you liable for the creditor's attorney fees, and (5) prevent you from getting a discharge in bankruptcy.

Keep your protection plan simple and back it up with good reasoning. It's also quite important to have a good reason why the transfers you make are in furtherance of your estate planning. If you fail to satisfactorily explain this to the court, you could have problems; if your protection plan is too complicated and poorly explained, there's a high likelihood the judge won't understand it, and a bad ruling will be made against you. There's also a good chance that the judge will find that you defrauded the creditors. Indeed, the best asset protection plans are simple and straight forward plans, such as an irrevocable trust set up for the benefit of your children.

There are some individuals who are crusaders, vigilantes, or activists; and if you're one of them, then you're at a very high risk of a lawsuit, and it's absolutely imperative that you take immediate steps to protect yourself now. If you like to teach people a lesson and your attitude is "let them sue me, I won't give them a dime," then this guidebook is for you. But first make sure you are indeed judgment protected before embarking on your crusade!

If you don't have a protection plan in place, you're playing Russian roulette with your finances and assets. Remember, little mistakes can have big consequences. Asset protection is legal according to the US Supreme Court provided it doesn't run afoul of the fraudulent conveyance laws.[1]

Contact your state or local bar association for a lawyer who specializes in asset protection. This is a field where you want to get good advice. Surprisingly, many lawyers know very little about asset protection. Stay clear of attorneys who are just general practitioners. There's an old saying: a little bit of knowledge can be dangerous. This applies to asset protection. Most general attorneys know very little about asset protection. They could give you bad advice, which would then make your asset protection plan essentially a "house of cards." It would never survive a creditor attack. Your best bet is to deal with an expert in asset protection planning. Would you go to a pediatrician to have surgery to remove a brain tumor? Of course not. Pay for some good advice from an asset protection lawyer before you begin your asset protection planning. It's money well spent. Remember, asset protection is to protect your property, not to save you income taxes, and it's not about tax planning. Also, a good asset protection plan will work well in all fifty states, even though each state may have different laws that dictate how much a creditor can get from a judgment.

And finally for those of you who say, "It can't happen to me, I won't get sued," my response is don't be so presumptuous to think that you are somehow immune from lawsuits. Just driving an automobile puts you at substantial risk for a lawsuit. What if you say something bad about someone and get sued for slander? What if someone trips and falls with serious injuries on your property? What about an employee of yours who makes a serious mistake and you end up getting sued under the legal doctrine of respondeat superior? Folks, the list goes on and on. Some of you might argue that this is just too complicated to understand and so you just put it off. My response is that a lot of people take vitamin pills, but few really understand how vitamins work. Here's the bottom line: however you might feel about not needing a protection plan, you must simply have one because the risk of not having a protection plan is just too great. By the way, it really is not complicated at all. This guidebook clearly explains how to set up a protection plan, even a low-cost plan that works well for most people. Offshore trusts are more expensive to operate, but seldom are they required for most people. Only if you have a high net worth or desire maximum protection is an offshore trust worthy of consideration. Let's begin, and I'll show you how to get started. It's really very simple.

THE US LAWSUIT EXPLOSION

The US Constitution ensures that everyone, including foreigners, is able to seek justice through the US court system if they believe they have been wronged. There are now more lawsuits in the United States than any other place in the world. The United States is the lawsuit capital of the world.

According to the *Economic Journal*, Americans spend more money on lawsuits than any other country in the world, and twice as much on lawsuits than on new automobiles.

In the United States, the losing party does not have to pay the winner's attorney's fees. However, in most European countries, the loser in a lawsuit must pay most of the winner's legal fees. This is one reason why the United States has so many lawsuits.

In 2002, over sixteen million lawsuits were filed in state courts across America and trial lawyers earned an estimated forty billion dollars, according to the State Court Guide to Statistical Reporting. The good news, if any, is that the number of state lawsuits for 2011 is estimated to have fallen to fifteen million. In 2011, there were 289,252 federal civil cases filed in the US District Courts according to Judicial Business of the US Courts.

What is the chance that you might get sued sometime in the next year? Some of you who may have read other asset-protection books might quote a well-known author who says you have a one in five chance of being sued next year. But let's look at the statistics to see if this is an accurate figure. Today, the estimated population for the United States as of November 2012 was 314,789,023 with 25 percent of that total estimated to be under eighteen years of age.[2] Children under age eighteen seldom get sued, and if they do, it's their parents or legal guardian who is ultimately responsible. That leaves about 236 million adults. Over the past ten years, the number of lawsuits has hovered around fifteen to sixteen million. Dividing 236 million adults by 15.5 million lawsuits works out to about a 6.5 percent (or one out of fifteen) chance of getting sued sometime in the next twelve months. Folks, don't believe everything you read; and in my opinion, authors should be required to back up their statistics. If you see a statistic that isn't referenced to a verifiable source take it with a "grain of salt."

Tort (personal injury) litigation now costs the United States more than an estimated $250 billion.[3]

In 2010, there were 1,225,452 lawyers in the United States, according to the American Bar Association Market Research Department—more per capita than any other country. That's approximately one attorney for every 254 Americans! According to the Bureau of Labor Statistics, in May 2010, the national wage estimate calculated the mean annual salary for lawyers at around $129,440.

Approximately one out of every six jury awards is for more than $1 million, and more than 7 percent of US companies have paid out more than $5 million in the past five years.[4]

The largest jump in lawsuits has recently occurred in the health-care industry where doctors have been steadily paying higher malpractice premiums to defend against potential litigation. According to a Harris Poll, nearly four out of five doctors report that they've ordered more tests than they normally would due to litigation fears. Nearly half of US hospitals reported that the lawsuit crisis has caused a loss of physicians and cutbacks in emergency rooms.

Most people believe they won't be sued. Unfortunately, that's not the case. Over 40 percent of people involved in auto accidents in 1997 retained a lawyer, and a decent-sized judgment can easily devastate a person's finances.

Lawsuits can happen to anyone. For example, a fourteen-year-old sues her friend for losing her iPod, the music industry sues a twelve-year-old for illegally downloading music from the Internet, and lawyers sue fast-food restaurants and snack food manufacturers for making us fat.

According to former US Alabama Congressman Terry Everett, frivolous lawsuits alone are estimated to cost two hundred billion dollars a year. According to a Harris Interactive Poll, more than three out four people surveyed feel that the fear of frivolous lawsuits discourages people from performing normal activities. Additionally, six out of seven people don't trust the legal system to protect them against frivolous lawsuits, and over half don't trust the legal system at all. Over three out four Americans surveyed agree that the court system is used by many people as a lawsuit lottery to start a lawsuit and see just how much they can win.

For over two hundred years the contingency fee system has allowed Americans to go to court who otherwise could not afford to pay the legal fees to obtain representation. The contingency fee system is most often used in personal injury and death cases, and the usual fee is based on a percentage of any monetary damages that are recovered—commonly 33 percent for cases that settle without a trial and 40 percent for cases that are resolved after a trial.

The Volunteer Protection Act of 1997 was passed to provide immunity for volunteers of nonprofits in the course of their charity work.[5]

Over sixteen million lawsuits are filed every year in the United States. California is one of the most litigious states in the nation. Nearly 1.4 million lawsuits are filed every year in California. It almost seems like everyone is suing someone else. Even a child can sue and be sued as well. Children, unlike adults, need to be represented by a guardian; it's called "guardian ad litem." Most contracts signed by a minor can be repudiated—declared null and void.

In 2010, Israel had the most attorneys in the world on a per capita basis—585 attorneys per 100,000 according to Israel's Courts Administration. America is number 2 at about 377 attorneys per 100,000.

Forum shopping is the practice by some litigants to have their legal case heard in a court that most likely will provide them with a favorable judgment. Some states, for example, are notorious as plaintiff-friendly jurisdictions and many lawsuits are filed in their jurisdictions even though there is little or no connection between the legal issues and the jurisdiction in which they are to be litigated.

In 2009, a lawsuit in New York succeeded in vacating over one hundred thousand credit card lawsuits on the basis of process-server fraud. Process-server fraud occasionally occurs, especially with debt collection and credit card lawsuits. The process server sometimes throws the lawsuit (summons and complaint) in the bushes, and if you're lucky, you'll eventually find the papers. In most other cases, your lawsuit is thrown in a dumpster, and the process server lies outright signing his name to an affidavit swearing you got served. Then one day, assuming the court papers don't get lost in the mail or aren't misaddressed, you discover a default judgment against you because you failed to answer your lawsuit.

Here's what happened in New York in April 2009: "Gutter service" describes a process server who delivers lawsuits (or lack thereof) on behalf of debt collection law firms and credit card companies. The problem is that the process server is not making the delivery. He's supposed to serve a defendant with a summons and complaint in accordance with the law but discards the papers usually in the trash and then falsely swears in an affidavit or declaration of service that he served the papers properly. Debt collection law firms cut ruthless deals with process servers, paying on average about six dollars for each lawsuit served. For such low rates, these law firms give the process server continuous business with up to hundreds of lawsuits a day to serve. Before long, the process server figures a better way to enhance his earning potential. Rather than drive around all day long and chasing people down to hand them a lawsuit, it makes more sense to throw the papers in a dumpster and falsely swear that the papers were properly served.

In April 2009, William Singler, the owner of American Legal Process in Lynbrook, New York, was arrested on charges of fraud and other felonies relating to illegal service of process. The indictment alleged that many process servers used by American Legal Process routinely and knowingly prepared false affidavits of service and falsely swearing that they properly served the lawsuit. In some cases, the affidavits showed that the process server was at two or more different locations at the same time! American Legal Process left thousands of New Yorkers completely unaware that credit card lawsuits had been filed against them or that a default judgment had been entered against them. That was until they learned their bank accounts were levied on or their paychecks garnished. Fortunately, a New York Supreme Court judge vacated all the default judgments.

What if this happens to you, a default judgment based on your never having received the lawsuit? A default judgment in these circumstances is relatively simple to vacate by an attorney.

You should notify an attorney as soon as you discover that a default judgment as been erroneously entered against you.

There's the ever-present threat of lawsuits. Humans are not perfect, thus they make mistakes and are always vulnerable to lawsuits. One lawsuit can literally wipe you out. What took you a lifetime to accumulate can be completely wiped out with one lawsuit. Don't be foolish and dismiss this as some remote possibility, something that happens to others. No matter how careful you are, you're going to make mistakes. And those mistakes can lead to a lawsuit. Preparation is your best tool. The United States is the lawsuit capital of the world. More lawsuits are filed in the United States than anywhere else in the world. With over sixteen million lawsuits filed every year in America, there is a strong likelihood that someday you will be hit with a lawsuit. When it happens, it will be a very unnerving experience. In some instances, people have fainted, had strokes, had heart attacks, and even had panic attacks. But this doesn't have to happen to you. I give you my highest assurances that if you follow the recommendations set forth in this guidebook, you'll essentially be fully protected from any significant devastation that could result from a lawsuit. There won't be any need for you to panic. I'll explain later exactly what you need to do and exactly how to handle the lawsuit.

In order to protect yourself from lawsuits, you have to prepare. But the timing of your preparation is critical to success. The law, with extremely few exceptions, prohibits you from engaging in lawsuit and asset protection once you are involved in a lawsuit. If you haven't planned ahead, then it's already too late (in the vast majority of cases) once you're involved in a lawsuit. Therefore, you must, and I stress the word *must*, begin the process of lawsuit and asset protection well before any lawsuit begins or is even threatened.

The lawsuit crisis in America has reached epidemic proportions and most Americans will eventually get sued. It's absolutely essential that you prepare before you get sued. Otherwise, it will be too late. You really can lose everything you worked so hard for over a lifetime in just a very short period of time. This guidebook will help you fight lawsuits and keep what is yours.

No matter how hard you try in life, you're going to make many mistakes. Unfortunately, in the United States there are many vindictive people who will sue you for just one of those mistakes. A lawsuit is therefore always lurking around the corner.

Jury trials are often unpredictable, and the verdict could instantly wipe out your life savings. You must take steps right now to protect yourself against a potentially devastating lawsuit. This guidebook will provide you with clear, simple, and concise instructions to give you *maximum* protection against lawsuits. It is my humble privilege to be able to help you become fully protected against lawsuits. No one should lose their home to creditors. This is truly barbaric and evil and spills over from medieval times.

SHOCKING LAWSUITS

Jury verdicts are often unpredictable. Strong cases are occasionally lost due to technical errors, misreading the jury, and unrealistic expectations. On the other hand, weak cases can sometimes yield large jury awards if the jury wants to teach someone a lesson. Our legal system is often referred to as a giant crapshoot. There's the famous McDonald's lawsuit, which resulted in a multimillion-dollar verdict for an old lady who was partially responsible for spilling hot coffee on herself. Most people simply can't understand how a jury would return such a large verdict for spilling coffee. It turns out there's more to the story.

The McDonald's Spilled-Coffee Lawsuit—What Really Happened? [6]

Ms. Stella Liebeck sustained third degree burns—the most severe—to her groin, inner thighs, and buttocks. She was hospitalized for eight days, during which time she underwent skin grafting and debridement treatments. She was in severe pain. Ms. Liebeck attempted to settle her claim with McDonald's for $20,000, but they refused. She eventually filed suit. Her lawsuit discovered that McDonald's was keenly aware of the "hot-coffee" problem. McDonald's produced documents showing more than seven hundred claims by people who were burned by its hot coffee between 1982 and 1993; some involving third degree burns similar to Ms. Liebeck. This history documented McDonald's knowledge about the extent and nature of this hazard. Whereas other fast-food restaurants kept their coffee at 165 °F, McDonald's routinely kept theirs at 185 °F. McDonald's own quality assurance manager testified that a burn hazard exists with any food that is served above 140 °F. McDonald's was repeatedly warned that their coffee was too hot. Several lawsuits were filed, and many complaints were made from people who scalded themselves with hot coffee. That's because

McDonald's set their coffee temperature at 185°F whereas the minimum requirement for fast-food restaurants was just 165°F. In fact, most other fast-food restaurants kept their coffee temperature at 165°F. When the jury learned that McDonald's failed to lower their coffee temperature despite repeated lawsuits based on previous injuries from excessively hot coffee temperatures, they decided to act. The jury decided to teach McDonald's a lesson. They handed down a multimillion-dollar verdict against McDonald's, not so much as to reward the old lady who burned herself but to punish McDonald's and teach them a lesson.

A jury awarded Ms. Liebeck $200,000 in compensatory damages but reduced it to $160,000 because they found her 20 percent at fault for the spill (contributory negligence). The jury also awarded her $2,700,000 in punitive damages, equal to two days of McDonald's coffee sales. This was eventually reduced to $480,000, even though the judge called McDonald's conduct reckless, callous, and willful. In lieu of an appeal, Ms. Liebeck and McDonald's eventually settled the lawsuit for an undisclosed amount. Now that you know the rest of the story, the jury award doesn't seem so outrageous.

So occasionally, the jury may want to teach the defendant a lesson and award the plaintiff a windfall judgment. You might be asking at this point what measures are available to avoid jury trials and have the judge decide the case. It is certainly true that landslide awards are seldom handed down by judges. However, to have a judge decide the lawsuit including the verdict, both sides need to make the request. All it takes for a jury trial is a request by just one of the parties to the lawsuit, either plaintiff or defendant. Many plaintiffs opt for a jury trial.

Sue the Pants Off Them Lawsuit [7]

A judge sued a dry cleaner for $50 million for losing his business suit. The dry cleaning establishment offered to settle the lawsuit, but the judge refused the settlement offer. When it was all over, the judge's lawsuit was thrown out of court. Here are the details of this bizarre case:

Pearson v. Chung is the infamous case known as the "pants lawsuit." This was a lawsuit filed in 2005 by Judge Roy L. Pearson, Jr., an administrative law judge in the District of Columbia in the United States over a pair of pants that a dry cleaner supposedly lost. Pearson sued the DC dry cleaning establishment, Custom Cleaners, for over $67 million for what he claimed was the loss of a pair of pants. On May 3, 2005, Pearson allegedly left a pair of gray pants that could be distinguished by a unique trio of belt loops on both sides of the front waistband. The judge's pants were mistakenly sent to another dry cleaner. After a couple of days delay, the pants were offered back to the judge. However, Judge Pearson refused to accept the pants claiming they were not his despite confirmation by the cleaner's records, tags, and the judge's receipt. Judge Pearson demanded to be compensated for the price of the pants, an amount of over $1,000, which the Chungs refused at first. As a result, Judge Pearson filed a lawsuit in the District of Columbia's Superior Court. The case went to trial on the basis of two of Judge Pearson's claims. The first claim concerned the issue of the ownership of the pants. The second claim was on the issue of signs posted outside the business advertising "Same Day Service" and "Satisfaction Guaranteed," which Judge Pearson claimed to be misleading.

Over time, the Chungs presented three settlement offers in the amounts of $3,000, $4,600, and $12,000, all of which were rejected by Judge Pearson.

The owners of the business, South Korean immigrants Jin Nam Chung, Soo Chung, and their son Ki Chung were considering moving back to South Korea. They put their plans on hold after a website was set up to accept donations for the Chungs' legal defense.

On May 30, 2007, Judge Pearson reduced his damages to $54 million rather than $67 million. Among his damages were $500,000 in attorney's fees, $2 million for "discomfort, inconvenience, and mental distress," and $15,000, which he claimed would be the cost to rent a car every weekend to drive to another dry cleaning service.

The remaining $51.5 million would be used to help other dissatisfied DC consumers sue businesses. Judge Pearson also redirected his lawsuit from the missing pants to seek removal of window signs for "Satisfaction Guaranteed" and "Same Day Service." Judge Pearson claimed the signs were fraudulent. The Chungs' lawyer, Christopher Manning, denied that the signs were fraudulent and portrayed Judge Pearson as a bitter, financially insolvent man. At trial, Judge Pearson admitted that he had only $1,000 to $2,000 in the bank due to divorce proceedings and was collecting unemployment.

Judge Pearson's case went to trial in June 2007, and he lost. The verdict was in favor of the Chungs. Moreover, a DC commission voted against reappointing Judge Pearson to his administrative judicial post with a salary of $100,512 because he lacked the necessary "judicial temperament." On May 2, 2008, Judge Pearson filed suit against Washington DC claiming that he had been wrongfully terminated for exposing corruption within the Office of Administrative Hearings. Judge Pearson sought $1 million in compensation for lost wages and punitive damages as well as his job back, claiming that his termination was retaliation for filing suit against the Chungs. On July 23, 2009, federal district Judge Ellen Segal Huvelle dismissed Pearson's May 2008 lawsuit claiming that the District of Columbia had not broken the law by not reappointing him as an administrative law judge. Judge Pearson lost his appeal when the DC Circuit ruled against him on May 27, 2010.

The Chungs attempted to recover $83,000 in attorneys' fees and impose sanctions but withdrew their motion after recovering their costs through fund-raising. The Chungs sought sanctions in an attempt to pressure Judge Pearson to stop litigating. But it didn't work. On August 14, 2007, Pearson filed a notice of appeal to his lawsuit against the Chungs.

On December 18, 2008, a three-judge panel of the DC Court of Appeals that heard Judge Pearson's appeal announced they were rejecting it. But Judge Pearson wasn't finished yet. On January 6, 2009, Judge Pearson filed a petition with the DC Court of Appeals, requesting an *en banc* hearing this time by the full nine-judge panel.

On March 2, 2009, the DC Court of Appeals rejected his request to have the case reheard by the full panel. Judge Pearson's final option was to ask the US Supreme Court to hear the case. The ninety-day deadline for seeking Supreme Court review elapsed without Judge Pearson filing a petition for *certiorari*. Judge Pearson's appeal options thus exhausted, the long-running dispute finally came to an end.

Chris Manning, the attorney for the Chung family, stated that the experience for the Chungs has become the "American nightmare"—an ironic reference to the American Dream. Citing a loss of revenue and emotional strain from the lawsuit, the Chungs announced on September 19, 2007, that they have closed and sold the dry cleaning shop involved in the dispute. The Chungs still own one additional dry cleaning shop and have stated they will be focusing their attention and resources on their remaining shop.

The "Wrongful Life" Lawsuit

Here's a story from the city of New York, and I think you will understand why so many doctors are worried about frivolous lawsuits.

Nancy DiGeronimo is a devout Jehovah's Witness. Because of her religious convictions, she will not accept blood transfusions. Unfortunately, during childbirth, Ms. DiGeronimo had severe complications and nearly died in the delivery room. Her obstetrician, Dr. Allen Fuchs, ultimately had to transfuse blood to save her and the baby. Dr. Fuchs says she consented, and her husband signed a consent form. Ms. DiGeronimo says she doesn't remember consenting to the blood transfusion.

Afterwards, Ms. DiGeronimo sued Dr. Fuchs for saving her life and that of her baby. It took five long years of litigation before the judge finally threw out the lawsuit. The judge said, "The plaintiff's argument, taken to its logical conclusion, is that the doctor should have allowed her to die rather than give her an 'allogenic' blood transfusion. Since the plaintiff's transfusion saved her life, this action is analogous to one for 'wrongful life' against the doctor.

However, there is no cause of action for 'wrongful life' in the State of New York."[8]

This story is an exemplar of the fact that people in high risk occupations need to worry about lawsuits, and they need to protect themselves. One can only obtain so much insurance and try to anticipate so many risks. Asset protection is a necessary evil in our litigious society.

The Oprah Winfrey Lawsuit [9]

Texas Cattlemen vs. Howard Lyman and Oprah Winfrey:

This was the first lawsuit to test "Food Slander" laws. The original trial was in February 1998 in Amarillo, Texas. The April 1998 verdict was for Oprah and Howard and was appealed to the Fifth Circuit Court by Cactus Feeders, et al. A unanimous decision upheld the trial court verdict. A "rehearing" was denied. Another suit was then filed in State Court by Cactus Feeders, et al., which was identical to the previously decided in Federal Court. Howard then removed the case from State Court to Federal Court (as he is not a resident of Texas and this is his right under law). On August 27, 2002, a federal judge dismissed the case with prejudice, effectively ending the case.

Here's what started the lawsuit: In April of 1996, Mr. Lyman (former cattle rancher and now president, Voice for a Viable Future) appeared on Oprah to discuss mad cow disease, food production, and the rendering process. When Mr. Lyman explained that cows are being fed to cows, Oprah exclaimed that it had just stopped her cold from eating another hamburger.

The Oprah show aired on a Monday, and beef futures—which had been in a steep decline due to drought, oversupply, and a number of complex factors—fell further on Tuesday, the "Oprah crash." The cattle industry was apparently outraged.

A short time later, some Texas cattlemen, led by billionaire Paul Engler, owner of Cactus Feeders, Inc., filed suit against Oprah and Lyman. The lawsuit alleged Lyman and Oprah had violated a Texas law, which forbids someone from "knowingly making false statements" about agricultural business. The cattlemen have alleged that Oprah is responsible for the decline in beef futures.

On February 29, 1998, a Texas jury found Howard Lyman and Oprah Winfrey not liable for comments made on the national show about eating beef.

Thirteen states, including Texas, have passed laws designed to silence and intimidate anyone who exposes unsafe and unhealthy factory farm and slaughterhouse practices. These so-called "food disparagement" laws make it a crime to criticize food and how it is produced.

All in all, frivolous lawsuits cost American businesses over $865 billion per year, according to the Pacific Research Institute. That's a whole 2.2 percent of the United States' annual GDP spent on tort costs, compared to the United Kingdom's 0.8 percent and Japan's 0.8 percent.

The state of Mississippi recently passed a bill that puts a cap on non-economic damage (e.g. pain and suffering) awards at $500,000. California has a non-economic damage cap at $250,000. Despite these advances, frivolous lawsuits will continue to plague American courts for the foreseeable future. To protect yourself, obtain and maintain sufficient liability and umbrella insurance. Also, run your business in a corporation. Furthermore, you should routinely check your business for any potential hazards and fix them, no matter how slight. Do your absolute best to make sure that your employees and partners are people you can trust. Lastly, watch what you say. Personal and non-contractual agreements may come back to haunt you.10

The "Eenie, Meenie, Miny, Mo" Lawsuit[11]

In 2003, two women sued Southwest Airlines after a flight attendant said, "Eenie, meenie, miny, mo, pick a seat, it's time to go." They claimed that the attendant was racist since one version of the rhyme contained a racial slur, a fact the attendant, who was merely trying to be cute, was unaware of. The judge dropped the case.

Make Annoying Phone Calls and Lose Your Home Lawsuit

There was even a lawsuit in California where the defendant was accused of making annoying phone calls (which were actually business calls), and he eventually lost his home.

Breasts Were Like "Cement Blocks" Lawsuit [12]

A Florida therapist claimed that he suffered mental and physical pain at his bachelor party after a lap dancer's large breasts, which he stated were like "cement blocks," struck him during her dance. He then sued for $15,000—on People's Court, of all places—and lost.

The Repaint Job Lawsuit [13]

An Alabama man who discovered that parts of his new BMW had been repainted by the dealership to conceal damage from acid rain was awarded over $2 million in damages.

The Jackass Lawsuit [14]

A Montana man who changed his name to Jack Ass in 1997 sued Viacom, the makers of the TV show Jackass, claiming defamation of character. He sued for $10 million to regain his reputation. The case was dismissed.

The McDonald's Milk Shake Lawsuit [15]

In 1993, a New Jersey man spilled a McDonald's milk shake that he had between his legs while driving as he was reaching into the passenger seat to get the rest of the meal out of the bag. He claimed that McDonald's should have warned him about the dangers of eating while driving. He lost.

The Biggest Lawsuit Winner of 1998 [16]

The biggest lawsuit winner in 1998 was Russian inventor Anatoly Sverdlin. A Texas state court awarded him $1.5 billion after his business partners forced him out of a company he founded.

The $250 Million Starvation Lawsuit [17]

Bryan Sellers, eighty, was dying of emphysema and so his daughter placed him in a nursing home in Bedford, Texas. The nursing home starved Mr. Sellers. A jury found that he died from malnutrition and awarded his daughter $250 million, the largest verdict against a nursing home.

Jury awards exceeding $50 million have become so commonplace. "Now, you can have a $50 million award and it is not even in the newspaper," said Victor Schwartz, general counsel to the American Tort Reform Association.

The Ford Ranger Rollover Accident Lawsuit [18]

Punitive damages made up $120 million of the $144.9 million verdict in a Ford Ranger rollover accident in Jackson, Mississippi.

The $525 Million North Carolina Rapist Lawsuit [19]

There was even a $525 million verdict against an imprisoned North Carolina rapist, but it's unlikely the victim will ever see a dime because the defendant is imprisoned for life and has no way to pay.

Experts admit such outrageous verdicts usually are reduced on appeal or by settlement.

The Bubbles Lawsuit [20]

Early on the morning of July 7, 2001, a prankster dumped detergent into Canal Park's Fountain of Wind in Duluth, Minn., that formed a mountain of bubbles. Later that morning, passerby Kathy Kelly walked into the suds and slipped into the fountain, sustaining a laceration to her left lower shin. Due to her diabetes the cut later became infected, resulting in a $43,000 medical bill. Kelly sued the city because it had not cleaned up the suds or posted warning signs, despite the fact that municipal workers had received a telephone call 4 hours earlier concerning the hazard. In March 2004, a jury found the city 70 percent responsible and Kelly 30 percent responsible for the injury, awarding $125,000 to Kelly. The fountain is now encircled by a railing.

Blame the School Lawsuit [21]

For many Americans, joblessness is an unfortunate side effect of a bad economy. New York native Trina Thompson, on the other hand, blamed her unemployment on the school she attended. In 2009, the 27-year-old sued her alma mater, Monroe College, for $72,000 when she was unable to find a job three months after graduating with a bachelor's degree in information technology. Thompson blamed the school's Office of Career Advancement for not working hard enough to place her in a job after graduation, despite her solid attendance record and a 2.7 grade point average. According to the lawsuit filed in the Bronx Supreme Court, Thompson sought to recoup the $70,000 she had spent in tuition, plus $2,000 for the stress of her job search.

The Trespasser's Lawsuit [22]

It's mind boggling to believe that anyone could win a lawsuit for being injured while trespassing on someone else's property. But that's exactly what happened to two Lancaster, Pa., teens who were severely burned atop a parked railroad car in 2002. While out skateboarding, Jeffrey Kline and Brett Birdwell illegally entered property owned by Amtrak and Norfolk Southern Corp. and climbed on top of a boxcar in order to get a view of the city. An exposed electrical wire suspended above the train jolted Klein with 12,500 volts of electricity, causing severe burns over 75 percent of his body. Birdwell received burns over 12 percent of his body when he ran to assist his friend, whose clothes were on fire. In the October 2006 trial, a jury declared that, although they were indeed trespassing, the 17-year-old boys bore no responsibility for the accident. Instead the blame fell entirely on Amtrak and Norfolk Southern for failing to post signs warning of the danger from the exposed electrified wires that power the locomotives. For medical costs, pain and suffering, and "loss of life pleasures," the teens received a combined award of $24.2 million.

Blame the Restaurant Lawsuit [23]

In 2009, 20-year-old Chelsea Hess met some friends at a sports grill in Bluffton, S.C., and was served alcohol, in violation of the legal drinking age of 21 in the state. Despite being intoxicated, she drove away from the restaurant after 1 a.m. and soon lost control of her car, rolling it off the road. Hess, who was not wearing a seat belt, was thrown 20 feet from the vehicle, sustaining serious injuries that made her a paraplegic. Instead of taking responsibility for her actions, Hess filed a lawsuit against the sports grill and the South Carolina Department of Transportation (SCDOT) in December 2011. She accused the sports grill of negligence for serving her the alcohol without first verifying her age and ensuring that she was not already inebriated. Hess also blamed SCDOT, claiming that a defect in the shoulder caused her to flip her Mitsubishi. The department's failure to maintain the shoulder or mark the damaged area, according to the lawsuit, amounted to negligence. In response, SCDOT reasoned "that any injuries and/or damages sustained by the Plaintiff were due to and caused by the sole negligent, grossly negligent, reckless, careless, heedless, willful and wanton acts and/or omissions of Plaintiff."

A Doppelganger Lawsuit [24]

Some people might be honored to resemble a famous athlete—but not Allen Heckard. The Portland, Oregon man said he had been mistaken for basketball legend Michael Jordan almost every day for 15 years—and was sick of it. In 2006, he sued the former Chicago Bull along with Nike cofounder Phil Knight (for promoting Jordan) for a combined $832 million, claiming personal injury and emotional pain and suffering. Heckard, an African-American with a shaved head and an earring in his left ear, did look somewhat like Jordan, except he was also 6 inches shorter and eight years older than his more famous counterpart. He soon dropped the lawsuit, because it was clear that Heckard's case didn't have a leg to stand on.

The Wendy's Severed Finger Lawsuit [25]

In March 2005, Anna Ayala filed a claim against a Wendy's franchise owner in San Jose, Calif., alleging that she had found a severed fingertip in a bowl of chili that she ordered at a Wendy's restaurant. The bad publicity that resulted cost the fast-food chain approximately $21 million in lost sales and cut business at some northern California locations by as much as 50 percent. But the authorities found no evidence of missing fingers at the accused restaurant or anywhere along Wendy's supply chain. Suspicion soon turned on Ayala, who was eventually arrested and found guilty of attempting to extort money from Wendy's. She served four years of a nine-year sentence, and, as a condition of her probation, was banned from ever returning to the restaurant that she sued. And where did the finger come from? It was traced to Brian Rossiter, a co-worker of Ayala's husband, who lost it in a work accident and gave it to the couple to settle a $100 bet.

The Good Deed Lawsuit [26]

On July 31, 2004, Colorado teens Taylor Ostergaard and Lindsey Zellitti decided to stay home from a dance in order to bake cookies for their neighbors. Wanting their good deeds to remain anonymous, the girls knocked on the doors of their neighbors and ran away, leaving packages behind with heart-shaped gift tags that read, "Have a great night. From the T and L Club." At 10:30 p.m., the girls dropped off a package at the home of Wanita Renea Young. Startled by the "shadowy figures" on her doorstep, the 49-year-old woman called the police, who arrived to find nothing to suggest that a crime had been committed. Still, the experience reportedly gave Young an anxiety attack and she was admitted to the hospital the following day. Ostergaard and Zellitti apologized to Young, and their families even offered to pay her medical bills. But instead of forgiving the well-intentioned teens, the disgruntled woman sued them. A Durango judge awarded Young almost $900 for medical expenses but denied her demand for nearly $3,000 in punitive damages, including lost wages and new motion-sensor lights for her porch. When the ruling made national headlines, Ostergaard and Zellitti received donations from across the United States to help pay the judgment.

The Sue Yourself Lawsuit [27]

Inmates have a lot of time to think, and a Chesapeake, Va., prisoner used his time to come up with an exceptionally innovative lawsuit. In 1995, Robert Lee Brock sued himself for $5 million, claiming that he violated his own civil rights when he was arrested two years earlier for breaking and entering and grand larceny. "I partook of alcoholic beverages in 1993, July 1st, as a result I caused myself to violate my religious beliefs. This was done by my going out and getting arrested," wrote Brock in the lawsuit he filed in U.S. District Court. But because he had no income in jail, Brock asked that the state pay him the multi-million dollar settlement. Judge Rebecca Beach Smith dismissed his claim as "ludicrous" but acknowledged his "innovative approach to civil rights litigation."

Keep Your Eyes on the Road Lawsuit [28]

While driving to an appointment, one of your employees remembers he needs to contact a coworker regarding a meeting. He dials the number on his cell phone, and briefly takes his eyes off the road. In that instant, a vehicle in front of him shifts lanes, and he strikes it, seriously injuring a 78-year-old woman…Under exactly this scenario, a jury awarded a $21 million judgment against Dykes Industries of Little Rock, Arkansas.

Let the Train Hit You and Sue

On one occasion, a woman in a car drove part of the way across the train tracks (of Southern Railway, which is now Norfolk Southern after a merger) and then decided she couldn't make it, so she backed up. Then she apparently decided the train wasn't going as fast as she thought, so she decided to try to beat it anyway, so she sped forward. The train hit the car. The details are sketchy, but it is believed she was badly hurt and a couple of small children in the car were killed. The woman then sued the railroad and won.

Our litigious society has forced product manufacturers to protect themselves by posting conspicuous warning labels on their products. Some are funny and others are ridiculous, but the warning labels have been designed to stand up in court. Here's a sampling:

- Superman and Batman costumes for children come with this warning label: "Wearing of this garment does not enable you to fly."
- A clothes iron comes with this: "Warning: Never iron clothes on the body."
- The instructions for a medical thermometer warn: "Do not use orally after using rectally."
- A Slush Puppy cup warns: "This ice may be cold."
- The box of a five-hundred-piece puzzle states: "Some assembly required."
- Over-the-counter PMS medication warns: "Warning: Do not use if you have prostate problems."
- Cans of Easy Cheese contain this instruction: "For best results, remove cap."
- A warning label on over-the-counter sleeping pills warns: "Warning: May cause drowsiness."
- Self-defense pepper spray has this warning: "May irritate eyes."
- The Harry Potter toy broom cautions: "This broom does not actually fly."
- A bicycle manufacturer posted a warning that read: "When operated, this product moves."

LAWYERS AND THE LEGAL SYSTEM

The lawyers in America have created a unique fee system called the "contingency fee," which is not found anywhere else in the world. The advantage to this unique system is that it gives many people who otherwise could not afford to hire an attorney an opportunity to sue. The main problem is that it allows too many frivolous lawsuits to get filed because lawyers know that many lawsuits are settled for economic reasons; it's cheaper to settle than to fight a lawsuit. Consequently, Americans are at much greater risk for a lawsuit compared to any other place in the world. Every day, more than eighty thousand lawsuits are filed in the United States. It's absolutely essential therefore that you prepare yourself against lawsuits, and this guidebook is your best place to start.

Never Ignore a Lawsuit—A default judgment will go on your record and creditors will go after your property. Today it's easy to sue. In fact, there are a number of "matchmaker" websites, which attempt to match clients with lawyers.[29] One site even has attorneys who will take your case for free.[30] And there's one Internet site that will give you a cash advance on your prospective settlement.[31]

Can debtors go to prison? According to most asset-protection books, the answer is *no*. But this is not the correct answer. Based on a recent US Supreme Court decision in *Turner v. Rogers*, the correct answer is *yes*. We now have the return of debtor's prisons where thousands of Americans have been jailed for not paying their bills.

Since 1833, federal imprisonment for unpaid debts has been illegal in the United States. Because of "sloppy, incomplete or even false documentation," many borrowers facing jail time don't even know they're being sued by creditors. For example, here's what happened to Illinois-resident Robin Sanders while driving home. She was pulled over for allegedly having a loud muffler. But after a warrant popped up on the computer, the officer arrested Sanders, and she was taken straight to jail. Sanders stated, "That's when I found out [that] I had a warrant for failure to appear in Macoupin County. And I didn't know what it was about." It turned out that Sanders owed $730 on an unpaid medical bill. She says she didn't even know a collection agency had filed a lawsuit against her.

Sometimes a company will sell its debt to a collection agency who then files a lawsuit against the debtor requiring a court appearance. A notice to appear in court is supposed to be given to the debtor, but that doesn't always happen. If the debtor fails to show up, a bench warrant is issued for his or her arrest.

In more than a third of all states, borrowers who don't pay their bills can be jailed, even though debtor's prisons have been explicitly banned by state constitutions.

Take Sean Matthews for instance. He was a homeless New Orleans construction worker who was incarcerated for five months for a $498 debt while his jail time cost the city six times that much. Some jailed debtors are even forced to pay for their room and board, adding to their financial woes. Lately, stories of surprise arrests for unpaid debts have been reported in Indiana, Tennessee, and Washington. In Kansas City, one man ended up in jail after just missing a furniture payment. The Federal Trade Commission received more than 140,000 complaints related to debt collection in 2010, and they've taken ten debt collection agencies to court for their improper practices in the past three years.

Since 2010, more than five thousand arrest warrants have been issued for deadbeat debtors. Many debtors and judges know little about debtor's rights, and this results in debtors being intimidated into a pay agreement. Creditors' attorneys are often aggressive and they usually leverage some kind of payment. Debt collection is big business—the industry is set to grow by 26 percent over the next three years.

If you think you can't go to jail merely because you owe someone money, you're wrong. Failing to pay child support is contempt of court and will land you in jail. You won't even be entitled to a public defender.[32]

Indeed, all debtors held in jail on civil contempt are legally entitled to an opportunity to conform with the court order in question or explain why it is impossible to do so.

Here's what the US Supreme Court had to say about debtor's prison. The United States Supreme Court in *Bearden v. Georgia*, 461 US 660 (1983), made it clear that courts cannot imprison an indigent person for failure to pay a criminal fine unless the failure to pay was "willful." This is often ignored in the South. Take for example the Municipal Court in Gulfport, Mississippi. In an effort to crack down on people who owed misdemeanor fines, the City of Gulfport employed a fine collection task force. The task force canvassed predominately African-American neighborhoods, rounding up many people who had unpaid court fines. After arresting and jailing them, the city of Gulfport processed these people through a court proceeding at which no defense attorney was present or even offered. After hearings lasting no more than a minute or two, many people were jailed for months. While the city ended up filling their coffers, it also overpacked their jail with hundreds of people who couldn't pay, including sick people and the physically and mentally disabled.

A new trend is "room and board" for inmates in jails and prisons. Ora Lee Hurley spent nearly a year in a Georgia prison due to her inability to pay a $705 fine from an old drug conviction. The court ordered Ms. Hurley incarcerated until her fine was fully paid. While in prison, Ms. Hurley was employed full time at a restaurant, which sent her paycheck directly to the Department of Corrections to pay for her room and board. The Department took nearly every penny of her earnings, and she was left with only twenty-three dollars each month to buy sundries and to pay her fine. Thus, Ms. Hurley was being confined in perpetuity. She was eventually let out of prison after an outside organization petitioned for her release.

In some cases, jails have even charged inmates for room and board before they were ever convicted of any crime. For seventeen years, the Clinch County Jail in Homerville, Georgia, charged inmates a daily room and board fee of eighteen dollars even though this was in fact prohibited by law. Many inmates were too poor to pay the fees upon their release, and so the sheriff required them to sign promissory notes that they had to pay in installments or otherwise be returned to jail. On several occasions, the sheriff charged inmates thousands of dollars, failing to return their money even when the criminal charges were dismissed. Legal action ultimately required the sheriff to return the illegal fees.

Before 1833, debtors in the United States could go to prison. In nineteenth century England, debtors regularly went to prison. In fact, Charles Dickens was sent to prison for his unpaid debts. However, it's still possible to be sent to jail or prison for contempt of court if you willfully fail to comply with any court order. For example, a court order requiring you to turn over money from an offshore bank.[33] However, as long as you comply with court orders, you need not worry about going to jail.

Court orders—the court can't make you do something that you're unable to do. Let's say you have an offshore trust in the Cayman Islands where your trustee has sole signatory on a bank account. There's no way you can get the money out yourself because you can't sign on the bank account. Only the trustee can. So if the judge orders you to hand over (repatriate) money from the offshore bank account to the creditors, well then it's impossible for you to comply. This is called the "impossibility defense." However, there's one exception. If it turns out that this is a *self-created* "impossibility defense," then you could go to jail (see chapter 37).

KISS (Keep It Simple Smarty)—Judges occasionally get confused with complex plans, so just keep it simple. Moreover, complex plans arouse suspicions of fraud.

Our legal system allows everyone to have their "day in court" after they've been injured or harmed in some way. One advantage to the US legal system is that it allows some people who would otherwise never be able to afford legal services to get attorney representation. On the other hand, the disadvantage is that this system allows too many frivolous lawsuits to get filed since lawyers know that most lawsuits (over 90 percent) eventually settle, even the frivolous ones. Consequently, Americans are at a much greater risk for lawsuits compared to anywhere else in the world. Therefore, it's absolutely essential that you prepare yourself for a lawsuit and you're at the right place to begin.

Our legal system is extremely adversarial, and emotionally charged trials can affect jury decisions, which can result in vindictive windfall awards. The occasional large windfall awards are sometimes based on a "Robin Hood" mentality—"Take from the rich and give to the poor." Punitive damages are usually awarded where there's malice, fraud, or oppression. In most cases, punitive damages can't be discharged (eliminated) in bankruptcy. Many jurors are low- to middle-class wage earners who see the upper-middle class as "rich." Jurors know that even a middle-class working person will earn several million dollars over his or her lifetime! Please remember, jury verdicts can be unpredictable!

Our legal system is based primarily on the British system of law. However, one major exception involves legal fees. Under the British system of law, the loser reimburses his opponent's legal fees. That's not the case in America where, with the exception of contracts that provide for reimbursement of legal fees, the loser is not required to reimburse his opponents' attorney's fees. There is no contingency-fee payment plan anywhere in the world outside of America. The downside is that there are some attorneys who for economic reasons will accept frivolous lawsuits on a contingency-fee basis. However, most attorneys will take a case on a contingency-fee basis if they feel you have strong likelihood of winning. Lawsuits are a full-time business in America. The United States is the only country in the world that permits attorneys to take cases on a contingency fee—no fee unless the plaintiff wins the case. In all other countries, attorneys are not allowed to take a case on a contingent-fee basis. Moreover, in many countries the plaintiff must post a cash bond with the court in order to pay the defendant should he lose the case.

There are 202 ABA-approved law schools in the United States[34] with close to 150,000 law students and an overabundance of attorneys. There's a myth (which I'm exposing) that states that two out of every three lawyers in the world practices law in the United States. That's simply not true. The figure is probably closer to around 20 percent. [35] As of June 2008, approximately 26 percent of lawyers were self-employed, practicing either as partners in law firms or in solo practices. In May 2008, the median annual wages of all wage-and-salaried lawyers were $110,590. The middle half of the occupation earned between $74,980 and $163,320. Median annual wages in the industries employing the largest numbers of lawyers in May 2008 were:

Management of companies and enterprises	$145,770
Federal Executive Branch	$126,080
Legal services	$116,550
Local government	$82,590
State government	$78,540

Every year, roughly one out of ten Americans is sued. Physicians are the frequent target for lawsuits:

Nationwide, 40 percent of all physicians have been sued.
The average obstetrician/gynecologist in New York has been sued eight times!
Nationwide, the average jury malpractice verdict is $1,330,000!
In New York, the *average* jury malpractice verdict is $4,000,000!

Accountants and accounting firms now face over three thousand lawsuits seeking more than $13 billion in damages. Huge judgments have caused several firms to go bankrupt.[36]

If you have a business, watch out. That's because every business person is exposed. Liability can sometimes come from what is least expected and can be based on new and unanticipated legal theories. Numerous Federal laws have been enacted to protect the environment and wildlife. If you buy property that is contaminated, you could be sued by the government to clean it up. This happened to the partners of a major law firm when they were notified of their responsibility to clean up toxic waste on raw land they purchased. The clean-up cost was projected at over $70 million!

There's a great deal of advertising in the competitive market of personal injury attorneys. These attorneys typically use a contingency-fee arrangement that allows people who would otherwise be unable to afford an attorney to file a lawsuit. On the other hand, it also substantially increases the number of lawsuits in the United States. Our legal system is complex, and thus most attorneys tend to specialize. Anyone is entitled to represent themselves in a lawsuit. However, your best bet is to be represented by a competent and experienced attorney. In fact, if you operate a business as a corporation or limited liability company, and your business is sued, then your business must be represented by an attorney. You are not permitted by law to individually represent your business. In these cases, your business or professional liability insurance company (assuming you have business insurance which you should have) will automatically provide your business with legal representation (see chapter 8).

Lawyers are always looking for new legal theories in order to advance their lawsuit retinue. Professionals, such as doctors, are often the target of lawsuits. The reason is primarily threefold. First, all doctors are perceived as being rich, even though many are not (and most people are naturally envious of their perceived wealth); secondly, doctors are generally viewed as being extremely smart (so they're not allowed to make any mistakes); and thirdly, many people have unrealistic expectations from their doctors and the medical establishment and expect perfect outcomes. Unfortunately, when a medical mishap occurs, these three factors come into play and often the result is a medical malpractice suit. That's why it's so imperative for any practicing professional to protect themselves with plenty of professional liability insurance. To practice medicine otherwise is courting a potential financial disaster that could easily wipe out the doctor's life savings

Testing, testing, testing—No what I really mean is reality testing, reality testing, reality testing: Lawyers lie! Plaintiff's lie! And witnesses lie! A 2002 study conducted by University of Massachusetts psychologist Robert S. Feldman "found that 60 percent of people lied at least once during a 10-minute conversation and told an average of two to three lies," according to the Journal of Basic and Applied Social Psychology.

Ninety-one percent of American physicians are practicing "defensive medicine" by ordering more tests and procedures than what is necessary in order to protect themselves against malpractice lawsuits according to a study published in the June 28, 2010, online issue of the *Archives of Internal Medicine*.

Attorneys will often advise their physician clients to document everything, just in case they're sued. Even if a mistake occurs, they must not destroy any of the records—that's obstruction of justice. Also, you should never lie because that could cripple your case. Lawyers routinely advise against admitting any liability. My recommendation is, if ever in doubt, always immediately consult your attorney. And don't ever admit anything! I guarantee it will come back to haunt you. Before ever admitting any liability, always seek a professional legal opinion.

Many books have been written about lawyers. The truth of the matter is that good lawyers are hard to find, and when you find one, they're usually fully booked and unable to handle your case. You then have to risk your case on a mediocre lawyer where there's a good chance something could go wrong. It's a risk that, in my opinion, is totally unacceptable. That's why it is so critical for you to have plenty of liability insurance. The insurance company handling your lawsuit will be responsible for your legal representation at their expense.

The sad fact is that many lawyers are dishonest and incompetent. Most state bar associations are weak and feeble because when they mete out discipline, it's usually just a "slap on the hand" punishment that has little deterrent effect. In many ways, the legal profession is like a private club where the lawyers are chummy with the judges, and the routine is "wink, wink, and nod, nod." Some attorneys even have illegal ex parte communications with the judges. Folks, what I'm describing here is nothing other than blatant corruption.

Let's face it; our society is made up of a large number of ignorant people. History reveals that less than 1 percent of world's people have ever made significant contributions or inventions to aid society.

Arbitration is a form of alternative dispute resolution (ADR) and is an alternative to a jury or bench (judge) trial. The parties to a dispute refer the matter to an arbitrator who renders a decision—the award. It is a settlement technique in which a third party reviews the case and imposes a decision. There are other forms of ADR such as mediation, a form of settlement negotiation facilitated by a neutral third party, and nonbinding resolution by experts. Arbitration is often used for the resolution of commercial disputes. Arbitration is also frequently employed in consumer and employment matters, where arbitration is part of an employment or commercial contract.

Arbitration can be either nonbinding (voluntary) or binding (mandatory). Binding arbitration can only arise from a law or from a contract in which the parties agree to waive any right to a lawsuit and to submit disputes to arbitration. Nonbinding arbitration, on the other hand, is similar to mediation. However, the major distinction is that whereas a mediator will try to help the parties find a middle ground on which to compromise, the nonbinding arbitrator will only determine liability and, if appropriate, will provide an assessment of damages payable to the plaintiff. A nonbinding arbitration award can be appealed to a (de novo or new) jury trial (also called a trial de novo).

In some situations, a lawsuit can be transferred from limited to unlimited jurisdiction with court approval where the judgment is the sky's limit. Ouch!

Here's something most people don't realize: in some cases, an appeal that involves a completely new trial can result in an outcome that is considerably worse than the original trial! You should never forget the saying "Quit while you're ahead."

In some cases, a lawsuit can occasionally be transferred from state court to federal court by the plaintiff, but the plaintiff must first dismiss the state lawsuit (without prejudice); and in some circumstances, the defendant can transfer (or remove) a lawsuit from state court to federal court.

There's another strong advantage to being judgment protected. If you're absolutely forced to represent yourself (which I don't recommend at all) because of a serious financial problem, then the lawsuit is much less dangerous than would otherwise be because even if you make a serious legal blunder and lose the case, the plaintiff's judgment would essentially be uncollectible.

Please remember never to forget that the courts are always on the lookout for fraud.

In some cases, your assets can be attached before there is a judgment. The Due Process Clause in the US Constitution protects your property. In most cases, you can lose your property only to judgment creditors who won a lawsuit against you and obtained a judgment against you. In some rare situations, a plaintiff may be able to "freeze" your assets with a prejudgment attachment. In California, only commercial plaintiffs that have a contract with you can attach your property and only to the extent of your property in California. Any property outside of California cannot be attached. This is one good reason to keep your property out of California. There is no prejudgment attachment in Small Claims Court. Attachment does not apply to mortgages on your home. Furthermore, the underlying lawsuit must be a commercial claim against your business, trade, or profession. Community property can be attached—another good reason for eliminating community property. Moreover, the plaintiff must post a minimum $10,000 bond. The good news is that prejudgment attachments are uncommon, and you have the right to a hearing before any of your property is attached. In some IRS situations, and in some divorce proceedings, your assets can be "frozen" prior to a final judgment. Therefore, in most situations, you have several years warning before you lose any of your assets. That's because it usually takes several years before a final judgment is rendered.

Men are more likely to engage in crime according to Department of Justice Statistics. This is true even though they are a lesser percentage of the overall population. The *Find Law* survey reflects this result as well with 10 percent of men reporting having been a defendant in a criminal case. Only 4 percent of women reported being in the same position.

Over fifteen million lawsuits will be filed this year in state courts throughout America at a cost of over $1.8 billion, which is one lawsuit for every twelve adults in America. That works out to one new lawsuit every two seconds. That's over forty-three thousand every day and the number keeps growing. Opportunists make careers out of filing lawsuits, knowing that the expense of defending against these attacks is so high, a settlement will likely be offered. How do these opportunists find out you're worth suing? Your bank, brokerage, and credit card transactions provide a remarkably detailed account of who you are and what you own. These records may be subpoenaed in a lawsuit and used against you.

For instance, if you loan a vehicle to a friend who injures someone or damages his property, you can be sued. Also, did you know that if you lend money to someone to purchase a vehicle, you may be responsible for any damages or injuries that person causes in an accident?

HOW CREDITORS SEIZE ASSETS

Most collections attorneys are by their very nature aggressive. Some are also dishonest. The Fair Debt Collection Practices Act (FDCPA)[37] can protect you in some instances. Certain judgments related to consumer debts are protected under the FDCPA. For instance, by law, you can tell a debt collection agency or collection attorney to leave you alone. Also, if you are represented by an attorney, a collections attorney cannot contact you but must contact your attorney. On the other hand, if you are not represented by an attorney and your judgment is a nonconsumer debt such as a business debt or a judgment related to a tort (a wrongful act), then the collections attorney can contact you directly unless you are represented by an attorney. If you feel that the collections attorney is harassing you, you can go directly to court to seek a protective order. (If self-represented, you may want to contact an attorney to help draft a motion for a protective order in order to stop the collections attorney from continued harassment.)

The FDCPA broadly defines a debt collector as a third-party person who collects debts and now includes collections attorneys.

The FDCPA's definitions of *consumers* and *debt* specifically restricts the coverage to personal, family, or household transactions. Commercial debts owed by businesses including individuals for business purposes are specifically exempted from the FDCPA.[38]

The FDCPA prohibits the following conduct:

1. Contacting consumers by telephone outside of the hours of 8:00 a.m. to 9:00 p.m.
2. Communicating with consumers in any way (other than litigation) after receiving written notice that the consumer wishes no further communication or refuses to pay the alleged debt, with certain exceptions, including advis-

ing that collection efforts are being terminated or that the collector intends to file a lawsuit or pursue other remedies where permitted.

3. Causing a telephone to ring repeatedly or engaging any person in telephone conversation repeatedly or continuously with intent to annoy, abuse, or harass.
4. Communicating with consumers at their place of employment after having been advised that this is not permitted by the employer.
5. Contacting a consumer known to be represented by an attorney.
6. Communicating with the consumer or pursuing collection efforts during the period of time between receiving a consumer's written request for verification of a debt or information (name and address) on the original creditor (made within the thirty-day validation period) and before the debt collector mails the consumer the requested verification or original creditor's name and address.
7. Misrepresenting the debt or a debt collector's misrepresentation that he or she is an attorney or law enforcement officer.
8. Publishing the consumer's name or address on a "bad debt" list.
9. Seeking inflated amounts not permitted under a contract or under applicable law.
10. Threatening arrest or legal action that is prohibited.
11. Abusive or profane language used in the course of collecting a debt.
12. Revealing or discussing the nature of debts with third parties is prohibited (other than the consumer's spouse or attorney). Note that collection agencies are only allowed to contact neighbors or coworkers in order to obtain location information.
13. Only the debt collector's address and business name if such name does not indicate that he is in the debt collection busi-

ness can be used on any envelope when communicating with a consumer.

14. Reporting false information on a consumer's credit report or threatening to do so is prohibited.

The FDCPA requires debt collectors to do the following:

1. Identify themselves and notify the consumer, in every communication, that the communication is from a debt collector and in the initial communication that any information obtained will be used to effect collection of the debt.
2. Give the name and address of the original creditor (company to which the debt was originally payable) upon the consumer's written request made within thirty days of receipt of the initial collection notice.
3. Notify the consumer of their right to dispute the debt within thirty days following the "initial communication" notice by the debt collector.
4. Provide verification (the amount owed and the name and address of the original creditor) of the debt if a consumer sends a written dispute or request for verification within thirty days of receiving the "initial communication" notice, then the debt collector must either mail the consumer the requested verification information or cease collection efforts altogether.
5. Any consumer disputes must also be reported by the creditor to the credit bureau(s) that reports the debt.
6. Any lawsuit filed by a debt collector may only be in a place where the consumer lives or signed the contract. (However, the consumer can sue the debt collector in other more convenient venues.)

Aggrieved consumers are permitted to file private lawsuits in a state or federal court to collect damages (actual, statutory, attorney's fees, and court costs) from third-party debt collectors. Moreover, the FDCPA is a strict liability law, which means that a consumer need not prove actual damages in order to claim statutory damages of up to $1,000 for each violation of the FDCPA plus reasonable attorney fees. The debt collector may, however, escape penalty if he shows that the violation(s) was (were) unintentional and the result of a "bona fide error" that occurred despite procedures designed to avoid the error at issue.

In California, a judgment debtor can be subpoenaed to court for a debtor's exam no more than once every six months. A debtor's exam requires a judgment debtor to answer questions under oath and to provide documents, where available, to the creditors. The information gleaned at the debtor's exam helps the creditors locate the debtor's assets so they can satisfy their judgment against the debtor. Legally, a debtor's exam is termed an Order of Examination and is a court process to aid enforcement of a monetary judgment.

The party (usually the debtor but occasionally a third party) being examined will be required to furnish information to aid in the enforcement of a monetary judgment. The judgment creditor or their representative may ask questions relating to the following:

1. Personal financial assets.
2. Property owned by the judgment debtor that is possessed or controlled by the third-party examinee.
3. Debt(s) owed to the judgment debtor by the third-party examinee.
4. Property owned by the defendant that is possessed or controlled by the third-party examinee.
5. Debt(s) owed to the defendant by the third-party examinee that is subject to attachment.

Creditors use many procedures to assist in their collection efforts. We'll discuss these ways later in this book. A main advantage to not having any creditors is that it allows you to sue as a plaintiff knowing full well that no creditor can usurp your judgment. If you have creditors, they could force you to hand the judgment over to them.

Creditors have an armamentarium of tools to help collect their judgment—debtors' exams (which could include handing over the cash in your wallet at your debtor's exam to the creditors!), liens, lis pendens, garnishments, bank levies, subpoenas (including the inspection of your safe deposit box), turnover orders, seizure orders (including your cash), writs of execution, receiverships, auctions, involuntary bankruptcies, various court orders, seizing your tax refunds, life insurance, stocks, bonds, coin/stamp collections, jewelry, cars, boats, airplanes, debts owed to you could be diverted to the creditors as well as accounts receivable, etc.[39]

A money judgment[40] is a final outcome (determination) in a lawsuit.[41] Money judgments are entitled to accrue interest.[42] In order to stay (postpone) enforcement of a money judgment, the debtor needs to (1) appeal the judgment *and* (2) post a bond (which is not necessary for a small claims case).[43] In California, judgments are valid for ten years and can be renewed once only for an additional ten years for a total of twenty years.[44] A monetary judgment allows the creditor to easily establish a lien on the debtor's property.[45] A judgment lien on real property is one of the quickest, simplest, and least expensive enforcement procedures available to the creditor. The lien is automatically created simply by recording an abstract of judgment, a certified copy of the judgment, or a 42 USCA § 652(a)(11) interstate lien form. Recordation is simple and inexpensive, and the judgment debtor has to pay off the lien in order to sell or refinance his property!

Real property interests that are exempt from a judgment lien:

1. Rental payments received by the debtor;
2. A leasehold (lease) under 2 years;
3. A beneficiary's interest under a trust;
4. Real property attached by the creditor that is transferred before judgment is entered; and
5. A declared homestead exemption.[46]

If the judgment debtor has real property in more than one county, the judgment creditor must record an abstract of the judgment or interstate lien form in each of those counties.

A judgment lien generally requires the recording of an abstract of the money judgment. [47]

The debtor must be notified of the judgment lien on his real property.[48] Basically, a "first in time" rule applies: Priority goes to the first-recorded abstract of judgment.[49] A lien sale will result in the sale of your real property, including your home, provided a lien has been properly recorded on your home by the creditors.[50] Business property of the debtor is also subject to a lien, but an ordinary lien sale is not possible.[51]

Unlike a real property judgment lien or writ of execution, which must be issued by the court clerk, a judgment lien on personal property is filed with the secretary of state. A judgment lien on personal property also gives the judgment creditor priority over unsecured creditors without the necessity of levying execution. However, in levying execution, secured creditors would have priority and could file third-party claims which might defeat the execution levy. A judgment lien on personal property is one of the least expensive enforcement methods.[52]

The most common method of enforcing a money judgment is to levy on the judgment debtor's property under a writ of execution. In most cases, execution can be used to reach virtually all of a judgment debtor's property interest. This includes real property and most tangible and intangible personal property. An execution levy may also reach a debtor's property interests in the possession or control of a third person or a debt owed the judgment debtor by a third person. The levying officer executes the writ by taking the property into custody (actually or constructively). The execution levy creates a lien on the real or personal property levied upon. And for priority purposes, the lien "relates back" to the date a prior effective judgment or attachment lien was created. Subsequently, the debtor's property can be sold at an auction (execution sale) and the proceeds applied to satisfy the judgment.

Some of the debtor's property is exempt from execution. State and federal laws provide generous exemptions protecting the property of judgment debtors from execution. For example, in California, the homestead exemption for a judgment debtor's home may be up to $125,000. In Florida and Texas, the judgment debtor has an unlimited homestead exemption and thereby gets to keep his home (see chapter 35).

An execution levy can be very expensive. If tangible personal property is seized, it must be moved to storage and held for sale. Levying officers may require substantial deposits to cover these costs. Even though enforcement costs can be added to the judgment, they may be difficult to collect. Furthermore, execution sales almost always bring in much less money than their market value. Another serious drawback to execution is that it may force the debtor to file for bankruptcy.

Only a "money judgment" recorded in California is enforceable by writ of execution.[53] A state tax lien (technically not a "money judgment") may also be enforced by writ of execution.[54]

A money judgment cannot be enforced against the following types of property by writ of execution:

1. An alcoholic beverage license.
2. A partnership interest held by the judgment debtor where the partnership itself is not a judgment debtor. However, partnership assets may be subject to execution if transferred in fraud of creditors or if the action is not subject to the Revised Uniform Partnership Act, and the creditor has been unable to collect under a previous charging order.[55]
3. The judgment debtor's interest as a member of a limited liability company where the limited liability company is not a judgment debtor.[56]
4. The judgment debtor's interest in a deposit in lieu of bond to the extent the deposit continues to be required for the judgment debtor to engage in business.[57]
5. A pending lawsuit.
6. A judgment in favor of the debtor that is not yet final (i.e., before expiration of time for appeal or, if an appeal has been filed, before determination of the appeal).

7. A debt, other than wages, owing to the debtor by a public entity.
8. The loan value of an (unmatured) life insurance, endowment, or annuity policy.
9. A franchise license granted by a public entity.
10. A trust beneficiary interest.
11. Any nonvested interest in property (including contingent remainders, executory interests, etc.).
12. Property in a guardianship or conservatorship estate.[58]

Judgments for possession or sale of real or personal property are enforced by writs of possession or sale rather than by writs of execution. But the procedural requirements for issuance of such writs are substantially the same as for writs of execution.[59]

There are special court orders that creditors can use to aid the execution of debtor property (facilitate a levy which the levying officer might otherwise be unable to make):

1. "Turnover" orders: Once a writ issues, the judgment creditor may apply to the court for a "turnover" order directing the judgment debtor to transfer to the levying officer the property sought to be levied upon. Turnover orders are enforceable by contempt and may be used to obtain possession of either tangible personal property that is sought to be levied upon by taking it into custody or documentary evidence of title to property sought to be levied upon (e.g., certificate of ownership of automobile) or of a debt sought to be levied upon (e.g., a promissory note).[60] After a judgment is entered, the judgment creditor can apply for a "turnover order" (court order) directing the judgment debtor to transfer the property and/or documentary evidence of title to the creditor.[61]
2. Seizure orders: The levying officer cannot seize property kept in the judgment debtor's home or other "private place" without a court order authorizing such seizure. Such an order may be granted even before the writ has issued, but there

must be "probable cause" to believe that property sought to be levied upon will be found at the place described.[62]

3. Orders to preserve value of assets levied upon: The court may appoint a receiver or order the levying officer to take any action necessary to preserve the value of property levied upon. For example, if the court determines that the property is perishable or will greatly deteriorate or depreciate in value, it may order the property sold by the levying officer without complying with the statutory provisions otherwise applicable to execution sales.[63]

After a writ of execution is issued, it must be delivered to the levying officer with instructions and the required fee. [64] There are four basic methods by which a writ of execution can be levied on property so as to create an execution lien thereon:

1. Physical seizure of the property—The levying officer must seize and take custody of the tangible personal property that is in the judgment debtor's possession (However, if tangible personal property is in the possession or control of a third person, i.e., someone other than the judgment debtor, the levying officer may not seize it. Rather, the third person must be served with a copy of the writ and notice of levy.)
2. Garnishment—A notice of levy must first be served on the judgment debtor's employer that directs the employer to garnish the employee's (judgment debtor's) wages up to 25 percent (the maximum amount in California)
3. Recording a copy of the writ and notice of levy—This is recorded in the recorder's office to levy upon real property interests including crops, timber, and minerals.
4. Delivery of a copy of the writ to the levying officer—Property that is already in the custody of the levying officer (e.g., under attachment) is levied upon by delivering a copy of the writ to the levying officer—a so-called "book levy."

A notice of levy is one of the documents that must be served on the judgment debtor when (or promptly after) the levy is made.[65]

The lien begins on the date of levy and continues until:

1. two years after the date of issuance of the writ, unless the judgment is sooner satisfied,[66] or
2. the ten-year period for enforcement of the judgment elapses,[67] or
3. the lien is renewed or continued, [68] or
4. enforcement of the judgment is stayed and bond is filed when required.

The levying officer will release property from levy upon written instructions from the judgment creditor's attorney of record (or the judgment creditor in pro per) or upon receipt of a certified copy of a court order for release.[69] A release may also occur by operation of law as where the judgment creditor fails to oppose a claim of exemption or third-party claim. Likewise, when the levying officer has collected the full amount necessary to satisfy the writ, all other property under the levy must be released.

There are several methods by which a judgment debtor may attempt to prevent property levied upon from being sold (or collected) by the levying officer:

1. Filing a motion to recall and quash the writ of execution—The court can recall and/or quash a writ of execution improperly or inadvertently issued and release any liens or to vacate an execution levy (i) if the writ was improperly or inadvertently issued (e.g., where judgment fully paid), (ii) after issuance of the writ the judgment was vacated, (iii) the writ failed to account for legitimate offset against payment due, (iv) the judgment was not enforceable by execution, (v) the property levied upon was not subject to execution, (vi) the lien is extinguished in connection with a stay of enforcement, (vii) the judgment was satisfied by agreement or "sub-

stituted" performance—e.g., agreement that lump-sum payment would discharge installment judgment.

2. Seeking a stay of execution—A trial court may stay enforcement of a money judgment for up to ten days beyond the last date on which a notice of appeal could be filed (e.g., to allow time to perfect an appeal or for the judgment debtor to arrange to pay the judgment). The stay may be granted regardless of whether an appeal is actually filed or is expected to be filed.[70] A trial court may also order enforcement stayed where the judgment debtor has a counteraction pending against the judgment creditor on a disputed claim. If enforcement of the judgment is not stayed, the judgment debtor may be deprived of the right of offset and, with a judgment-proof debtor, of the right to recover anything at all. [71]
3. Filing a timely exemption claim.
4. Encouraging a third person to file a third-party claim.

As stated previously, the perfecting of an appeal and the posting of a sufficient undertaking (bond) are ordinarily required to stay enforcement of:

1. A superior court money judgment[72]
2. A (CCP § 998) settlement offer to pay court cost (unless such costs constitute CCP § 1033.5—"routine costs")[73]
3. Judicial arbitration for court costs pursuant to CCP § 1141.21 (unless such costs constitute CCP § 1033.5—"routine costs")[74]
4. A judgment directing the assignment or delivery of personal property or the sale of personal property upon foreclosure of a mortgage or other lien[75]
5. A judgment directing the sale, conveyance or delivery of possession of real property in possession, or control of the appellant or the party ordered to sell, convey, or deliver possession of the property[76]
6. A judgment appointing a receiver[77]

7. An individual judgment debtor may still be able to prevent the levied property from being sold by filing a timely claim of exemption.

The California Constitution mandates that the legislature protect "a certain portion" of debtors' property from forced sale.[78] The broad purpose is to protect enough property from enforcement to enable judgment debtors to support themselves and their families. Exemption laws are liberally construed in the debtor's favor. The EJL exemptions may be claimed only by natural person judgment debtors, i.e., not by partnerships, corporations or other entities.[79] Generally, an exemption must be claimed by the judgment debtor within the time and in the manner prescribed by the EJL. If not timely claimed, the exemption is waived, and all of the property is subject to enforcement of a money judgment.[80] Exception: Property that is described by an exemption statute as "exempt without making a claim" cannot be reached by any procedure for enforcement of a money judgment.[81] A homestead exemption may be claimed anytime by the judgment debtor; and if there is a *judicial* sale of the debtor's home, the court must apply the homestead exemption to the debtor's property if it is absent.

A judgment creditor is allowed to timely file an opposition to a debtor's claim of exemption[82] but must:

1. file with the court a notice of opposition to the Claim of Exemption (Judicial Council Form EJ-170), notice of motion for an order determining the claim of exemption, and notice of hearing on Claim of Exemption (Judicial Council Form EJ-175); and
2. file with the levying officer (preferably by personal delivery or certified mail, return receipt requested) copies of each of these documents. (The levying officer will file the judgment debtor's claim of exemption and any attached financial statement with the court.)[83]

The EJL property exemptions may be claimed by the judgment debtor or person acting on the debtor's behalf, e.g., a garnishee, the judgment debtor's agent, or a public or private retirement plan.[84] An exemption for community property may be claimed by either the judgment debtor or his or her spouse regardless of whether or not the spouse is also a debtor under the judgment.[85]

To claim an exemption, the judgment debtor (or spouse or other person where applicable) must file an original and one copy of a Claim of Exemption with the levying officer.[86]

After being served with the notice and claim of exemption, the judgment creditor may oppose the claim. If the creditor files an opposition, a court hearing within twenty days[87] must be held to determine whether the exemption should be allowed. If opposition is not timely filed, the property will be released whether or not the exemption claim is valid.[88]

As stated previously, state and federal law protects some of the debtor's property—exempt property. In most cases, an exemption claim must be filed in a timely manner in order for the property to properly protect under state and federal law. See chapter 35, "Exempt Property," for a full discussion.

Federal Law Regarding Wage Garnishment[89]

More than 25 percent of the employee's wages can be withheld to satisfy a support judgment (e.g., family support) pursuant to an earnings assignment order for support[90] and support payments (earnings assignment orders) have priority over any type of wage garnishment![91] Folks, this is where a "friendly" divorce comes in combined with generous family support payments (see chapter 14).

The Wage Garnishment Law does not apply to self-employed debtors. If you're self-employed, watch out! The creditors could take more than 25 percent of your earnings. Therefore, you should make yourself an employee of your own business in order to cap any wage garnishment at 25 percent of your earnings.

Interestingly, persons who form professional corporations (e.g., doctors, dentists, lawyers) are by law not self-employed because they are employed by their corporations. Therefore, an incorporated professional's wages can be garnished but only up to the extent of 25 percent of earnings. Corporate dividends, bonuses, and other future payments can be reached by an assignment order.

The wages of a state or local employee or public officer can be garnished.[92] Federal law permits the salaries of federal employees to be garnished. [93] To implement a wage garnishment, the creditor must serve the judgment debtor's employer with a proper earnings withholding order.[94] There are two other types of earnings withholding orders:

1. "Withholding order for taxes": A "withholding order for taxes" is an earnings withholding order issued to collect a state tax liability.[95]
2. "Withholding order for support": A "withholding order for support" is an earnings withholding order issued to collect delinquent amounts under a child or spousal support judgment. The order must indicate "on its face" that it is a "withholding order for support."[96] Generally, a withholding order for support automatically ends one year after the employee stops working for the employer.[97] Only one half of a judgment debtor's disposable earnings are exempt from garnishment under an earnings withholding order for support (as opposed to 75 percent for nonsupport withholding orders).[98] However, in some situations, the court may make an "equitable division" of the judgment debtor's wages by taking into account the needs of all persons whom the judgment debtor is required to support (e.g., both the debtor's former spouse and present family).[99] The court may order more or less than 50 percent of the judgment debtor's wages to be withheld, so long as the maximum amount withheld does not exceed the maximum permitted under federal law.[100]

In addition to the automatic exemption for nonsupport withholding orders, that portion of an employee's earnings necessary for the support of the judgment debtor or his or her family (including a spouse or former spouse) is exempt from nonsupport earnings withholding orders. Thus, under appropriate circumstances, an employee may be able to exempt all of his or her earnings from a nonsupport withholding order.[101]

To obtain this exemption, the judgment debtor must file a timely claim of exemption with the levying officer. If the judgment creditor fails to oppose the claim, the exemption is automatically granted, and the earnings must be released. A claim of exemption can be made by the judgment debtor any time during the withholding period.[102]

A judgment creditor wishing to oppose the claim of exemption must file a notice of opposition with the levying officer within ten days after the date the notice of claim of exemption was mailed.[103]

An earnings withholding order can be obtained by filing an application and the original writ of execution directly with the levying officer (not the court) in the county where the order is to be served. The earnings withholding order must promptly be issued by the levying officer. The debtor can always go to court to dispute the wage garnishment.[104]

Federal restrictions dictate the maximum amount that may be withheld from an employee's earnings may not exceed the lesser of: (1) 25 percent of the employee's wages for that week, or (2) the amount by which the wages for the week exceeds thirty times the federal minimum hourly wage. In most cases, no more than 25 percent of the employee's wages can be garnished. This means that at least 75 percent of an employee's wages are effectively exempt from all nonsupport-earnings withholding orders, and no claim of exemption need be made.[105] An even smaller amount may be withheld if an earnings assignment order for support payments (e.g. family support) is in effect against the same earnings. Folks, make sure you pay a large family support payment in order to keep the creditor's wage garnishment low.

By definition, your wages ("disposable earnings") subject to garnishment are those remaining after deduction of any amounts required by law to be withheld. These include deductions for social security, federal and state income taxes, state disability insurance, and payments to public employee retirement systems.[106]

The automatic wage exemption does not apply to:

1. any court order involving a chapter 13 bankruptcy proceeding or
2. any debt for federal tax. [107]

State Laws Regarding Wage Garnishment

The law also allows states to impose more lenient wage garnishment than the federal government. In fact, Texas prohibits all wage garnishments![108] (Let's move to Texas.) Florida prohibits wage garnishment on "all of the disposable earnings of a head of family whose disposable earnings are less than or equal to $750 a week."[109]

How Debtors Can Protect Themselves from Wage Garnishments

Once you receive your exempt wages (typically the remaining 75% of your salary), you must then place this money in a *separate* bank account in order to protect it. If you commingle this money with any of your other bank accounts, it will lose protection.

You can also increase your tax withholdings which will then result in less money going to your creditors as well as yourself. In theory, you should then get a larger tax refund. However, your creditors may be able to attach your tax refund. So this plan may not pan out. Please check with your tax advisor before going this route.

You can form a new company and request that your employer pay your new company instead of you, explaining that you are working for your new company. Since your new company is not a judgment debtor, it is not subject to your wage garnishment. There could be some pitfalls. First, your creditor could challenge your new company under the Alter Ego Doctrine and the court could disregard it as a sham. Second, your employer may not be amenable to paying your company based on the fact that you got hired, not your company. Now if you happen to be self-employed at your own company, you could stop paying yourself and instead have your company (1) give you periodic loans or (2) give you stock dividends or (3) put your family to work for your company and pay them generously and in turn they will support you!

Debtor's Examinations

Usually, only a debtor can be examined in order to ascertain the whereabouts of the debtor's property that the creditor can seize for sale to satisfy the judgment. In some situations, a third party who has possession or control of the debtor's property may also be examined with the court's approval. An examination of a judgment debtor or third party is the equivalent of a post-judgment deposition. An examination can be used to identify property in the possession or control of the judgment debtor or a third person (e.g., a nondebtor spouse) to learn about property the debtor has or may obtain in the future and to require the debtor or third person to turn over property to the levying officer. Upon service of an examination order, the judgment debtor must appear in court "to furnish information to aid in enforcement of the money judgment."[110] A third person (e.g., a nondebtor spouse) may be ordered to appear for examination upon the judgment creditor's application showing to the court's satisfaction that the third person is in possession or control of property in which the judgment debtor has an interest.[111] In addition, any person with knowledge leading to enforcement of the judgment (e.g., debtor's bookkeeper, accountant or nondebtor spouse) can be subpoenaed to testify before the court or a referee in an examination proceeding in the same manner as a trial witness.[112] However, the assertion of the marital privilege by the nondebtor spouse should permit the nondebtor spouse from testifying against you. Similarly, discussing these matters with your attorney will protect your privacy as your attorney cannot be compelled to testify against you pursuant to attorney-client privilege.

An order to appear for an examination must be personally served by a sheriff, marshal, or a registered process server. If the examinee fails to appear, the court may issue an arrest warrant requiring the examinee to appear in court and explain the nonappearance.[113] Even if service is improper, i.e., the order to appear for examination was left on your doorstep, I strongly recommend you appear for the debtor's exam. Otherwise, the court could issue a bench warrant for your arrest, and only later after spending time in jail will you have an opportunity to explain to the judge about the improper service. It's just easier to appear. Moreover, upon a finding that the examinee did not have a good reason for failing to appear, the court must award the judgment creditor reasonable attorney fees incurred for the examination proceeding. Now you have extra fees added to your jail experience, and those fees are added to your judgment. [114]

After the examination, the creditors may apply for a "turnover order" in which the court orders a debtor to deliver nonexempt property to the levying officer to be applied to satisfy the judgment.[115] Turnover orders are enforceable by contempt.[116]

A judgment creditor may serve written interrogatories on a judgment debtor to obtain information to aid in enforcement of a money judgment.[117]

A judgment creditor may serve an inspection demand on a judgment debtor to obtain information to aid in enforcement of a money judgment.[118]

If a third person possesses or controls property that the debtor owns or owes money to the debtor, then the judgment creditor may sue the third party to apply the property or debt to the money judgment.[119]

If a judgment debtor has a right to any future payment, a court may order an assignment of all or part of such right to a judgment creditor.

The court may appoint a receiver to enforce a judgment upon a showing by the judgment creditor that the appointment is a "reasonable method to obtain the fair and orderly satisfaction of the judgment."[120]

The debtor's assets in a general or limited partnership or in a limited liability company cannot be directly seized on a money judgment rendered against a partner or member personally. In other words, the partnership or limited liability company assets are not subject to execution unless the judgment is against the partnership or LLC itself. To reach a debtor's partnership or LLC interest, the judgment creditor must obtain a "charging order" to assign those interests with the amount of the judgment. This makes the creditor an assignee or lien holder of the debtor's interest in the partnership or LLC.[121]

If a state or local public entity owes any money to the debtor (e.g., income tax refund), then there are special procedures the judgment creditor can utilize to seize the money.[122]

Under the law, a judgment creditor is permitted to assign (transfer) the judgment to a third person. Through such an assignment, the assignee (transferee) acquires all the rights and remedies possessed by the assignor for the enforcement of the debt, subject, however, to the defenses that the judgment debtor had against the assignor.[123]

Occasionally, a judgment debtor changes his or her name after a judgment is entered. When this happens, it will be necessary to amend the judgment to reflect the judgment debtor's current name. A California court may use "all the means necessary" to carry its jurisdiction into effect.[124]

If a judgment debtor is a beneficiary of a trust, that interest is not subject to execution.[125] Rather, the judgment debtor's beneficial interest in a private or charitable express trust may be reached only by obtaining a court order.[126]

Contingent remainders, executory interests and other nonvested property interests held by a judgment debtor may not be reached by execution.[127] However, a judgment creditor may obtain a court order applying such interests to satisfy a money judgment. The court has discretion to determine how best to protect both the judgment debtor and creditor (i.e., prevent a "sacrifice sale" while preserving the creditor's rights). This may include imposing a lien on, or requiring sale of, the judgment debtor's interest.[128]

Debtor property held in a guardianship or conservatorship estate is not subject to any procedure for enforcement of a money judgment. However, if the guardian or conservator refuses or fails to pay the judgment, the judgment creditor may petition the court having jurisdiction over the guardianship or conservatorship for an order requiring payment.[129] If the judgment creditor dies, the judgment may be enforced under normal applicable procedures by the judgment creditor's executor, administrator, or successor in interest.[130]

Third-Party Claims

Occasionally, a third party (neither the debtor nor the creditor) claims ownership or possession of real and/or personal property or a superior security interest in or lien on personal property levied upon under writ of execution, writ of attachment, prejudgment, or postjudgment writ of possession (including claim and delivery proceedings[131] or writ of sale).[132] A third-party claim may also be filed where the claimant has an equitable right to the property (real or personal) levied upon. A third party may also claim legal or equitable title to, or a right of possession to, real or personal property under levy may file a claim with the levying officer. This halts the levy process and forces the levying officer to release the property unless the judgment creditor files an undertaking (bond) or obtains a restraining order. A third party may also claim a superior security interest in or lien on personal property (or security interest in fixtures) and must follow substantially the same procedures as for claims of title or possession.

Either the levying creditor or third-party claimant may petition the court for a hearing to determine the validity of the third-party claim and the proper disposition of the property.[133] The time for filing the petition is very short, and if the petition is not timely filed, the court that entered the judgment loses jurisdiction to entertain the summary proceedings.[134] Additionally, during these proceedings, the property levied upon may be sold, delivered, or released by the levying officer if proper undertakings have been filed by the creditor and/or third party (or a deposit made by the creditor).[135] To prevent this, the court may order the sale stayed or enjoin any transfer or other disposition of the property until the hearing is concluded.[136] The parties are entitled to only a bench trial with all due process protections.[137]

A nonmoney judgment (requiring real or personal property to be sold or transferred to the judgment creditor) is enforceable in essentially the same manner as a money judgment and is pursuant to writ of possession or sale. This writ allows the levying officer to take possession of or sell property to enforce the judgment.[138]

Judgments for possession of personal property are often obtained where a creditor or lessee cannot peacefully repossess its collateral or leased property by private means. Such judgments may be enforced by levying a writ of possession of personal property by obtaining a court order directing the debtor to transfer the property to the judgment creditor or by appointment of a receiver in an appropriate case.[139]

The levying officer levies a writ of possession for personal property by seizing the property specified in the writ and taking it into custody in the same manner as an execution levy. Thus, the judgment creditor must advise the levying officer where the property is located. After obtaining custody, the levying officer must deliver the property to the judgment creditor.[140]

If personal property is located in a "private place" (e.g., a home), the levying officer must first obtain a seizure order before forcibly taking custody of the property.[141] If personal property is used as a dwelling (e.g., a boat or mobile home not affixed to land), the levying officer must comply with special service requirements, and a court order is required to remove the occupants.[142]

Instead of taking custody of inventory, equipment and other personal property of a going business, the creditor may instruct the levying officer to place a keeper in charge of the business.

A judgment for possession of real property is enforced by levying a writ of possession for real property. Levying a writ of possession of real property requires service of the writ on the judgment debtor and, if necessary, removal of the occupants from the property. The evicted occupants must remove all of their personal property from the premises by the time the judgment creditor takes back the property. Any personal property remaining on the premises can be sold by the judgment creditor in its entirety.

A judgment requiring the sale of real or personal property (e.g., in a judicial foreclosure action to enforce a security interest) may be enforced by levying a writ of sale or a receiver may be appointed.[143]

If a money judgment is included in a judgment for possession or sale (e.g., costs and attorney fees), the writ of possession or sale may be enforced by the levying officer as if it were a writ of execution to satisfy such judgment (unless a judgment for sale orders otherwise).[144]

Sister State Judgments

A judgment from another state (sister state) is entitled to the same "full faith and credit" in every court within the United States. A sister state judgment cannot be enforced in California until it is "domesticated" (or registered) as a California judgment in accordance with the Sister State Money-Judgments Act[145] or by bringing an action to establish the judgment in California.[146] Thus, a writ of execution may not issue on an out-of-state judgment until it is entered as a California judgment, and recordation of a sister state judgment in California will not itself create a real property judgment lien.

Under the Sister State Money-Judgments Act (SSMJA),[147] a money judgment obtained in another state may be filed with a California court, and a California judgment is thereby immediately entered, entitled to the same force as any California judgment. The SSMJA does not apply to federal court judgments.[148] Instead, federal court judgments are enforceable by registration in a California federal district.

After the SSMJA application is filed, the court clerk must enter a judgment for the amount remaining unpaid under the sister state judgment plus the accrued interest at 10 percent per annum (beginning on the filing date) plus the amount of the filing fee.[149] However, the judgment creditor generally must wait at least thirty days after serving the debtor with notice of entry before commencing enforcement proceedings (including obtaining issuance of a writ of execution). This gives the debtor time to file a motion to vacate the judgment.[150] The judgment debtor has thirty days following service of the notice of entry of judgment to vacate the judgment (but equitable relief may be available after this time expires).

Although the SSMJA is far more efficient to enforce sister state money judgments, a separate civil action must be used to enforce most sister state nonmoney judgments.[151]

Family law support orders are enforceable under the "Uniform Interstate Family Support Act" (UIFSA) and only for money support judgment.[152] The application should be filed in the county where the judgment debtor resides.

Satisfaction of a judgment must be filed immediately with the court by filing an acknowledgment of satisfaction of judgment.

A final money judgment is satisfied upon full payment of the amount necessary to satisfy the judgment or the judgment creditor may accept a lesser amount in full satisfaction of the judgment.[153]

A judgment debtor or owner of real or personal property subject to a judgment lien created under a money judgment may serve a demand on the judgment creditor's attorney of record that the creditor execute and deliver an acknowledgment of partial satisfaction of the judgment. If the judgment has been partially satisfied, the creditor must comply with the demand within fifteen days after actual receipt.[154]

Beginning January 1, 2013, a new government rule will take effect. The largest debt collection agencies[155] will be policed by the federal government[156] to make sure they comply with debt collection laws and follow ethical practices.

Can a Creditor Collect a Debt Against a Deceased Debtor?

Yes, a creditor can collect a debt against a deceased debtor, but the collection effort is against the deceased debtor's (decedent's) estate. If the creditor[157] had a prior judgment when the debtor was alive, then in most cases there would be a judgment lien against the debtor's property. However, if the creditor does not have a judgment against the debtor, then he or she would have to present a claim against the decedent's estate according to the particular state probate laws that govern presentment of a claim. In some cases, the creditor must apply to administer an estate in order to present his or her claim. The time to file a claim (statute of limitations) is often very short, so it behooves the creditor/claimant to know the procedural requirements of his or her jurisdiction and act expeditiously. The statute of limitations generally starts to run from the date of death, not from when an estate is actually opened.

In some cases, family members purposely delay opening the decedent's (deceased debtor's) estate until after the statute of limitations has run (expired) in order to time-bar all creditors' claims that would be presented once the estate is actually opened. In order for the creditor/claimant to protect his or her claim, it is strongly recommended that immediately following the death of the debtor, or as soon as the debtor's death is discovered, a demand letter and/or invoice statement in the name of the decedent must be mailed, preferably by certified or registered mail, to his or her last known address and to anyone appointed as the individual's caregiver, guardian, or power of attorney, if known. The reason for sending a demand letter is an exception exists under the presentment statute of most states that will deem a creditor's claim timely filed if the person who is eventually appointed the executor or administrator is actually in receipt of a written notice of the claim within six months from date of death. Sending the demand letter by certified or registered mail helps to prove that the appointed representative was in receipt of the written notice within the required time period. Typically, the debtor's estate rejects the claim. Then the creditor must immediately file a lawsuit against the debtor's estate as the statute of limitations for a rejected claim is usually extremely short.

An alternative option for a creditor if no estate is timely opened is to apply to administer the estate,[158] him or herself as a creditor, within the statute of limitations. Courts will often accept an Application for Authority to Administer an Estate along with a creditor's claim being filed simultaneously in order for the claim to be timely filed. The purpose in allowing the creditor to force open the estate is to put the known heirs and/or family members on notice that an estate application has been filed to liquidate the decedent's assets to pay his or her debts.

In summary, a creditor can collect a debt against a deceased debtor by filing a claim against the debtor's estate but the manner in which a creditor protects his or her interest is governed by individual state laws on presentment of a claim and the local court rules.

WHAT YOU NEED TO KNOW ABOUT A LAWSUIT

In order to establish a meritorious lawsuit, two requirements must be met: (1) there must be liability (or responsibility) and (2) there must be damage (or injury/harm). For example, suppose you run a red light and hit another car broadside causing a broken arm to the driver of the car you hit. You are liable because you illegally ran a red light and caused damage, namely physical damage to the car as well as a broken arm, pain and suffering, medical bills, lost wages, etc., to the driver. You can be 100 percent liable, but if there are no damages, then there can be no bona fide lawsuit. For example, suppose I'm playing golf, and I accidentally hit a golf ball out of the golf course and the ball hits your car window without breaking it or in any other way damaging it and simply bounces off the window. I'm certainly 100 percent liable because I hit the golf ball that hit your car window, but since there was no damage, there won't be (or shouldn't be) a lawsuit. On the other hand, there could be a situation where there's no liability and full damage. Suppose you're driving a car when suddenly it begins to hail and a giant hail ball breaks your car's windshield. Obviously, there's complete damage to your windshield, but no one's liable (because this situation is considered an act of God) and thus no one is responsible for the damage. Consequently, there won't be a lawsuit since there's no one to sue. However, in a situation where you're partially liable and you caused some damage, then you certainly could be sued. The important thing to remember is that in order to initiate a meritorious lawsuit, there must be some liability and some damage. You can also be liable for omissions (something you failed to do) as well as acts that you commit. For example, with regard to omissions, suppose you're driving and happen to see your friend walking to the shopping mall. As a friendly gesture, you offer a ride to your friend and he accepts. He hops into your car, and you disregard the fact that he failed to secure his seat belt. Shortly thereafter, you're involved in an automobile accident and your friend gets hurt. Your friend could sue you because as the driver of the car, it was your responsibility to make sure he was wearing a seat belt. You were negligent by failing to make sure your friend was wearing his seat belt (an omission under the law) and thus you are liable.

Now let's take a case where you're sued because you were liable and caused damages. The person (victim) you injured is called the plaintiff, and you are the defendant. Attorneys will often take a personal injury case on a contingency-fee basis. But before this happens, the plaintiff will have to explain the details to the lawyer who may immediately accept the case or may decide to do some research before accepting the case. Additionally, the attorney might do an asset search of the defendant, or some additional legal research to determine the strengths and weaknesses of the case. There's also the statute of limitations to consider, which is the window of time that the plaintiff has to file the lawsuit. If you wait too long, you may be barred forever from filing your lawsuit. The following table represents some general statutes of limitations:

Chart 1

The Statute of Limitations for all 50 States including District of Columbia

State	Statute	Written Contract	Oral Contract	Injury	Property Damage
Alabama	Ala. Code § 6-2-2 et seq.	6	6	2	6
Alaska	Alaska Stat. § 09.10.010 et seq.	3	3	2	6 (real property); 2 (personal property)

Arizona	Ariz. Rev. Stat. Ann. § 12-541 et seq.	6	3	2	2
Arkansas	Ark. Code Ann. § 16-56-101 et seq.	5	3	3	3
California	Cal. Civ. Proc. Code § 312 et seq.	4	2	2	3
Colorado	Colo. Rev. Stat. § 13-80-102 et seq.	6	6	2	2
Connecticut	Conn. Gen. Stat. Ann. § 52-575 et seq.	6	3	3	2
Delaware	Del. Code Ann. tit. 10, § 8101 et seq.	3	3	3	2
District of Columbia	D.C. Code § 12-301 et seq.	3	3	3	3
Florida	Fla. Stat. Ann. § 95.011 et seq.	5	4	4	4
Georgia	Ga. Code Ann. § 9-3-20 et seq.	6	4	2	4
Hawaii	Haw. Rev. Stat. § 657-1 et seq.	6	6	2	2
Idaho	Idaho Code § 5-201 et seq.	5	4	2	3
Illinois	735 Ill. Comp. Stat. 5/13-201 et seq.	10	5	2	5
Indiana	Ind. Code Ann. § 34-11-2-1 et seq.	10	6	2	6 (real property); 2 (personal property)
Iowa	Iowa Code Ann. § 614.1 et seq.	10	5	2	5

Kansas	Kan. Stat. Ann. § 60-501 et seq.	5	3	2	2
Kentucky	Ky. Rev. Stat. Ann. § 413.080 et seq.	15	5	1	5 (real property); 2 (personal property)
Louisiana	La. civil code § 3492 et seq.	10	10	1	1
Maine	Me. Rev. Stat. Ann. tit. 14, § 751 et seq.	6	6	6	6
Maryland	Md. Courts & Jud. Proc. Code Ann. § 5-101 et seq.	3	3	3	3
Massachusetts	Mass. Ann. Laws ch. 260, § 1 et seq.	6	6	3	3
Michigan	Mich. Comp. Laws § 600.5801 et seq.	6	6	3	3
Minnesota	Minn. Stat. Ann. § 541.01 et seq.	6	6	6	6
Mississippi	Miss. Code. Ann. § 15-1-1 et seq.	6	3	3	3
Missouri	Mo. Rev. Stat. § 516.097 et seq.	5	5	5	5
Montana	Mont. Code Ann. § 27-2-2021 et seq.	8	5	3	2
Nebraska	Neb. Rev. Stat. § 25-201 et seq.	5	4	4	4
Nevada	Nev. Rev. Stat. Ann. § 11.010 et seq.	6	4	2	3
New Hampshire	N.H. Rev. Stat. Ann. § 508:1 et seq.	3	3	3	3

New Jersey	N.J. Stat. Ann. § 2a:14-1 et seq.	6	6	2	6
New Mexico	N.M. Stat. Ann. § 37-1-1 et seq.	6	4	3	4
New York	N.Y. Civ. Prac. Laws & Rules § 201 et seq.	6	6	3	3
North Carolina	N.C. Gen. Stat. § 1-46 et seq.	3	3	3	3
North Dakota	N.D. Cent. Code § 28-01-01 et seq.	6	6	6	6
Ohio	Ohio Rev. Code Ann. § 2305.03 et seq.	15	6	2	4
Oklahoma	Okla. Stat. Ann. tit. 12, § 91 et seq.	5	3	2	2
Oregon	Or. Rev. Stat. § 12.010 et seq.	6	6	10	6
Pennsylvania	42 Pa. Cons. Stat. Ann. § 5501 et seq.	4	4	2	2
Rhode Island	R. I. Gen. Laws § 9-1-12 et seq.	10	10	3	10
South Carolina	S.C. Code Ann. § 15-3-510 et seq.	3	3	3	3
South Dakota	S.D. Codified Laws Ann. § 15-2-1 et seq.	6	6	3	6
Tennessee	Tenn. Code Ann. § 28-3-101 et seq.	6	6	1	3
Texas	Tex. Civ. Prac. & Rem. Code § 16.001 et seq.	4	4	2	2

Utah	Utah Code Ann. § 78-12-22 et seq.	6	4	4	3
Vermont	Vt. Stat. Ann. tit. 12, § 461 et seq.	6	6	3	3
Virginia	Va. Code Ann. § 8.01-228 et seq.	5	3	2	5
Washington	Wash. Rev. Code Ann. § 4.16.005 et seq.	6	3	3	3
West Virginia	W. Va. Code § 55-2-1 et seq.	10	5	2	2
Wisconsin	Wis. Stat. Ann. § 893.01 et seq.	6	6	3	6
Wyoming	Wyo. Stat. § 1-3-102 et seq.	10	8	4	4

For some ongoing (continuous) situations, there are no statutes of limitations. For example, suppose you broke off an engagement and your former lover keeps on making harassing telephone calls to you. In this situation, there is no statute of limitations because the continual harassing telephone calls constitute a continuous tort (nuisance). However, once the harassing calls stop, then the statute of limitations begins from the date of the last harassing call that was allegedly made to you.

After the lawyer accepts your case, he must then prepare and file the complaint (lawsuit) with the clerk of the court in the civil division (not criminal division) of the court. After the complaint has been filed, it must then be served (delivered) on the defendant. The reason for this is to give the defendant proper notice of the lawsuit. The original complaint is generally served by personal delivery using a registered process server or (less frequently) by any person (eighteen or over) who is not a party (neither the plaintiff nor the defendant) to the lawsuit. Occasionally, the complaint is left with a person who has an association with the defendant, and this called a subservice. Additionally, when a subservice is made, the process server must also mail an extra copy of the complaint directly to the defendant.

Another less common way to serve the complaint on the defendant is to mail it directly to the defendant together with a waiver of service (delivery). This is the general procedural method used sometimes in federal lawsuits. If the defendant decides to accept a waiver of service, then he must sign the form and mail it back to the plaintiff indicating a waiver of service. There are two main advantages for the defendant to waive personal service: (1) The defendant won't be bothered by a process server, and (2) in a federal lawsuit, the defendant will be given sixty days instead of the usual twenty-one days to answer the complaint.

A third way to notify a defendant occurs in cases where the plaintiff is not sure exactly where the defendant lives but knows the county where the defendant resides. In these particular instances, a plaintiff is permitted to publish a notice in a local newspaper and run the notice usually for four weeks. This method termed service by publication is infrequently used. The downside with this type of service is for defendants who do not read the local newspaper (which is common these days because of the Internet), so then there will be no way for the defendant to learn about the lawsuit. Fortunately, the service-by-publication method is seldom used; and if the defendant does not know about the lawsuit and a default judgment is filed against him, then the defendant can most likely get the default judgment vacated (removed) by the court.

I have a very important message regarding service (delivery) of the complaint. Please don't play "cat and mouse" with the process server and try to hide from the lawsuit. First of all, purposely evading service of process really gets judges mad. And secondly, the process server could get frustrated and damage your property, or he simply could toss the summons and complaint into the bushes without you ever knowing about it and then lie to the court by falsely stating that you were properly served. What happens next is that you receive a default judgment from the court because you failed to respond (answer) to the lawsuit. You might have trouble convincing the court that you never received the lawsuit when you attempt to vacate the default judgment on the basis of improper service of process.

Every jurisdiction has its own laws regarding service of legal papers. Generally, a summons and complaint (lawsuit) must be personally served upon the defendant. However, in some cases, a substituted service (subservice) is made upon another person at the defendant's residence or place of business/employment. For small claims lawsuits, service of the complaint may be made by US mail. In unusual circumstances, service by publication may be authorized by court order when an individual cannot be located in a particular jurisdiction.

Process service in a lawsuit generally refers to delivering the summons and complaint to the defendant. Proper service of the summons and complaint establishes personal jurisdiction of the court over the defendant. In the federal courts, service of process is governed by Federal Rules of Civil Procedure 4. Service on a defendant who resides in a foreign country is more complicated.[159]

You must be given proper notice to a lawsuit in which you are named as a defendant. Due process as guaranteed under the Fifth and Fourteenth Amendments to the United States Constitution requires that federal and state governments provide notice to all defendants of a pending lawsuit. Improper service means inadequate notice—a violation of your due process.

In most lawsuits in the United States, personal service is required to prove proper service. Most states allow substituted service in almost all lawsuits unless you are serving a corporation, LLC, LLP, or other business entity; in those cases, personal service must be made by serving the summons and complaint on the "registered agent" of a business entity. In most states, the summons and complaint must be visible to the person being served, e.g., not in a sealed envelope. If the defendant refuses to accept service or flees or closes the door, and the defendant has been positively identified as the person to be served, then the summons and complaint may be "drop" served, and this is considered a valid service. Personal service of process has been the hallmark for initiating litigation for nearly a century, primarily because it guarantees actual notice to a defendant of a legal action against him or her. Personal service of process remains the most reliable way to ensure compliance with constitutionally imposed due process requirements of notice to a defendant.

In most states, any person eighteen years of age or older and not a party to the lawsuit may serve the summons and complaint on the defendant. Most jurisdictions permit service to be made by a sheriff, marshal, or constable. There are licensing requirements for private process servers in New York City, Alaska, Arizona, California, Florida, Illinois, Montana, Nevada, and Oklahoma, Rhode Island, and Texas. Georgia requires a court order before a private person can serve legal papers.

When a defendant is unavailable for personal service, many jurisdictions allow for substituted service. The summons and complaint is left with another person of suitable age, such as a cohabiting adult or a teenager. Under Federal Rules of Civil Procedure, substituted service must be made at the residence of the defendant. In many states, where substituted service is effected, a second copy of the summons and complaint must also be mailed to the defendant. Substituted service often requires the process server to show that ordinary service was impracticable and that due diligence was made to attempt personal service and that substituted service will reach the party and effect notice.

In unusual circumstances, another method of service is "service by publication," which gives "constructive notice" to a defendant who is intentionally absent, in hiding, or unknown, and only when allowed by a judge's order based on a sworn declaration of the inability to find the defendant after "due diligence."

Service by mail is permitted in many US jurisdictions for defendants located in some US states and some foreign countries.[160]

Some jurisdictions allow voluntary waiver of service. The defendant voluntarily acknowledges receipt of the summons and complaint without the need to be served by a process server. Waiver of service is strongly encouraged by the US federal courts. Under

Federal Rule of Civil Procedure 4(d) (2), when a defendant refuses to waive service "without good cause," the defendant can be held liable for the cost of personal service. However, in most state courts, individual service by a process server is the best way to effect service of process as it easily comports with due process.

Most jurisdictions require business entities—such as corporations, LLCs, general and limited partnerships—to have a registered agent for acceptance of service in each jurisdiction where they are active. The identity of the agent for service can usually be found with the appropriate secretary of state. If the registered agent can't be found, the summons and complaint can usually be delivered directly to the appropriate secretary of state.

Typically, once service of process has been completed, the process server or other qualified individual must file a "Proof of Service" or "Affidavit of Service" with the court or mail one to the plaintiff to file with the court. It is signed by the process server and operates as prima facie evidence that service of process was effectively made.

If procedures for service of process are not rigorously followed, then a defendant in a court hearing can use the affirmative defense of "I was not served" as this often represents a successful affirmative defense in any lawsuit. If the court agrees that the defendant was not properly served, then the plaintiff has to start all over to effect proper services on the defendant.

In nearly every state of the United States, with limited exceptions, process servers are restricted from trespassing on property as a means of serving process. Such invasions, no matter how innocuous, are regarded as not only invalid but illegal and may result in penalties for offenders. Most gated communities and apartment buildings are required to allow process servers to enter.

In California, "registered process servers" are granted "a limited exemption against trespassing." Washington State also grants a limited exemption or affirmative defense against trespassing. This allows process servers to enter private property for a reasonable period of time to attempt service of process. Moreover, in California, gated communities (with or without security guards) must allow a registered process server to enter for service of process upon presenting valid identification and indicating to which address the process server is going. Often, the security guard contacts the resident and alerts them that a process server is on his way to their residence.

Most jurisdictions have a deadline for completing service of process after filing the summons and complaint. In the US District Courts and in New York, service must be completed no later than 120 days after filing the summons and complaint. In Hawaii, a civil lawsuit must be served within six months after filing. In California, service must be completed within sixty days after filing. Dies non juridicum is a prohibition some states impose restricting the delivery or serving of legal documents on Sundays, holidays, and/or election days, which can be exempted by court order.

New York's City Council recently passed a bill that requires process servers to use a GPS log every time they attempt service of process. The legislation also ensures that deceitful process servers who dump papers instead of serving them—a trick known as "sewer service"—could be liable if the people they were supposed to serve decide to sue them. The registered process servers must electronically log their attempts to serve papers using some kind of GPS device and keep those records for seven years.

Bottom line: Don't evade the process server. You don't have to open your door when the process server comes to your residence. Just tell him or her to leave the legal papers under the doormat or next to the front door.

Getting hit with a lawsuit is a traumatic event. There can be no doubt about that. Your first question might be: "Will I get wiped out?" To answer this, you'll first need to carefully review the complaint (lawsuit) to figure out what the basis for the complaint is and what you might have done wrong to get hit with a lawsuit. Even if you determine that you might not get wiped out, it could still happen. Our legal system is unpredictable and fickle. I had an arbitration award of $20,000 against me that literally turned into a $2 million judgment! That happened despite my attorney's repeated assurances that the original lawsuit was filed in limited jurisdiction where judgments are capped at $25,000, and I could not possibly get wiped out.

Lawsuit protection is more than just protecting you against getting wiped out. It's also meant to protect you against the emotional stress that comes along with a lawsuit. In fact, protecting against emotional stress may be just as important as not getting wiped out. Lawsuit protection, therefore, is an absolute must for anyone living in America today. America is the lawsuit capital of the world. Americans have the highest risk of getting sued in the world. If you live in America, this book is for you. Please make no mistake; you must take immediate steps to protect yourself against the lawsuit epidemic, which is quickly engulfing America. Prepare now before it's too late. Getting hit with a lawsuit is an attack. It's a personal attack on you! A lawsuit that you're unprepared to handle can be devastating. The emotional stress which commonly results from a lawsuit often leads to health problems as well. Some of these problems include insomnia, hypertension, depression, anger, and confusion. Some people have even had strokes and heart attacks from the stress of a lawsuit. There is very little written on the adverse health consequences from a lawsuit. And there's practically nothing written about how to prevent those health problems and the stress that comes from being sued. That's until now. This chapter will discuss what has never been written about—the preemptive steps you can take to lessen or even eliminate the stress of adverse health problems associated with being sued.

Did you know as a parent of a child under age eighteen, you could be held responsible and sued for their misdeeds?

A lawsuit is a civil action as opposed to a criminal action brought in a court of law in which a plaintiff claims to have incurred a loss as a result of a defendant's actions, and demands a legal and/or equitable remedy, i.e., a monetary award and/or nonmonetary judgment such as repossession of property. If the plaintiff wins the suit, then a judgment will be entered in the plaintiff's favor, and a variety of court orders may be issued to enforce a right, award damages, or impose a temporary or permanent injunction to prevent an act or compel an act. Declaratory judgments may be issued to prevent future legal disputes. A lawsuit may involve the state to be treated as if it were a private party in a civil case.

Many lawsuits involve torts. No, this isn't some kind of French pastry. A tort is simply wrong behavior that usually causes an injury or harm. For example, specific torts include assault, battery, defamation, libel, negligence, product liability, trespass, and intentional infliction of emotional distress. There are three general tort categories: (1) intentional torts (e.g., intentionally making false statements about someone); (2) negligent torts (e.g., accidently causing a car accident); and (3) strict liability torts (e.g., a manufacturing defect that results in automobile tire blowouts leading to numerous injuries).

Tort law is designed to compensate victims (plaintiffs) for their losses and also occasionally to prevent future losses by punishing the defendants. There are compensatory damages, that represent the actual money the plaintiff lost, and there are also punitive damages. Punitive damages are what the defendant has to pay as his punishment for being malicious or oppressive or acting fraudulently. In an effort to rein in outrageous punitive damages, the US Supreme Court placed limits on the amount someone can recover in punitive damages.[161]

When you're hit with a lawsuit, the first thing you should do is contact your insurance carrier. Then you should review the lawsuit point by point and counter every allegation with your own response. Your lawyer (appointed by the insurance company to represent you) will then advise you. If the insurance company won't accept your claim (which will be very infrequent), then you'll need to retain your own attorney. It's important to inform your attorney that you are judgment proof so that information can be quickly conveyed to the plaintiff. If you're lucky, the plaintiff may get "cold feet" and immediately dismiss the lawsuit against you.

There's a 25 percent chance that you will have a catastrophic lawsuit sometime during your lifetime![162]

Some contracts you sign may require mediation before you can file a lawsuit in the event of a dispute.

There are two court systems in the United States: state court and federal court. If your lawsuit involves someone from another state (known as a diversity case) and has damages over $75,000, then you may file it in federal court; or if it involves federal law or the US Constitution (known as federal-question jurisdiction), then you are allowed to file it in federal court. On the other hand, if your lawsuit involves only state law or the state constitution, then it must be filed in state court. Unless, of course, your lawsuit involves both federal and state laws, in which case you can go to either state or federal court.

The summons informs a defendant that he or she is being sued and asserts the power of the court to hear and determine the case. It also tells the defendant of the necessity to answer the complaint by a certain deadline, and failure to do so could result in a default judgment.

Once you've been served, you must respond to the complaint usually within twenty to thirty days (depending on the jurisdiction) by filing a responsive pleading. One type of responsive pleading is called an answer. In that document, you might totally deny the complaint, deny certain parts of it, point a finger at someone else not named in the complaint, point out technical problems with the complaint itself. Your answer's main purpose is an attempt to modify the complaint.

Alternatively, you may file a motion to dismiss the lawsuit if

1. there is no legally sufficient claim in the complaint that warrants the award the plaintiff is requesting,
2. the court lacks the subject matter jurisdiction or personal jurisdiction for the case,
3. the court isn't of the proper venue, or
4. there has been a problem with the service of process itself.

You may also file a countersuit against the plaintiff, which makes the plaintiff the counter defendant. This begins a new complaint process; however, the two cases will be heard as one lawsuit.

If you don't respond to the lawsuit, then the plaintiff will get a default judgment against you, and the plaintiff will then become the judgment creditor and you'll be the judgment debtor. It's best to respond to the lawsuit even if you're judgment proof.

Discovery is the process of gathering all of the evidence and information, no matter how trivial it may be, from all parties involved as well as third parties outside of the suit. It can be information about the facts of the case, documents that may be important to the case, background information on the parties involved, names of others who might know more—anything that is germane to the lawsuit. Information from a conversation that would never be admitted in court can also be part of the discovery process. The justification for this is that it might lead to admissible evidence as a result of the knowledge gained from a discussion among the defendant, witnesses, or others related to the case.

While discovery is expansive, there are some things, however, that are protected by privilege:

1. The marital privilege—Conversations between spouses are privileged because of the importance of free communication between a husband and wife.
2. Doctor-patient privilege—Conversations between doctors and patients are privileged unless the patient is suing for personal injury.
3. Penitent-clergy privilege—Conversations with religious counselors are privileged.
4. Attorney-client privilege—Conversations between attorneys and clients are privileged unless the client is suing his attorney for malpractice.
5. Tax returns—Certain financial information can be privileged, but exceptions can apply.

There are five general categories of discovery:

1. Requests for production of documents
2. Requests for admissions
3. Depositions
4. Interrogatories
5. Requests for an Independent Medical Examination (IME)

The judge will schedule case management conferences (CMCs) during the lawsuit. These can cover things like the status of discovery (i.e., whether it is moving along as it should be), settlement potential (i.e., whether there is a chance for settlement at this stage), or resolving any discovery disputes that may be arising. Motions can also be filed if any of the discovery requests are not being met. For example, a motion for more responsive answers can be filed. This type of motion requires documentation of each discovery request, the response, and the reason the response is inadequate. Additionally, a motion to compel can be made if opposing counsel refuses to cooperate in discovery, and the information requested is important to the case. Sanctions can be requested with discovery motions to offset additional legal costs.

In the request for production of documents, each attorney requests documents that will help him prove his case. These documents can include business records, traffic or police reports, or anything else that might apply.

Requests for admissions are requests your attorney will make of those involved on the opposing side of the suit to state under oath that certain facts are true or untrue. This is to save time and money gathering evidence and to back up facts that are either obvious or prove that documents are authentic.

Interrogatories (or form interrogatories) are questions the attorneys prepare to send to the other party to answer. The answers to these questions can become part of the sworn testimony used in the lawsuit, so they are quite important.

Depositions are live interviews (question and answer sessions) the attorneys have with the other party, witnesses, or any third-party who may be able to provide information for the lawsuit. They are the most important part of discovery because this is where attorneys find out what the opposition is going to say in his or her testimony as well as assess his or her ability as a witness. A critical part of all depositions is that the witnesses tell the truth—untruths (even minor ones) can come back to haunt them at the trial. Juries focus on those kinds of things. A witness's credibility can be weakened when even minor discrepancies crop up. Many lawsuits have been lost when a witness's credibility has been impeached. Bottom line: always tell the truth at your deposition and your trial.

Independent Medical Examinations (IMEs) are medical examinations made by a neutral physician who is not involved with anyone in the lawsuit and is not the treating physician. IMEs are occasionally performed for personal injury cases.

Motions to quash may be filed if one party is trying to get protected information from the other party during discovery. If the judge allows the information to be admitted, then another motion (motion to seal matters produced upon discovery) can be filed.

If either party of the lawsuit doesn't provide information he is supposed to provide, then the judge can also impose a sanction against him. This means he will be fined for not providing the information. The sanction can be against either the attorney or the client. It depends on which person is refusing to provide the information.

The primary purpose of a trial is to resolve disputed facts in the lawsuit. If there are no disputed facts, then a motion for summary judgment can be filed. A summary judgment means the judge reviewed the undisputed facts, applied the law, and made a ruling—expediting resolution of the case and saving you time and money.

A motion for judgment can be made after the trial has started but before the case goes to the jury and allows the judge to render a judgment. Like the summary judgment, this motion is used when there aren't any facts that are disputed in the case. If testimony in the trial has resolved the disputes (at least to reasonable minds), then the motion for judgment will probably be accepted and the judge will rule—if not, the judge will deny the motion.

A motion for judgment notwithstanding the verdict (JNOV) is a motion filed when the jury's verdict is unreasonable and clearly contradicts the facts. In most jurisdictions, in order to file a motion for judgment notwithstanding the verdict, you must have previously filed a motion for directed verdict after all of the evidence had been heard. If the judge denied the motion and sent the case to the jury, and the jury's verdict was totally unreasonable, then a motion for judgment notwithstanding the verdict can be filed.

Often before a case goes to trial, discussions take place for settlement. Factors to consider include, does the defendant have the money you are demanding for damages? If not, is there any use in going to trial? Do you and your attorney think you have a good chance of winning? If not, then settling might be your best option. Another factor to consider is that your attorney's fees may end up being higher than what you are awarded by the judge or jury.

An important point to remember is that disputed facts require a trial for resolution. There's no way around this.

A settlement ends the lawsuit with a written document known as the "dismissal with prejudice," and the defendant is "released" from the lawsuit. If a settlement is not reached, then the court will set a trial date. There are two types of trials: (1) A bench trial where the judge decides the case or (2) a jury trial where the jury decides the case.

The trial consists primarily of deposing witnesses where the plaintiff's attorney and the defendant's attorney ask the witnesses a number of questions to determine the truth of the disputed facts. This is called testimonial evidence. Additionally, nontestimonial evidence is introduced at trials as well. In civil cases, the plaintiff has to prove his case by a preponderance of the evidence. That means 51 percent or greater. In most states, punitive damages must be proven by "clear and convincing" evidence, which falls between the "preponderance" standard and "beyond the reasonable doubt" standard. This might be comparable to 75 percent or greater.

After the presentation of all evidence, the case will either go to the judge (in a bench trial) or to the jury (in a jury trial). Sometimes a jury is deadlocked, and no decision can be reached. This results in a mistrial. In civil cases, this happens infrequently. In most cases, a decision by the jury is reached. If the plaintiff wins the lawsuit, a judgment is entered in favor of the plaintiff. If the defendant wins, then he gets to go home relatively intact. Suppose the plaintiff wins. Then the fun begins. If you have prepared properly, you will be judgment proof, and the fun will begin for you. Otherwise, the plaintiffs will have fun. The decision is yours. By the way, even if the plaintiff wins at trial, you can file posttrial motions to get the judgment thrown out. Should that fail, you can always appeal.

Criminal law involves wrongful acts committed against society. State and/or federal governments prosecute and punish the criminal defendant. On the other hand, civil law spells out duties that exist between individuals. Many civil lawsuits involve torts (wrongs).

A tort, French for "wrong," is wrongful conduct or behavior that results in an injury or some form of harm. Part of doing business today and part of everyday life is the risk of being sued. Liability insurance to protect against the cost of lawsuits is an ever-increasing expense for most businesses and people. For example, an employee who allegedly gets injured on the job can sue his or her employer for having an unsafe working environment. A consumer, who allegedly gets injured while using a product, can sue the product manufacturer for making a defective product. A patient who allegedly received incorrect medical treatment can sue the physician. The common ground of all these cases is the alleged wrongful conduct by one person that injures another. Tort law covers such wrongful conduct.

There are three major categories of torts:

1. Intentional torts include assault, battery, conspiracy, conversion, defamation, false imprisonment, fraud, infliction of mental distress, libel, misrepresentation, invasion of right to privacy, trespass against land and personal property, nuisance, and infringement on trademarks, patents, and copyrights.
2. Negligence torts include malpractice. Negligence is an unintentional failure to exercise the care that a reasonably prudent person would exercise. The area of tort law known

as negligence involves harm caused by carelessness, not intentional harm.

3. Strict liability torts are "no fault" torts or liability without fault, which include workers' compensation and products liability.

WHAT YOU MUST DO TO PREVENT A LAWSUIT

First of all, a little common sense is in order. Generally speaking, if you're respectful and friendly toward others, then there's less of a chance of getting sued. It's a well-known fact that doctors with poor bedside manners get sued much more often than doctors with good bedside manners. Also, try to be conscientious and try to do a good job in order to minimize errors. This helps too. Even minding your own business helps; but please remember, don't be fooled by the "whistle-blower" laws that in theory have been designed to protect you but in realty can come back to haunt you. Keeping your home clean and free of hazards can help prevent lawsuits. For example, if there are children's toys scattered around the entrance to your home, and someone happens to trip and injures himself, you could be sued. Also, don't engage in any criminal activity because your victims could turn around and sue you. Criminal defense attorneys often advise their clients to plead no contest to misdemeanor plea agreements because a "no contest" plea can't be used against a defendant in any future civil lawsuit. A civil suit can easily arise from a crime, and a "no contest" plea from you means the victim has the burden of proving his or her case in a civil suit whereas if you plead "guilty" to a crime, then the victim or victims don't have to prove their case and can use your guilty plea automatically to win their lawsuit.

The law requires a defendant to mitigate (lessen) his or her liability. For example, suppose you run a textile mill and discover there are microscopic cotton fibers in the air that could cause respiratory ailments in your workers. The law clearly requires you to fix the problem. If you do it soon enough, you may be able to avert a lawsuit. But if you do get sued, the damages will likely be less since you took steps to quickly remedy the problem. Most attorneys will tell you to never admit liability because your admission could be used against you in a lawsuit with potentially serious consequences.

Driving safely also lessens the risk of a lawsuit because there's less of a chance you'll cause an accident. Physicians should always obtain a signed consent from their patients, which apprise them of any risk from a medical procedure. Where known risks exist, you have a legal duty to disclose that information to others. If not, you could get sued. Good Samaritan laws protect you in emergency situations where you provide life-saving heroic measures. Disclosure of a known risk is absolutely essential; it helps tremendously to prevent lawsuits. Warning labels are also necessary. Release of liability forms, risk disclosures, and the duty to notify are important ways to help prevent lawsuits. Once unknown risks are discovered, it behooves you to disclose those risks in order to avoid potential liability. Also, you must exercise due diligence when hiring, otherwise you could get sued for negligent hiring. You should have an employee operations manual for the workplace. There must never be any sexual discrimination in the workplace. Teachers can't hit students because corporeal punishment is illegal in most jurisdictions, and the schools they work for could get sued. Some government employees (who work under color of state law) have qualified immunity or absolute immunity (judges and politicians). Be careful what you post on the Internet otherwise you could get sued for libel and/or defamation. A frivolous lawsuit can get you sued for abuse of process or malicious prosecution. A stunt or practical joke that goes terribly wrong can also get you sued. When in doubt, always check with an attorney.

An asset protection plan that you record, and thus make known to others, acts as a shield against lawsuits. That's because many attorneys, before accepting a case, will perform an asset search to see if you own a house and other valuable assets. If the attorney sees that you don't own a home or discovers a transmutation agreement, then he or she will be less inclined to prosecute a lawsuit against you, especially on a contingency-fee basis. Therefore, visible asset protection will often protect you against lawsuits. The old adage "An ounce of prevention is worth a pound of cure" fits perfectly well with the sound recommendations given in this guidebook. Before you're hit with a lawsuit, I strongly urge you to consider implementing the strategies and recommendations contained in this guidebook. The best time to begin your asset protection planning is:

1. *before* you're threatened with a lawsuit,
2. *before* you're actually involved in a lawsuit, and
3. *before* you have any existing creditors.

If all three of these conditions apply to you, then you can start right *now*! Otherwise, it could be too late! Please don't procrastinate. Repeat: do *not* procrastinate. If you wait until you're hit with a lawsuit, you could easily get wiped out. This is not a game, folks. Don't fool around. If you live in America, lawsuits are lurking just around the corner. You must take action now!

Lawsuit protection directly protects against lawsuits while asset protection indirectly protects against lawsuits. Preventive measures include the following:

1. No criminal activity, including fraud and deceitful conduct.
2. Sometimes an honest and heartfelt apology will prevent a lawsuit, but first check with your attorney or insurance company before making an apology because it could be construed as an admission of liability.
3. Acting friendly and treating others with respect and dignity will often prevent lawsuits.
4. Minding your own business and avoiding saying negative things about others will also help to prevent lawsuits.
5. Common sense and decency can prevent lawsuits.
6. Doing good work and minimizing mistakes is a helpful way to prevent lawsuits.
7. Removing and eliminating safety hazards prevents injuries and thus avoids lawsuits.
8. Risk disclosures and warning labels steer people away from danger and prevents lawsuits.

9. Obeying all laws, rules, and regulations is a wise practice for avoiding lawsuits.
10. And finally, perhaps the simplest and best way to protect against lawsuits is to purchase plenty of liability insurance. Don't skimp on liability insurance. Liability insurance will protect you most of the time against lawsuits. The few cases where it doesn't is the reason you still need lawsuit and asset protection.

Tort lawsuits in the United States cost $248.1 billion in 2009, which is roughly $808 per person.[163] About sixteen million lawsuits are filed in the United States each year at an estimated cost of about $150 billion, or 2.5 percent of the Gross National Product.[164] The chance of one of these lawsuits being directed at you grows yearly.

The liability insurance provided by most automobile and property policies almost always pays for accidental injuries to another person or to another person's property. But coverage in most plans is usually limited to between $100,000 and $300,000. That's why you need umbrella insurance, which picks up where standard policies leave off, extending and broadening standard liability coverage. An umbrella insurance policy increases liability limits, most commonly to $1 million, on current property or automobile policies. Typically, umbrella policies also extend protection to situations in which you would not normally be covered such as libel, slander, defamation of character, false arrest, or invasion of privacy. Umbrella insurance supplements your standard automobile and homeowners policies, so most insurers require you to maintain specific coverage amounts on your property and car policies and that may require you to increase the liability amounts on your current coverage to qualify for the umbrella insurance. The cost of umbrella insurance is very reasonable, usually about $200 to $300 a year for a $1 million policy. In my opinion, you must have umbrella insurance for maximum protection.

About 67 percent of all state tort lawsuits are from automobile accidents.[165] About 33 percent of homeowner's claims are from dog bites, a figure that translates into an estimated annual payout of $1 billion.[166]

Bear in mind that liability coverage does more than just protect you from lawsuits. It will protect you from financial loss if someone gets injured in your home or automobile. And suppose a friend who injures himself on your property, for example, may not want to sue you but will want his medical bills covered. Liability insurance will pay the medical bills without your being responsible.

If you have high net worth, then you must have an umbrella policy because you will more likely be a target for litigation, and you have much more to lose. So be sure to protect yourself with a good umbrella insurance policy. Since 1991, the average compensatory award exceeded $700,000 and has grown every year since then. About 40 percent of compensatory judgments exceed $100,000 and more than 10 percent are over $1 million. These figures do not include punitive awards or legal fees. Liability insurance pays for judgments up to your policy limit and includes legal expenses as well. Legal expenses today easily cost tens of thousands of dollars and your liability policy automatically covers these expenses. It's up to the insurance company whether to settle the case or fight the lawsuit. However, the cost of your legal defense will not be deducted from your liability limit. Your liability limit is reserved for settlement or judgment payments.

If you run a home-based business, you will most likely need a business liability policy in addition to any personal coverage you have. That's because a personal liability policy will not cover any injuries incurred while someone is on your property for the purposes of conducting business. Business liability insurance is broader than professional liability coverage, because it covers workers in the event of a lawsuit. If you engage in any high-risk activities, such as race car driving or skydiving, you will need a "rider" for coverage for related accidents or property damage that will require additional premiums. And most importantly, make sure your liability limit matches or exceeds your total worth. Do you want to lose your house or other assets because you failed to spend a couple of extra hundred bucks for ample insurance?

To protect against lawsuits, corporations often use warnings, disclaimers, notices, disclosures, and consent forms. Here are some ways to protect your business from a lawsuit:

1. Always be prepared for a lawsuit, and never let anyone take you by surprise. This guidebook will help you to prepare for a lawsuit.
2. All agreements should be in writing. In fact, most states have a statute of frauds which nullifies certain contracts that are not in writing. Do yourself a favor, and get all contracts in writing. It's something that you just have to do for protection. Also, make sure the written agreement specifies how disputes will be resolved. Many contracts these days specify that the parties agree to binding arbitration in order to avoid a lengthy and expensive legal battle.
3. Always make certain an attorney reviews all of your written agreements. A loophole in your contract can be disastrous. A good attorney will be able to spot these potential loopholes and will be able to help modify your contract so that these potential pitfalls can be averted.
4. It's all about customer service, customer service, and customer service. Treat your customers with the utmost respect, and you'll come out a winner. Often customer lawsuits are not about money but because they felt they were slighted or treated unprofessionally. Consider compromising with the customer, even if you know you're right and the customer is wrong, it's often cheaper than going to court. And very importantly, even though you're right and the customer is wrong, extending a discount, offsetting a bill, and offering a sincere apology will often avert a lawsuit, even a small claims one.
5. Spend money wisely, and that includes business liability insurance. Business liability insurance is your friend.

Literally, it's pennies on the dollar for protection. Don't skimp on good liability coverage.

Many lawyers will tell you a lawsuit is a crapshoot. You can be perfectly in the right, but the jury could rule against you. It happens all the time. Even the cost of defending yourself against the lawsuit could be so prohibitive that it would be cheaper for you to settle out of court. But why would you settle if you're in the right? Nothing is certain. We live in a very litigious society, and everyone is exposed to the risk of a lawsuit. That means everyone needs protection. This guidebook will show you how to achieve *maximum* protection. If you own a business, lawsuits can come from your customers as well as from government organizations who may charge you, for example, with a statutory violation for alleged pollution or hazardous waste dumping.

A judgment made against your business could not only wipe out your business but could also reach all of your personal assets as well.

To protect you personally, corporations and limited liability companies (LLC) provide *limited* liability to their owners. For example, simple negligence will protect the owner of a corporation or LLC against personal liability. However, gross negligence will not. Also there is a growing trend in employment law to hold managers and supervisors personally liable for discriminatory decisions.

Recent court decisions are holding human resource managers, supervisors, and business owners personally liable for their actions under some employment laws. The basic corporate veil limiting personal liability no longer totally protects you. Fortunately, you are not liable under every employment law. Public employers may be personally liable for claims under the federal Civil Rights Act.[167] In *Knussman v. Maryland*,[168] the court upheld a jury's finding that the state personnel officer was personally liable for $375,000 in emotional damages caused by her failure to grant leave to a male employee because of his gender. Similarly, in *Alexander v. Fulton County*,[169] the Eleventh Circuit upheld a jury's finding that a sheriff was personally liable for intentionally making racially based employment decisions and assessed over $500,000 in punitive damages against her and the county employer.

Many state courts have found supervisors liable for tort claims (wrongful acts) such as defamation, intentional infliction of emotional distress, invasion of privacy, negligent training, fraud, and misrepresentation.

Here's what you can do to protect yourself against these employment lawsuits:

1. Make sure your company carries Employment Practices Liability Insurance (EPLI).
2. Make sure you are fully complying with all federal and state employment laws.
3. Maintain up-to-date written policies that comply with the law and be certain to follow them.
4. Any questions or concerns about your decisions should be discussed with your appropriate corporate legal counsel.
5. Your decisions, especially negative ones, should always be completely explained in writing.
6. Always keep written records of your decisions.

Business owners, managers, and licensed professionals can be personally sued for any action taken as part of your business or profession, regardless of your business structure. That's why you must protect your personal assets.

Money you have in qualified Employee Retirement Income Security Act (ERISA) plans is protected from creditor seizure and in bankruptcy. Simply stated, creditors cannot touch ERISA retirement plans in bankruptcy, regardless of how much they are worth. Furthermore, Individual Retirement Accounts (IRAs), pension plans, 401(k)s, Social Security, and other benefits receive the same protection from creditors in bankruptcy. And with the new Bankruptcy Abuse Prevention and Consumer Protection Act of 2005 (BAPCPA), even non-ERISA tax qualified plans, including traditional and Roth IRAs, 403(b) and 457 plans are protected if the debtor can prove that the fund from which they receive payment or may receive payment is tax exempt. (See chapters 35 and 47.)

One way of avoiding estate taxes is by gifting money or other assets to your children at a rate of no more than $13,000/year per child (or $26,000 if you are a married couple). More than this will incur gift taxes.

In cases where you have no insurance coverage, your legal defense in a lawsuit could easily cost you over $100,000 beginning with an initial retainer of $10,000 to $25,000 and with an hourly rate ranging anywhere from $250 to $450 per hour. So even if you eventually win the lawsuit, you still lost!

So how do you prevent getting hit with a lawsuit? The secret is to be like a poor impoverished person—don't own anything! When the plaintiffs and their lawyers discover that it's simply not possible to squeeze any money from you, they'll go after bigger and better things and they won't waste any time trying to come after you. In essence, that's how you kill a lawsuit.

Summary

There's a lot of material here, and it's quite overwhelming the first time you see it. My suggestion is for you to reread either the entire book at a later date or review specific chapters that interest you. You're probably wondering, "What should I do first?" (See Appendix A.) For starters, make an appointment with your insurance agent or go online and/or check the Yellow Pages for an insurance agent. Check to make sure your agent is state licensed and whether there is any pending or past disciplinary action against the insurance agent. If there is, it could be a red flag, and you may want to choose a different insurance agent. If for any reason you are disappointed with your insurance agent, switch agents. There are lots of insurance agents, and you can easily find an insurance agent who is happy to help you. Make an appointment as soon as possible with your insurance agent for a complete review of your insurance needs. Explain to your agent that you want plenty of liability insurance to protect yourself against lawsuits and other claims. This can usually be accomplished quickly. The next order of business involves your home. If you're renting, then you need renter's insurance and an umbrella insurance policy. If you own your home, then the first order of business is to determine whether your homeowner's insurance is up to date and that you're fully protected against liability claims and property and casualty claims such as fire, theft, and earthquakes (if you live in an earthquake zone). And don't forget flood insurance (if you live in a flood-prone area) where you have to get flood insurance directly from FEMA (the Federal Emergency Management Agency). If your home is owned as community property or in joint tenancy, then you'll need to transfer it so that it will be less likely available for creditor seizure in the event you lose a lawsuit. It's also critical that you find an attorney who specializes in real estate law or asset protection. Your house should either be transferred to the least vulnerable spouse using a quitclaim deed or a transmutation agreement (which is used in community property states like California) or by transferring it to an entity like a trust or a corporation, which may be even be better. Here's the bottom line: you must take proactive steps now to protect your home. The sooner the better. Also be sure to record the transfer document in the recorder's office of your county. After the transfer is made, please follow these three rules: (1) record the transfer, (2) record the transfer, and (3) record the transfer.

After obtaining liability insurance and transferring your house, you can now take a deep breath and relax a bit. The next order of business is less urgent but nonetheless very important. If you are self-employed, you must operate your business either as a corporation or limited liability company. As stated previously, I believe that a C corporation is the best way to run your business. Please make an appointment with an attorney who specializes in business law and forms corporations and limited liability companies for his or her clients. Once your company is formed, the next step to take care of involves your automobiles. You should transfer the ownership of your vehicles to the least vulnerable spouse. Also, if you have a joint or community bank account, you'll need to close it and open two new separate bank accounts for each spouse. Additionally, most of the money should be placed in the personal bank account of the least vulnerable spouse. After these tasks are completed, you can now coast. For most people, you're now in great shape. If you want the ultimate protection plan, then you'll have to step up to an offshore (irrevocable) trust, which is a bit more complicated and more expensive but will provide you with the best satisfaction and luxury of being "bulletproof"—essentially impervious to creditor attack, provided it does not run afoul of the fraudulent conveyance laws.

WHAT TO DO AND NOT DO WHEN YOU GET SUED

Now that you've been sued, the "clock" starts to run. In most cases, you have only thirty days to answer (respond to) the lawsuit. In federal court, you have just twenty-one days to answer the lawsuit unless you agree to waive personal service of the summons and complaint. In that case, the court gives you a full sixty days to respond. *Never*, and I repeat never, ignore a lawsuit even if it appears to be frivolous! My suggestion is for you to pursue the following course of action: (1) Carefully read the complaint and write down any arguments you may have which contradicts or refutes any of the statements made in the complaint; (2) immediately give a copy of the complaint to your insurance carrier along with a copy of your opposing arguments, if any; (3) additionally, provide a copy of the complaint with your opposing arguments to your attorney; (4) remember to keep a copy for yourself of the complaint with your opposing arguments; and (5) regularly follow up to get a status report each week with the insurance company and/or with your attorney. It's very important to stay on top of this to make sure your complaint is timely answered. This is critical as the complaint must be answered before the "clock" runs out, which typically is just thirty calendar days in state court or twenty-one days in federal court.

If you've taken the time to implement a lawsuit protection plan as suggested in this guidebook, then you're in great shape. There's really no need to get all worked up if you get sued. First of all, the lawsuit filed against you could very well be a frivolous suit brought on by a disgruntled individual. If that's the case, then the suit against you can easily be dismissed by your insurance company or your attorney. To repeat, it's very important for you to carefully examine the complaint in detail. Often there are errors that only you can identify. So your first task is to take notes and write down rebuttal information for every key point in the complaint. This information is critical, so be sure to tell your insurance carrier or your lawyer. It's also important to realize that in most cases, your liability insurance company will handle your lawsuit. The insurance company will even hire an attorney for you at no cost to handle your case. It's really important to contact your insurance carrier immediately once you've been served with a lawsuit. Don't delay. In most cases, you must respond to the lawsuit within thirty days for state cases and twenty-one days for federal cases. If you fail to respond by the deadline, you will lose the lawsuit through a default judgment. Moreover, your insurance company may not accept your late claim after thirty days. Therefore, I strongly urge you to contact your insurance company immediately whenever you get sued.

In the unlikely event that your insurance company won't handle your claim (lawsuit), then your next step is to quickly find an attorney to handle your lawsuit. If you don't have an attorney, then you must act quickly to hire one. The Internet and the local Yellow Pages are two good places to start. You can also contact the State Bar Association and your local County Bar. Some attorneys will give you a free initial consultation. But it's best to call first. If possible, try to visit at least three attorneys. Bring a copy of the lawsuit and your rebuttal information. Let the attorney know that you'll need to evaluate a few more lawyers before making a final decision. Be sure to take notes at each attorney visit. Afterwards, check your notes to help you decide which attorney will best represent you. Here are some key questions to ask the attorney: (1) How long have you been in practice? (2) Do you carry malpractice insurance? (A "no" answer raises a serious red flag.) (3) Have you ever been sued for malpractice? (4). Have you had any disciplinary action taken against your license? (5) What is your specialty, if any? (6) Have you handled similar cases to mine? If the answer is yes, then ask, "How many?" What is your fee arrangement? Occasionally, one of your friends might suggest a good attorney. Be sure to inform the attorney that you are judgment proof. This information alone could put the "brakes" on a plaintiff's lawsuit. Once the plaintiff's attorney learns that you are judgment proof, he could get cold feet, especially if he has taken the case on a contingency-fee basis; and the lawsuit could quickly get dismissed. Moreover, a quick low-priced settlement could be in the offing once the revelation is made that you are judgment proof. So be sure to mention this important information to your attorney.

There are various ways to respond to the lawsuit. Your insurance company or your attorney, or you (if you're representing yourself, which I strongly discourage) will try to get the lawsuit dismissed (in some places this is termed a demurrer). If this proves unsuccessful, then you must file an answer to the complaint. If the lawsuit survives an attempt at dismissal, then it must be answered. The defendant(s) can generally deny all or some of the allegations in the complaint. If the defendant has some legitimate or legal reason for doing what the allegations state, then this is asserted by the defendant and is termed an affirmative defense.

After the complaint has been answered, the next stage of the lawsuit is called discovery. Discovery is the mutual exchange of information, documents and evidence between the plaintiff and defendant. Discovery consists of depositions, interrogatories, requests for admissions, subpoenas, and in some cases medical examinations. After discovery is completed, and there are no legal disputes regarding the evidence, one or both parties can ask the judge to decide the lawsuit in what is known as a Summary Judgment. However, in many cases, there are usually some material disputes between the plaintiff and defendant. In these cases, a trial will be held to resolve the disputed matters. If neither party requests a jury, the judge will decide the lawsuit. If at least one party requests a jury, then there will be a trial before a jury, and the jury will resolve (decide) the disputes and render a judgment. After the judgment, the losing party often appeals the judgment (verdict). This can be a time-consuming and expensive process. It should also be noted that at any time there can be a settlement between the parties. The settlement has to be approved by the court, and over 90 percent of all lawsuits settle.

Please remember, *never* ignore the lawsuit! Do not contact the plaintiff yourself, even for a possible settlement discussion. Notify your attorney or insurance company at once about the lawsuit. And *never* admit liability. Also, review the lawsuit and give your records to your attorney and/or to the insurance company. And one more thing to remember, please don't panic. If you follow the advice given in this guidebook, there's absolutely no need for you to panic at all. Lawsuit protection and asset protection provides peace of mind. It really does.

Now let's suppose you've been sued, but unfortunately, your assets are still in your name. The question is: should I start to transfer my assets? My response is that it's better to do something rather than nothing in this particular situation. If you do nothing and you lose the lawsuit, your creditors will take away your assets like picking low-hanging fruit from a tree. On the other hand, even if you commit a fraudulent conveyance, your creditors will have to initiate a new lawsuit to avoid (unwind) the transfer. If your mobile liquid assets have been sent offshore, then that adds another layer of difficulty for the creditors. The downside is that the judge can order you to repatriate the assets and should you refuse; you could be jailed for contempt of court. If that possibility exists, my recommendation is for you to head for the nearest airport and purchase a one-way ticket out of America.

WHAT IS THE EASIEST AND SIMPLEST WAY TO PROTECT AGAINST LAWSUITS?

Insurance—This is one of the most important things you must have, plenty of insurance in order to protect yourself against lawsuits and other claims. Yet this is overlooked by so many people. Many people don't realize insurance covers them against most types of lawsuits. Asset protection seminars (also known as "road shows") seldom mention anything about insurance because the promoters (salesmen) don't make any money selling insurance (since they're attorneys, not insurance agents). They make money by selling you their services whether legal services or financial services or some other form of service. I can't overemphasize the fact that whether or not you like insurance, or even if you don't believe in it, you must have plenty of liability insurance to protect you. It may help to think of insurance as a "necessary evil." Please, just do yourself one big favor and purchase plenty of liability insurance. You get the biggest bang for your buck with liability insurance. It literally costs pennies on the dollar for coverage. Don't skimp on the coverage either. (Disclaimer: I have no ownership interest whatsoever in any insurance company, thus I have no conflict of interest when making the recommendation that you purchase adequate insurance.) Here's the bottom line: having adequate liability insurance is the single best way to protect yourself against lawsuits and to protect your assets as well. If you do nothing else, please get plenty of liability insurance! It's the single best hedge against risk. This is because for relatively little money (the premium) you get protection against great loss (the liability coverage). It really gives you "the biggest bang for your buck." (In Spanish, the word for insurance is *seguro*, which means security.) Yes, insurance can give you security and peace of mind.

Experts say insurance is the first line of defense against a lawsuit. Standard homeowner's and professional malpractice policies cover general liability and provide an attorney to defend you should someone fall on your property or claim you were negligent in your profession. In addition, an "umbrella" liability policy that kicks in when regular insurance benefits are exhausted will handle most large claims.

Asset protection planning is a supplement to liability insurance. Liability insurance also protects you against a fraudulent transfer claim. If you get sued, your insurance company will defend it and pay to settle it. Please remember that you must file a claim within strict time limits otherwise your insurance carrier may not honor your claim.

There are many different forms of insurance and literally thousands of insurance companies to pick from. How do you go about choosing? First of all, not all insurance companies are alike. Some insurance companies with cheap rates (premiums) balk at paying claims. Having an insurance company that doesn't pay claims is basically like not having insurance at all. So this obviously won't do. You need to have insurance with companies that are financially sound, have a good record of paying claims on time, have competitive rates, treat their customers with respect, and have good industry ratings.[170]

The types of insurance you should get all depend on what your needs are. I will discuss the various types of insurance that are available and the purpose they primarily serve.

- Business insurance—Liability, sex discrimination, employment.
- Homeowner's insurance—Include an additional rider for jewelry, art, cash, and guns.
- Renter's insurance
- Automobile/motorcycle insurance
- Umbrella insurance—Slander, defamation, libel.

- Director's and officer's insurance
- Errors and omissions insurance
- Life insurance—Include funeral expenses
- Disability insurance
- Worker's compensation insurance
- Property and casualty insurance
- Aircraft insurance
- Boat insurance
- Medical insurance—Hospital, doctors
- Dental insurance
- Optical insurance
- Car rental insurance
- Viatical insurance
- Flood insurance
- Earthquake insurance
- Legal insurance
- Malpractice insurance
- Mortgage insurance
- Surety bonds
- Long-term nursing care

Always read the fine print of any contract you sign, and watch out for exclusions and waivers. Always be sure to pay your premiums on time.

Auto/home/business/life/umbrella. Having no insurance is just like playing Russian roulette with your finances. If you can afford liability insurance, then you really must get it. Not getting liability insurance, in my opinion, is an act of irresponsibility. Even being underinsured is much better than having no insurance at all. For example, let's suppose there's a lawsuit against you with ten claims, and just one of those ten claims is covered by your insurance, then under the law, your insurance company is obligated to defend you against the *entire* lawsuit although you'll be responsible for paying the other nine (noninsurance-covered) claims yourself. By being relieved of having to pay the legal fees for the entire lawsuit, you'll be saving yourself a lot of money too. That's why it really does pay to have liability insurance coverage. It's the easiest and simplest way to protect against lawsuits and other liability claims!

Here are some important reasons why you must have insurance:

1. Insurance protects against lawsuits and other claims.
2. The insurance company pays for your legal representation.
3. If you don't have insurance, then you must decide either to pay for outside legal representation or otherwise you have to represent yourself in court which is often foolish.
4. If a lawsuit contains multiple claims, some which are covered by your insurance and other claims which are not, the insurance company is nonetheless obligated under the law to represent you for the entire lawsuit although you'll have to pay for the claims not covered by insurance.
5. Insurance companies often use skilled law firms who can artfully negotiate settlements or can fight the lawsuit for you.
6. Plaintiffs usually (but not always) settle lawsuits for no more than the policy limit of your insurance.
7. Insurance is often required in order to do business with other companies.
8. Not having insurance can be viewed as being socially irresponsible and could hurt your business. For example, in California, under the law attorneys must inform prospective clients whether they carry malpractice insurance. Uninsured attorneys lose potential clients.
9. Insurance is an excellent way to hedge (or mitigate) against risk often for pennies on the dollar. For example, a $1 million umbrella insurance policy can be had for as little as $200 to $300 each year which is less than one dollar per day!
10. And finally, there's the emotional aspect of having insurance that provides security (the word for insurance in Spanish is "el seguro" for security) and peace of mind which is a very important consideration, especially in today's litigious (lawsuit-happy) society.

Business Liability Insurance

Incredibly, nearly four out of every five small US businesses are structured as a partnership or sole proprietorship.[171] This form of ownership is dangerous because it puts your business and personal liabilities at risk. Owning business liability insurance protects both your business and your personal assets.

A common misconception regarding a corporation or a limited liability company (LLC) is that a business owner is protected from personal liability and liability insurance is unnecessary. These entities provide *limited* but not complete liability. You can still be personally liable if:

1. you have acted in an irresponsible or illegal manner,
2. you do not operate your business as a separate legal entity,
3. you have personally injured or harmed someone, or
4. you have signed a personal guaranty for a loan.

Business liability insurance protects your small business in the event of a lawsuit for personal injury or property damage. In most cases, it will cover the damages from a lawsuit together with the legal fees. There are several types of business liability insurance:

1. General Liability Insurance—This form of business liability insurance is the main coverage to protect your business from: injury claims, property damages, and advertising claims. General liability insurance also known as Commercial General Liability (CGL) may be the only type of business liability insurance you need depending on your business situation.
2. Professional Liability Insurance—Business owners providing services will need to consider having professional liability insurance known as errors and omissions insurance. This coverage protects your business against malpractice, errors, negligence, and omissions. Depending on your profession, it may be a legal requirement to carry such a policy. Doctors require coverage to practice in certain states. Technology

consultants often need coverage in independent contractor work arrangements.

3. Product Liability Insurance—Small businesses selling or manufacturing products should be protected in the event of a person becoming injured as a result of using the product. The amount of coverage and the level of risk depend on your business type.

Every licensed professional should have insurance. It's a known fact that quite a few attorneys don't carry malpractice insurance possibly because they believe they can defend themselves in a malpractice suit. While that may be true, those attorneys should consider that their time is money too. For example, if an attorney has to spend fifty to one hundred hours involved in a lawsuit, and they bill their fees at $200 per hour, then there then they are sacrificing $10,000 to $20,000 of their income defending themselves in a lawsuit. Also, a judgment against an attorney may be more damaging and difficult to ignore. An attorney subject to a turnover order must relinquish the money he would normally get from his client trust fund and hand it over to the creditor. Furthermore is the fact that even with a newly formed professional corporation, the attorney is still subject to the original turnover order. By law, all attorneys must place the retainer fee in a client trust fund that they can subsequently withdraw funds from through their billing. The turnover order allows the creditor to intercept the money the attorney would normally get and places that money into the creditor's hands. Therefore, a creditor can easily seize money from the attorney's client trust fund with a turnover order from the court. Attorneys who practice without malpractice insurance are taking an incalculable risk which, in my opinion, is very foolish.

Some professionals require bonding through the use of surety bonds that fall under license and permit bonds. These bonds are generally required to obtain a license or permit in any city, county, or state. The license bond is used to ensure that a professional service provider is qualified to do business and will abide by whatever state law, statute, ordinance, or regulation requires.

Professional corporations (abbreviated as PC or P. C.) are corporate entities formed by licensed professionals such as attorneys, architects, engineers, public accountants, and physicians. Professional corporations do not usually afford the professional person(s) the same degree of limited liability as an ordinary business corporation or limited liability company. Professional corporations are often formed as part of a law firm or a medical practice. The professional corporation does not allow professionals to be free from personal liability from the result of his or her professional actions, but it does allow other shareholders or directors to be protected from the actions of the professional.[172]

Malpractice Insurance

There are two types of malpractice insurance: (1) claims-made and tail coverage and (2) occurrence coverage.

Claims-Made Coverage:

As long as you continuously renew your claims-made policy, you can file a claim for any incident that occurred any time from the policy's start date. For example, your claims-made insurance began in 1995, and you have renewed your policy continuously since then with no lapse in coverage. A patient you treated in 1997 sues you. Since you've renewed your policy continuously since 1995 and it is currently in force, you are still protected for that 1997 incident.

With a claims-made policy, any claim you file covers you from the start date of your insurance.

The premiums in the initial years of a claims-made policy are generally less than those of an occurrence policy offering similar coverage. In general, a claims-made policy will save you money over an occurrence policy after just three years. With a claims-made policy, the limits of liability are those in effect when the claim is made. For example, in 1995, your claims-made policy had limits of liability of $100,000/$300,000. Then, in 1998, you increased your limits to $1 million/$3 million, and a patient you treated in 1997 files a malpractice claim against you in 1998. Therefore, the current

$1 million/$3 million limits apply because those are the limits in place when you reported the claim.

Tail Coverage for Claims-Made Policies:

If you decide to discontinue your claims-made policy, tail coverage is available to extend your claims reporting period and should be seriously considered. Tail coverage is optional protection that allows you to file claims after your policy has ended for alleged injuries that occurred while your policy was in force. It is necessary only if you discontinue your claims-made policy. Tail coverage is a one-time fee that's calculated as a percentage of your annual premium. When you purchase tail coverage, your policy's existing limits of liability are extended to pay claims reported in the future. Tail coverage is necessary to protect yourself from future claims and will provide you long-term protection and peace of mind. For example, in 1995, you purchased a claims-made policy. In 1998, you discontinued your policy and purchased tail coverage to extend your claims reporting period. In 1999, a patient you treated in 1996 files a malpractice claim against you. Since you purchased tail coverage, you can file that claim in 1999 for the 1996 incident.

Occurrence Coverage:

The occurrence policy protects you against incidents that occur while the insurance is in force, not when the claim is filed. For example, you purchase an occurrence policy in 1994 and discontinue the policy in 1996. A patient you treated in 1995 files a malpractice claim against you in 1998. Since the patient was treated in 1995 while the insurance was in force, you can file the claim in 1998 for the 1995 incident. The occurrence coverage insurance automatically protects you for any incidents that occurred while you were a policyholder. This means that you can report claims anytime so long as the incident occurred while you had insurance coverage.

With an occurrence policy, the limits of liability are those that were in effect at the time of the incident. For example, in 1993, your occurrence policy had limits of liability of $100,000/$300,000. Then, in 1998, you increased your limits to $1 million/$3 million. A patient you treated in 1994 files a malpractice claim against you in 1998. The $100,000/$300,000 limits of the 1994 policy year apply because those were the policy limits at the time of the alleged incident. Tail coverage is unnecessary with an occurrence policy because you can always file a claim after the insurance is discontinued so long as the incident occurred while your policy was in effect.

One way to lower insurance premiums is to take higher deductibles. Insurance is supposed to be used for major losses, so it makes sense to have high deductibles. Also, be sure to have high liability limits and err on the side of a higher liability limit. Be extremely careful using cheap insurance companies; they may not pay your claims! You must use a good reputable insurance company that pays claims! Never skimp on insurance.

What should you do if you're considered high risk? Unfortunately, you'll have to pay a much higher premium; but if the rates are prohibitive, then you should probably consider a lower liability coverage limit with a high deductible for a lower premium. One of the reasons to do this is because plaintiffs often settle for the maximum policy limit of your insurance. Having some insurance is therefore much better than having no insurance at all. In so many situations, insurance is really the only way to offset liability risk.

Many businesses are targets for lawsuits. They seem to act like a magnet that attracts lawsuits. That's why you *must* have business liability insurance. But business liability insurance isn't foolproof and in some instances you may face claims that are not covered by the business insurance policy. That's why as an added measure of security, you need to implement a lawsuit and asset protection plan.

Umbrella insurance is generally so inexpensive and gives you so much more protection that it would be foolish to pass it up. Most auto insurance companies provide a maximum of $500,000 for liability coverage. In my opinion, this is probably insufficient for a major automobile accident with major injuries or multiple victims or even death. In order to have more liability coverage for your automobile(s), an umbrella insurance policy is the best way to increase your coverage to at least $1 million or more. Additionally, your umbrella insurance policy will also cover you against slander and defamation and will provide extra homeowner's coverage as well. This coverage usually costs less than one dollar per day (about $200 to $300 per year). You really shouldn't pass it up. So please do yourself a favor and carry umbrella insurance for peace of mind.

While insurance may be a necessary evil, in reality, insurance is a necessary component to a lawsuit protection plan. Without adequate insurance, your lawsuit protection plan is incomplete, and you'll only invite problems.

Life Insurance

There are basically two types of life insurance: term and whole life/universal. Term life insurance is like renting the insurance. You don't build any cash value, and the insurance will expire at a predetermined future date. If you should happen to die while the term insurance policy is in force, your beneficiaries (likely your spouse and/or children) will get the insurance money. Since there's no cash value on a term life insurance policy, it's of no value to a creditor. Furthermore, your beneficiaries' payment of the death benefit does not make them responsible for any of your debts.

On the other hand, whole life insurance or a universal life policy does build cash value and could be subject to a creditor's collection efforts. Under federal bankruptcy, the cash value of a life insurance policy is protected (exempted) only up to $8,000.[173] States also exempt the cash value of life insurance, which varies considerably from Maine's meager amount of $4,000[174] to Hawaii's and Florida's unlimited amount.[175]

Remember, if a corporation purchases life insurance for its employees, it's tax deductible.

In order to fully protect your life insurance, don't own the policy yourself. In most cases, you can always transfer the ownership of your life insurance policy if necessary. Instead, you can have the least vulnerable spouse own the policy, or better yet, you can set up an irrevocable trust and place the life insurance with trust. This type of trust is called an Irrevocable Life Insurance Trust (ILIT).

Besides protection from creditors, an ILIT also provides estate tax benefits as well as tax-free proceeds to beneficiaries outside the decedent's estate. Since you no longer own the policy, it's outside your estate. The insurance premiums must be paid by the Trust. An alternative would be to fully fund the insurance and then transfer it to the ILIT. Interestingly, the gift tax is for present transfers, and the IRS does not consider a transfer of life insurance to an ILIT a present gift. Therefore, you won't have to pay a gift tax when you transfer your life insurance to the ILIT. This is based on a court decision[176] where your beneficiaries have to be given an opportunity every year to withdraw money from the ILIT. However, in most cases, your beneficiaries would probably decide to forego a withdrawal of money from the ILIT. The tax code also provides that if you should die within three years of setting up your ILIT, the value of the death benefit reverts back to your estate. There's also another type of trust that can protect against creditors and if combined with an ILIT makes for an extremely strong asset protection tool; it's called a Beneficiary Defective Spendthrift Trust (BDST).[177] (See chapter 32.)

Insurance Ratings

There are a number of insurance-rating companies, such as A. M. Best and Standard & Poor's, which provide insurance company ratings to help consumers make more informed decisions. If you're in the market for insurance, you should look for an insurance company that's been around a while with a proven ability to pay claims. Every state has a department of insurance that monitors the financial status of insurance companies and regulates their practices.

Insurance companies are rated by the following insurance-rating companies:

- A. M. Best Insurance Company Ratings
- Moody's Insurance Company Ratings
- Standard & Poor's Insurance Company Ratings
- Tower Hill Insurance Company Ratings
- Weiss Insurance Company Ratings

Lloyd's of London is the world's specialist insurance market where members join together as syndicates to insure risks.

Offshore (captive) insurance companies provide large US corporations with insurance coverages they need but are unable to obtain economically through the mainstream insurance market thus reducing their costs.

I recommend that you obtain insurance quotes online and consult with an independent insurance agent to ensure you receive the right coverage at the lowest price. Finding the right liability insurance company requires some research and perseverance. It makes a difference which company you choose, because you want an insurance company that is reliable and financially stable so as to have peace of mind.

Before you begin looking for liability insurance, you should determine exactly what type of coverage you need. If you are a healthcare professional, then medical professional liability insurance is right for you. If you are a lawyer, a consultant, a broker, an accountant, an agent, an architect or an engineer, errors and omissions (E & O) insurance is the protection you need. For a consumer, you need automobile liability coverage, homeowner's coverage including adequate liability coverage, and an umbrella policy with a minimum of $1,000,000 of liability coverage. For business owners, business liability insurance is a must.

One of the most efficient ways of shopping for liability insurance is through Internet marketplaces where you can get free no-obligation quotes from multiple insurance companies. It's important to compare the quotes offered by different insurance companies. Price should be one of the guiding factors contributing to your decision, but it shouldn't be the only one. In fact, the cheapest quotes are not worth considering since they usually offer inadequate coverage and often fail to pay claims. Make sure you choose an insurance company that offers the coverage you need for an affordable premium and has a track record of paying claims.

Another significant factor in your search for the best liability insurance company should be the financial strength and reliability of the insurance company. Fortunately, there are ways to check how stable and trustworthy an insurance company is. A. M. Best is one of the major agencies providing unbiased insurance company rating services. You should look for a credit rating of A++ (Superior) or A (Excellent). The higher the rating, the more reliable and financially stable it is.

Carrying no liability insurance is a recipe for disaster. Your failure to protect against lawsuits invites a financial catastrophe with the loss of your hard-earned money and assets. It's absolutely essential that you carry plenty of liability insurance. With all due respect, you're acting stupidly if you don't carry liability insurance, and this also demonstrates great irresponsibility on your part. I understand there may be a few situations where you just can't get any liability insurance coverage because it may be prohibitively expensive or may not be available. (For example, several years ago, obstetrician-gynecologists in Florida were unable to get malpractice coverage because it was so prohibitively expensive.) You may be in a situation where you are considered high risk because of previous claims you submitted and are no longer able to afford the insurance coverage. However, in most instances, people can get liability insurance; and there's really no good reason not to obtain it. Please do yourself a favor and get plenty of liability insurance for *maximum* lawsuit protection.

WHY YOU MUST SEPARATE AND PROTECT YOUR ASSETS

Always separate and protect your assets. For example, if you get sued, will your neighbor have to worry? Not unless he owns part of your house.[178] If you're at high risk for a lawsuit, you should never own a home. Let your spouse own the home. Or your home can be owned by an offshore trust or a family limited partnership (FLP) or a limited liability company (LLC). The guiding principle here is to disperse your assets by separating them and to protect them by disinheriting them through an asset transfer—get the assets out of your name as well as any ownership interest. That's the guiding principle here.

Before I address the issue of why you must separate your assets, I need to explain the concept of "safe assets" and "dangerous assets." First of all, what is an asset? An asset is simply property that belongs to you, either actually or constructively. An actual asset is simply property that you own outright. For example, let's say you buy a computer and register it in your name. That computer belongs to you. You can also have equitable (or constructive) ownership in property. For example, let's say you are a sixteen-year-old beneficiary of a trust that owns a house, and the trust deed (contract) stipulates that the house will transfer to you upon attaining age twenty-one. The law declares that you have an equitable (or constructive) ownership interest in the house. Assets can be further defined as "safe" and "dangerous." A "safe asset" is an asset that is unlikely to attract a lawsuit. For example, a "safe" asset would be a one-hundred-share stock certificate of Google Corporation. This is an asset which has value, but you're not going to get sued for owning Google stock. The stock, in and of itself, is not going to attract a lawsuit. Other examples of safe assets would be your home, bank account, brokerage account, jewelry, and coin/stamp collection, etc. On the other hand, a "dangerous asset" could very well get you sued. Dangerous assets are assets that often attract lawsuits (whether or not the asset itself is intrinsically dangerous). Common examples of dangerous assets would be your business, your automobiles, and surprisingly (in my opinion) being a male. (I'll explain shortly.) Businesses are frequently the target of lawsuits, so it goes without saying that you need plenty of business liability insurance. Automobiles are involved in over thirty thousand deaths each year (in 2010 there were 32,885 fatalities) and about 2.5 million injuries annually. There are millions of lawsuits each year involving motor vehicle accidents. The only effective way to protect against an automobile-related lawsuit is to carry plenty of automobile liability insurance with a high liability limit. The reason men attract a disproportionate large number of lawsuits is because they are much more predisposed to criminal activity compared to women. There are roughly ten times more male prisoners, parolees, and ex-felons in the United States compared to women. Also, there are many men with anger management problems who perpetrate violence and criminal activity, and this often leads to lawsuits. And finally, more men run businesses than women, and as previously stated, businesses are a frequent target for lawsuits. An excellent example of a "dangerous asset" would be an asbestos manufacturing company that you own which produces insulation. Since scientists have discovered that your insulation causes lung cancer, your company is going to get hit with multiple lawsuits, and you'll probably go out of business and lose everything. These examples show how assets can be divided into "safe" and "dangerous" categories.

We can also categorize assets into "mobile" and "immobile" categories. For example, your house is an "immobile" asset. You can't physically move your house. It stays put. Money and jewelry are "mobile" assets that can be easily and quickly transferred. These are assets that don't stay put. If necessary, they can even be quickly secreted to hidden locations and put out of the reach of creditors without their knowledge. Unfortunately, from an asset-protection perspective, your house is locked into place by its physical location and by its title in the recorder's office. Another potential problem is that your home could have a lot of equity (value) that would obviously be very attractive to a creditor. Therefore, your home is a fixed asset that requires special treatment. As a result, you must take important steps to protect your home. Whatever you do, don't overlook your home and leave it vulnerable to creditors. Please take my advice and protect your home now. Don't procrastinate. If you're not presently facing any lawsuits and you don't have any outstanding judgments or current creditors, then you can take immediate steps right now to legally protect your home. Transferring your home when you have current creditors is both criminally fraudulent (fraudulent conveyance) as well as a civil fraud. While it's unlikely that you'll ever be criminally prosecuted for a fraudulent transfer, it's much more likely that a court will avoid (rescind) the fraudulent transfer, thereby making it available for creditor seizure. My advice is to refrain from any type of transfer during these situations.

As a general rule, you must always separate your dangerous assets from your safe assets. There is one exception to this rule, and it involves automobiles. This is especially the case where your automobiles are fully paid for and you hold title to the automobiles and they have significant value of over $10,000. In this situation, you should transfer the ownership of the automobile(s) to the least vulnerable spouse. But please remember to make sure you always have plenty of automobile liability insurance! A transmutation agreement or even a prenuptial agreement can effectively separate the dangerous assets from your safe assets. (This is more fully discussed in chapter 12.)

The primary reason for separating your assets is to keep your valuable safe assets away from creditors. This is true because the valuable safe assets should be separately owned by the least vulnerable spouse or should be owned by a separate legal entity such as a trust, FLP, or LLC. In the vast majority of cases, the least vulnerable spouse, FLP, LLC, or trust will never become a judgment debtor, and therefore the property will never be seized. On the other hand, a business (which is a dangerous asset) or someone at high risk for a lawsuit can easily lose their property to a creditor. It therefore makes good sense to keep as few assets as possible in a business or with a high-risk individual. That's because a creditor would have very few assets to go after. Remember, be sure to keep most of your assets and the all of the valuable safe ones with the least vulnerable spouse or alternatively in an FLP, LLC, holding corporation, or a trust. Once your assets have been separated into safe and dangerous ones, they must be separately owned as well! This is the only way to protect the safe assets from the dangerous ones. In community property states like California, transmutation agreements are an excellent way to separate assets. (See chapter 12.)

For example (and I'm not being sexist, but just using a stereotypical example), suppose the husband owns a meatpacking factory with twenty employees, which uses dangerous meat-cutting machines. His wife is a homemaker caring for their two children. In this scenario, it's highly unlikely the wife is going to get sued, except possibly for an automobile accident. Therefore, the wife should carry a large amount of automobile liability insurance. On the other hand, the husband has an enormous amount of potential exposure to lawsuits. First, there is the ever-present possibility of employee injury, so he must carry workmen's compensation. Secondly, if the factory-processed meat is ever accidentally tainted with E. coli bacteria and inadvertently shipped out, then some people will undoubtedly get very sick and could possibly die. You can bet what follows next will be a series of lawsuits. Thirdly, a visitor could slip and fall in the factory should an employee accidentally spill liquid on the factory floor. You can bet that a lawsuit will result. I'm sure you get the picture now. The husband's business is a potential lawsuit minefield. That's why the husband must incorporate his business and have plenty of business liability insurance. He also has to make sure his wife separately owns all of the safe assets such as the home and other valuable assets.

You must separate and protect your assets much like multiple fortresses. Who should own the cars, especially the valuable ones?

This can be a difficult question because expensive cars are both dangerous and valuable. But the driver who causes an accident can be directly sued even if he doesn't own the car. The solution here is to have plenty of automobile liability insurance and to register the ownership of the car in the name of the least vulnerable spouse, often the wife. How about guns? Who should be the registered owner? Since guns are relatively inexpensive and they are exempt property, the most vulnerable spouse should own them, and this is often the husband. What if the wife owns the gun and the husband uses it to shoot someone? This is an example of a situation that can go from bad to worse: the husband uses his wife's gun to shoot someone and guess who gets sued? Both husband and wife.

Here's a concept you won't find anywhere else—safe people versus dangerous people. Dangerous people will often attract lawsuits and, hence, should not own many assets and certainly should *never* own any of the safe and valuable assets.

Please remember to always separate safe assets from dangerous (liability-generating) assets, and dangerous (liability-generating) assets should always be held in separate entities. For example, you would never have two apartment complexes owned by the same limited partnership. In this case, you would need two separate limited partnerships or another form of legal entity.

USE MULTIPLE LAYERS OF PROTECTION FOR MAXIMUM FORTIFICATION

The more layers of protection you use, the stronger your lawsuit and asset protection plan is. Here's a simple example: suppose you want to protect your new car against auto theft. The first thing you'll want to do is to install an auto alarm in your car and paste decals on your car windows warning of an alarm system in your car. The next step you'll take is to use a club-like device that is clearly visible on the steering wheel of your car. What you have now done is to advertise to everyone, including a potential auto thief, that your car has at least two layers of protection—an alarm and a club-like device—that would have to be circumvented in order to steal your automobile. The auto thief would have two major obstacles to overcome in order to steal your car: (1) He would have to disarm the auto alarm, and (2) he would have to remove the club-like device from the steering wheel (at a minimum) in order to steal your car. Additionally, there's always the possibility there could be other antitheft devices unbeknownst to the potential car thief. For example, there could be a Low Jack (GPS tracking) device that he might not know about. All in all, these are strong deterrents that make it highly unlikely your car will ever be stolen.

Now let's carry this concept over to the area of lawsuit protection and asset protection. You need to do the same thing to protect all of your assets, including your home. And it really is not that hard to accomplish nor expensive to do! This guidebook will easily guide you to *maximum* lawsuit and asset protection that's quick, easy, and above all, inexpensive. On the other hand, many asset-protection seminars and asset-protection attorneys will typically cost you thousands of dollars, and they will often drag their feet for months or even years before your protection plan is fully implemented. That's because many attorneys are just too busy to do a good job, or they purposely want to squeeze you for more money.

It goes without saying that the more layers of protection you have, the more difficult it is for your creditors to collect on their judgment against you. In cases where attorneys perform asset searches on you, this could stop a lawsuit from ever getting off the ground.

In cases where a lawsuit has just begun, your attorney can inform the plaintiff's attorney that you are "judgment proof" or "judgment protected" and this information could, in and of itself, quickly derail a pending lawsuit. Folks, the first layer of protection *must* be plenty of liability insurance. This is a critical first step. If you do nothing else, I implore you to get plenty of liability insurance. This could literally save you from financial disaster. However, liability insurance is not always foolproof. As you may know, there can be a number of exclusions in your insurance policy. That's why you need additional layers of protection besides insurance. Separation of your safe and dangerous assets is another critical layer of protection, and be absolutely certain you have separate owners for your safe and dangerous assets. Do not commingle safe assets with dangerous assets! The owner of the safe assets (almost always the least vulnerable spouse like the wife) should have absolutely no ownership interest involving the dangerous assets. The dangerous assets must be separately owned from the safe assets. Also, you must be very careful not to accrue or build an ownership interest in the other spouse's separate assets. For example, if the husband pays the mortgage on his wife's house, he could become a part owner of wife's house! (See chapter 12 on how to avoid this pitfall.)

Another strong layer of asset protection is to use an irrevocable trust or better yet an offshore trust. (See chapters 32 and 34.) A family limited partnership (FLP) while not as strong as an irrevocable trust or an offshore trust can nonetheless still provide a strong layer of asset protection as well as estate tax advantages. (See chapter 15.) A business should always be operated as a corporation or limited liability company (LLC) in order to obtain limited liability protection.

The irrevocable offshore trust is a strong vehicle for asset protection. If structured correctly and timely formed, it's virtually impossible to mount a successful attack on an offshore trust. (Many centuries ago, in medieval England, even the king couldn't interfere with a trust whose beneficiary was the church!) The successful key to all of this is timing. You *must*, and I repeat *must* act: (1) *Before* you are threatened with a lawsuit, (2) *before* you are sued, and (3) *before* you have creditors.

Once you have been threatened with a lawsuit, or once you've been sued, or once you have creditors, it's legally too late to initiate an asset protection plan because then you would be in violation of the fraudulent conveyance laws. (There are some exceptions to this. See chapter 22.)

Here is a useful "seat belt" analogy: your car comes equipped with seat belts, air bags, and some models even have anticollision radar. Obviously, your car protects you with multiple layers of protection. You shouldn't even think of driving without buckling up. The same holds true with asset protection. Your liability insurance is analogous to your seat belt, and the other measures of lawsuit protection are like your air bags and anticollision radar. Just like buckling up before driving, you shouldn't even think of living in society today without having liability insurance and a lawsuit and asset protection plan.

NINE COMMUNITY PROPERTY STATES WHERE YOU CAN LOSE EVERYTHING

There are nine community property states where you can lose everything: Arizona, California, Idaho, Louisiana, Nevada, New Mexico, Texas, Washington, and Wisconsin. These states are dangerous for judgment debtors. These nine states favor creditors. But the good news is that you can do something about it. Please read on.

If you live in any one of these states, you must take immediate action now to protect yourself. These states and their courts are very friendly to creditors. They also happen to be very biased against debtors. Debtors are definitely at a disadvantage in these nine states. Here's why. The community property laws basically state that all property acquired during marriage belongs equally to both spouses, except for gifts and inheritances, and this is termed "community property." Even if property acquired during marriage is titled in the name of just one spouse, the creditors could make a showing that the property in question really belongs to the "community." For example, let's say the husband has a judgment against him and is therefore a judgment debtor. Even though the husband and wife may have purchased a house in California and decided to title the house in the wife's name, the creditors could make a showing in court with an explanation to the judge that the down payment and/or mortgage payments came from community funds and therefore there's a community-property interest in the house despite the fact that the house is titled solely in the wife's name. Based on these circumstances, the court would probably decide that the house is indeed community property. So even though the wife is not a debtor, and the house is titled in her name, the house can nonetheless be sold off by the creditors because it's community property, and the husband (who is a judgment debtor) has an interest in it. The way to get around this problem is through the use of a transmutation agreement (postnuptial agreement), which divides community property into separate spousal property during the marriage. (Please see chapter 12.) Another way to avoid this problem is to execute a prenuptial agreement (before the marriage), which will maintain separate spousal property during the marriage and will prevent the formation of community property. I'll explain how to do this later. A transmutation agreement should always be recorded even if no real estate is involved. This too will be explained later. The transmutation agreement accomplishes two things: first, it operates to divide community property into the separate property of both spouses, and secondly, it abrogates (extinguishes) any future community property by the spouses. This is something that is vitally necessary for you to do if you happen to live in a community property state. Another great feature of a transmutation agreement is that no consideration is required for the transfer of property. Basically what this means is that you can transfer your property just like a gift. There doesn't have to be any exchange of money, and it doesn't even have to be equal (fifty-fifty).

This is the legal definition of community property: all assets acquired during the marriage belong equally to the husband and wife except for any property acquired *before* the marriage and all inherited property and gifts acquired during the marriage which is separate spousal property. A community property state is very much like a general partnership (see chapter 23) where joint and several liability can prove disastrous. Joint and several liability is the legal principle whereby liability of a group can be borne by any individual of the group to a creditor.

There's another important reason why community property is so terrible. In a community property state, like California, the wages of a nondebtor spouse could be garnished! Before that can happen, a court order would be required. But nonetheless, the idea that an innocent spouse who has no judgments against her or him would have their wages garnished is anathema to the concept of justice. Folks, this is really upsetting. But wait, there's more. The separate bank account of a nondebtor spouse could be levied on and the money transferred to the creditor. This too would require a court order. Is there anything you can do to prevent this? Yes. It's critical that you and your spouse consummate a transmutation agreement and record it in your local recorder's office. The sooner you do this, the better. The transmutation agreement must clearly state that you and your spouse are abrogating (eliminating) all community property and dividing the community property into separate spousal property and that this condition shall continue throughout the marriage. Basically, what you are doing is opting out of community property, which is permitted under the law.

Community property laws vary considerably between states. For example, California generally lumps all property into the community whereas Nevada splits community property in half so that the spouse who was not sued cannot lose his or her share to the creditors.

Joint and several liability is a form of liability that is used in civil cases where two or more people are found liable for damages. The winning plaintiff can collect the entire judgment from any one of the parties or can collect from any one or all of the parties in various amounts until the judgment is paid in full. In other words, if any of the defendants do not have enough money or assets to pay an equal share of the judgment, the other defendants must make up the difference. Basically, you can be stuck with the judgment if you have "deep pockets" and the other partners don't have enough money to pay the judgment. General partnerships are very dangerous because if the partnership is sued successfully, then all the partners of the partnership are equally responsible for the judgment. Similarly, in a community property state like California, if just one spouse is sued successfully, then both spouses are equally responsible for the damages. This is like being found guilty by association! It's not fair, but it is the law. That's why you *never*, and I absolutely mean *never* form a general partnership. If you happen to live in a community property state, then you must immediately take legal steps to abrogate (abolish) community property by using a transmutation agreement. Folks, this is really important information, and I certainly hope you heed my advice. The bottom line: community property states create significantly more risk of possibly losing your assets. You must take proactive steps now to abrogate (abolish) community property. This must be done *before* you are threatened with a lawsuit, *before* you are actually sued, and *before* you have creditors.

Community property is just like a general partnership because just one spouse with a judgment can cause the loss of the entire community property. Community property is like putting "all your eggs in one basket." Community property is divided upon divorce, annulment, or death. Joint ownership is automatically presumed by law in the absence of specific evidence that would point to a contrary conclusion for a particular piece of property.

In California, a marital dissolution (divorce) requires a fifty-fifty division of community property[179] meaning that the focus then shifts as to whether particular items are to be classified as community or separate property. In other jurisdictions, such as Texas, a divorce court may decree an "equitable distribution" of community property, which can result in an unequal division of property. In noncommunity property states, property may or may not be divided by equitable distribution. Generally, the property that each spouse initially brings into the marriage or receives by gift, bequest, or devise during marriage is separate spousal property and not community property. Division of community *debts* is not necessarily the same as division of community *property*. For example, in California, community property is required to be divided "equally" while community debt is required to be divided "equitably."[180]

Transmutation agreements can also be used to convert separate spousal property into community property. For asset protection purposes, this is not a good idea. Property that is owned by one spouse before the marriage is the separate property of that spouse unless the property is "transmuted" into community property.

In the United States, there are nine community property states—Arizona, California, Idaho, Louisiana, Nevada, New Mexico, Texas, Washington, and Wisconsin. Puerto Rico as well as several Indian jurisdictions permit property to be owned as community property Alaska makes community property optional. In community property states, each spouse technically owns an undivided one-half interest in the property. In noncommunity property states, generally speaking, property is separate property unless both parties agree to make it community property through a community property agreement or a community property trust.

Community property laws vary from state to state. For example, in some community property states ("American Rule" states) income from separate property stays separate. In other community property states ("Civil Law" states) the income from separate property becomes community property.

Community property has certain federal tax benefits.[181] In general, community property often results in lower federal capital gain taxes after the death of one spouse when the surviving spouse then sells the property because of a step up in the basis (value) of the property, which decreases the amount of capital gains tax that has to be paid. Some states have created a newer form of community property called "community property with right of survivorship." This is similar to joint tenancy with right of survivorship.

As I have repeatedly stated, community property states are dangerous places in which to live without a valid transmutation agreement that has been recorded in the recorder's office of the county where you live. A remarkable example of this involved the 2011 Los Angeles Dodgers ownership dispute in which Frank McCourt paid his ex-wife Jamie McCourt approximately $130 million in a settlement over a dispute about whether the Los Angeles Dodgers were community property after the trial court ruled that the McCourts' prenuptial agreement was declared invalid.[182] The McCourts' invalid agreement was prepared by a lawyer based in Massachusetts shortly before they moved to Los Angeles. Folks, make sure you use a competent attorney in the state where you live or plan to live for drawing up a proper transmutation agreement. The transmutation agreement has to be done right.

Questions regarding whether property is separate or community property are not always clear. For example, where a spouse owns a preexisting business when marrying, it is clearly separate spousal property at the time of the marriage. But if the business continues during the marriage, then what of the additional property acquired during marriage? How about the labor contributed by both spouses? Were some of the funds that were used to pay for the business, community funds, or separate property funds? That's why you need a transmutation agreement or a prenuptial agreement. It avoids major headaches in the marriage.

Community property can consist of any type of property, including real property, such as your home and personal property such as bank accounts, stocks, bonds, and cash.

A pension or annuity may have first been acquired before a marriage. But if contributions are made with community property funds during marriage, then the proceeds are partly separate property and partly community property. Upon divorce or death of one of the spouses, there are rules for apportionment. This is termed commingling. (See chapter 28.)

Stocks options are quite difficult to determine in community property states, especially if the marriage is terminated before the stock options are exercised (cashed in).

Quasicommunity property is a determination made when one spouse dies or if the couple divorces and applies to assets located in a noncommunity property state in which a community property state where the couple now lives recognizes this out-of-state property as community property. However, in California, assets acquired while married and domiciled in a noncommunity property state does not become community property just because the married couple moves to California. It is the event of divorce or death while living in California that allows that state to treat such property as quasicommunity property. In other words, before the death of a spouse or before a divorce, the property outside of California in a noncommunity property state is *not* community property.[183] Only at the time of a spousal death or a divorce does this property become community property. If this sounds confusing, it is. As of 2007, only Arizona, California, New Mexico, and Washington have such quasicommunity property laws.

WHY YOU MUST HAVE A TRANSMUTATION AGREEMENT

Transmutation agreements, which involve real property (real estate), *must* be recorded to be effective against third parties. If you live in a community property state (see chapter 11), then you definitely need a transmutation agreement (or a prenuptial agreement before marriage) to abrogate (abolish) community property. Regardless of whether you live in a community property state or not, it's best to keep your assets separate. Spouses should never own any property jointly and that goes for your bank account as well. So the bottom line for everyone—no joint ownership of any assets at all. Furthermore, the least vulnerable spouse (often the wife) should own the valuable assets like the house, cars, bank accounts with the most money, brokerage accounts, etc. What if you're concerned about a future divorce and you feel uncomfortable giving your least vulnerable spouse the most valuable assets? A good alternative would be to establish a trust (see chapters 32 and 34) or possibly a family limited partnership (see chapter 17).

I strongly recommend you insert a special clause in your transmutation agreement to prevent a resulting trust: "If community property funds or the personal funds of the nonowning spouse of the real property are used to pay the mortgage, it shall be considered a *gift* and no resulting trust shall form therefrom. Additionally, it shall not affect this agreement."

A California transmutation agreement is a written marital contract that changes the ownership of a particular piece of property effective from the date of the agreement. The reason why it's so important to have a transmutation agreement is because simply deeding property or changing the documents of title on stock or other assets may not change ownership rights in California between spouses. California statutes and the courts have specific rules that must be followed to change community-held property into separate spousal property. For example, simply changing the ownership of stock from one spouse to the other without some written statement of intent has been held to be inadequate to transmute the stock from one spouse to the other. Even a simple quitclaim deed may be ambiguous about the intent of the spouses.

A transmutation agreement must be in writing, and it must be specific in order for it to be valid. I strongly urge you to use an attorney who is familiar with transmutation agreements so that your agreement will stand up in court. A transmutation agreement is not required to be notarized. However, by notarizing the spousal signatures, you will avoid later claims of signature forgery. If the transfer involves real property or an asset of substantial value, notarization of the signatures is highly recommended.

A postnuptial agreement is similar to a transmutation agreement, but additionally, it also sets out how spousal property will be divided in the event of a divorce and can also address issues of spousal support. A postnuptial agreement is similar to a premarital agreement but is entered into during marriage rather than before marriage. Because of the complexity of California law dealing with how property is divided after a divorce, if one of the spouses to a marriage has a premarital business, or any premarital assets of significance, then it is imperative that the parties execute a valid premarital (prenuptial), postnuptial, or transmutation agreement. These agreements cannot bind the spouses to custody or child support. A California prenuptial agreement can provide for spousal support, if any, in the event of a divorce.

All states set family support payments or alimony based upon a mathematical calculation that is required by federal law. The mathematical calculations most typically accepted by the courts come fromDissoMaster (support calculation tool) and Xspouse (property division and arrearage calculation tool).

Spouses can enter into legally binding contracts with one another.[184] In California, the property rights of husband and wife may be altered by a premarital agreement or other marital property agreement.[185] Also, the spouses can change the character of their property from community property to separate property or vice versa using transmutation agreements.[186]

Additionally, marital agreements preserve the estate of a spouse intact for his or her heirs and free from succession claims of the surviving spouse.[187] Marital agreements must comply with general contract law. There must be no undue influence, duress, or fraud. Also, there is no statute of limitations because marital agreements procured through undue influence remain voidable for the duration of the confidential relationship.

In California, transmutation agreements must now be made "in writing," and the advantaged spouse has the burden of proving the transmutation agreement was not the product of undue influence. Furthermore, a real property transmutation must be recorded in order to be valid against third parties. Transmutation agreements are subject to the laws governing "fraudulent transfers."[188] (See chapter 21.)

A transfer made or obligation incurred by a debtor is fraudulent[189] as to a creditor whether the creditor's claim arose before or after the transfer was made or the obligation was incurred if the debtor made the transfer or incurred the obligation as follows:

1. With actual intent to hinder, delay, or defraud any creditor of the debtor
2. Without receiving a reasonably equivalent value in exchange for the transfer or obligation, and the debtor either:

    (A) Was engaged or was about to engage in a business or a transaction for which the remaining assets of the debtor were unreasonably small in relation to the business or transaction

    (B) Intended to incur, or believed or reasonably should have believed that he or she would incur, debts beyond his or her ability to pay as they became due.

Fraud is difficult to prove. Therefore, the courts have established guidelines that when established become "red flags" for fraud. These guidelines are termed the "Eleven Badges of Fraud" and consist of the following:

1. Whether the transfer or obligation was to an insider
2. Whether the debtor retained possession or control of the property transferred after the transfer
3. Whether the transfer or obligation was disclosed or concealed
4. Whether before the transfer was made or obligation was incurred, the debtor had been sued or threatened with suit
5. Whether the transfer was of substantially all the debtor's assets
6. Whether the debtor absconded
7. Whether the debtor removed or concealed assets
8. Whether the value of the consideration received by the debtor was reasonably equivalent to the value of the asset transferred or the amount of the obligation incurred
9. Whether the debtor was insolvent or became insolvent shortly after the transfer was made or the obligation was incurred
10. Whether the transfer occurred shortly before or shortly after a substantial debt was incurred
11. Whether the debtor transferred the essential assets of the business to a lienholder who transferred the assets to an insider of the debtor

The more badges of fraud you commit, the greater the likelihood you'll be convicted of a fraudulent conveyance. If the court believes you committed a fraudulent conveyance by illegally transferring property, say for example, to your spouse to avoid a creditor's claim, then watch out.

In California, a transmutation agreement doesn't have to be made for consideration. However, with that said, the division of community property needs to be somewhat fair and equitable to pass legal muster. Also, it's highly unlikely that one spouse can disavow complete ownership of the community property.

One very important thing to remember in a family asset transfer is the possibility of death of the spouse or family member or possible dissolution of the marriage or a court judgment. Provisions must be made for such an event. For example, if the wife receives the family home pursuant to a transmutation agreement, then she should have a will that bequeaths the home to her children in the event of her death. Bottom line: even after the asset transfer, there's still work to be done—plan for the unexpected.

During retirement, you can use a transmutation agreement to reaffirm community property because you are now considerably less vulnerable to lawsuits as a result of not running a business any longer. The advantage here is when the first spouse dies, the property value is "stepped up," which reduces future estate taxes when the remaining spouse dies.

Prenuptial Agreements

The following is brief information regarding prenuptial agreements. The divorce rate is approximately 33 percent for first marriages and 50 percent for second or third marriages. Basically, a prenuptial agreement is a contract between two fiancées about to wed that describes how assets will be distributed in the event of divorce or death. Most people about to wed should have a prenuptial agreement, especially if the following factors apply:

- You have assets such as a home, substantial cash, stocks, or retirement funds.
- You own a business or part of a business.
- You stand to receive an inheritance.
- You have children and grandchildren from a previous marriage.
- One of the fiancées is much wealthier than the other.
- One of you will be supporting the other.
- You have to support elderly parents.

- You have or are pursuing a degree or license in a lucrative profession.
- You could see a big increase in income because your business is taking off.

Talk to your fiancée about the need for a prenuptial agreement before the engagement. To help ensure an enforceable agreement, both parties need their own lawyers, and most importantly both parties must *fully* disclose their assets. If it's later discovered that either person has hidden something, a judge can toss out the contract. A prenuptial agreement must also be signed well in advance of the wedding, at least one month in advance of the wedding to negate any suspicion of coercion or duress. A valid prenuptial agreement must also be fair and equitable and will not leave one of the parties destitute. Moreover, make sure you have a proper written agreement.[190]

Use only matrimonial attorneys who specialize in prenuptial agreements in the state where you will reside. You cannot waive child support payments. Generally, a will cannot supersede or preempt a valid prenuptial agreement. The prenuptial agreement should be witnessed, preferably by an attorney. A copy should be kept by a third party, such as an attorney or CPA. Prenuptial agreements should be reviewed and possibly modified every few years. The prenuptial agreement could conceivably be rescinded after a number of years into the marriage.

A prenuptial agreement can protect your assets and can also make sure that the people you want to inherit your assets actually get them. Moreover, neither the divorce court nor your spouse will make the final decision as to who gets your assets. Without a prenuptial agreement, the law in community property states[191] requires that all property, with some exceptions, accumulated during the marriage will be divided equally; and in most other states, assets are divided up according to what the court deems fair (which may not be fair to you).

WHAT YOU MUST DO TO PROTECT YOUR HOME

After you obtain adequate liability insurance, the next item for asset protection purposes is your home. Unfortunately, when it comes to lawsuits and judgments, your home (metaphorically speaking) is your Achilles' heel. Collections attorneys know this all too well. That's why it is absolutely imperative for you to protect your home. I can't overemphasize this strongly enough.

If you absolutely want a foolproof method to thwart a plaintiff who may eventually become a creditor of yours from ever obtaining your home, then you'll probably have to sell your home quickly and send the proceeds (money) offshore to your trust. That's why you *must* take immediate action to protect your home. I just can't overemphasize this point strongly enough. Most people do not want to sacrifice their home in a forced sale in order to thwart creditors. Therefore, the next thing to do after you are fully insured is to fully protect your home.

If you have already transferred your home to a trust, family limited partnership, limited liability company, or a corporation, then you are now a renter; and you should have a lease agreement with the new entity that now legally owns your home. If you insist on not having a lease agreement and you continue to make the mortgage payments on behalf of the new legal entity (owner), then by all means you *must* make those mortgage payments as a *gift* and clearly write this on your check that it's a "gift." Otherwise, you will accrue an ownership interest in this new legal entity and that creates the "deadly" resulting trust (see chapter 29). My strong recommendation is to use a standard lease agreement (which you can easily procure from a stationary store or from the Internet). Once your home has been legally transferred, the owner (lessor) of the new legal entity and the spouses (lessees) execute a lease agreement.

Every legal structure (whether a family limited partnership, limited liability company, trust, or corporation) should have its own business bank account. (See chapter 24.) Once a real-property transfer is made, it must be notarized (transmutation agreement, quitclaim deed, grant deed, trust deed) and then promptly recorded in the local recorder's office. A transfer of real property can always be challenged as a fraudulent conveyance but only up to a certain point in time, which is dictated by the statute of limitations. In California, a recorded transfer of real property has a four-year statute of limitations. An unrecorded transfer in California has a seven-year statute of limitations. I'll take the four-year statute of limitations any day over the seven-year statute of limitations. After four years, your transfer can no longer be challenged or defeated in any way by the creditors. It's as good as gold. The statute of limitations will completely block your creditors even if the transfer was in fact a fraudulent one! Here's some useful information that's not well known regarding a homestead exemption after you've been sued or have a judgment. You can still record a valid homestead exemption during a lawsuit or even after a judgment. With a judicial (court-ordered) sale of your home, you'll get to keep the homestead-exemption money up to the statutory limit after the sale.

Please remember, if you transfer your home to a legal entity, you better have a very good business reason for doing so. Otherwise, the court won't recognize its legitimacy, and basically you'll have a "house of cards" (no pun intended). If it's not for a business purpose, then your home won't be fully protected. The truth is that most homes held by FLPs or LLCs are not for business purposes. Since the FLP and the LLC probably won't work well for most homeowners, you are then left with two other options. Fortunately, these two remaining options are quite good for asset protection. The first would be to use a transmutation agreement to transfer your home to the least vulnerable spouse. If your marriage is stable and strong, this would be a very good choice. For others, you should transfer your home to an irrevocable trust, either a domestic or foreign trust. A foreign trust would be the better choice for asset protection purposes. Placing your home in an irrevocable trust would ostensibly be for estate planning purposes; a legitimate purpose for establishing a trust. The bottom line is that your best options for protection of your home would be to use either a transmutation agreement or an irrevocable trust.

Basic Forms of Home Ownership

There are several types of basic home ownership that range from providing *no* asset protection to *limited* asset protection that the vast majority of US homeowners use. They are the following:

- Joint tenants
- Joint tenants with right of survivorship
- Tenants in common
- Tenants by the entirety
- Community property

Joint Tenants

In noncommunity property states, both husband and wife are named on the deed to their home. From an asset protection standpoint, this is dangerous. From a tax point of view, this is highly disadvantageous. Unlike community property, there is no step up in basis upon the death of the first spouse (tenant). As a result, more taxes will have to be paid, especially on greatly appreciated assets. Moreover, there is loss of estate tax protection. Either spouse (tenant) can transfer the home to a third party *without permission* from the other spouse (tenant). Consequently, this puts the home at risk. Joint tenancy disinherits all heirs, except the remaining spouse, regardless of any will or trust. In other words, joint tenancy supersedes any will or trust. There is even the possibility of a gift tax from the transfer of a home into joint tenancy. In small estates, joint tenancy avoids probate.

Compared to community property (which has no asset protection features), joint tenancy in which a husband and wife have fifty-fifty ownership, a judgment against one of the spouses would result in a loss of half the home rather than the entire property if held as community property. However, the creditor could sell the entire home but only receive half its value (equity).

The bottom line: this is a dangerous form of home ownership from an asset protection standpoint because a creditor who substitutes for one of the debtor spouses can *sell the entire asset without permission from the other spouse.*

Joint Tenancy with Right of Survivorship (JTWROS)

From an asset protection view, joint tenancy should never be used because owning property as "joint tenants" gives each spouse the right to use the "whole" house with rights to occupy the entire property and the right to sell the entire house. Furthermore, joint tenancy gives the right to each spouse to transfer his or her interest in the property *without asking* permission from the other spouse. The survival rights, such as when the first spouse dies, means the share of the deceased spouse automatically becomes that of the other spouse. Joint tenancy is a common form of co-ownership for personal residences.

When the first spouse dies, the entire home becomes that of the other spouse. Also, a major problem is that joint tenancy is subject to the full loss of the home in a lawsuit. So if one of the spouses gets sued and loses, the entire home is at risk and may cause the forced sale of the entire home to satisfy the judgment. You should never hold title to a home as a joint tenant with right of survivorship. Never rely on co-ownership as a way to protect your home. It never works. A joint spouse (tenant) automatically inherits the home.

There are six characteristics to joint tenancy:

1. Each tenant (spouse) acquired or was vested with the title at the same time.
2. Each tenant (spouse) acquired title by the same instrument or deed or action.
3. Each tenant (spouse) owns an equal and undivided interest.

4. Each tenant (spouse) has the right to possess the "whole" house (dangerous in cases of frivolous litigation).
5. Each tenant (spouse) has the right to survivorship.
6. Interest may not be transferred by will.

Tenants in Common

Tenancy in common has the following characteristics:

1. Each spouse has a separate but undivided interest in the home. Each spouse has his or her own deed/title to his or her share.
2. Ownership interest in the property may be varying in proportions, that is, fractional shares, e.g., one-third or one-half.
3. A spouse's interest in the home may be transferred by will.
4. Each spouse has an equal right to possession.

The downside is that there's the ever-present risk of separate ownership. This is the most common type of shared ownership and is widely used to transfer property tax free. If both spouses get sued and a judgment is entered against them, then the creditors can seize the home. On the other hand, if just one spouse is sued and a judgment is entered against him or her, then there would be limited asset protection with this type of home ownership in as much that the entire house could not be seized, and the nondebtor spouse's share would continue to be retained. The ultimate disposition of the house in these situations is often unpredictable.

Tenancy by the Entirety

Tenancy by the entirety exists in some states, which permits a special kind of home ownership between married couples such that each spouse has the right to enjoy the underlying home completely, and when one of the spouses dies, the other spouse automatically inherits the entire home. About half of the states have this type of home ownership. The common feature is that the innocent (nondebtor) spouse's share (interest) of the house is protected from creditors. However, if the innocent spouse dies, that leaves the remaining debtor spouse with sole ownership of the home and then the creditor can seize the home. But if the debtor spouse dies first, that leaves the remaining innocent spouse in sole possession of the home and the creditor will no longer have any ability to seize the home. In other words, it's all over for the creditor with regard to the home. On the other hand, if both spouses are sued and judgments entered against both of them, then the entire house can be sold by the creditor. And with a divorce, it depends who ends up getting the house. If the innocent spouse gets the house, the creditor won't be able to seize it; whereas if the debtor spouse gets the house, the creditor will be able to seize it. Tenancy by the entirety has the following characteristics:

1. Tenancy by the entirety may only be created by husband and wife.
2. Tenancy by the entirety automatically provides the right of survivorship.
3. Neither spouse may transfer or convey title to a third person without consent of the other spouse.
4. Title converts to tenancy in common upon divorce.

Community Property

Community property of the home is property owned together by both spouses regardless of who purchased the home until separation or divorce. This type of property exists in the following community property states: Arizona, California, Idaho, Louisiana, Nevada, New Mexico, Texas, Washington State, and Wisconsin. As a general rule, the home is owned jointly and equally by each spouse. This type of home ownership offers no asset protection and in fact is dangerous. Married couples should seriously consider using a transmutation (postnuptial) agreement to replace this type of home ownership. (See chapter 12.) There are a few exceptions to community property:

1. Property received by one spouse through gift or inheritance is his or her separate property.
2. Property received through separate property owned by the spouse outside the community property rules, i.e., rents on separate investment real estate.
3. Property through ownership by partnership, trust, corporation, or limited liability company.
4. Property acquired separately before marriage normally remains separate property unless it is commingled during marriage.

Homestead Exemptions

Homestead exemptions are laws designed specifically to protect the value of a home from property taxes and creditors. Homestead exemptions can be found in all state statutes and is an automatic benefit in some states. In states where the homestead protection is not automatic, homeowners must file a claim. The primary features of homestead exemptions are typically to prevent the forced sale of a home to meet creditor obligations and to reduce property taxes. Homestead exemption laws typically have the following main features:

- They prevent the forced sale of a home to meet the demands of creditors (however, in most cases, homestead exemptions do not apply to forced sales to satisfy monetary judgments exceeding the value of the mortgage and homestead exemption (i.e., "exposed equity"), mortgages, mechanics liens, or sales to pay property taxes).
- They provide an exemption from property taxes, which can be applied to a home.

Texas, Florida, Iowa, Kansas, Oklahoma, Arkansas, and Washington DC have unlimited homestead protections in terms of the value of property that can be protected. Texas's homestead exemption has no dollar value limit and has a 10 acres (4.0 hectares) exemption limit for homesteads inside of a municipality (urban homestead) and 100 acres (40 hectares) for those outside of a municipality (rural homestead). The rural acre allotment is doubled for a family: 200 acres (81 hectares) can be shielded from creditors in Texas for a rural homestead. Both the Kansas and Oklahoma exemptions protect 160 acres (65 hectares) of land of any value outside of a municipality's corporate limits and 1 acre (0.40 hectares) of land of any value within a municipality's corporate limits. Most homestead exemptions cover the land including fixtures and improvements to it, such as buildings, timber, and landscaping.

In the majority of states, the real dollar value of "protection" provided by these laws has diminished as exemption dollar amounts are seldom adjusted for inflation. The protective intent of such laws, with some notable exceptions stated above, has been eroded in most states.

On the other hand, New Jersey and Pennsylvania have no homestead exemptions. Most states have homestead exemption limits anywhere between $5,000 and $550,000. Federal Bankruptcy currently limits your homestead exemption to $125,000 [192] regardless of your state's exemption amount. Please remember, if the creditor is your mortgage lender and forecloses on your home, you won't get the homestead exemption. In other words, the mortgage loan supersedes your homestead exemption. Moreover, the federal government, such as the IRS can take your home without your getting the homestead exemption. And don't forget the forfeiture laws where your home can be seized lock, stock, and barrel. Most states can also take your home for unpaid taxes under a tax lien sale, and you won't get the homestead exemption.

Some states will forfeit your homestead exemption if you transfer your home to a living revocable trust (LRT), family limited partnership (FLP), limited liability company (LLC), corporation, or any other legal entity. Also, the homestead exemption typically protects against debts incurred *after* the homestead exemption is claimed.

Are your homestead proceeds (money) vulnerable to creditor seizure after receiving it? Unfortunately, many states do not protect the money you receive from your homestead exemption. For instance, in California, your homestead money is transiently protected just for six months after receiving it before your creditor can come after it. This means you better do something quickly otherwise you will probably lose it. Now would be a great time to open that offshore bank account.

The bottom line: In many states, the homestead exemption is only available to individuals and married couples.

Situations Where Your Homestead Exemption Does Not Apply

If your creditor is your mortgage lender or the government; or your home has been seized under the forfeiture laws, then your homestead exemption will not apply. If you fail to pay your mortgage, your lender will foreclose and your homestead exemption won't be effective. If you owe back taxes to either the state or federal governments, your homestead exemption won't be effective. If you lose your house to forfeiture, your homestead exemption won't be effective. Also, if you fail to list your home as an asset in your bankruptcy petition, then your homestead exemption will not apply. In some cases, you must record a homestead exemption in order to receive it.

Equity Stripping

Equity stripping refers to extracting exposed equity, typically from your home, by having a lien placed against the property. Most commonly, the homeowner gets a home equity line of credit (HELOC) from his or her bank or from another lender. This is very similar to a second mortgage. In fact, a number of homeowners elect to take out a second mortgage on their homes rather than obtain a HELOC. In either case, the bank or lender records a trust deed on the property and gives you the money. The trust deed is recorded at the local recorder's office. By not having any exposed equity, your home becomes less attractive to a plaintiff/creditor. Some homeowners may elect to have a friend or relative record a lien on their property. A few even have one of their own companies record a lien on their property. But these loans are not "arm's length" transactions, and a court most likely would avoid (unwind) these transactions as a sham. The bottom line is to use a legitimate lender or bank to give you a second mortgage or a HELOC. Please remember to do this before you are threatened with a lawsuit, have pending litigation, or have present creditors. Otherwise, the court will consider this a fraudulent conveyance/transfer. Also, with a HELOC, don't wait to draw down on your line of credit when creditors arrive on your doorstep. Otherwise, the court would consider this a fraudulent transfer/conveyance.

For further security, once you draw down on your home equity, you might consider investing the money in an offshore annuity where it would be extremely safe.

Some asset protection experts advocate keeping your home fully mortgaged with little or no equity except perhaps with an amount under the homestead exemption. However, in a rapidly rising real estate market, you'll have to keep refinancing your home either with a second or even third mortgage or with a home equity loan. Nevertheless, you still might not be able to keep up with the rising equity in your home. Paying down a mortgage gets to be really expensive over the years. You're actually making the bank rich. For example, a $300,000 mortgage could easily cost you about $1.2 million when amortized over a thirty-year period. Even though the interest payments are tax deductible, you'll still end up paying about two-thirds of the interest payments yourself. This is a very expensive way to protect your home. The only real advantage of having a home without any exposed equity is that you can legally transfer your home during a lawsuit or even shortly after a judgment (but before a lis pendens or lien attaches) without triggering a fraudulent conveyance! That's because a home which is fully mortgaged (so that there's no exposed equity) is by legal definition not an asset of yours. (See chapter 22.)

When you buy or sell a house or other real property, the deed is recorded. Most people don't know that technically under the law, you're not required to record the deed. But if you don't record the deed, you would be taking an enormous risk because third parties would have absolutely no knowledge of the property transfer. Therefore, your transfer would not be binding on third parties. And if a subsequent transfer were made and recorded, it would have precedence over your earlier unrecorded transfer. The bottom line is that you must *always* record the transfer of real property—no exceptions!

There's another very important reason why you need to record a real property transfer. It has to do with the statute of limitations for a fraudulent conveyance. The statute of limitations is the period of time your creditor has available to challenge your property transfer as a fraudulent transfer (also known as a fraudulent conveyance). The shorter the period of time to challenge or contest the transfer, the better it is for you. When the statute of limitations has run out (expired), your transfer is forever safe from a creditor's fraudulent conveyance lawsuit. This is true even if the transfer was, in fact, made as a fraudulent conveyance! If a lawsuit is filed alleging a fraudulent conveyance, it will be thrown out of court (legally speaking, dismissed with prejudice.) This will happen well before the judge even considers the merits (the details) of the case. Bottom line: the expiration of the statute of limitations will forever save your property transfer. Your transfer is as good as gold and can't be avoided (undone). Well then, with this in mind, it makes perfect sense to have the shortest possible statute of limitations as it applies to fraudulent transfers. In California, there are two different time periods for the statute of limitations with regard to a fraudulent conveyance. One is for recorded transfers. When you record a transfer in your local recorder's office, the statute of limitations is just four years long. On the other hand, if you don't recorder the transfer, the statute of limitations can be as long as seven years. The one major exception to this involves an unrecorded transmutation agreement of real property. That's because an unrecorded transfer of real property in a transmutation agreement is not effective against third parties. What this means is that there is no statute of limitations for an unrecorded real property transfer in a transmutation agreement. For example, your creditors can always challenge the transfer of your home that was made in an unrecorded transmutation agreement.[193] The bottom line: always, and I mean *always*, record a real property transfer (for most people this means their personal home). If you fail to record the transfer of your home, you could lose it to your creditors! My strongest advice is to *always* record your transfers; that way you get the shortest statute of limitations.

Personal information can be redacted (edited) for privacy concerns when you file your documents in the recorder's office. But *always* record your transfers, especially your real estate!

1. Protect your home—Your home can very well be your financial Achilles' heel if you don't take immediate steps to protect it now. Creditors and collection's attorneys know this all too well. They know that your dream home is precious and dear to you, and they know they can apply tremendous pressure to force you to capitulate (surrender) mostly on their terms. They can squeeze you, and they can make you squirm. Unfortunately for you, you just can't physically move your house, at least not in most cases. Your permanent fixed dream home in the United States is under the jurisdiction of the US courts. Whereas an automobile, boat, or even an airplane of yours could easily and quickly be transported out of the country and hidden, thereby rendering it no longer under the jurisdiction of US courts. However, this is not the case with your home. Even if you smuggle your car, boat, or plane of the country, your continued presence in the United States subjects you to the jurisdiction of the US courts, and you could be held in contempt of court and perhaps even jailed. You need to be very careful if you do this because it's a fraudulent conveyance, which would likely violate a court order. Before making any transfers during litigation, you're well advised to get a legal opinion from an attorney. Ultimately, you may have to flee the United States to fully protect yourself, but we're getting way ahead of ourselves. Returning to the predicament involving your home,

> you must—and I just can't stress this enough—take steps to fully protect your home from creditors. There's an old saying, "Timing is everything." And the best time to protect your home is during a quiescent (quiet) period. What does this exactly mean? It means a time during your life when you haven't been threatened with a lawsuit, when you're not actually being sued and when you have no current judgments or creditors. If all of these conditions apply to you, then you're ready to begin the process of fully protecting your dream home from creditors. One word of caution though. If your home is financed with a mortgage and you don't make your scheduled mortgage payments, then the mortgagee (usually the bank or mortgage company) will eventually foreclose on your home and there's little you can do to stop it. Although you may be able to slow down the foreclosure process, eventually the bank will repossess your home. Therefore, always make sure you pay your mortgage payments on time.

There are several ways to protect your home from future creditors, and I strongly advise you to consult an attorney to make sure everything is done absolutely correctly. For most people, the way to protect their home is through a property transfer that is properly recorded in the local county recorder's office in order to be effective against third parties. Even though the law (amazingly) doesn't require a transfer of real property to be recorded, you must—and I stress must—record the transfer of your home in the county recorder's office. Another point to consider: most mortgages have a "due on sales clause" written into the contract. Check your mortgage agreement to see if it contains "a due on sales clause." Some mortgages are assignable, which means that they can be assumed when transferred. You'll have to check your mortgage agreement carefully to see if it can be assigned. If you live in a community property state (like California) and use a transmutation agreement or a quitclaim deed to change your community property home into the separate property of one of the spouses, then you don't have to worry about a "due on sales clause" because it doesn't apply. However, if you transfer your home to a family limited partnership or limited liability company or even a trust or corporation, then a "due on sales clause" might apply. However, since these transfers don't normally utilize an escrow company or title insurance company or even an exchange of money, it's unlikely the bank will ever know about the transfer, and therefore the bank (mortgagee) will not enforce the "due on sales clause" unless you have a low fixed interest rate at a time when the prevailing interest rates are higher or are rising. Then the bank may come after you and enforce the due on sales clause. If you have an adjustable mortgage interest rate, then it's unlikely the bank will enforce the "due on sales" clause. But make sure that the mortgage payments continue and are promptly made to the bank by the new entity (family limited partnership, limited liability company, trust, or corporation) that now legally owns your home. Otherwise, the bank could foreclose on the house. There will be more on this later. However, if you continue to make the mortgage payments yourself, you could be creating a dangerous resulting trust, which could result in the loss of your home![194] Bottom line: you must not continue to pay the mortgage on your home once it has been transferred (to a legal entity) because if you continue to make the mortgage payments, you'll establish a beneficial ownership interest (in the legal entity) and a resulting trust will form. A court can use this resulting trust to confiscate your home and give it to your creditors! [195]

The first thing to do if you haven't done so already is to record a homestead exemption on your personal home. The two best states for homestead exemptions are Florida and Texas where you have an unlimited homestead exemption of your personal residence! What this means is that regardless of how much your house is worth, even if it's worth millions of dollars, your judgment creditors can't take it away from you. However, if you're not fortunate enough to be living in Florida or Texas, then your homestead exemption will be seriously limited. Any value above the homestead exemption will be exposed to potential creditor seizure. Your creditors could take your home away to satisfy their judgment against you depending on the amount of value over and above the homestead exemption and any encumbrances, such as mortgages and lines of credit. This is called exposed equity or value "above water."

The next thing to do depends on many other factors. But perhaps the easiest thing for most people to do is to transfer their home to the least vulnerable spouse often to the wife as her separate property. (See chapter 12.) In community property states (like California), you should use a transmutation agreement to safely and legally transfer property. In noncommunity property states, homes held in joint tenancy should be transferred by quitclaim deed to the least vulnerable spouse. Remember to always, and I mean always, record the transfer of your home. There are simply no exceptions to this ironclad rule. Now I'm sure some husbands or wives may feel uncomfortable transferring their home to the other (least vulnerable) spouse. One alternative is to form a family limited partnership and transfer the home by a quitclaim deed to the family limited partnership. (See chapter 16.) A better option is to transfer your home to an irrevocable trust or an offshore trust. While family limited partnerships (FLPs) have been in existence for a long time and there's a lot of case law to help protect you, they're not as strong as an irrevocable trust or an offshore trust. Also, it is important to remember that you must have a legitimate *business* purpose for placing your home in an FLP. Generally speaking, the family home has no good reason to be held in a business entity. Moreover, a homestead exemption may not apply to your family limited partnership. If you decide to use an offshore trust, you should probably set up a limited liability company (LLC) that is owned by the offshore trust and then transfer the house by a quitclaim deed directly into the LLC. However, there is much less case law on limited liability companies so you're on shaky legal ground here. Please remember that a single-member LLC is subject to reverse piercing if its sole member is a judgment debtor. It's unlikely that your offshore trust would be a judgment debtor. It may be better to form a corporation and have it owned by the offshore trust and then transfer the house by a quitclaim deed directly into the corporation. There's extensive case law on corporations, and the law is well-established. The main downside with using a corporation to hold your home involves taxes. If your home appreciates in value, you may have to pay corporate taxes on the capital gains. The profits might also have to be distributed as dividends, which you would pay personally, and is the basis for double taxation with corporations. Furthermore, removing the home from the corporation would likely require taxes to be paid. This is an area for a knowledgeable tax and/or business attorney, which I encourage you to seek. Also, it's unlikely you can claim the homestead exemption when your home has been transferred to a limited liability company or a corporation. Before you legally transfer your home to a trust, I suggest you speak to a qualified attorney who specializes in real estate law and/or trust law. If your home is transferred to a limited liability company, corporation, family limited partnership, or a trust, and you wish to finance it or even refinance it, you'll probably have to obtain a commercial loan. And finally, it's critical to remember the new entity is entirely responsible for the mortgage payments. This is extremely important. If you continue to pay the mortgage payments yourself, you will almost certainly be forming a resulting trust with potentially disastrous consequences. (See chapter 29.) Once the home is transferred, the question which naturally arises is this: do I own the house that I still live in, or am I now a renter? Once your house has been transferred to a trust, family limited partnership, limited liability company, or corporation, then you legally become a renter, and the new entity becomes the owner of your home.

As previously stated, an extremely strong way to protect your home is with an offshore trust and C corporation combination. The C corporation is a holding company for your home, which in turn is owned by the offshore trust. In this arrangement, the offshore trust owns all of the stock in the C corporation. You'll need a lease agreement between the C corporation (lessor) and you and/or your spouse (lessee[s]). You'll then pay rent from your personal bank account made payable to the corporation's business bank account. The corporation's business bank account then directly pays the mortgage. The offshore trustee could even hire you to manage the corporation or alternatively the trustee could hire an outside management agency to run the corporation.

As previously discussed, a home with a lot of debt (mortgage) helps to protect against lawsuits, but you end up paying a very high price to finance that mortgage debt. For example, a $300,000 mortgage amortized over thirty years will cost you about $1.2 million. That eats away at your equity like a cancer. That is a very expensive way to protect against lawsuits. There are better ways to protect your home than to saddle it with a lot of debt, and that also allows you to build up equity in your home safely. The solution is to transfer your home, preferably to an irrevocable trust during a quiescent period when your transfer will not run afoul of the fraudulent conveyance laws.

If you need to additionally encumber your home, say with a home equity loan or second mortgage, then use a third party such as a bank since a court of law will view the encumbrance as a bona fide loan. Some people set up their own company, either a corporation or LLC, and use it as a loan company to further encumber their home. This is much like transferring money from your left pocket to your right pocket and is viewed with much suspicion by by the courts. In fact, your creditors will probably make a claim of a fraudulent loan and will seek a restraining order against you to prevent your loan company from foreclosing on your home. Once there is a lis pendens or a lien on your home, it is extremely difficult to further encumber your home or to refinance it. If you're desperate and there's a lis pendens on your property, you may be forced to either have your bank foreclose on your property or you can try to set up your own loan company and quickly make a loan, and then wait a short while to foreclose on your own property when the loan repayments are not forthcoming. All of this is quite complicated, and you are strongly advised to have professional assistance, such as a real estate attorney or other qualified financial planner assist you. Moreover, as in this example, you must act quickly before the creditors find out what you are doing. Therefore, this is another strong reason why preplanning well before you're hit with a lawsuit is your best bet.

I also have another word of caution. A transfer of real property could trigger a reassessment of your property taxes. The rules are complicated, so it's best to check with your county's assessor's office or a qualified real estate attorney.[196]

The Due-on-Sales Clause Regarding Your Mortgage

In many cases, where you retitle your home, there may be a due-on-sales clause with your mortgage lender. (The one major exception is with a transmutation [postnuptial] agreement which will not typically trigger a due-on-sales clause.) While technically your mortgage loan can be called, which means it has to be completely repaid immediately, should you sell or transfer your home, this doesn't often happen. First, so long as you pay your mortgage promptly, it's unlikely your mortgage lender will know about the sale or transfer. The exception to this is when you sell your home to a third party, and the sale goes through an escrow company. Also, if you have a mortgage interest rate above the prevailing interest rates, then your mortgage lender will not likely call your loan for obvious reasons: they are making more money from you because of the higher interest rate you're paying. On the other hand, if the prevailing interest rates are higher than what you are paying, then your mortgage loan could be called.

How Does Retitling Your Home Affect Your Title Insurance?

You should review the terms and conditions of your title insurance. In general, your title insurance is more likely to continue using a grant deed rather than a quick claim deed to transfer your home. You are encouraged to seek the services of a real estate attorney for further assistance in this area. Please remember, when using a grant deed, there needs to be consideration in exchange for the transfer. This is not the case when using a quitclaim deed.

Will Your Living Revocable Trust Void the Homestead Exemption?

The good news is that many jurisdictions allow you to hold your home in a living revocable trust and still qualify for the Homestead Exemption. However, if you no longer control the home or if you place the home in your children's names, you may no longer qualify for the exemption. However, there are some jurisdictions where you may lose your homestead exemption. In some areas, your homestead exemption will also reduce your property taxes, but to qualify, the home must be your primary residence and you must own it.

Qualified Personal Residence Trust

Residence trusts generally should not be used for asset protection purposes but instead may be used to transfer a grantor's residence out of the grantor's estate at a low gift tax value. Once the trust is funded with the grantor's residence, the residence and any future appreciation of the residence is excluded from the grantor's estate.

Single-Member LLCs Shouldn't Be Used to Hold the Family Home Unless Owned by a Foreign Asset Protection Trust

An excellent asset protection plan for the family home is the LLC/FAPT combination. You begin by transferring the family home to a Single-Member LLC, which in turn is 100 percent owned by the foreign asset protection trust (FAPT). This makes for an extremely strong asset protection plan. If you use a single-member LLC in any other way, it could prove dangerous. Here's why: In 2010, the Florida Supreme Court ruled that a creditor of a single-member LLC had remedies extending beyond the charging order and that the creditor could execute upon the assets of the single-member LLC in order to satisfy the sole member's debt.[197] In sum, an assignee of the membership interest of the sole member in a single-member LLC becomes a member himself and doesn't need the consent of anyone else to liquidate the LLCs assets.

Single-Member LLCs no longer provide asset protection when the sole member is in bankruptcy. A Colorado Bankruptcy Court[198] ruled for the first time that the assets of a single-member LLC could be used to pay the personal debts of the debtor (also the sole member of her LLC) to her creditors. The debtor filed for bankruptcy, not her LLC.

Folks, it's clear that you should not be the sole member of your LLC. Let your offshore trust own the LLC.

When All Else Fails, Foreclose on Your Home

As a last resort, when the creditors begin to close in on you and everything looks bleak, you may just want to go to your mortgage lender and tell them to foreclose on your property. This procedure will probably get your creditors very upset because it reduces the amount of money they can get from your home. Remember, foreclosures typically sell for 70–80 percent of the home's appraised value.

HOW A FRIENDLY DIVORCE CAN SIDESTEP YOUR CREDITORS

A "friendly" divorce can be done at any time, even during or after a lawsuit, but there could be problems. Nevertheless, one very good reason for a "friendly" divorce is to sidestep your creditors. Property transfers made pursuant to a divorce while a lawsuit is pending or even after a judgment can be attacked by your creditors as a fraudulent conveyance. Creditors can even use an uncommon legal maneuver that allows them to intervene in your divorce but only for contesting who gets the property—spouses or the creditors. The divorce (legally termed a marital dissolution), which legally terminates the marriage, is nonetheless unaltered. The primary advantage to a "friendly" divorce during a lawsuit or even after a judgment is for court-ordered family support or alimony payments (which you definitely want to have) that must be paid first before your creditors can get paid. Under federal law, family support payments or alimony payments must first be completely paid *before* any of your wages are garnished by your creditors! Federal law prioritizes family support and alimony payments, which preempts garnishment, so that your family will be paid first before your creditors can take any money from your wages. And if your creditors garnish your wages, the most they can get is 25 percent of your wages. What happens if you're not an employee receiving wages but instead you're self-employed with a salary? It's simple. If you're doing business as a corporation or limited liability company (which you must do), then you can make yourself an employee of your company and pay yourself whatever amount of wages you so desire. Those wages would then be subject to a maximum 25 percent garnishment but only after family support or alimony payments have been fully paid. On the other hand, self-employment income is not capped at 25 percent but is completely unprotected from creditor seizure. In theory, your creditors could confiscate all of your self-employment income. Let's take an example. Suppose you get a monthly wage of $6,000 and your family support payments are $4,000 each month. Your take-home pay is $2,000 per month, and this amount could be subject to a 25 percent creditor garnishment of $500 each month. You could either go to court to argue that the remaining $1,500 that you receive every month is inadequate for the "necessities of life" and in certain high-cost areas of the country, you're likely to win your argument and then you could probably get the garnishment either partly reduced or completely eliminated. The bottom line: a great way to sidestep your creditor's garnishment is to use a "friendly divorce" with court-ordered family support payments or alimony.

And here's an additional bonus: even though you're legally divorced, there's arguably no law to prevent you from living with your ex-spouse and your children under the same roof! Your ex-spouse can even support you too! And there's not one darn thing your creditors can do to stop this! (I just love happy endings, don't you?)

Can a divorce involving a property transfer that occurs during a lawsuit but before a judgment is recorded be avoided as a fraudulent conveyance? More than likely yes because it hinders creditors.

In a divorce, when one spouse decides to keep the home, the other spouse typically signs a quitclaim deed, which severs any claims he or she may have to the property. However, using a quitclaim deed after a divorce only removes the other spouse's name from the home's title; it does not remove his or her name from the mortgage and thus the nonowning spouse is still responsible for the mortgage! One way to take a spouse's name off the mortgage is to refinance the mortgage. Another way is to execute a release of liability. However, not all lenders allow releases of liability and not all spouses (depending on their credit) qualify for them. Moreover, if the mortgage balance is greater than the value of the home (which means the home is "under water"), a release of liability is simply not possible.

HOW TO PROTECT ASSETS DURING A DIVORCE

Here are some steps you should consider when trying to protect your assets during a divorce:

1. Identify everything that was given to you as a gift or family heirloom.
2. Identify everything that you inherited.
3. Identify community property.
4. Hire a professional appraiser.
5. Figure out how you will split retirement and physical assets.

Use a camera to record and to identify all gifts and family heirlooms given to you as well as all inherited property. You should make a list of all items, which were given to you or inherited before and during the marriage, and take pictures of these items prior to removing them from the residence. This legally is your separate property. After you have compiled your list, you should then remove all your personal items to a location that is not easily accessible to your spouse. Your spouse will be within his or her rights to claim any items you leave behind in the residence and do not immediately claim. If you or your spouse left the residence voluntarily, either of you is entitled to return at any time and retrieve belongings. If the locks have been changed, and there is no stay-away order, you are within your legal rights to have a locksmith open the doors. Your next step will be obtaining, if possible, written proof of who gave you the items and when they were received.

Community-property assets refer to any and all property shared by you and your spouse, during marriage such as your home, furniture, appliances, automobiles, etc. If you claim any of these items as your own separate property, then it's important to take pictures of these belongings well before you remove these items. Photographs are especially valuable if there are expensive items that you would like to have but did not have the ability to remove, and you feel your spouse may try to take them. All photographs should be kept in a secure location not readily accessible by your spouse.

You should hire a professional, independent appraiser because division of property during a divorce is determined by the fair market value of the disputed items to ensure one party is not being favored over the other during settlement. An appraiser will be necessary to determine accurate estimates. You may need to consult with your attorney for a qualified appraiser. It is critical that an independent appraisal be straightforward and unbiased for the protection of assets during the divorce. In addition, you may need an independent accountant for appraisal purposes as well. You may need an estate planning consultant or financial analyst when considering how to divide assets prior to a divorce settlement. For example, if you are thinking about selling your home, then it may be wise to do so prior to the divorce settlement since you are entitled to deduct up to $500,000 of the sale from capital gain taxes. Selling the home after the divorce is final reduces your tax deduction to $250,000 of the sale from capital gains taxes. Retirement assets and stocks should also be discussed. If you and your spouse choose to split the retirement benefits you must sign a Qualified Domestic-Relations Order (QDRO), which notifies the pension sponsors how to pay the benefits. Although you cannot take stocks in your spouse's name, you may be entitled to the proceeds once they are sold.

Not every state splits assets fifty-fifty in a divorce (marital dissolution). For example, some states, such as New York, are known as "equitable distribution" states. "Equitable" means "fair" and assets will not be divided right down the middle based on their fair market value. Division of assets according to New York divorce law states that all property obtained prior to the marriage still belongs to the individual and all property obtained afterwards will be distributed by the court based on established guidelines.[199]

If you are considering divorce, it is wise to consult a lawyer as soon as possible to ensure the protection of your assets and your rights as they pertain to individual state law.

THE NOT-SO-POWERFUL FAMILY LIMITED PARTNERSHIP[200]

The family limited partnership ("FLP") is a legal structure that does not provide its purported powerful asset protection. Nonetheless, the FLP is useful for reducing or even eliminating estate taxes. Additionally, the FLP can still effectively impede some inexperienced creditors with the incorrect notion that a charging order will result in the creditor paying taxes on phantom income.[201] Because of this, salesmen for the longest time have hoodwinked the gullible public into believing that the FLP along with charging orders were part of a powerful asset protection scheme that was essentially "bulletproof." The truth is that the FLP is not "bulletproof," the FLP in some circumstances can be foreclosed by the creditors, and the charging order does not require the creditors to pay taxes on phantom income.

If you decide to utilize an FLP, then the FLP agreement should contain a special clause: "The General Partner has the unfettered discretion to retain earnings of the partnership with distribution to the individual partners."[202] There's also a legal provision called the charging order (CO), which makes the creditor an assignee of the partner's interest in the partnership. However, contrary to the pervasive myth, the creditor is not responsible for paying taxes on phantom income.

Family limited partnerships have been around for a long time, and there is a lot of case law, which firmly establishes some asset protection features of a family limited partnership along with legal ways to either reduce or eliminate estate taxes. Please remember to set up a family limited partnership before you're threatened with a lawsuit, before you're involved in a lawsuit, or before you have any creditors, then your family limited partnership should be able to withstand all creditor challenges. The structure of a family limited partnership is composed of one or more general partners and one or more limited partners. The limited partners have no control or any managerial responsibilities involving the partnership. They are simply passive investors or owners. They cannot lose more than their original contributions (investments) to the partnership. They are not liable for the partnership entity itself. On the other hand, the general partners are liable for the partnership because they manage and control the partnership and potentially they have unlimited liability in that they can lose substantially more than their original contributions. Because of the risk of unlimited liability, many experts now recommend that a corporation or limited liability company substitute for the general partners of the family limited partnership. I definitely concur and recommend that if you use a family limited partnership, then the general partner should be a corporation or limited liability company. I also recommend that the most vulnerable spouse (often the husband) should not have any association or ownership interest in the family limited partnership. Also, please remember that the limited partners must not participate in the partnership's management since that would eliminate their limited liability and place them in the same position as a general partner—exposure to unlimited liability.

Note: a general partner can also be a limited partner. In your family limited partnership operating agreement, you should have a clause that states the following: "The general partner in his or her unfettered discretion retains the right to reinvest the profits of the family limited partnership back into the family limited partnership without distribution of the profits to the limited partners." What this means is that the limited partners may not see any of their money returned to them (at least not initially) but rather see their money stay within the family limited partnership. The reason for this is simple. If one of the limited partners becomes a judgment debtor, then the creditor can go to court and get a charging order which allows the creditor to become an assignee of the limited partnership. This means that if the limited partner (debtor) gets a check (disbursement) from the family limited partnership, he or she would then be required to turn the check over to the creditors because of the charging order. However, once a charging order is issued by the court, the general partner would not issue any checks to any of the limited partners but rather would reinvest the money back into the family limited partnership. This would prevent the creditor from getting any money at all. One downside to the family limited partnership involves the rarely used involuntary bankruptcy was which can force a family limited partnership to liquidate its assets in order to pay a creditor's claim. (See chapter 47.) However, the likelihood of this happening is remote, and you shouldn't be deterred from using a family limited partnership. In addition, there's a nice feature of family limited partnerships that helps reduce your income taxes. You can deduct a portion of the value of your family limited partnership from your income taxes. This can be a little tricky so please consult a professional tax consultant. Salesmen who hype FLPs will tell you that you can get income tax discounts of 40 percent or more. The reality is that these large discounts will probably get you audited by the Internal Revenue Service (IRS). A more realistic figure is probably somewhere in the neighborhood of 20 percent. Bottom line: the family limited partnership has some usefulness in asset protection and estate planning, but it isn't "bulletproof." Because of the complexities of FLPs, a skilled attorney familiar with FLPs should be utilized for the proper formation of your FLP.

Where should you form your family limited partnership? If your family limited partnership is a holding company for your home, you should consider forming your FLP either in the states of Nevada or Delaware. If your family limited partnership is formed for business purposes, then you should form your FLP in Delaware, but you'll also need to register your FLP in the state where you are conducting your business. However, in order to prosecute a lawsuit, your business entity must be currently registered in the state were you conduct your business or where it holds assets. The reason why so many people form their businesses in Delaware, even though they may not live there, is because the state courts where they reside often follow the laws of the state where the business entity was originally formed. This legal principle is termed comity. Here's an example: say you live in California and you form a Nevada FLP. You'll also need to register your Nevada FLP with the secretary of state in California in order to do business or to prosecute lawsuits in California.[203] You can then transfer your assets to your FLP. If your FLP is ever sued in California, the court will usually follow Nevada law as they apply to FLPs, rather than California law, because your FLP was originally formed in Nevada. The states of Nevada and Delaware have some of the most favorable business laws in the United States. I would definitely recommend that you set up a family limited partnership in either Nevada or Delaware to take advantage of their favorable business laws.

Naming your family limited partnership is extremely important. Please remember to use names that don't attract attention. For example, don't use your own name and never use the word *family*. Instead, use names like ABC pension fund, especially if you have a lot of money in the business entity.

There's a little known way to add significant protection to your asset protection plan by strategically using multiple FLPs. For example, you can divide an apartment building into four separate limited partnerships for enhanced protection whereas most people would simply use just one FLP for the apartment building.

One word of caution, partnerships or LLCs, which hold personal property, may be subject to a reverse piercing claim.[204] Therefore, entities holding personal assets should be formed in Delaware, which allows business entities to be formed for any lawful purpose.

Assets that would otherwise be attractive to creditors are rendered unattractive by transferring them to an FLP in exchange for FLP interests. Following the transfer, the transferor owns just the interests in the FLP rather than the transferred assets themselves. The family limited partnership is a popular way to turn attractive assets (e.g., a duplex) into unattractive assets. The asset becomes less attractive to a creditor because by transferring the duplex into the limited partnership, the remedy for the judgment creditor changes.

The judgment creditor cannot force the sale of the duplex. Instead, the judgment creditor's remedy is with a charging order,[205] and this only allows the judgment creditor to become an assignee and to receive any distributions to which he would be entitled.[206] In other words, the creditor only gets what the general partner decides to distribute, which typically is nothing.

Another *big scam* promulgated by a number of salesmen is using an offshore trust to own the FLP's limited partnership shares. In an emergency as the theory goes, the FLP assets can be liquidated and quickly transferred overseas to your offshore trust. The problem is that the debtor still resides in the United States and thus the court maintains *in personam* jurisdiction over him or her. As such, the court can compel the debtor to repatriate the assets back to the United States. And if the debtor refuses, then he or she could be held in contempt of court. The way around this quandary is for the debtor to be prepared to flee the jurisdiction of US courts by becoming a permanent ex-patriot by leaving the United States.

One strong advantage with FLPs is that sometimes an FLP will be utilized for estate tax savings (rather than an income tax savings) based on a claimed reduction in value of the limited partnership interests because of the limitations placed on the limited partner's ability to control the operations of the partnership. (See chapter 17.)

A creditor of a corporation or a creditor of a private individual can levy on the stock of the corporation or the bank account of the individual, respectively, and get the entire interest in the asset. However, creditors of limited partnerships and limited liability companies are not allowed to seize the entire asset, at least not initially. Instead, the collection laws limit the creditor to a "charging order."[207]

Only "safe assets" are typically held inside an FLP. Most contributions of property, even appreciated property to a partnership, are exempt from taxes.[208]

Even if all they own is a 1 percent general partner interest, an FLP allows senior family members to keep total control and management of the FLP's assets. Thus, a person can transfer his or her estate yet still keep control over the assets. FLPs enable families to pool investments. Family limited partnerships allow the transfer of FLP interests more easily than transferring undivided interests in the underlying assets. Folks, please remember that if you transfer your home to an FLP, it has got to be for a legitimate business purpose. Estate planning may be an acceptable business purpose for your situation. Please discuss this with a professional advisor. Also, some potential downsides to consider with your home in an FLP include but may not be limited to loss of your mortgage interest deduction, loss of your homestead exemption, loss of your capital gains exemption, your lender may call your mortgage loan by exercising the due on sales clause, you may have to get a commercial loan to finance the home, and your title insurance may be void.

Typically, senior family members/general partners like the ability that FLPs give them to control the FLP while making gifts of FLP interests to family members. If the parent of a limited partnership is both the general partner (GP) and the only limited partner (LP), then a court may deem that since the parent owns all the interests, there is no partnership and the parent simply owns the FLP's assets outright (thus negating the charging order protection and any hoped-for tax benefits). Some salesmen actually form this type of entity for asset protection purposes!

An *individual* should never be a general partner of the FLP. That's because if an individual dies, or is sued, the management of the FLP may be thrown into disarray and the potential exists for an heir or creditor to take control of the FLP's assets. It's best to use an LLC (or C corporation) as the general partner for the FLP. Moreover, any creditor can go after the personal assets of the general partner in order to satisfy a judgment against the limited partnership. Bottom line: the parent(s) should never be the general partner(s). Corporate control of the FLP is critical in order for the FLP to withstand any court challenges. That is because the protective feature of the charging order relies upon the general partner not to make distributions to a limited partner's interest for the benefit of a creditor. However, if the parents get sued, the creditor could probably persuade the court to enter an order compelling the parents to make a distribution to the limited partner, thus totally subverting the charging order protection.

Just like with investing, diversify your assets by utilizing multiple FLPs. Don't put all of your assets in one giant FLP. You should have no more than one million dollars in any one FLP; and at most, you should have no more than 10–20 percent of your total assets in FLPs. For large amounts of assets, use *offshore trusts*, *offshore corporations*, and *offshore LLCs*.

Charging order protection only works for assets legitimately transferred to the FLP. It does not, nor will it ever work for assets that have been fraudulently transferred (conveyed) to the FLP. It's imperative that you thoroughly understand this concept; you will never succeed in a fraudulent transfer, no matter what!

A sound operating agreement is essential for your FLP and should be drawn up by an experienced attorney. Please don't use the cookie-cutter fill-in-the-blanks operating agreement that salesmen tout will work just fine for you. What are you going to do when it doesn't hold up in court? You'll realize it's a house of cards that the promoter duped you into buying. Please form your FLP in business-friendly states like Delaware and Nevada that limit the creditor's remedy to a charging order and does not easily allow liquidation of the partnership interests to satisfy creditors. For added protection, the limited partners of the FLP should be spendthrift trusts where the beneficiaries are your children. The parents should gift assets annually to the limited partners to the maximum extent so that the LP interest accrues continually until the children have a 100 percent interest. This will avoid future estate taxes.

Watch out for salesmen who may encourage you to have an offshore trust for ownership of your limited partners' interest. The problem here is that this arrangement will cost you a lot more money than by simply having a domestic trust for your limited partners' interest. Moreover, if you fraudulently transfer assets, this offshore arrangement will not protect you. The court has jurisdiction over you, and it's only a simple matter for the judge to find you in contempt and throw you in jail. (See chapter 37.)

It's a sad fact that most "road shows" with all of their glitz and fancy salesmen are glorified con men with a serious conflict of interest. They're much more interested in making money for themselves than in helping you set up a bona fide asset protection and estate plan. Folks, stick with an experienced professional attorney with training and experience in business and taxes who will give you sound legal advice and will draw up legal documents that will survive in a court of law. Most salesmen will sell you a "house of cards" that will collapse in the court house. Let this be fair warning—I told you so!

In most cases, the parents manage their FLP. For additional asset protection, it may make sense to hire an outside third-party management firm to manage and operate the FLP. Just make sure you do due diligence on the management firm, and check to see if they are bonded. You don't want them running off with your assets. You have to weigh the additional cost with the added benefit of increased asset protection. In fact, courts look more favorably on your FLP when managed by an outside third party. This is something worth considering.

Be careful when one of the spouses/general partners is high risk. Make sure that their FLP general partner interests are held as sole and separate property and not community property. This way, if one spouse/partner suffers bankruptcy, then the other is not dragged in and the bankruptcy trustee cannot force the dissolution of the FLP. In my opinion, it's much safer for a high risk spouse to be neither a general partner nor a limited partner of an FLP.

Living Revocable Trusts (LRTs) offer absolutely *no* asset protection whatsoever because they are *revocable* entities. As such, a court could compel the debtor to revoke the trust. Never use a living trust in any FLP or for any type of asset protection.

The family limited partnership has the following attributes:

1. Limited protection of assets.
2. Shifting income.

3. Transferring wealth efficiently.
4. Maintaining parental control, but only if a general partner.
5. Limiting payroll taxes.
6. Reduction of income taxes and estate taxes.
7. Valuation discounts of partnership interests.
8. Maintains separate property useful for pre-martial planning.

Any of the following may be a partner of an FLP: individuals, corporations, LLCs, custodianships for children, trusts, or other partnerships.

Flexibility of who may be a partner of an FLP is quite unrestricted when you compare it with who may be a shareholder of an S corporation. All S corporation stockholders must be individuals, estates, specifically described organizations or trusts.[209]

The general partner manages the business of the FLP, its investments, and its day-to-day activities. Although limited partners are not responsible for partnership liabilities, general partners of an FLP are liable for partnership debts. An individual general partner is personally responsible for partnership liabilities. Please note that if the FLP is funded with liability producing assets, it is advisable to use a trust,[210] LLC,[211] or a corporation[212] as a general partner rather than an individual family member.

Trusts can become limited partners.[213]

A general partner is dissociated from the FLP in the event of

1. bankruptcy,
2. death, or
3. general partnership interest is charged or foreclosed by creditor.

Therefore, the FLP should provide for a successor general partner in case any of the foregoing events occur.

A limited partner is dissociated from the FLP in the event of death.[214]

The Big Lie Exposed—Creditors with Charging Orders Do Not Have to Pay Tax on Undistributed (Phantom) Income!

Here's one of the biggest hoaxes in the annals of asset protection that salesmen routinely promulgate; they state that Internal Revenue Service (IRS) Ruling 77-137 treats the creditor with a charging order as a substituted limited partner for tax purposes; and as a result, the judgment creditor is saddled with the tax consequences resulting from ownership without the capacity to force dissolution of the partnership or distributions from the partnership. The salesmen further emphasize that the creditor with a charging order has to pay taxes on undistributed income! And all of this supposedly acts as a powerful deterrent that keeps creditors away from your limited partnership. The problem is that this is one huge lie. And thanks to Mr. Jay Adkisson, this lie has been exposed. Thanks, Jay! One other thing to watch out for—some advisors make an offshore trust one of the limited partners of a (domestic) partnership. This is potentially dangerous because the trust could fall under the jurisdiction of a United States court.

Income from the partnership or LLC that is retained by the entity rather than distributed to its partners or members is called "phantom income." Lienholders do not pay income taxes on phantom income. Therefore, the creditor, who is a lienholder, is not liable for taxes on phantom income. This exposes the big lie perpetrated by the salesmen of FLPs: that the creditor with the charging order pays income taxes on undistributed income from the FLP.[215]

A judgment creditor who obtains a charging order is an assignee of a limited partnership interest who has *not* acquired "substantially all of the dominion and control over the interest of a limited partner" and thus is *not* "treated as a substituted limited partner for Federal income tax purposes."[216]

For example, when a debtor receives a distribution from a limited partnership or an LLC, the charging order lien then redirects the distribution to the creditor. The debtor pays income tax on the redirected distribution, and the creditor may or may not pay income tax on the distribution he receives. The reason the debtor pays income tax on the distribution is because the IRS considers this as if the debtor physically received the money and then paid the creditor. Whether the judgment creditor pays tax on this distribution depends on the nature of the judgment. For example, if the judgment arose from unpaid wages, the creditor will also pay tax on the distribution as it is received because it will be treated as income to the creditor. If the judgment was for something like damages for personal injury, the creditor would probably not have to pay taxes on the money received.

Charging Order Protection May Be a Misnomer

Folks, don't fall into the trap of thinking that a charging order will protect you. The law is always changing and court decisions occasionally make new law called *case* law or *decisional* law. Here's what can be said in a "nutshell." Limited partnerships and limited liability companies are subject to charging orders. Depending on the state where you live, there are three possible scenarios that can result from a creditor's charging order:

1. Typical charging order *protection* which only allows a creditor to receive distributions that a limited partner or member would normally receive.
2. Foreclosure upon the limited partner's or member's interest or which divests the limited partner or member of his or her interest in the partnership or LLC. The creditor steps into the debtor's shoes. However, the creditor cannot dissolve the partnership or LLC and basically has no voting rights.
3. Dissolution of the partnership or LLC. Some states allow a creditor with a charging order to dissolve and liquidate the partnership or LLC in order to satisfy his or her judgment. Where's the protection? There is none!

Folks, it's important to understand that you need to carefully review your state's laws regarding charging orders. And if your partnership or LLC was formed out of state, the laws where it was formed may not be respected (legally termed comity) in your home state. Please discuss this with a knowledgeable and competent professional before embarking on the formation of any limited partnership or LLC.

Tax Treatment of Family Limited Partnerships

Family limited partnerships are nontaxable (tax pass through) entities. Taxes are therefore the individual responsibility of the partners, not the partnership entity. FLPs permit the individual partners to obtain valuation discounts for tax purposes. FLPs allow intrafamily income shifting so that income can be shifted away from the high tax bracket parents to the low tax bracket children. FLPs reduce the size and tax value of assets, thereby permitting "leveraged gifting" and "valuation adjustments" to reduce estate and/or gift taxes. An FLP can provide estate tax savings because the value of FLP interests are reduced as a result of the limitations placed on a limited partner's ability to control the operations of the partnership.

Another scam involves salesmen's enticements for huge IRS tax discounts with your FLP's limited partnership interests. Salesmen often suggest that you can take 40–50 percent discounts or more off your FLP, but the truth of the matter is that these huge discounts are major red flags that will probably get you audited and then you'll probably end up paying heavy IRS tax penalties. Realistically speaking, a reasonable FLP discount of 15–25 percent will probably pass muster with the IRS, but don't expect the salesmen to tell you this.

An FLP can be dissolved. For tax purposes, an FLP will be terminated if no part of any business, financial operation or venture of the FLP continues to be carried on by any of its partners.[217]

Must Family Limited Partnerships Have a Business Purpose?

The family limited partnership must have a business purpose.[218] However, this is contradicted under the Uniform Limited

Partnership Act (ULPA) pursuant to ULPA §104(b) which states that "this Act does not require a limited partnership to have a business purpose."

Just as a corporation must be operated as an entity separate and apart from its owners to prevent a creditor from "piercing the corporate veil," an FLP also must be operated separate and apart from its partners to prevent a court or the IRS from discarding it. Partners should use FLP assets only under a rental or lease arrangement.

All filings and registrations must be undertaken properly, a written partnership agreement entered into, tax returns filed, and the assets of the FLP must not be commingled or treated as if they are assets of the general partner.

Creditor's Remedies Involving Family Limited Partnerships

• *Charging Orders*

A partnership interest is personal property and thus an individual with a personal judgment can lose his partnership interest to a judgment creditor. A judgment creditor of a partner may obtain a charging order, charging the partner's FLP interest. However, the judgment creditor has only the rights of an assignee (without all of the dominion and control over the limited partner interest). An assignee (creditor) is entitled to receive distributions to which the assignor would be entitled but is not entitled to participate in the conduct of the partnership. Generally, the FLP operating agreement prohibits the creditor (assignee) from becoming a substituted partner. The creditor can have a receiver appointed to receive distributions from the FLP.

A judgment creditor's remedy against a partner of an FLP is to obtain a charging order. The charging order directs the FLP to turn over all distributions that would normally have gone to the debtor-partner and instead must be handed over to the creditor. After the charging order is issued, the debtor-partner remains a partner but is not entitled to receive distributions or liquidating proceeds until the order is satisfied. Instead, the FLP must deliver to the creditor any money or property that would otherwise be distributed to the debtor-partner. However, if the FLP agreement gives the general partner discretion as to when and how much to distribute to the partners, the general partner may decide not to make distributions when a partner has creditor problems. Or he may not distribute to that one partner. If there are no distributions, then the creditor with the charging order gets nothing from the FLP.

Charging order[219] protection as some of you may know is touted by many asset protection experts as an extremely powerful asset protection tool. Unfortunately, this is a myth. A creditor of a partner in a limited partnership can only get a charging order against the interest of the partner. As a result, the creditor cannot acquire the partnership (or LLC) interest of the debtor and therefore cannot acquire the assets of the partnership (or LLC). As a result, the creditor traditionally has to wait until the manager or general partner makes a distribution in order to get paid. Of course, in most cases, the general partner (or manager) has authority to delay distributions. However, contrary to widespread misinformation, the creditor does *not* have to pay income tax on the undistributed (phantom) partnership income![220]

Charging order protection is for the benefit of nondebtor partners or members who need protection from the creditors (of debtor partners or members). With regard to single member LLCs, there are no other nondebtor members to protect. One court[221] held that the charging order protection does not apply to single-member LLCs. This means that a single-member LLC cannot be counted on to provide charging order protection and thus should not be used for asset protection purposes. The bottom line: Single-member LLCs don't provide any asset protection at all. Moreover, outside of bankruptcy, a creditor could use the Uniform LLC Act provisions to foreclose on the lien created by a charging order and then dissolve the LLC followed by liquidation of its assets to satisfy the judgment.

As for legitimately formed multiple member LLCs and partnerships, those entities would most likely receive charging-order protection. Membership interests in LLCs and partnership interests are afforded a significant level of protection through the charging order mechanism. The charging order limits the creditor of a debtor partner or a debtor member to the debtor's share of distributions without conferring on the creditor any voting or management rights.

On the other hand, there are many cases where multiple-member LLCs and partnerships have not received charging order protection when they were formed to hinder or deter creditors. In these cases, the courts have permitted foreclosure against the partnership interest or they have appointed receivers to dissolve the partnership and pay the proceeds to the creditor. To avoid these pitfalls, your family limited partnership should be set up for valid estate planning (and incidentally they can save some estate taxes, too) or business reasons during a quiescent period. Consequently, due to the recent trend of diminishing asset protection involving partnerships and LLCs, and in order to gain solid asset protection, one needs to utilize irrevocable and offshore trusts because LLCs or partnerships *alone* will not fully protect your assets.

The general partner does not owe a duty to the creditor of a charging order because there is no fiduciary relationship between them. The creditor of the charging order is merely an assignee and has not been substituted into the partnership.[222]

Charging orders are often onerous to the judgment debtor and the other partners of the FLP. Besides directing that the FLP to pay the debtor's share of any and all distributions to the creditor, the charging order may prohibit the FLP from making loans to any partner or anyone else, from making capital acquisitions without court approval, and from entering into or consummating any sale or encumbrance of any interest without court approval.

If the only purpose of the family limited partnership is to protect assets, a court may determine that a creditor's remedy is not limited to obtaining a charging order.

The law regarding charging orders is evolving, and there is a definite trend toward allowing judicial foreclosures of charging orders. Furthermore, multipartner FLPs or multimember LLCs where "there are no nondebtor partners/members to protect" may be liquidated to pay creditor claims based on recent trends.[223]

- *Judicial Dissolution and Liquidation of the FLP*

A creditor (assignee) can seek judicial dissolution of the FLP. Moreover, a court may order a foreclosure upon the interest subject to the charging order at any time. The purchaser at the foreclosure sale has the rights of a transferee. However, some states have not enacted the foreclosure procedure. The following states prohibit foreclosure of the FLP: Alaska; Arizona; Delaware; Florida; Minnesota; Nevada; New Jersey; Oklahoma; Virginia; and Wyoming.

It's best to use Delaware or Nevada to form your FLP. That's because some jurisdictions (other than Delaware or Nevada) do not limit the creditor's remedy to a charging order, thus allowing a judgment creditor to attempt a wide variety of possible remedies to get at the FLP assets to satisfy its judgment. Moreover, if any of your FLP assets are located in a jurisdiction that does not limit the creditor's remedy to a charging order, then your assets could be subject to seizure. Avoiding this potential problem is simple—use a Delaware or Nevada FLP.

There is a trend by courts to allow for judicial foreclosure of a charging order. Judicial foreclosure permits a judgment creditor with a charging order to sell his "assignee" interest. This creates a means by which the judgment creditor can at least partially satisfy collecting on his debt.

In California, a judgment debtor's interest in an FLP may be foreclosed upon and sold if the foreclosure does not unduly interfere with the partnership business.[224] Creditors can foreclose on a family limited partnership. For example, in California, case law and statutory law specifically allow a creditor to foreclose on an FLP in addition to the charging order remedy.[225] As opposed to the charging order remedy, a foreclosure of the FLP is a potentially highly destructive. For example,let's say you own the entire FLP worth $500,000. At a later date, a judgment is entered against you for $100,000. The judgment creditor decides to foreclose on your $500,000 FLP. But his judgment is only for $100,000. Yes, he can do this. Now this is where it gets interesting. By foreclosing on your FLP, the creditor is legally entitled to distributions without regard to the amount of the judgment, in this case $100,000. The creditor could eventually get paid the full value of your FLP—$500,000! In this unfortunate situation, your only recourse would be to pay off the creditor's judgment at its full amount—$100,000. So you can see that the FLP could literally force you to pay the creditor more than his judgment. Ouch! Recent court decisions make the FLP a poor choice for asset protection planning. Moreover, FLP creditors are entitled to all assets held by the FLP. For this reason, care must be taken to avoid mixing safe assets (stocks, bonds, and cash) with dangerous assets (apartment complexes, and businesses).[226] (Hypothetically, if the creditor's remedy was solely limited to a charging order, then he would be entitled to distributions equal to the amount of the judgment. When and if he was ever paid, this amount including interest, the creditor's judgment would be satisfied.)

In states other than California, case law and statutory law are not entirely clear and as such, reliance on the charging order protection is speculative at best and, therefore, dangerous. Even when the state where the partnership is formed specifically prohibits foreclosure, rules regarding jurisdiction may dictate that the law of the plaintiff's residence state may control the applicable law. In other words, the court may use its own state laws rather than the laws of the state where your partnership was formed. Many factors are considered by the courts in determining jurisdiction and the applicable law, and it's difficult to predict the choice of law that will prevail in any litigation.

However, the FLP may still be useful in certain situations for asset protection. Based on recent case law, only a qualified expert should form FLPs for their clients. The FLP needs to be correctly structured so that neither a charging order nor a foreclosure can be applied to the FLP.

How to Fund a Family Limited Partnership

Upon forming an FLP, the partners (generally the husband and wife or entities controlled by them) contribute investment assets to the FLP. FLPs can be funded by gifting cash or business (and investment) assets directly to the partnership. FLPs should NOT be funded by personal assets. Real property can be transferred to an FLP by either of the following:

1. A general warranty deed (in mortgage states).
2. A grant deed (in deed of trust states).
3. A quitclaim deed is *not* recommended because it may make it more difficult for the FLP to transfer the property.

Since only business or investment property should be placed into the FLP, the partnership should not be used to protect a personal residence. If a partner continues to use his or her home, then he or she must pay rent to the FLP. The FLP then pays the mortgage.[227] Rent is not tax deductible to the partner, but the income to the FLP is taxable. This FLP income then is taxable to the FLP partners through the K-1 (tax form) according to their percentage ownership. In addition, putting a personal residence into an FLP will cause the loss of the homestead exemption and loss of the $250,000 ($500,000 if married) capital gains exclusion.

Business property sold to an FLP should be documented by a bill of sale and the FLP should pay for insurance on these items. Often the FLP will then lease the equipment back to the operating business. Since the equipment is only leased by the operating business, if the operating business loses a major lawsuit, the equipment is not lost as it still belongs to the FLP. This is much like a sale-leaseback agreement.

Personal property should not be held by an FLP unless the partner pays rent.

LEGALLY AVOID ESTATE TAXES WITH A FAMILY LIMITED PARTNERSHIP

Family Limited Partnerships (FLPs) not only provide limited asset protection but can also save you money on estate taxes. One of the benefits of an FLP is that it allows for accelerated gifting through the use of tax discounts of the FLP's assets.

FLPs are often formed with a spousal-owned LLC (or a C corporation) as a 1 percent general partner, and the 99 percent limited partners would be the children and occasionally grandchildren. You and your spouse can then slowly gift and thereby increase the Limited Partnership units to your children and grandchildren while continuing to be the General Partners that control the FLP. Through this incremental gifting and through the discounting of the ownership shares, your children (and grandchildren) eventually end up owning all of the FLP's assets that they would otherwise have received through your estate after you and your spouse die. This puts your assets into the hands of your descendants before you and your spouse die while at the same time it avoids any payment of estate taxes. The author's motto is: "Distribute wealth before death." The bottom line: The assets of the FLP go to your children (and grandchildren) free from estate taxes! This is a great loophole, which bypasses estate taxes. Moreover, as general partners of the FLP, you still retain complete control of the FLP and its assets during your lifetime.

There are two types of discounts of partnership shares/units: One is the loss of *marketability* because the partnership interest is no longer marketable in the open market place, and the other is the "*minority interest*" discount because your children have no voting rights. Typically, FLP assets can be discounted from 20–40 percent of their normal market value. (However, with the use of a special "freeze" partnership, you may be able to obtain even larger discounts. See chapter 58: Advanced Techniques.)

With corporations, the failure to capitalize or to undercapitalize (fund) the corporation can lead to problems involving asset protection and tax benefits, and the same is true with FLPs. You need to adequately capitalize your FLP and that means transferring business assets to the entity. Failure to do so will deprive you of the asset protection features of the FLP as well as any added tax benefits. In addition, you must legally maintain your FLP by payment of annual dues. Failure to pay the annual dues will place your FLP in legal default, which means that it simply ceases to exist as a legal entity under state law as well as IRS rules. Your FLP must have a proper operating agreement, and failure to do so deprives your entity of any legal status. In simple terms, the court will not recognize your FLP as a legal entity.

Thou shall not commingle personal assets with business assets. Your FLP is a business entity. As such, your personal home should *not* be placed in your FLP. Salesmen who tout placing your personal residence in your FLP are providing bad advice to you. Moreover, your FLP should not be paying for any personal expenses, e.g., utilities, clothing, educational expenses, etc. The use of the FLP for personal purposes or commingling personal assets with the FLP's business assets could result in your FLP being disregarded for tax and asset protection purposes.

Please remember this important concept: your FLP is a business and must be treated as a business. Furthermore, it's not a good idea to even call your FLP a *family* limited partnership. A better idea is to name it simply as a *limited partnership*, and treat it as a business entity. If you need to borrow money, the limited partnership should draw up a loan document and loan you money at prevailing interest rates. Alternatively, the limited partnership can loan money to other entities of yours; and they, in turn, can loan you money. Please discuss this with a skilled attorney because if you don't do the loan correctly, the asset protection features could be quickly lost under an alter ego theory or by a creditor piercing the corporate veil. Never use the limited partnership for personal use, such as placing your personal residence in the limited partnership. A number of salesmen conduct "road shows" around the country by selling FLPs for your personal residence. These disingenuous salesmen will tell you to transfer your home to an FLP and then you'll be "bulletproof." Folks, these salesmen are selling you a "house of cards." The best thing you can do is to avoid these con men like the plague.

Watch Out for the Internal Revenue Service

Family limited partnerships can be used to reduce the size of an estate for estate tax purposes. The attractive feature of the FLP is that the value of any asset in the FLP—an apartment building, a business, even Google stock—can be discounted because selling partnership shares in the market place is difficult.

Your FLP should be able to stand up to an IRS audit, provided you did more than just set it up to reduce estate taxes. Also, as stated previously, you should not discount your partnership too drastically. Watch out for anyone suggesting discounts of more than 25 percent. It seems the IRS has settled on a discount of 25 percent in cases that it litigated.

The key principle to withstanding an IRS audit is to have a legitimate business interest for the FLP—beyond the discounts—for forming the family limited partnership.

Another factor to consider is timing, that is, when you formed your FLP. Setting up an FLP on a parent's deathbed could result in an IRS audit.[228]

Another point to remember is not to put all of your assets in the FLP. That's because if you put all of your assets in the FLP, at a later date, you may have to reach into the FLP for some reason, such as to obtain cash to make nursing home payments.[229]

Another important point to remember is to let some time lapse[230] between putting assets into your FLP and giving partnership interests to your children and taking the discount. Otherwise, the IRS could rule the whole amount was a taxable gift. Parents must *gift* the Limited Partnership interest to their children. Failure to do so will result in higher estate taxes as well as potential exposure to the claims of the parents' creditors. (Instead of directly gifting limited partnership interests directly to your children, it may be safer to gift those interests to a spendthrift trust. This would help militate against any charging order that could potentially interfere with the transfer of limited partnership shares to your children, especially claims against the limited partnership interest by the child's creditors and ex-spouses.)

You should also utilize the services of a qualified appraiser in order to obtain a fair market valuation of your FLP. The FLP valuation will assist you in discounting your *gifted* limited partnership interest in order to avoid estate taxes.

There are no guarantees here, but if you plan and structure your FLP carefully, you're ahead in the game. Please remember to maintain your FLP as an ongoing legitimate business. Regular business meetings with recorded minutes are necessary. Partnership distributions should be made in a professional manner. Unfortunately, some people fail to do this. And poor administration can invite an IRS audit. Most of this could be avoided by talking to your lawyer periodically to see if your FLP is being run properly.

THE LIMITED LIABILITY COMPANY

The limited liability company (LLC) is a hybrid legal entity similar to a partnership but with the limited liability of a corporation. For income tax purposes, it has "pass-through" tax treatment for its owners. Moreover, the IRS now lets an LLC elect to pay taxes either as a sole proprietorship or as a partnership or as a corporation by filing IRS Form 8832. However, if there is more than one member (owner), the "pass through" tax treatment does not have to be proportionate to the percentage (%) equity ownership. For example, two members may have a fifty-fifty equity ownership, but for tax purposes, they may report seventy-five–twenty-five. The LLC is the only legal entity that allows this departure. The LLC must also decide how it wants to be taxed, either as a sole proprietor, partnership, or corporation. Also, the profit distributions can vary with any percentage profit sharing under the LLC umbrella unlike a common partnership at fifty-fifty split. Please note that the operating agreement is very important for an LLC. Also, asset transfers to an LLC could trigger a gift tax. Therefore, it's important to consult with a qualified attorney before you set up an LLC.

Recent court decisions have eroded some of the asset protection features of the LLC. For instance, some courts have allowed reverse corporate piercing for single-member LLCs. Moreover, creditors have, in some cases, been able to foreclose on an LLC to satisfy its judgment. However, in most cases, the sole remedy of the creditor is a "charging order" against the member, similar to an FLP. (See chapter 16.)

Like a corporation, the members of an LLC are given limited liability. In cases of ordinary negligence, the law provides immunity for its members and will absolve all of its owners of any liability for business debts and court judgments and legal settlements obtained against the LLC. An investor in an LLC normally has at risk only his or her share of capital paid into the business.

An LLC has the following advantages:

1. Shareholders/investors are not personally responsible for LLC debts.
2. Unlimited number of membership units (similar to corporation stockholders).
3. Ease of transfer of LLC membership interest. (Some publicly traded shares are LLC membership units.)
4. Ease of raising capital by issuing additional membership units.

The limited liability company with multiple members avoids double taxation (corporate taxes and personal taxes) because the members are partners for taxation purposes, and therefore it is a pass-through entity flowing directly to a member's personal taxes. The LLC itself does not pay any taxes.

LLCs can even register their shares with the Securities and Exchange Commission as publicly traded securities.

Additionally, there is the little known family limited liability company (FLLC) and the Xtreme LLC (XLLC). Personally, I believe it is better to use a C corporation rather than a limited liability company. Corporations have been around for hundreds of years, and there's a lot of case law on the legal books involving corporations. Courts are very familiar with workings of corporations, and corporate attorneys are very comfortable forming corporations for clients and rendering legal advice. On the other hand, LLCs are the "new kid" on the block, and there is a dearth of case law on the books. Moreover, recently California courts have rendered rulings against single-member LLCs that all but eliminate any asset protection features they once may have had. The bottom line: LLCs are risky from an asset protection perspective. You're much better off with a C corporation. That's why I no longer advise using LLCs.

HOW TO PROTECT YOUR OTHER ASSETS

For most people, after their personal residence, the next most valuable assets that could be seized by creditors are their bank accounts and their cars. In my opinion, you must have several bank accounts because of the principle that you don't put all of your "eggs in one basket." By playing it extra safe, you might even want to have an offshore bank account just in case you need to make an emergency transfer of money. Also, be sure to have separate bank accounts for each spouse. The least vulnerable spouse (often the wife) should have the largest bank account. (I know that some husbands might be a little squeamish about this). Every one of your business entities must have its own separate bank account. (See chapter 9.) For example, if you operate a business as a C corporation, then the corporation must have its own separate bank account. If your home is owned by a (holding) corporation, then the (holding) corporation must have its own separate bank account. If you have a lot of money, then you may want to form a corporation to act as a holding company for your money. If you have more than $25,000–$50,000, you should seriously consider establishing an offshore bank account. In most cases, as little as $1,000 will open an offshore bank account. If you have more than $10,000 offshore, you must report this on your income tax return, using schedule B. However, you don't have to report this information for any total amounts (adding up all offshore accounts) under $10,000. My suggestion is to open an account with $1,000–$5,000 to begin with. It would be very unlikely for your (holding) corporation bank account to be the subject of any lawsuit because all it is doing is just holding your money in the bank. To play it extra safe, I wouldn't write checks from this account. What you ought to do is to periodically transfer money from the (holding) corporation bank account to your smaller personal accounts and then write checks only from your personal bank account. Basically, what you're attempting to accomplish is to hide your corporate bank account at least until you may have to divulge its existence in the discovery phase of a lawsuit. The (holding) corporation's (domestic) bank account should be formed in Delaware rather than Nevada. The reason is that there is less Internet information about Delaware corporations compared to Nevada corporations. The secretary of state of Delaware, for example, discloses far less information about its corporations than the secretary of state of Nevada. Therefore, for greater privacy, form your corporation in Delaware.

The reason for the secret corporate bank account is because occasionally a plaintiff can obtain a prejudgment attachment order from the court after allegations of fraud are made. Prejudgment attachments are rare, but they can happen. You would not want your bank account frozen with a prejudgment attachment. Hence, the reason for the "secret" corporate bank account. If you get sued and you're unable to get the lawsuit thrown out (dismissed), then you can quickly wire money out of your corporate bank account (which holds most of your money) and whisk it safely to your offshore bank account. If you get a judgment against you, and your creditors find out about your offshore bank account, they could get a court order to force you to repatriate (return) the money to the United States. However, long before that happens, you can form an offshore trust and transfer your offshore bank account to the trustee. (See chapters 34 and 37.) Be very careful if you transfer funds during a lawsuit because the judge could hold you in contempt and throw you in jail. It has happened before.

I don't ever recommend joint accounts except perhaps as a custodian for a minor child. In community property states (like California), a transmutation agreement can effectively abrogate community property and then you and your spouse can establish separate bank accounts. Spouses should never have joint bank accounts. That's because of the legal principle of joint and several liability. (See chapter 23.)

How do you protect your automobiles? Well, if you're like me, you lease an automobile. Problem solved! There's no way any creditor will ever be able to seize your leased automobile. It's just not possible and that really frustrates your creditors. Most people don't know that you can even rent cars on a long-term basis. For example, Avis Rent a Car has a "mini lease" program, which offers renewable monthly contracts for eleven months with unlimited mileage! Rates are competitive, and if you do a lot of driving, for example, like being in sales, then this is something definitely worth your consideration. Typical auto leasing can penalize you if you drive more than fifteen thousand to twenty-five thousand miles per year. So if you do a lot of driving, check out the rental car agencies. What can you do if you own one or more expensive automobiles free and clear? Your expensive automobiles should be registered in the name of the least vulnerable spouse. (See chapter 20.) Always be sure to carry plenty of automobile insurance (the liability component protects you against lawsuits) and additionally you should also have an umbrella insurance policy as well. (See chapter 8.) In my opinion, you can't have too much automobile liability insurance. What happens if you're financing your automobiles? The title to the automobile will be held by the finance company until your note is paid in full. During this time, the creditors won't be able to seize your automobile. Also, over time, most automobiles depreciate in value and this will help you. My suggestion for you is to make sure that when the time comes for you to get title to your automobile (when the automobile loan has been fully repaid), you should make sure that the least vulnerable spouse acquires the automobile title. You may have to contact the finance company ahead of time to make any necessary changes to the loan documents so that this happens correctly. Another possibility is for you to sell the car when the automobile loan has been fully paid, and any profits are paid directly to you. After your car is sold, you can then make arrangements to lease or rent an automobile. There's a personal exemption for one automobile of yours, which in the state of California is limited to $2,500 in value. If your primary car is worth less than $5,000, then it's unlikely to be seized.

First of all, you have a personal exemption of $2,500, and secondly, the creditors will have to post a bond in order to auction your car off. This costs money, and so therefore it's not very feasible for your creditors to sell your primary car if its value is under $5,000. On the other hand, if your primary car is worth considerably over $5,000, then there's a good chance it could be seized by the creditor.

An automobile you own, especially an expensive model, is a double-edged sword. On one hand, it's a valuable asset that could be seized by a creditor, and on the other, it's a dangerous asset because it causes accidents and exposes you to liability. That's why you need automobile insurance and the more the better. What about your teenage children driving your car? In almost all jurisdictions, the parents or the legal guardians are liable for their children's actions or omissions.[231] The ideal solution is for you to transfer title of your least-expensive automobile to your child as soon as he or she turns eighteen and basically give him or her use of that car and be sure to maintain full automobile insurance coverage on your child as well. Remember, this is the concept of separating and protecting assets. (See chapter 9.) Also, teenagers are high risk drivers according to the Department of Transportation. While your sixteen- and seventeen-year-old teenagers are driving, be sure to have plenty of automobile insurance as well as an umbrella policy, as you, the parents or legal guardian, are liable for any of their accidents. Unfortunately, there's not much else most of us can do. Having your sixteen- and seventeen-year-olds driving around in your car is a period in your life where you pretty much have to "hold your breath" and hope for the best and prepare for the worst. Remember, that's why you need plenty of insurance, especially during this critical period.

Other valuable assets of yours in most cases can be secreted (smuggled) to destinations where your creditors will never look and never find (provided you keep your mouth shut!). While this constitutes a fraudulent conveyance after you've been threatened with a lawsuit or during the pendency of a lawsuit, or when you currently have creditors, it happens more often than you think. Desperate people resort to desperate measures and that includes committing fraud. Many asset protection books published by licensed attorneys go so far as to advertise that they will commit fraud on behalf of their clients for an extra fee, often in the amount of $25,000–$50,000. These unscrupulous attorneys can also help you "break the law" by backdating legal documents and otherwise assisting (aiding and abetting) you in the perpetration of a fraudulent conveyance! In fact, I personally know of one attorney who lost his law license by the California State Bar for this type of fraud. However, very few attorneys are ever criminally charged for aiding and abetting a fraudulent conveyance. So perhaps this is why some attorneys fearlessly advertise and perform this type of fraud. To this day, I find it all quite amazing. Alas, it seems a lot of people are committing fraudulent conveyances—both attorneys and debtors. Remember, desperate people do desperate things, and this can often lead to disastrous consequences. It's much better to plan ahead, so you have the upper hand and you can score the ultimate victory! Kill the lawsuit! Defeat the creditors! Don't forget the old adage: "The best defense is a strong offense." This guidebook gives you the complete instructions to mount a strong and formidable offense.

The bottom line: As for your cars, you can always lease or rent long term. Many autos can be financed, and after you pay off the note, your automobile in most cases will have depreciated enough so that won't attract creditor attention. Also, be sure your automobiles are registered in the name of the least vulnerable spouse and have plenty of liability coverage on the automobiles. Remember to always separate your safe assets from your dangerous assets. Expensive safe assets like bank accounts, stocks, bonds, life insurance, etc., should always be owned by the least vulnerable spouse or otherwise placed in a legal entity such as an irrevocable trust, a family limited partnership, limited liability company, or corporation. Some expensive items like art and coin collections can "disappear" to your offshore trust or temporarily be given to relatives for safekeeping. There are so many possibilities.

THE LEAST VULNERABLE SPOUSE

The spouse who is least vulnerable to lawsuits should own the safe and valuable assets *separately* from the other spouse. This is critical to a lawsuit and asset protection plan. In many cases, the wife is the least vulnerable spouse. If this is unacceptable because of potential divorce concerns, then you should utilize an irrevocable trust or another legal entity such as a family limited partnership, limited liability company, or a corporation.

If we extend the concept behind the least vulnerable spouse, it leads to the least vulnerable person who potentially can be sued, and this usually is a nonrelative trustee, provided the beneficiary of the trust is not vulnerable to lawsuits. Remember, the beneficiary of a trust has an equitable ownership in the trust. There's legal title to property as well as equitable title to property.

Bottom line: The least vulnerable spouse is a simple concept that works well. Trust me, use it!

FRAUDULENT CONVEYANCES— TIMING IS EVERYTHING

Fraud is difficult to prove and so too are fraudulent conveyances. So the courts use what are called "Badges of Fraud" to help them decide if a fraudulent conveyance was committed. A "Badge" is essentially a suspicious sign that may indicate a fraudulent intent. The following is the archetypal list called the "Eleven Badges of Fraud" to help the courts decide if the defendant perpetrated a fraudulent transfer (conveyance):

1. The transfer was to an insider.
2. The debtor retained possession or control of the property transferred.
3. The transfer was disclosed or concealed.
4. Before the transfer was made, the debtor had been sued or threatened with suit.
5. The transfer was of substantially all the debtor's assets.
6. The debtor absconded.
7. The debtor removed or concealed assets.
8. The value of the consideration received by the debtor was not reasonably equivalent to the value of the asset transferred.
9. The debtor was insolvent or became insolvent shortly after the transfer was made.
10. The transfer occurred shortly before or shortly after a substantial debt was incurred.
11. The debtor transferred the essential assets of the business to a lienholder who transferred the assets to an insider of the debtor.

The more Badges of Fraud that the court can pin on you, the greater the likelihood you committed a fraudulent conveyance. Moreover, any asset transferred during a lawsuit is a major red flag that, in and of itself, could be the swing vote to prove you committed a fraudulent conveyance. Don't, and I repeat don't, transfer any significant assets during a lawsuit. You'll only raise a red flag that would strongly indicate to the court that you committed a fraudulent conveyance. If the judge thinks you transferred property to avoid paying a debt, you could be in trouble. However, just because your transfer triggers one or more Badges of Fraud doesn't necessarily mean that it constitutes fraud. The court will look at the whole situation, especially in the context of something that might occur in the normal course of business. If your transfer was done for a business purpose, then the court will probably find in your favor, meaning that it won't consider your transfer a fraudulent conveyance.

Here's an interesting paradox. Criminal fraud is an "intent" crime, which means that it requires intent on the part of the perpetrator. This certainly makes sense. In California, for example, a fraudulent conveyance is not only a tort (a civil wrong) but is also a misdemeanor.[232] However, there's a special type of fraudulent conveyance (see below) that can involve your transfer even when you acted innocently and without any intent whatsoever to deceive or to defraud your creditors! It's called a *constructive* fraudulent conveyance. So in theory, your *constructive* fraudulent conveyance could represent criminal fraud. This doesn't make sense.

Generally speaking, you're free to transfer any of your assets' subject to the laws of fraudulent conveyance. Basically, as long as you haven't been threatened with a lawsuit, don't have any pending lawsuits against you, and don't have any current creditors, then you are freely permitted to transfer any or all of your assets without fear of committing a fraudulent conveyance. I call this the quiescent (quiet) period in your life, and it's the best time to make any necessary transfers for your lawsuit and asset protection plan. Don't wait until it's too late, or you'll be sorry.

There's a common fallacy amongst collections attorneys and asset-protection experts that a debtor who transfers a house with equity (value) of as little as one dollar can lose the entire house to the creditors. In other words, the incorrect thinking here is that the creditor can get the *entire* house at some later date (regardless of the current equity or value) if the original transfer made by the debtor is determined by a court to have been a fraudulent conveyance. However, there's a little-known statute [233] in California that entitles the creditor of a fraudulent transfer to only the value of the asset at the time the transfer was made. In the example above, the creditor would only be able to recover one dollar, no more, regardless of the home's current value. Using another example, let's suppose the debtor who transferred his home in 1998 had exposed equity (value) of $7,700 (not including his homestead exemption or the mortgage) But in 2006, when a final ruling came down from the court, the house had appreciated in value and now had $600,000 in exposed equity. Even though the house is worth much more in 2006, the creditors could only get $7,700, which was the exposed equity at the time the fraudulent conveyance (transfer) was made in 1998.

Real property, such as your home, that is transferred to an offshore trust can be avoided (undone) in a fraudulent conveyance action (lawsuit) because a US court has jurisdiction over your home for the simple reason that it's located here in the United States. If you're desperate, and you don't care about committing a fraudulent conveyance, then you can always quickly wire money offshore to your trust, and you can even go so far as to ship (air freight) portable assets to your offshore trust well out of reach (jurisdiction) of US courts. Depending on how desperate you are, you can even quickly sell your home and when escrow closes, you can have your money wired to your offshore account. However, if there is a lien or lis pendens on your property, then you've got some serious problems. In those cases, the escrow company probably won't release any money to you until it is cleared by the court.

Fraudulent conveyance (transfer) lawsuits are typically brought by creditors or by bankruptcy trustees.

There are two types of fraudulent conveyance (transfer)—"actual fraudulent conveyance" and "constructive fraudulent conveyance."

An "actual fraudulent conveyance" typically involves a debtor who often, when attempting to avoid a creditor, gifts his assets usually to an "insider" and leaves himself nothing to pay his creditors. A "constructive fraudulent conveyance" does not relate to fraudulent intent but rather is a transfer by the debtor that took place for less than reasonably equivalent value if the debtor is insolvent at the time of the transfer or becomes insolvent (which under the Bankruptcy Code, exists when the sum of the debtor's debts exceeds the fair value of the debtor's property, with some exceptions) or is left with unreasonably small capital to continue in business as a result of the transfer. In other words, a constructive fraudulent conveyance exists whenever you sell or even give away your property for less than its fair market value *and* you are either insolvent when you made the transfer *or* the transfer made you insolvent. Courts have ruled that the sale of property for at least 70 percent or greater of its appraised value represents "fair market value."[234] For example, where the debtor has transferred a $100,000 item only to have received $50,000; or in a business, the business should have ceased trading earlier to preserve capital (wrongful trading). In a successful fraudulent conveyance suit, the plaintiff is entitled to recover the property transferred or its value from the transferee (recipient) who has received a gift of the debtor's assets. (Subsequent transferees may also be targeted although they generally have stronger defenses than immediate transferees.)

Some asset protection experts say that asset protection planning is like wine; it gets better with age. This is true only up to a certain point. What does this really mean? What this refers to is the statute of limitations as it applies to a fraudulent conveyance. Whenever a transfer has been made, it can only be challenged by creditors (who are the only ones who can do this, which legally is termed "standing"). But there is a strict time limit when the transfer of an asset can be attacked and the challenge comes in the form of a fraudulent conveyance lawsuit. For instance, in California, a *recorded* transfer can only be challenged by creditors up to four years after it has been recorded. Only creditors (which in most cases are plaintiffs with a judgment) who have legal standing to file a fraudulent conveyance lawsuit can initiate an action against a debtor. After four years, your *recorded* transfer is as good as gold; it can never be challenged or avoided (set aside) as a fraudulent conveyance.

What happens if you have a *recorded* transfer that is two years old and you just got sued? Since most lawsuits can easily drag on for well over two years you should just sit tight. By the time a final judgment is entered against you, your recorded transfer is going to be well over four years old, and any fraudulent conveyance lawsuit would be time-barred (prohibited). However, there are cases and states where courts have tolled the statute of limitations in order to allow the plaintiffs/creditors to initiate a fraudulent conveyance action after they obtain a judgment.

Fraudulent conveyances (transfers) are governed by two sets of laws that are generally consistent. The first is the Uniform Fraudulent Transfer Act (UFTA) that has been adopted by most of the states. The other law is found in the federal bankruptcy code.

The UFTA and the bankruptcy code both provide that a transfer made by a debtor is fraudulent as to a creditor if the debtor made the transfer with the "actual intention to hinder, delay or defraud" any past, present, or future creditor of the debtor.[235]

The bankruptcy code authorizes a bankruptcy trustee to recover the property transferred fraudulently for the benefit of all the creditors of the debtor if the transfer took place within the relevant time frame (usually within two years of filing for bankruptcy). The bankruptcy trustee is also permitted to use the UFTA if the state in which the transfer took place has adopted it and the transfer took place within its relevant time period (the time period under the UFTA is typically four years before an action is brought to recover the assets). Creditors may also pursue remedies under the UFTA without the necessity of a bankruptcy.

A *constructive* fraudulent conveyance amazingly doesn't even involve fraud and can happen to honest debtors because this type of transfer does not involve any actual wrongdoing! The term is an oxymoron since it only has to do with an asset transfer for less than its actual value. For example, let's say your home has a value of $300,000 and you sell it for $150,000. Under the law, this would be a *constructive* fraudulent conveyance. Another situation is where the parents transfer their home without any consideration (that is, for no money) to an adult child in order to keep the home out of probate. Later, when the parents file for bankruptcy, they learn that the bankruptcy trustee will avoid (undo) the transfer. In order to keep the home, the adult child (owner of the home) must pay the bankruptcy trustee an amount equal to the equity in the home or the parents' total debts (whichever is greater) either directly to the chapter 7 bankruptcy trustee or in payments (installments) to a chapter 13 bankruptcy trustee; otherwise, the bankruptcy trustee will sell the home to pay the creditors. Ironically, had the parents kept their home (or recovered title to their home), they could have applied their homestead exemption and would either have kept their home or at least would have recovered an amount equivalent to their homestead exemption.

Even good faith purchasers of property who are the recipients of fraudulent transfers are only able to keep the money they paid for it and no more.

In the corporate world, fraudulent transfers often occur with leveraged buyouts (LBOs). The owners of a failing corporation will get a corporate loan using its assets as collateral. Then the company announces a buyout. The stock skyrockets, and the corporation uses the loan proceeds to purchase the officers' and directors' stock at highly inflated prices. The creditors of the corporation are then left with a corporation having little or no unencumbered assets left upon which to collect their debts.[236]

Also remember, if you transfer assets for less than fair market value, it's a taxable gift. To determine fair market value, get a professional appraisal.

The Uniform Fraudulent Transfers Act (UFTA)

Most states have adopted this act, which refers to fraudulent transfers (conveyances). A fraudulent transfer is a transfer of a debtor's asset for the purpose of obstructing or defeating a creditor from obtaining that asset in order to collect on a judgment. The UFTA updated and replaced an earlier version called the Uniform Fraudulent Conveyances Act (UFCA).

The UFTA is a claim made by the creditor against a transferee (recipient) of an asset. It governs the rights of the creditor against a transferee who is not a judgment debtor. The UFTA is powerful because where there are conflicts in the law; the UFTA will supersede the other law. Generally, the UFTA assists creditors in having a transfer set aside. However, a good faith transferee is usually able to keep the asset.

Some courts have misinterpreted the act's statute of limitations. The UFTA states that the four-year statute of limitations *begins* "after the transfer was made or the obligation was incurred." However, some courts have held that the statute of limitations *begins* when the plaintiff/creditor has obtained a judgment.[237] Because of this problem with the statute of limitations, some creditors forum shop for the best jurisdiction in order to give them a more favorable statute of limitations period whereas debtors and transferees seek to keep the assets in states that give them the four-year statute of limitations provisions.[238] The statute of limitations also includes "one year [to file your claim] from when the transaction could reasonably have been discovered by the creditor." Folks, this is why you must record your transfers in the local recorder's office; it puts all third parties on notice and so therefore it nixes the one-year discovery statute of limitations that could potentially extend the claim-filing period a very long time. (But see endnote 187.)

A claimant under the UFTA does not have to have a judgment but must be a creditor to have standing to bring a claim.

The UFTA applies the "Badges of Fraud," and any Badge of Fraud is highly suspect. Transfers to insiders, and by insolvent debtors, and *constructive* fraudulent conveyances are highly suspect. To protect yourself, always transfer assets for adequate ("reasonably equivalent value") consideration. In most cases, consideration equals cash. Remember, there is no consideration with gifts. Therefore, gifting will get you in trouble. Moreover, funding a trust is essentially the same as gifting because it requires no consideration.

The UFTA specifically excludes the following transfers:

1. Valid liens.
2. Exempt property (where transferred property is located).
3. Tenancy by the entireties.

When a claim is brought under the UFTA, the court must first determine if the transfer from a debtor to a third-party transferee was fraudulent. If so, does the transferee have a good faith defense? [239] If the transferee does not have a good faith defense, then the court must decide what remedies to impose: a judgment creditor may get the court to order execution upon the transferred assets or the proceeds of the transfer. This remedy is not available to creditors that have not yet obtained a judgment. However, all claimants (judgment creditors and nonjudgment creditors) can get the court to avoid the transaction, attach the assets, enjoin the assets from further transfer, appoint a receiver to take charge of the assets.

A Fraudulent Conveyance constitutes a civil tort as well as a criminal act. Under the Uniform Fraudulent Transfer Act (UFTA), a Fraudulent Conveyance is a crime:

"(a) a transfer made or obligation incurred by a debtor is fraudulent as to a creditor whether the creditor's claim arose before or after the transfer was made or the obligation was incurred, if the debtor made the transfer or incurred the obligation: (1) with actual intent to hinder, delay, or defraud any creditor of the debtor."

Bottom line: Fraudulent transfers will not be tolerated by the UFTA. Legitimate transfers, especially those for "reasonably equivalent value," are likely to survive challenge. If the debtor receives equivalent cash in return for the transfer, the creditor can collect from the debtor (against that asset). Thus, the creditor's position has not been substantially impaired, so there is no reason to unwind the transfer. In most instances, your gifts will be avoided until the statute of limitations runs (expires). Most legitimate business transactions should survive creditor challenge. The possible remedies the court can impose is to avoid (invalidate) the transfer and restore title to original owner, freeze the asset, appoint a receiver, award damages such as attorney's fees and costs and possibly award punitive damages, and recover any proceeds received by the transferee (recipient of the transfer).

THE FRAUDULENT CONVEYANCE LOOPHOLE

In most cases, there seems to be an exception to almost every law. For example, it's against the law to kill someone *except* in self-defense. Likewise, regarding fraudulent conveyances, there are a few interesting exceptions.

Folks, there's one point which is very important to remember. There is a way to make a transfer during a lawsuit or when you have creditors that can *never* be considered a fraudulent transfer. Even some of the experts forget this. So long as you receive fair market value for your asset when you sell it, you will not have committed a fraudulent conveyance. This brings up an interesting point. I once ran into an individual who declared bankruptcy. He told me he sold his home for fair market value, and therefore he did not commit a fraudulent conveyance. He subsequently took the proceeds of the sale and hid the money. The bankruptcy trustee queried him as to the whereabouts of the money he had received from the sale of his home. He lied and told the trustee that he lost all of the money through gambling in a Las Vegas casino. The trustee believed him. He wittingly pulled off a successful bankruptcy fraud. Now don't get me wrong, I'm not advocating fraud or any criminal activity for that matter, but I recount this story to show you other possibilities.

There's a little-known method which few asset protection experts and real estate attorneys know that allows a debtor to *legally* transfer his or her home during a lawsuit! And even if the debtor is sued for a fraudulent conveyance, he or she can get the lawsuit thrown out (dismissed). It's based on numerous federal and state published decisions. California Civil Code section 3439.08 (b) states that a transfer deemed fraudulent is only fraudulent up to the value transferred. But what happens if the debtor fraudulently transfers property with no value? A fully encumbered asset has no value. Let's suppose I own a $1 million Picasso statue, which I'm using as collateral for a $1 million loan. The $1 million statue is now fully encumbered. There's no equity in the statue because it is fully encumbered. And fully encumbered property by legal definition is not an asset of the debtor because it has no value for the debtor. What happens if I transfer the statue? Have I committed a fraudulent conveyance? Numerous federal and state courts have said "no." A California court decided in *In re Mehrtash* that a creditor needs to be injured by the conveyance (asset transfer) that it seeks to invalidate. However, if the debtor transfers property with no value, then the creditor has not been injured. Furthermore, the *Mehrtash* court stated that the UFTA implicitly requires that a creditor demonstrate that he or she has been injured by a transfer.[240]

A federal court in Pennsylvania stated, "Moreover, numerous courts in other jurisdictions in which the issue has arisen have stated as though it were axiomatic the requirement that a creditor be *injured* by the conveyance it seeks to invalidate"[241] (Emphasis added). As stated previously, numerous other courts have followed this "axiom."[242]

I'd rather have protected assets that will eventually go to my heirs, such as my children and other relatives than exposed assets that can potentially go to creditors. Therefore, the transfers are done in furtherance of estate planning. The US Supreme Court stated in a public opinion that asset protection is legal, subject to the laws of fraudulent conveyance.[243]

As I have said all along, in almost all cases, once a lawsuit is begun (or even threatened), you are no longer legally permitted to transfer your assets. That's because the transfer of your assets actually hinders your future creditors, and that's illegal. It's even a criminal offense! But you're unlikely to be criminally prosecuted unless you fraudulently transfer a very valuable asset. Also, if you happen to be lucky enough to have a fully encumbered home with no exposed equity, then you are in the enviable position to transfer your home without triggering a fraudulent conveyance. By legal definition, any of your property that's fully encumbered (that has no equity or value) is *not* your "asset"! Hurray, that's wonderful! Therefore, what this means for you is that you can *legally* transfer any fully encumbered property of yours at any time, even during a lawsuit without committing a fraudulent conveyance! If you are ever sued for a fraudulent conveyance in this situation, you can get the lawsuit tossed out (dismissed with prejudice). The legal cases that can support you are found in endnotes 186–188. Folks, this is really great news, and you are unlikely to find this information in any other asset protection book! What if your property has some exposed equity? For example, if your $425,000 house has $10,000 of exposed equity ($425,000–$75,000 [the California homestead exemption for a married couple]–$340,000 mortgage = $10,000), can you then transfer your home legally during a lawsuit? The answer is no because it is considered an asset due to the $10,000 of exposed equity. Would there be any advantage to illegally transferring your home with $10,000 of exposed equity during a lawsuit? Yes, in most cases, at least in California because of a California law that states for purposes of a fraudulent conveyance that only the *value* of the asset transferred is available to your creditors. In this example, if the creditors were ever able to succeed in setting aside your transfer as a fraudulent conveyance, the most they could possibly recover would be $10,000 regardless of the asset's present value. Now let's suppose you expect the value of your home to rise in the next few years, it would then probably be a very good idea to transfer your home now rather than wait later as it becomes more valuable, and this is true even if the transfer is made as a fraudulent conveyance.

In the Western United States (Ninth Circuit Federal Jurisdiction), you may be able to transfer your home in a bankruptcy with an unrecorded transmutation agreement. Remember, a transfer of real property in a transmutation agreement must be recorded in order to be effective against third parties. Therefore, an unrecorded transmutation agreement involving a real property transfer is not valid against third parties. However, the Ninth Circuit Court of Appeals allowed an unrecorded transmutation agreement to be effective against third parties in a bankruptcy proceeding. It's complicated and it's not entirely foolproof. I therefore strongly suggest you use an expert bankruptcy attorney for this method. The transfer is based on *Finalco, Inc. v. Roosevelt*, 87 F.3d 311 (Ninth Circuit 1996).

There may be one other way to transfer your property during a lawsuit, but it's very risky and probably unlikely to help you. I mention this for the sake of completeness. It involves transferring your assets to a limited liability company and is based on the *US Shoe Company* case in the Southern Alabama federal district. What you are really doing here is hindering your creditors and thus the courts are apt to rule this fraudulent conveyance.

By the way, if you transfer your home with any exposed equity (value), your creditors can also seek punitive damages in addition to their requested attorney fees in their fraudulent conveyance lawsuit against you. All together, these damages could be quite large; in fact, they could be much larger than the value you transferred. So the take-home lesson here is to be careful.

You can make any transfer of any asset of yours without triggering a fraudulent conveyance only if all three the following conditions apply:

1. You have not been threatened with any lawsuit.
2. You are not a defendant in any current lawsuit.
3. You do not have any existing creditors.

THESE BUSINESSES SHOULD NEVER BE FORMED

Sole Proprietorships

In my opinion, you should never operate any business as a sole proprietorship. In fact, sole proprietorships are so dangerous that they should be outlawed. First of all, sole proprietorships offer absolutely no liability protection whatsoever. A judgment against your sole proprietorship will not shield you personally. In fact, your personal assets are at risk of seizure and sale to satisfy the judgment of the sole proprietorship. Any judgment involving the sole proprietorship will pass right through to its owner. If your sole proprietorship is sued, then you automatically are personally sued as well. That means your business assets along with all of your personal assets are vulnerable to creditors if a judgment is rendered against your sole proprietorship. This really is the worst possible situation to be in. If you happen to live in a community property state like California and you have neglected to take steps to separate your community property, then your community property is also vulnerable to seizure by the creditors. You really can't do much worse than this. Unfortunately, there are also some sole proprietors who operate without business insurance. This is a ticking time bomb waiting to explode—a potential major disaster. This is so self-destructive; and worse yet is the fact that so many sole proprietors are operating just this way—without any business insurance. And these same people also have their personal property held in joint and/or community ownership. Please, if you fit this picture, then you must act immediately to correct this dangerous situation. There's no need to panic, but here's what I suggest you do. First, call your insurance agent, or if you don't have an insurance agent, then go online or check the yellow pages of the telephone directory to find an insurance agent and sign up for business liability insurance. Also, let your insurance agent know that you're going to roll your business over to a corporation sometime during the next thirty to sixty days. I no longer recommend limited liability companies (LLCs) because there's very little case law on this type of entity and single-member LLCs are vulnerable to reverse corporate piercing.[244] The next thing to do is to contact a licensed attorney who specializes in forming corporations. After a consultation with the attorney, your corporation should be up and running in a short while. Then you'll set up your business bank account and contact your insurance agent to begin business liability coverage on your newly formed business. After this is completed, your lawsuit and asset protection plan should be quite strong.

A sole proprietorship is a business operated either by a single individual or by a husband and wife team. Sole proprietorship is the automatic default business for all businesses with a single owner that have not been established as a corporation or limited liability company. Sole proprietorships are the most common type of business. They are also the easiest to operate because unlike a corporation or a limited liability company, sole proprietors are not required to file any documents with the state to begin the company. By default, the name of the sole proprietorship is the same as the legal name as the owner. Alternatively, sole proprietors may elect to operate under a fictitious business name. In some states, sole proprietors are required to file a fictitious name certificate with the city or county clerk's office where the sole proprietorship is located and/or post a newspaper notice in a local newspaper.

A sole proprietorship can even be formed by default without even realizing it. For example, if you become a contractor or a salesperson or just freelance, then you automatically become a sole proprietor.

Owners of a sole proprietorship have unlimited liability for claims made against the business and debts accumulated by the company. This means that besides the business assets, the sole proprietor's personal assets—home, automobiles, etc.—are vulnerable to business debts and judgments. This makes a sole proprietorship extremely risky to operate. Sole proprietors should therefore operate a business as a corporation or LLC in order to afford them limited liability, which protects their personal assets against business lawsuits and other business-related debts.

The Internal Revenue Service treats a sole proprietorship as a pass-through entity, which means profits and losses go directly onto the owner's tax returns. Thus, there is no need to file any business tax forms. The one small advantage of a sole proprietorship is that sole proprietors are not taxed twice on business profits as is the case with a corporation.

Sole proprietors have full control and responsibility for making any and all decisions for the business. There is no requirement for voting or holding meetings, and there is no need to have a separate business bank account. Sole proprietorships also have a hard time raising capital and obtaining loans and credit. Sole proprietorships cease to exist when the business owner passes away, retires, or decides to sell the business.

General Partnerships

A general partnership is a business that you definitely want to avoid. You should never join any general partnership. General partnerships should also be banned and outlawed because they are very dangerous from a liability standpoint. General partnerships involve the (unfair) legal principle of joint and several liability. If just one of the partners in the general partnership "screws up," then the whole general partnership can get sued. Don't walk, but run away from general partnerships as fast as you can. Simply put, you must avoid general partnerships. They cause major trouble. Did you know that *any* general partner can commit the entire general partnership and all other general partners to any legal contract (e.g., a loan)? All general partners are therefore jointly and severally liable.

Since all partners of a general partnership are jointly and severally liable, this means that if a lawsuit is filed against the general partnership and not all of the defendants (partners) are served, the plaintiff may proceed against those defendants who are served as if they were the only defendants.[245]

If the lawsuit is successful, then the general partnership gets hit with a judgment, and all of the general partners are personally responsible for the judgment as well as the general partnership itself. This is literally a classic case of "guilt by association." You could be the best and most conscientious partner in the partnership and do everything just right, and all it takes is for one partner to "screw up." All your good work is down the drain. And this feature is a real sore point for the general partnership. Suppose, as one of the partners of the general partnership, you own a lot of *personal* (not business) assets. In other words, you're the one with the "deep pockets." The result is you could end up losing everything you own (that is, your personally assets) just because another general partner "screwed up" and even though you did nothing wrong yourself! I guarantee you will definitely have a bad day. Folks, stay clear of the general partnership. Avoid it like the plague. This is one business entity that definitely should be outlawed!

There's one more thing most asset protection books won't tell you: married couples living in community property states like California are much like a general partnership. That's why it's so critical to abrogate[246] this terrible situation, and the best way to do this during marriage is with a transmutation agreement. (See chapter 12.) Remember, before getting married in a community property state, you should have a prenuptial agreement to avoid acquiring community property during the marriage.

If you have a partner working with you, then by default you automatically have a general partnership. A general partnership can even be formed by oral agreement. There's no need for any written agreement. Remember, a simple handshake can seal the deal; you now have a general partnership. On the downside, you'll have to go to court to resolve any misunderstanding if an individual is under the impression that he or she is a partner in the business.

If you are named together with another individual on any legal document, such as title to real property, then by default it's a general partnership under the law. The small advantage to a general partnership is that are no filing requirements with the state, and tax treatment is pass-through, which means the profits and losses of the partnership go directly onto the partner's separate individual tax returns in proportion to the partner's contributions. Unfortunately, the death knell for general partnerships is joint and several liability, which means that each partner is personally liable to an unlimited extent for any act or omission of any other partner as well as being personal liable for all liabilities attributable to the general partnership. All it takes is for one partner to screw up, and all other remaining partners become liable. The United States needs to outlaw the general partnership. Remember, avoid the general partnership like the plague.

Single-Person Companies

Single person companies which include single-shareholder corporations (C corporations and S corporations) and single-member LLCs attract close scrutiny by the courts because they are often used as alter ego companies of their owners and are sometimes involved in fraudulent conveyances. Additionally, attorneys and financial advisors who assist their clients in forming these entities with a fraudulent intent can be named as civil conspirators in lawsuits.

Single person companies can provide the owner with limited protection against liabilities arising from the legitimate conduct of their company (limited liability) but cannot protect the owner directly from liability stemming from illegal activity, gross negligence, and improper use of the company. In other words, if the company does something wrong, the owner is not necessarily responsible. To reach the owner's *personal* assets, a plaintiff/creditor would have to "pierce the veil" of the entity showing one or more of the following:

- The entity was undercapitalized for its intended business purpose,
- company (corporate) formalities were not followed,
- the owner used the entity mostly for personal purposes,

- the entity did not serve a "bona fide" legitimate commercial or business purpose, and/or
- the entity lacked economic or commercial substance and was merely an alter ego of the owner.

Single-Member Limited Liability Companies

Single-Member LLCs are no longer protected from creditors because of reverse corporate piercing, in which a debtor's personal judgment may be satisfied by attaching the assets of his single-member LLC. Unfortunately, the vast majority of financial advisors are, in the opinion of the author, committing malpractice and rendering atrocious legal advice to their clients when they recommend the formation of a single-member LLC. Never form a single-member LLC!

A bankruptcy court has held that the charging order limitation serves no purpose with a single-member LLC because there are no nondebtor members to protect. The court thus allowed the bankruptcy trustee to sell the LLC's assets.[247] However, the bankruptcy court stated that the LLC's assets would not have been sold had there been any nondebtor members in the LLC. Remember, you *must* form a multimember LLC for adequate charging order protection.

ALWAYS FORM THESE BUSINESSES

Corporations and Limited Liability Companies

If you're self-employed and running a business, then you need to have some form of limited liability protection. This is much like state employees who have qualified immunity—partial protection from lawsuits—when working under the "color of law" in their official capacity as government workers. Should you commit a simple and unintentional mistake (the legal term for this is negligence), then limited liability protection will protect you against personal liability; and that extends to your personal assets. We all make occasional mistakes. If in the course of operating your business under a corporation or limited liability company, you make an honest and simple unintentional mistake, then through statutory law that's provided to corporations and limited liability companies you will not be held personally liable. You really need to have some form of limited liability if you run your own business. You're probably asking, "How can I get limited liability protection?" It's very simple. You need to operate your business as a corporation or limited liability company in order to get some form of limited liability protection. In order for this to work correctly, please use a licensed attorney who specializes in setting up corporations and limited liability companies. It shouldn't be very expensive or time-consuming to set up your company, and no more than one or two consultations should be required. Once you receive all the legal papers for your corporation or limited liability company, which includes the business certificate from the secretary of state, then you're ready to open a business bank account. It's extremely important and critical to always, and I mean always, to keep your personal bank account completely separate from your business bank account. Because if you don't, plaintiffs/creditors can allege that you are engaging in an "alter ego" company by commingling personal and business assets. In other words, your corporation is really a front for your personal operations rather your business operations. Guess what happens next if the court agrees with the plaintiffs/creditors that you have an "alter ego" business? You lose your limited liability protection and now you can be sued personally and your personal assets could be available for seizure by the creditors! Folks, you don't want this to happen. There's one other point to remember: you should *never* appoint the least vulnerable spouse to be a director or officer of your company. If your company ever gets sued, your spouse would likely be named as a defendant, and depending on the circumstances, her separate property could then be subject to creditor seizure as well as yours. You and your spouse must keep assets separate. By appointing your spouse as a director and/or officer of your company, you are in effect commingling your assets. For a small corporation that you own and run, it's best for you to be the director and all of the officers of the company yourself. For a small limited liability company that you own, it's best for you to manage it yourself or alternatively have a third party manage it for you. You should *never* have your spouse involved in the management of your limited liability company. Another point to remember is to always act professionally when you run your corporation or limited liability company. When you sign the company's checks, always add your title to your signature. For example, John Doe, president. Another very important point to remember, all signatories to your business bank account could be liable in a lawsuit and thus named as defendants. Therefore, your spouse should *never* be a signatory on your business bank account. Also, your office secretary should never be a signatory on the business bank account because he or she could also be named as a defendant. However, the corporate secretary can be a signatory. For larger companies that have more than one director and/or officer, you would be wise to purchase D and O (directors and officers) insurance for your corporation.

I am now of the opinion that it is better to run your business with a corporation[248] rather than a limited liability company (LLC).

To begin with, there's a tremendous body of case law regarding corporations that extends over hundreds of years. Courts and judges are very familiar with corporations. On the other hand, case law regarding LLCs is sparse, and some recent rulings eliminate liability protection for single-member LLCs. There is one small advantage of LLCs over corporations: with LLCs, you are not required to have an annual director's meeting. However, in my opinion, this small LLC advantage is outweighed by the four attributes of corporations: (1) limited liability, (2) perpetual existence, (3) centralized management, and (4) stock certificates. With limited liability companies, you're allowed to choose only two of these four attributes. Limited liability companies have no stock but rather a certificate of membership. A member of the limited liability company is an owner. Based on recent court decisions, you should have more than one member in your LLC in order to better withstand charging orders. In order for a court to establish an "alter ego" theory of liability (otherwise known as piercing the corporate veil), you must have some ownership interest in the corporation or limited liability company. If you're only a manager of an LLC with no ownership interest at all, then there cannot be any "alter ego" liability or piercing of the corporate veil. Who are the owners of a corporation? The owners of a corporation are its stockholders. If you own stock in a corporation, then by law, you are one of its owners. Directors and/or officers of the corporation are not obliged to be stockholders (owners) of the corporation. The directors' job is to appoint officers to run the corporation and to make corporate decisions that often have to be ratified by its stockholders, whereas the officers of the corporation are involved basically in the daily management of the corporation. Also, if your corporation has more than one director, it appears more bona fide before a court and thus it will probably be able to more successfully challenge any alter ego claim. It's important and legally necessary to keep track of the stockholders of the corporation. The proper and legal way to do this is to use a stock ledger and by keeping it up-to-date.

I must stress to you the critical importance of always keeping your business separate from your personal life. Never, and I mean *never* commingle your personal assets with your business. If you do, your corporation or your limited liability company will lose its limited liability protection. This is called the "Alter Ego Theory" otherwise known as "Piercing the Corporate Veil" in which the courts view your business as a front for your personal matters. Basically, the courts consider your business a sham. It's a form of fraud. So the courts will nullify your corporation's limited liability protection. Now your personal assets are on the line, meaning that a creditor can go after your personal assets to satisfy their judgment. Folks, this is something you definitely want to avoid. Play by the rules, and your personal assets will be off limits to the creditors. We all make mistakes, and your honest mistakes will not cause you to forfeit your personal assets. This is where corporate laws come in to protect you. Take advantage of this protection by using a corporation for its limited liability protection and keep your personal assets separate from your business assets. Please remember, when using a legal entity, it must always be done for a business purpose. No exceptions. For example, if you transfer your home to a corporation, there better be a business reason for doing so; otherwise, your asset protection plan will not hold up in court.

On the flip side, there is something called reverse corporate piercing. The way it works is through a one-member limited liability company. Remember, a member of an LLC is the owner of the LLC. A one-member LLC is owned by just one person. In theory, the one-member LLC is a separate legal entity and entirely separate from its owner. A personal legal judgment against an owner should be separate from the LLC. But what should be isn't always the case. Unfortunately, in some places like California, the courts now have authority to confiscate the assets of the one-member LLC to satisfy the personal judgment of its owner. It doesn't seem fair, and it's called reverse corporate piercing. That's why I don't like LLCs. Folks, I really believe you're better off with a C corporation. A sole-owner of a C corporation isn't subject to reverse corporate piercing as is the single-member LLC. However, a judgment creditor may be able to confiscate/seize your corporation's stock and thereby gain control over the company. Then the creditor can liquidate the corporation to satisfy the judgment. So therefore it seems that one-person entities no longer provide the liability protection once afforded. (See chapter 23.)

One of the best ways to protect your business against lawsuits is to have plenty of business liability insurance. It's important to keep as few assets as possible in the corporation or limited liability company. One way to distribute money legally out of the business is to employ your spouse and/or your children in the business. They should probably be hired as independent contractors rather than employees because, generally speaking, you will have significantly more protection against lawsuits if your workers are hired as independent contractors rather than employees. The legal principle of respondeat superior, where you are held responsible for the acts or omissions of your workers, is much more difficult to establish for independent contractors that you hire compared to employees who work for your company. But just make sure your family members are not doing any work that could expose them to liability. For instance, assign them to paperwork, bookkeeping, copying, answering the phone, etc. These are jobs that won't get them sued. You can pay your spouse any amount you want; however, unusually high salaries that don't comport with local market conditions might be viewed with suspicion from a court. My suggestion is to keep the salaries reasonable. As for your minor children, if they earn less than the standard exemption, there's no income tax for them and you are allowed to deduct their pay as well! This is a win-win situation for everyone.

Since there's considerably more decisional law involving corporations than limited liability companies, I strongly recommend you use a corporation rather than a limited liability company for your business. There are two types of corporations—C corporations and S corporations. In my opinion, the two best states to incorporate your business are Nevada and Delaware. It's also important to register your out-of-state (foreign) corporation in the state where you are doing business. Additionally, don't forget that you may need a business license even if you work out of your home. If your business does get sued and your liability insurance doesn't cover the lawsuit, you may have to declare bankruptcy or wind down the business into an empty shell. Don't dissolve the business because as a former owner you'll be personally liable for the corporation's debts during the next two years.

Unfortunately, limited liability protection won't help you at all if you commit gross negligence (an intentional or serious mistake for which you should have known better) or in instances of reckless misconduct or malice were you acted without regard to safety or acted irresponsibly or where you purposely tried to inflict harm. Moreover, all of these conditions are subject to punitive damages as well.[249]

Professional corporations are used mostly by attorneys and doctors and other professionals. They do furnish limited liability protection, provided they are operated professionally, i.e., personal and business assets are not commingled and corporate procedures are followed, etc.

Are there any income tax consequences regarding your attorney's fees, lawsuit settlements, and satisfaction of judgments? Attorney's fees involving business tort lawsuits and other business-related lawsuits that have some nexus (relationship) to your business or income-generating abilities are usually fully tax-deductible from your federal and state income taxes. Settlements and satisfaction of judgments (involving business-related matters) that your business receives are usually taxable to the business. However, settlements and satisfaction of judgments involving personal injuries are usually exempt from income taxes. Just to be sure, it's always a good idea to speak with your financial advisor or a tax consultant for a professional opinion regarding this matter.

Always look and act professionally with your corporation or limited liability company. And always sign your name with your corporate title. Don't let your office secretary (as opposed to your corporate secretary) sign on the business bank account; otherwise, he or she could be named in a lawsuit. Furthermore, look legitimate when you have a company, and keep your assets separate. And don't forget your business cards and stationary.

A newly formed company (corporation or LLC) must be adequately capitalized in order to be legally recognized. What does this actually mean? It simply means that you have to fund (transfer) money or other assets in sufficient amounts to start your company and before you begin corporate operations. A company that is not capitalized at all or inadequately capitalized (underfunded) will not be treated under the law as a separate legal entity (a "person") and thus there will not be any limited liability protection. This is known as the "alter ego" doctrine. Please don't overlook this when you set up your company. Your company *must* be funded adequately.

When you give money to a business, you can do it in one of three ways:

1. Gift—giving it away equals no ownership/no control.[250]
2. Loan—A loan document or promissory note or secured note equals expectation of money back with conditions attached and control.
3. Investment/ownership—may or may not have control by general partner or limited partner.

The court can only pierce the corporate veil for owners of the corporation, not the managers (unless they have an ownership interest in the corporation). Even a bankruptcy judge once got this wrong and charged the manager of a corporation under the alter ego theory when in fact he had no ownership interest whatsoever in the company! With regard to contract claims, it's extremely hard to pierce the corporate veil in Texas.

When a corporation is no longer doing any business, it's far better to keep the corporation as an empty shell rather than completely dissolving the corporation because by dissolving a corporation, the owners are usually liable for any remaining corporate debts. It's also important to keep your corporation's registration up to date with your secretary of state. An unregistered corporation is not allowed to prosecute civil lawsuits; however, an unregistered corporation is still allowed to *defend* against civil lawsuits.

It's also very important to use a name for your company that won't attract attention. And be sure to not use "family limited partnership" in the registered name of your limited partnership. Just use "limited partnership" at the end of the name when registering with the secretary of state. When capitalizing your corporation or LLC, a minimum of perhaps $5,000 to $10,000 in most cases would probably be adequate. The initial contribution could be in the form of a gift or a loan. In summary, naming your family limited partnership and/or limited liability company is extremely important. Use names that won't attract attention. For example, do not use your own name and do not use the word *family*. Instead, use names like ABC pension fund, especially if you have a lot of money in the business entity.

Single-member LLCs and single-owner corporations have significant drawbacks, so it is strongly recommended to use multimember LLCs and multiowner corporations. (See chapter 23.)

If asset protection of risky assets (e.g., rental property) is desired, you should form a limited liability company to own the property, and use an FLP to be the major (or even sole) member of the LLC.

In sum, it's a good idea to separate your physical assets from your money-making business. Always maintain the legal formalities of meetings and legal filings. Always avoid general partnerships. Never give a personal guaranty. And avoid boilerplate legal forms.

Where Should I Form My Company?

One of the questions most often asked by people wishing to form a new business is, "Where do I form the new company, in my home state or a business-friendly state like Nevada or Delaware?" In most cases, even if you do form your new company in Nevada or Delaware, you will also have to register it in your home state as a "foreign" entity. This naturally increases your expenses. If your "foreign" company is simply a "holding" company, say for real estate in your home state, then it's not absolutely essential that you register it in your home state. The downside of not registering in your home state is that your "foreign" company won't be able to prosecute any lawsuits in your home state although your "foreign" company would be allowed to defend against any lawsuits. The bottom line: If you're doing business in your home state, you can either form your company in your home state or you can form your company in a business-friendly state like Nevada or Delaware and register it as a "foreign" company in your home state. Please talk to a professional business attorney to decide on these options.

Do I Have to Pay State Income Taxes on My Out-of-State Company?

If your company has pass-through income treatment, like an S corporation or an LLC, then you will pay state income taxes on your out-of-state company unless you happen to live in a state that does not imposes state income taxes.[251] However, if you have a C corporation or an LLC that elects corporate tax treatment, and you engage in "corporate activity" in your home state regardless of the fact that your corporation was formed out-of-state, then you'll likely have to pay state income tax in your home state.[252] In order to avoid paying state income tax for income generated by your "foreign" company, your home state will determine where your business property is located, in your home state or out of state, and where your business' sales occur, in your home state or out of state. The bottom line: If you do any business in your home state, regardless of where your company is formed, you will likely pay state income taxes if your state so imposes such taxes.

There are two types of corporations, which will be reviewed separately. However, both types of corporations share the following attributes:

1. Shareholders are the legal owners of the corporation.
2. Directors operate the corporation, have regular meetings, and hire officers.

3. Officers, which include the president, vice president, corporate secretary, and treasurer, manage the day-to-day operations of the corporation.

The S Corporation

The S corporation is taxed as a pass-through entity directly to the shareholder(s).[253] But unlike typical pass-through tax treatment seen in an LLC, the individual shareholder(s) pay tax proportionately on the corporation's profits instead of the amount of money they receive. If some of the corporation's profits are not distributed to the shareholder(s) but rather are retained by the corporation, you are nonetheless still responsible for paying the tax. Undistributed income is also referred to as "phantom income." On the other hand, you can offset this somewhat because there's a legal way to downsize your 15.3 percent self-employment tax. You can divide the money you receive from your corporation between compensation and receipt of corporate profits. You only have to pay self-employment tax on your compensation. You don't have to pay any self-employment tax on the return of corporate profits. But make sure your compensation is reasonable. Otherwise, you'll be inviting an IRS audit.

The stockholders (shareholders) must be US citizens or permanent US residents and cannot exceed seventy-five in number. Moreover, all the stockholders must be natural persons; that is, no stockholder can be a legal entity. The S corporation is also not designed to be a holding company, but must be actively engaged in business.

The C Corporation

The C corporation is the most commonly used corporation. It should be used if you ever consider taking your company public. You can freely trade your stock with the C corporation without any approval. The C corporation is allowed to take many tax deductions which include, but are not limited to, workers' compensation, health insurance, life insurance, business insurance, tuition reimbursement, leasing, meals, travel, legal fees, management fees, employee compensation, director's fees, medical costs, advertising, etc. These tax deductions can save you a lot in taxes. The downside is that corporate dividends are taxed twice. The corporation pays tax on the dividends, and the shareholders pay personal income taxes on the dividends they receive. The way to avoid this dividend double taxation is simply not to distribute any dividends but rather pay out corporate profits in the form of employee compensation, which is totally deductible to the corporation. In fact, most small corporations simply omit any corporate dividends. Problem solved.

A C corporation is perhaps the easiest legal entity to help raise outside capital, especially commercial financing.

If corporate taxes are not paid, the IRS will come after the corporation. The IRS typically does not go after the officers or shareholders personally. However, if employee withholding taxes are not promptly submitted to the IRS, then you could be personally responsible.

The Limited Liability Company

Chapter 18 discusses the limited liability company (LLC) in detail. But briefly, the LLC is a relatively new legal entity with few court decisions. The few decisions that have come out are not good. Specifically, the single-member LLC does not provide good asset protection. The operating agreement is very important for an LLC. There is pass-through tax treatment for an LLC. Business formalities must be strictly followed. Some states limit an LLC's existence to thirty years. But you may be able through your operating agreement to allow your LLC to exist in perpetuity. Remember, members and managers have limited liability. A member of an LLC is an owner of the LLC and can only transfer his or her interest with the consent of the other members. LLCs can be dissolved.

USE YOUR CORPORATION LEGALLY

A few states cloak the transparency of beneficial ownership of legal entities such that some taxpayers can conceal their ownership interests for the purpose of evading tax obligations or facilitating other financial fraud and money laundering. The lack of transparency involving business entities in some states enables countless numbers of taxpayers to hide their noncompliance behind a legal entity. This noncompliance would include such things as the nonfiling of income tax returns and the hiding of taxable income—tax fraud. Billions of dollars are being lost annually to the United States Treasury by corporate and individual taxpayers seeking to hide income in foreign tax havens or shelter income by claiming it was earned in low tax jurisdictions.

The "beneficial owner" of a legal entity such as a corporation or an LLC is the person or group of individuals who ultimately owns or exercises effective control over the legal entity.

Privacy and protection against personal liability are important and necessary components of corporations, but it can also be used to hide the owner's identity. Delaware, Nevada, and Wyoming are the three states that offer company registrations with cloaking features—such as minimal information requirements and limited oversight—that rival those offered by offshore countries.

State laws govern the legal formation of business entities within their borders. However, most states do not require information concerning the *beneficial* ownership of the private business entity. On the other hand, publically traded companies whose securities are registered with the Securities and Exchange Commission (SEC) are subject to federal disclosure requirements regarding *beneficial* ownership.

Nevada does not share information with the IRS, and some noncompliant taxpayers take advantage of this situation. Nevada requires the resident agent to know the location of the stock ledger.

Bearer shares and nominee officers are particularly effective and popular in maintaining an anonymously owned entity. Bearer shares are issued by the corporation. Corporate ownership is established by the one who is the physical holder of the bearer share. Thus, in order to determine corporate ownership, one must actually determine who has physical possession of the bearer shares. Nevada and Wyoming are the only states that permit bearer shares in the United States.

Nominee officers make it very easy to establish a corporation and remain completely anonymous. While most states require that corporate officers have some meaningful relationship to the corporation, Nevada and Wyoming do not require this. A single nominee officer can serve as all of the officers for a Nevada or Wyoming corporation. The identity of the nominee officer is reported to the state, but this is essentially just a name on a piece of paper. Corporate owners, who wish to remain anonymous, can hold the title of vice president, which is not reported to the State, and hire a nominee officer to hold the other offices. With relative ease, corporate owners can funnel income to another similarly formed entity, and the only available information regarding that entity will be the nominee's name and address. These nominees often forward mail to a PO Box belonging to the true owner(s). Occasionally, some of these nominees claim they do not know the identity of the true owner, and in some cases, they could be telling the truth.

Some clients using the services of nominees are engaged in fraudulent activity in violation of tax and money laundering laws. The IRS is constantly on the lookout and criminal penalties are harsh.[254]

US shell companies are mostly organized in Delaware and Nevada.

Remember to adequately capitalize (fund) your corporation. Undercapitalization of any corporation, especially a sole-shareholder corporation will result in piercing of the corporate veil.[255] An undercapitalized corporation is not sufficiently capitalized to pay its liabilities, and it also lacks the ability to perform its designated business. Please note that a corporation that purchases business insurance is deemed to have been adequately capitalized. Sole-shareholder corporations (or single-member LLCs) are prone to veil piercing claims. Also, courts have recently pierced the corporate veil of a number of corporations primarily for lack of adequate capitalization.

A bankruptcy court[256] easily pierced the corporate veil because the defendant "corporation was undercapitalized, lacked separate books and did not keep its finances separate from the debtor's individual finances. The corporate formalities were not followed and the LLC is a mere sham which serves no legitimate business purpose." Moreover, the debtor "had misrepresented to the homeowner that the subcontractors had been paid and their liens released, when exactly the opposite was true," and thus the debtor's discharge was denied. Remember, never mix business and personal operations. Also, a business entity must be adequately capitalized, and a common weakness with single-owner and closely-held entities is undercapitalization. Adequate capitalization means that the company has sufficient assets to back up the business that it is conducting, and the debts that it is incurring. So if a business has creditors with claims up to $200,000 but only $100 in capital, there is not a chance that it will be determined to be adequately capitalized. Indeed, inadequate capitalization is the common Achilles' heel of single-owner and closely held entities; few are adequately capitalized or even have owners who have any idea what the level of adequate capital for their entity would require. But without adequate capital, no business entity is anything more than a paper sham at the secretary of state's office.

Please also remember to fully comply with all the "corporate formalities." This is especially true for sole-shareholder corporations because the owners can only have shareholders meetings with themselves!

Entering into a business transaction without the ability to perform is sufficiently wrong for veil piercing purposes. All business entities must be sufficiently capitalized for its ongoing operations and obligations. This means that a corporation or other entity should have at least sufficient cash to carry on its ongoing business activities and has sufficient assets to back its known liabilities. Business insurance is extremely important because the insurance can go towards capitalization of unknown or unsuspected liabilities, and sometimes even indemnification claims of this type.

Business Insurance

Business insurance is a must, especially liability insurance. Don't even think of operating your business without business liability insurance. Employers have been held directly and vicariously liable for criminal acts of violence committed by or against their employees and third parties. Some insurance carriers will cover the business for some criminal acts committed by employees while on the job. You can probably save money by bundling different types of insurance with a single carrier. Most insurance companies will give you a decent discount for multiple policies. You are well advised to buy as wide ranging insurance coverage as possible. Here are some various types of business insurance to consider:

- General liability business insurance for premise liability, such as an accidental injury on business property.
- Malpractice insurance for professionals such as physicians, dentists, and attorneys.
- Errors and omissions insurance for licensed professions such as insurance agents.
- Director and officer insurance for larger corporations which employ officers and directors.
- Workers compensation insurance is generally required by law if you have employees.
- Business property insurance covers you for business property loss or damage.

- Business discrimination insurance may be necessary if you have a large corporation where they may be a risk of discrimination.

How to Properly Handle Your Employees

In order to protect against claims of wrongful termination or discrimination, the following advice is given:

- Always protect yourself with proper and legal agreements.
- Your employment agreement should be an "At Will" agreement [257] that is clear and concise and might also include a noncompete or nondisclosure or nonsolicitation agreement.
- Every employee should be given a detailed employee manual.
- All performance reviews (at least annually) and any discipline (including a warning interview) must be in writing and kept for several years. Also, the employee and the manger or supervisor or employer should sign or at least initial the written record.
- You can always terminate an employee out of economic necessity.
- Arbitration agreements are useful because they are cheaper and quicker than litigation and less likely for a windfall award.

Summary

If you operate your company professionally, the corporate veil will protect you. Here's what you need to do:

1. It's important to set up your company correctly and properly maintain its records. Besides filing your Articles of Incorporation with the secretary of state, you'll need a corporate book, corporate by-laws, stock certificates with a stock ledger, initial corporate minutes, and afterwards, you must have regular director and shareholder meetings including minutes of the meetings.

2. Always document your business transactions and always use your company name and address on every business correspondence. Always sign your name with your corporate title.
3. You must establish a separate business banking (checking) account. Never forget to keep your business bank account separate from your personal bank account.
4. Always keep your business assets separate from your personal assets, and never commingle these assets.

WHY YOUR BUSINESS SHOULD HAVE FEW ASSETS

Your corporation needs to have as few assets as possible. And remember not to overload your business bank account. There's a second good reason for keeping just a few assets in your company. That's because if a creditor does happen to come along, there won't be much for him to get.

One great way to diminish the amount of corporate assets you have is by spreading income to your family members. The simplest way is to employ your family members. Put your family to work in your company, preferably as independent contractors.

Your business can even set up an IBC (International Business Company) in a foreign jurisdiction with the same name as your domestic business entity and then establish an offshore bank account for the IBC. From here, it's a simple matter to periodically wire money from your domestic business bank account to your IBC's offshore bank account. This is another great way to deplete your domestic company's assets (cash).

Also, your company becomes less attractive as a target of a lawsuit when it has few assets. And what assets it does have can be made even less attractive to potential creditors when those assets are leased. No creditor can attach any of your leased business assets as those assets don't belong to you. There's even an option for any assets that your company owns. It's called Equipment Equity Stripping, and it involves a bona fide lien holder to record a lien on your business property by using the Uniform Commercial Code (UCC) recording system with the secretary of state. This puts third parties on notice that your business property is encumbered, which makes it less attractive to a creditor. In exchange for the business property lien, your company will receive money for any equity in the business property by the lien holder. An arms-length lease agreement with an outside company is more favorably viewed by a court compared to a company you may have formed for the purpose of leasing equipment. In other words, the closer the relationship between you and the leasing company, the more it will be viewed with suspicion.

A lender, especially a friendly lender, can loan your business money and place a lien on your business. If you ever have problems with a persistent and recalcitrant creditor, your lender can foreclose on your business.

Factoring (Accounts Receivable Factoring or Invoice Financing)

Besides keeping few assets in your company, there's an additional way to help minimize the risk of a company lawsuit. It's called factoring. Basically, factoring is a financial transaction whereby a business sells its accounts receivable (i.e., invoices) to a third party (called a factor) at a discount. In "advance" factoring, the factor provides financing to the seller of the accounts in the form of a cash "advance," often 70–85 percent of the purchase price of the accounts with the balance of the purchase price being paid, net of the factor's discount fee (commission) and other charges, upon collection from the account client. In order to put third parties on notice and to inform the public of the lien against your accounts receivable, a Uniform Commercial Code (UCC) recording is made with the secretary of state. Additionally, this has the added effect of discouraging potential plaintiffs/creditors from suing against or collecting from your company.

For asset protection purposes, you should borrow sufficiently from the lender so that there is no significant equity remaining in your accounts receivable. Your creditor will not be able to attach a lien on your accounts receivable since it is already secured by the lender. If necessary, the lender can foreclose on your accounts receivable. Moreover, since you received fair value (by way of a loan), it cannot be deemed a fraudulent conveyance. What will you do with the loan? Perhaps you can send the money offshore to purchase an annuity.

LIMITED LIABILITY IS GOOD

Limited liability protects you personally in the event of ordinary negligence, which obviously can happen to anyone. This is basically just an honest mistake, and only your company can be sued. In the event that you are named as a defendant in a lawsuit, you can be personally dismissed upon a showing to the court that only ordinary negligence was involved.

Limited liability is a legal concept whereby a person's financial liability is limited to a fixed amount, most commonly the value of a person's investment in a company or partnership with limited liability. If only a company with limited liability is sued, then the plaintiffs are suing the company itself and not its owners or investors. A shareholder in a company is not personally liable for any of the debts of the company other than for the value of his or her investment in that company. The same is true for the members of a limited liability company and the limited partners in a limited partnership. (By contrast, sole proprietors and partners in general partnerships are each liable for all the debts of the business [unlimited liability].)

Please remember that any owner of a corporation or an LLC who gives a personal guaranty of the company's debts to those lending to the company will then be *personally* liable for those debts in the event that the company cannot pay.

The following are limited liability entities:

- Limited liability company (LLC)
- Limited partnership (LP)
- Limited liability partnership (LLP)
- Limited liability limited partnership (LLLP)
- C corporation
- S corporation

- Professional corporation (PC)

NEVER COMMINGLE ASSETS

Never, and I mean *never* commingle or mix your personal assets with your business assets. If you do, you could get yourself into serious trouble. You will have lost the coveted limited liability protection that comes with the corporation or limited liability company. Always keep your personal bank account completely separate from your business bank account. Here's an analogy: Let's say you live in a rural area and you depend on a well for drinking water. Would you ever think of dumping sewage in your well and thereby contaminating it? Of course not. Commingling your personal assets with your business assets contaminates your business assets, and thus your limited liability protection is lost. If you don't follow this critical rule, the court will "pierce the corporate veil" of your company, which will then expose you directly to personal liability. Then your personal assets would be vulnerable to creditor seizure. Folks, please avoid this scenario at all costs. Please follow these three rules: (Rule 1) Don't commingle personal assets with business assets, (Rule 2) Don't commingle personal assets with business assets, and (Rule 3) Don't commingle personal assets with business assets.

What should you do if your personal assets have been commingled with your business assets in your corporation or limited liability company? If your corporation or limited liability company has been "contaminated" by your personal assets, then you must dissolve your company and basically start all over with a fresh new company.

What exactly is "commingling"? Commingling of funds means that you are treating your business's money as your own personal money. Here are some examples of various ways to commingle funds:

1. Depositing checks made payable to your business into your personal bank account.

2. Making withdrawals from your business checking account to pay personal expenses.
3. Using the same bank account for your business and your personal needs.
4. Writing business checks for your personal expenses.
5. Mixing funds between your business and personal accounts.

"Piercing the corporate veil" simply means that you lost your limited liability protection in your business, and you are now personally held responsible for your company's debts. There are several factors that courts look at when deciding whether to pierce your company's veil and hold you personally liable on company debts and company lawsuits. One important factor is the presence of commingled funds. If you treat your business's money the same as your own, then you risk the exposure of your personal assets. As stated previously, you must keep your business separate from your personal matters and that includes everything from separate bank accounts to separate accounting and separate taxes.

Corporations and LLCs are legal entities, separate and distinct from the people who create and own them.[258] One of the principal advantages of forming a corporation or an LLC is that since the corporation or LLC is considered a separate legal entity (unlike general partnerships and sole proprietorships), the owners and managers have limited personal liability for the company's debts. Closely held corporations[259] and small LLCs are most likely to get their veils pierced unless they stringently adhere to corporate formalities.

If a court pierces a company's corporate veil, the owners (shareholders) of the corporation, or members (owners) of an LLC will be held personally liable for corporate debts. This allows creditors to go after owners' homes, bank accounts, investments, and other assets to satisfy the corporate debt. But courts will impose personal liability only on those individuals who are responsible for the corporation or LLC's wrongful or fraudulent actions; they won't hold innocent parties personally liable for company debts.

If you commingle personal and business assets or don't operate your corporation professionally or inadequately capitalize your corporation, the judgment creditor can pierce the corporate veil by alleging an "alter ego" theory of liability on its owner(s). Once in a while, a judgment creditor obtains a judgment only against a corporation and later discovers that the owner or owners of the corporation are using it as an alter ego. In this event, the judgment creditor may be able to amend the judgment to add the alter ego owner/owners as judgment debtor/debtors and enforce the judgment against them. A California court may use "all the means necessary" to carry its jurisdiction into effect.[260]

Amending the judgment to add a third party (judgment debtor) may be allowed where necessary to prevent "injustice" even though an "alter ego" liability is not involved.[261]

Limited liability protection could be lost if the owners fail to maintain a formal legal separation between their business and their personal financial affairs, which could cause a court to find that the corporation or LLC is really just a sham (the owners' alter ego). For example, if the owner pays personal bills from the business bank account or ignores the legal formalities that a corporation or LLC must follow by not holding regular corporate meetings, then a court could decide that the owner isn't entitled to the limited liability that the corporate business structure would ordinarily provide.

Also, limited liability protection could be lost if the owner(s) recklessly borrowed and lost money, made business deals knowing the business couldn't pay the invoices, or otherwise acted recklessly or dishonestly, then a court could find financial fraud was perpetrated and that the limited liability protection shouldn't apply. Additionally, limited liability protection could be lost if the company's creditors suffered an unjust cost. If someone who did business with the company is left with unpaid bills or an unpaid court judgment and the above factors are present, a court will try to correct this unfairness by piercing the veil.

Piercing the Corporate Veil

Piercing the corporate veil has now become somewhat of a misnomer because this legal principle has been recently extended to include limited liability companies (LLCs) and limited liability partnerships (LLPs). The most common factors that courts consider in determining whether to pierce the corporate veil:

1. Whether the corporation, LLC, or LLP engaged in fraudulent behavior.
2. Whether the corporation, LLC, or LLP failed to follow corporate formalities.
3. Whether the corporation, LLC, or LLP was inadequately capitalized (if the corporation never had enough funds to operate, it was not really a separate entity that could stand on its own).
4. Whether one person or a small group of closely related people were in complete control of the corporation, LLC or LLP. Closely held companies are more susceptible to losing limited liability status than large, publicly traded corporations because small corporations are less likely than their larger counterparts to observe corporate formalities, which makes them more vulnerable to a piercing of their corporate veil.

All corporations, LLCs and LLPs, including close corporations and single-member LLCs, *must* follow corporate formalities, which include the following:

1. Holding annual meetings of directors and shareholders or members.
2. Keeping accurate, detailed records (called "minutes") of important decisions that are made at the meetings.
3. Adopting company bylaws and making sure that officers and agents abide by those bylaws.
4. Keeping business and personal assets and expenses separate. Small business owners seem more prone than their larger counterparts to commingle their personal assets with those of the corporation or LLC.

If you are an owner (shareholder) of a corporation, a member of an LLC, or partner in an LLP, please take the following steps to ensure that a court won't pierce your corporate veil:

1. Comply with the formal rules for forming and maintaining a corporation or LLC.
2. Maintain a separate bank account for the corporation or LLC.
3. Don't commingle personal assets with those of the corporation or LLC.
4. Don't divert corporate or LLC assets for personal use.
5. Make a reasonable initial investment in the corporation or LLC so that it is adequately capitalized.
6. Purchase business insurance.
7. Do not personally guarantee payment of the corporation or LLC's debts.
8. Don't use the corporation or LLC to engage in illegal, fraudulent, or reckless acts.
9. Make sure the world knows it is dealing with a corporation or LLC by conspicuously identifying the company status (that is, "Inc." or "LLC") on all business cards, letters, quotes, invoices, statements, directory listings, advertisements, and all other forms of company communication.
10. When signing company documents, clearly state your representative capacity (such as, "John Doe, President, ABC, Inc.").

The bottom line: If the corporate owners, the members of the LLC, or the partners of the LLP can ignore the corporation, LLC, or LLP, respectively, then a creditor can also ignore it and seek the personal assets of the corporate owners, LLC members, or LLP partners, respectively. This certainly seems fair.

While it may be more common for small corporations to lose their limited liability protection via piercing of the corporate veil, large corporations nevertheless can lose it as well. Courts will often pierce the corporate veil of a large corporation when the officers or directors create a subsidiary corporation and transfer debts to that subsidiary. For example, the owners of a large corporation incorporate several undercapitalized subsidiaries (companies that do not have enough money to support their operations). The large corporation (called the "parent corporation") controls and finances the operations over the subsidiaries. Such subsidiaries are commonly called "dummy corporations" or "corporate shells." When creditors seek to collect debts from or enforce a court judgment against a dummy corporation, they are often out of luck because the dummy corporation does not have sufficient assets to collect. Often in these situations, a court will pierce the corporate veil of the parent corporation, which allows the creditor to collect directly from the personal assets of the owners or members of the parent corporation or LLC. This prevents the creditor from suffering an unjust disposition.

BAD TRUSTS

A trust consists of three parties: (1) The person who forms the trust is called the grantor, trustor, or settlor of the trust (all of these terms are interchangeable). The grantor gifts assets: property such as real estate, finances such as money and securities (stocks and bonds), and tangible assets such as art and jewelry to the trust. Once property is gifted to the trust, the trust legally begins its existence. (2) The person who manages the trust property is called the trustee. Sometimes there is a person who oversees the trustee to make sure the trustee is following the grantor's directives. This person is called the protector. And (3) the person who will eventually possess the trust property at a later date is called the beneficiary of the trust. The trust will last until the beneficiary receives the trust property, usually at a much later date. The instructions for managing the trust are clearly spelled out in a trust indenture.

Constructive Trusts

A constructive trust is a court-ordered remedy to correct a fraud in order to benefit a party that has been wrongfully deprived of his property due to another person who has obtained that property fraudulently. The basis for this court-ordered type of trust is premised on a fraudulent (wrongful) taking of someone else's property, often by deception.

For example: suppose you go to a dishonest jeweler who sells you what purports to be loose diamonds which he says retails for $15,000, but he'll sell them to you for a discounted price of $10,000. You make the purchase. A few months later, you need fast cash, so you sell your loose diamonds on eBay. However, before the sale is completed, the purchaser wants an independent appraisal. When the appraisal is made, you discover you were defrauded by the jeweler. You learn that you actually bought cubic zirconia rather than genuine diamonds, and the value of your gemstones is merely worth a few hundred dollars. You subsequently sue the jeweler and ultimately win. To remedy the fraud, the court will impose a constructive trust against the jeweler which essentially makes him the trustee of the $10,000 that you paid and makes you the beneficiary of the court-imposed constructive trust. With the constructive trust firmly established by the court, the court will then order the jeweler (trustee) to transfer the $10,000 to you (the beneficiary). Another example is a fraud lawsuit that alleges that the seller sold defective goods (known by the seller to be defective), the money you gave to the fraudster (seller) would then be held in trust to eventually be returned to you at a later date by court order. To summarize, a constructive trust is a court–imposed trust used to correct injustices caused by fraud.

Resulting Trusts

A resulting trust (which is not very well known even to the experts!) is also a court-imposed trust that is used not to remedy fraud but rather is used to infer the *intent* of the transaction. Here are a couple of examples that will help you to understand this concept: If I give you the down payment for a house (which is *not* a gift), and you make the mortgage payments for a house that is titled in your name, the court will determine that I have an ownership interest in the house by virtue of my down payment. This makes sense. In a lawsuit, the court will impose a resulting trust in which the legal title owner of the house, that is the one who is making the monthly mortgage payments, becomes the trustee of the resulting trust; and I, who made the original down payment to the house, become the beneficiary (or equitable owner) of the trust which holds (owns) the house. Once the court imposes the resulting trust, it can then order the trustee (the legal owner) to transfer the house to me (the beneficial owner). And when this happens, the creditors step in and take the house away from me in order to satisfy their judgment.

Let's say you lost your job and you are now having difficulty making your mortgage payments. When your kind neighbor learns of this, he steps in and helps make your mortgage payments. Folks, please be very careful of this situation because your neighbor could unintentionally be acquiring an ownership interest in your home! This could even result in the formation of a resulting trust. One way to legally get around this conundrum is for your neighbor to mark the mortgage payments that he makes on your behalf as a *gift*. This prevents the formation of a resulting trust because your neighbor wouldn't be acquiring an ownership interest in your home. If your neighbor intends to loan you money for your mortgage, then draw up a loan document. Your neighbor will then loan you money so you can continue to make the mortgage payments yourself.

The one sure way to defeat a resulting trust—and you should always do this even in doubtful situations—is whenever you give away money, always make sure that it is in either the form of a gift or a loan. If it's in the form of a loan, then make sure you have a loan agreement to document the nature of the loan. Moreover, when you gift money, you should clearly earmark it as a "gift." Gift money will automatically prevent a court-imposed resulting trust. However, you may be subject to a gift tax. Therefore, when writing a check or using any other document, please clearly note that the money you're giving is a "gift." On the other hand, if the money is a loan, then you must have a loan document to back that up. Now let's look at this situation from the court's point of view. If the court does not see any evidence that your money was a gift or a loan, then it can rightfully conclude that you have established an ownership interest in the property, much like an investor. Always let others know (which includes the court) what your intentions are when you give away money or make payments for something. This always includes gifts, loans, or investments. Gifting your money is analogous to a quitclaim deed because it absolves you of any ownership interest of the cash or property transferred.

Here's another example of a resulting trust that could easily happen to you if you're not careful, and it relates to the commingling of money. Let's say you transfer your home to an irrevocable offshore trust but continue to make the mortgage payments yourself. Can you identify why this could be a major mistake and what you should have done to prevent this? The mistake is that you should have immediately stopped making the mortgage payments after your home was transferred unless you clearly noted on your checks that the mortgage payments were made by you as a "gift" for the benefit of the trust.

However, another method can be used that will definitely prevent a resulting trust. It's a lease agreement between the new owner (lessor) of the home (in this case, the offshore trust) and you (the lessee). This would now make you a renter. Pursuant to the lease agreement, you would then make monthly rent payments to the offshore trust, who in turn would then make the mortgage payments directly to the bank. One word of caution: there could be a "Due on Sales Clause" in your mortgage agreement whereby the bank could call the loan; that is, the mortgage loan could be immediately due in its entirety.

In the previous example, by directly making the mortgage payments on behalf of the offshore trust without earmarking it is a gift or loan, the *result* is that you are accruing an ownership interest in the home that you just transferred to the offshore trust, hence the formation of a *resulting* trust. This happens because your mortgage payments reflect the fact that you are paying down some of the principal balance, which causes you to accrue an ownership interest in the property. Folks, this is something you shouldn't be doing, and something you definitely want to avoid. Paying the mortgage now becomes the responsibility of the new owner, in this case, the offshore trust. To continue with this example, assuming you continued to make the mortgage payments yourself, the court would then infer you had a beneficial interest in the home and would then impose a resulting trust designating the new owner, the offshore trust, as the trustee of the court-imposed *resulting* trust, and designating you as the beneficiary (equitable owner) of the home (trust property). Once the court imposes a *resulting* trust, it essentially orders the home returned to you and then the creditors will step in to seize the house for liquidation in order to satisfy their judgment. Folks, this example is based on a real incident, so please be careful.

Creditors and collections attorneys will often discuss constructive trusts when they believe you have a fraudulently retained interest in the home in which you are residing. But what practically no one ever discusses is the very little-known *resulting* trust, which can really foul up your plans. It's truly amazing that so little is mentioned about this rarely used court-imposed remedy, but you need to know what steps that you must absolutely take to avoid its treacherous pitfalls.

Some of you may probably be thinking that paying someone else's mortgage is such a small thing that it really shouldn't matter and certainly not result in the loss of a home. But it's not uncommon for some small mistakes to have huge and disastrous consequences. For example, would you ever think of putting a lighted match in your car's gas tank? Not unless your life insurance is fully paid up. So sometimes little mistakes can have catastrophic consequences.

Land Trusts

Land trusts are typically disadvantageous. They are mostly sold to the unsuspecting public by salesmen. The concept is to have the land trust own your property so that your name is no longer on the public rolls and for purported asset protection. The problem is that you transferred the property to the land trust using a deed (probably a quitclaim deed) that was recorded. Now there's a permanent paper trail. Any creditor can easily hire a private investigator and discover that you transferred your property to a land trust. Moreover, most land trusts are revocable self-settled trusts, which means you (the grantor) are also the beneficiary. There's absolutely no asset protection here. Moreover, if you transferred your property to the land trust for no consideration,[262] it could be challenged as a fraudulent conveyance. Also, in a bankruptcy, any transfers to a self-settled trust that occurred in the previous ten years can be avoided (undone). Please remember too that most mortgage agreements have a "due on sales" clause, whereby your bank or lender could call the mortgage loan on your property as result of the property transfer to the land trust. That means you would be obligated to immediately pay the total balance on your mortgage. All in all, please avoid land trusts unless it is recommended by a competent and professional attorney or financial advisor.

The bottom line is that land trusts do not afford asset protection because the trust is not irrevocable. Also, land trusts do a poor job hiding the identity of the true owner(s) of the property.

GOOD TRUSTS

A trust begins its existence not when it's set up, but once assets have been transferred into the trust. No consideration (which usually means money exchanged for assets) is necessary to transfer assets to a trust. In other words, your transfer of assets to the trust is a gift to the trust.

All trusts have three components: (1) the grantor of the trust, that is, the person who transfers assets to the trust; (2) the trustee of the trust, that is, the person who manages the trust assets; and (3) the beneficiary of the trust, that is, the person who receives or benefits from the trust assets.

The only trust that offers true asset protection is the irrevocable trust. Nevertheless, any and all transfers of assets to an irrevocable trust are still subject to the laws of fraudulent conveyance; so be sure that at the time you establish your trust and begin to transfer assets, that you haven't been threatened with a lawsuit, that you're not currently involved in a lawsuit, and that you don't have any existing creditors. If all of these conditions apply to you, then this would be an excellent time for you to set up your irrevocable trust. In your trust deed (contract) you should have the following clause (which most attorneys don't even know about!) that will provide you with extra protection: "Notwithstanding any other provisions of this trust deed, the trustor (grantor or settlor) is prohibited from ever becoming a trustee of this irrevocable trust. Furthermore, no court of competent jurisdiction can abrogate or otherwise modify this provision as it would constitute illegal and tortious interference with contract."

The creation of a trust can either be made during one's life or can be made by will upon the death of the creator. Once created, legal title of the transferred assets is vested with the trustee. There is pass-through tax treatment for the grantor of an offshore trust.

Generally, most trusts contain the following provisions:

1. The jurisdiction under which the trust is created.
2. The name of the grantor.
3. The name of the trustee.
4. The purpose of the trust agreement.
5. The name or names of the beneficiaries of the trust agreement.
6. A provision for a successor trustee.
7. The list of powers granted to the trustee by the grantor(s).
8. A list of prohibited trustee transactions.
9. A "flee" clause to move the trust assets from one jurisdiction to another in the event a lawsuit is filed where the trust is located.
10. A spendthrift provision limiting distributions to any beneficiary under duress.
11. The duration of the trust.
12. The name of a trust protector, required for offshore trusts.
13. The recompense for the trustee's services.
14. A provision to employ other financial experts, if needed.
15. Power to add or exclude beneficiaries.
16. Power to contract with others.
17. Power to borrow or lend, or both.
18. Power to withhold distributions.
19. Power to make alternative arrangements for incompetent beneficiaries.
20. Prohibition against direct ownership and operation of a trade or business.
21. Power to merge with other trusts.
22. Invalidity of any provision considered by local jurisdiction to be invalid, illegal, or unenforceable.

The Many Advantages of a Trust

1. Asset protection: Assets transferred to a trust no longer belong to the grantor. Thus, a creditor of the grantor won't be able to seize those trust assets, provided they were not transferred in violation of the fraudulent conveyance laws.

2. Tax planning: Income generated by trust assets are taxed according in the country of residence of the legal owners—the trustees. Moreover, inheritance tax would normally be eliminated because the trustees would not die upon the death of the grantor.
3. Avoiding probate: By establishing a trust, probate can be avoided because "death" will have no effect on the trust property which will continue to be held and managed by the trustees in accordance with the terms of the trust.
4. Confidentiality: Assets in a trust avoid probate which is a public procedure.
5. Avoiding forced heirship: In some jurisdictions, the deceased will not be permitted to leave property to anyone he wishes on his death. This problem of forced heirship can be avoided by a properly drafted trust.
6. Estate planning: Many people do not want their assets to pass outright to their heirs, whether chosen by them or prescribed by law, and prefer to make more complicated arrangements. These might involve providing a source of income for a widow for life or making provision for the education of children or providing a fund to protect members of the family in the event of sudden illness or other disasters. A trust is the most satisfactory and flexible way of making arrangements of this kind.
7. Providing for the weak: A trust provides a vehicle by which a person can provide for those who may be unable to manage their own affairs such as infant children, the aged, the disabled, and persons suffering from certain illnesses.
8. Preserving family assets: An individual may wish to ensure that the wealth he accumulated over a lifetime is not divided up amongst his heirs but instead is retained as one fund to accumulate further, with provision for payments to members of the family as the need arises while preserving some assets for later generations.

9. Continuing a family business: A person who has built up a business during a lifetime will often be concerned to ensure that it continues after death. If the shares in the company are transferred to trustees prior to death a trust can be used to prevent the unnecessary liquidation of a family company.
10. Gaining flexibility: The best laid plans can, in a changing world, rapidly become obsolete. A discretionary trust can be structured to provide for a system of management of property that is capable of rapid change as circumstances demand.

The Qualities Your Trustee Must Have

The courts regard a trust as creating a special relationship which places serious and onerous obligations on the trustees. Thus the law regards the special "fiduciary" relationship of a trust as imposing stringent duties and liabilities on the person in whom confidence is placed—the trustees—in order to prevent possible abuse of that confidence. A trustee is therefore subject to the following strict rules:

1. No private advantage—A trustee is not permitted to use or deal with trust property for private advantage.
2. Best interests of beneficiaries—Trustees must exercise all their powers in the best interests of the beneficiaries of the trust.
3. Act prudently—Whether or not a trustee is remunerated he must act prudently in the management of trust property and will be liable for breach of trust if, by failing to exercise proper care, the trust fund suffers loss. [263]
4. Duty to keep all beneficiaries informed of any material transactions of trust assets.

The concept of "possession" is the legal right to own and vested exclusively to the trustee. The trustee's power is derived from the grantor(s) by a written agreement (trust agreement). The most important person is therefore the trustee.

- *Factors to Consider When Choosing a Trustee:*

A true trustee is an independent person not related to the grantor(s) by blood or marriage or is an independent trust company, bank, or corporate body. It is common for a bank to be a trustee. The selection of a trustee is the most significant part of any trust agreement and often the most difficult decision. Here are some factors to consider when choosing a trustee:

1. The trustee more familiar with the financial and tax implications of your assets should be given weight.
2. The trustee's physical location in relation to the beneficiaries.
3. Relationship of the individual trustee to the grantor's family.
4. An understanding of the intrafamily dynamics of all the beneficiaries.
5. Familiarity with financial management and the financial ability and level of experience with the assets entrusted.
6. If it's a family business, the nature and familiarity of the business.
7. The willingness and vitality to serve as an impartial fiduciary.
8. The legal capacity to interpret and administer the agreement fairly to all beneficiaries.
9. The willingness to accept the appointment and the willingness to accept potential legal liability from disgruntled beneficiaries.
10. Succession planning for a successor trustee.

The following trustees may not be the best qualified to serve:

1. Corporate trustees or trust companies. They administer the trust assets but they are not responsive to the needs of the people they are hired to serve. Generally they are very slow and usually react in the interest of the trust company not their clients.
2. Banks as trustees. They are too slow in making decisions and are always afraid to make decisions without first consulting their legal department.

3. Lawyers have been trained to handle legal matters but generally have no financial experience or expertise in the management of assets. Even when they hire outside consultants in those financial roles, they often are way too expensive.
4. Accountants have been trained to accumulate information, but they aren't trained to make investment decisions. Generally they lack the qualities to administer and provide full service or to take legal liability to serve as trustees.
5. Family members as trustees. The problem is mistrust and a conflict of interest.

The Trust Protector

The trust protector is a person whose primary function is to protect the trust. Trust protectors are recognized in the following states: Alaska, Delaware, Idaho, South Dakota, and Wyoming.

Foreign trusts often have a trust protector, and a foreign trust protector is best for a foreign trust.

While a trustee can be a bank, trust company, or other financial institution, the trust protector on the other hand is usually a person close to the family, such as a CPA, accountant, or lawyer who is already the family consigliore.

The more common trust protector's powers are as follows:

1. Ability to remove or replace the trustee. Often this is the only power granted to the trust protector. In some cases, the protector can fire and replace the trustee, at will, without any explanation to the current trustee.
2. Ability to change the trust's situs (location) to take advantage of changes in the law or necessary steps to protect the beneficiaries.
3. Ability to resolve conflicts between co-trustees.
4. Ability to control spending over a certain amount. For example, amounts over $10,000 requiring two signatures of the trustee and the trust protector.

5. Ability to veto distributions to beneficiaries. The trust protector can override/veto the trustee and withhold distributions temporarily or permanently make other arrangements such as buy the assets necessary for the benefit of the beneficiary (buy a house, a car, sign a rental agreement, but have the trust own the assets, make loans or make other provisions).
6. Ability to veto investment decisions. This checking and balancing of investment decisions are based on the trust protector's experience, prudence, and the trust agreement guidelines in protecting the assets for the beneficiaries.
7. Ability to sue and defend lawsuits against the trust assets.
8. Ability to terminate the trust.

The trust protector's role is created by the trust agreement to add an additional layer of protection and is usually a person most familiar with the grantor's long-term financial and personal goals. A trust protector usually provides the balance of power between the trust agreement, the trustee, the grantor, and the beneficiaries. Neither the trustee nor the trust protector should be a family member nor anyone related to the family by blood or marriage. Both positions should be independent of each other acting in the long-term interest of the beneficiaries.

REVOCABLE TRUSTS

Except for a living will (a special type of revocable trust), you *must* definitely avoid revocable trusts. That's because a court can order you to revert the trust assets back to you which could then fall into the hands of your creditors. Bottom line: *never* form a revocable trust. Always establish irrevocable trusts. (See chapter 32.)

Revocable trust property in a revocable inter vivos trust is subject to creditor seizure during the debtor's lifetime because of the debtor's power of revocation. There is absolutely no asset protection using a revocable trust.[264] Upon the judgment debtor's death, no writ of execution may issue against the revocable trust property. Instead, the judgment creditor must file a claim with the trustee or executor (probate), or if no trust or probate proceeding is initiated, then a lawsuit against the decedent's beneficiaries.[265]

Gift tax laws may apply to transfers of assets to a trust.[266]

A-B (Spousal) Trusts

An A-B trust is a trust created by a married couple in order to eliminate or minimize estate taxes. An A-B trust is a trust that divides into two upon the death of the first spouse. It is formed with each spouse placing assets in the trust and naming as the final beneficiary any person except the other spouse. The trust gets its name from the fact that it splits into two separate trusts upon the death of the first spouse: Trust A = the survivor's trust and trust B = the decedent's trust. The surviving spouse has complete control over the survivor's trust, which contains his or her property interests, but has limited control over the assets in the deceased spouse's trust. However, this limited control over the assets in the decedent's trust will still enable the surviving spouse to live in the couple's house and draw income from the trust, provided these terms are stipulated in the trust. Upon the death of the surviving spouse, the property in the decedent's trust passes to the beneficiary(s) named in this trust.

As this property is not considered part of the second spouse's estate for purposes of estate tax, double taxation is avoided.

The A-B trust takes advantage of such features as a Step-Up in Basis (where the value of the property transferred to the successors of the trust is said to be the fair market value at the time of the transfer at death and not what the parents originally paid for it. This means less capital gains tax will have to be paid by the children when they sell the property).

It is important that each trust is drafted with absolute precision as the IRS has specified the exact wording to be used.

The bypass trust is typically created to achieve one or more of the following goals:

1. To maximize the use of the decedent's estate tax exclusion amount in order to minimize estate tax upon the death of the surviving spouse.
2. To ensure that the decedent's spouse's property will be disposed of in accordance with the decedent's wishes even if the surviving spouse remarries or chooses to adopt a different estate plan for the surviving spouse's assets.

An A-B trust is a living trust, and as such the trust remains revocable while both spouses are alive. Thus, the A-B trust confers no asset protection features whatsoever. When the first spouse dies, the A-B trust becomes irrevocable.

The downside to an A-B trust is related to accounting, legal and administration fees. Additionally, after the death of the first spouse, the A and B trusts requires separate tax returns. The A-B trust also limits the surviving spouse's rights to the trust property. A surviving spouse may feel entitled to all the property in the B trust and may wish to spend the trust principle. This may conflict with the beneficiaries of the trust who wish to conserve the trust assets. Because an A-B trust becomes irrevocable once the first spouse dies, an A-B trust should be created only after consultation with an estate planning professional.

IRREVOCABLE TRUSTS

The preferred method of holding all valuable assets is through an irrevocable trust or an intentionally defective irrevocable grantor type trust. Never be the trustee of your own irrevocable trust and *never* exercise any *control* over your irrevocable trust because otherwise the courts will not recognize your trust as an irrevocable trust.[267]

The reason an "irrevocable" trust is so powerful is because you have relinquished control. If you have control over a trust, the court could force you to repatriate the assets of the trust and turn the assets over to the creditors. You don't want that to happen. Please remember that you need to fund the trust in order to gain asset protection.

Bypass Trusts

A bypass trust is an irrevocable trust into which the grantor deposits assets and which is designed to pay trust income and principal to the grantor's spouse for the duration of the spouse's life. The transfer of grantor's assets to the bypass trust for the benefit of the spouse is a tax-free transfer under the currently unlimited marital deduction. At the grantor's death, the assets in the bypass trust are not included in the grantor's (decedent's) estate, effectively reducing the total value of the estate and therefore potentially limiting the estate taxes owed at the grantor's death. Bypass trusts are used as a legitimate tool to circumvent gift tax and to minimize taxation of assets upon death of a married couple. Bypass trusts are long-term planning devices.

Charitable Lead Trusts

A charitable lead trust is a trust designed to reduce the beneficiaries' taxable income by first donating a portion of the trust's income to charities and then, after a specified duration, transferring the remainder of the trust to the beneficiaries. Basically, the idea of a charitable lead trust is to reduce taxes of the estate left by the deceased, which is done by donating to charities from the estate until all taxes are reduced. Once this is accomplished, the estate is then transferred to the beneficiaries, who typically will face lower taxes.

Charitable Remainder Trusts

A charitable remainder trust is a form of trust in which the grantor places substantial funds or assets into an irrevocable trust with an independent trustee, in which the assets are to go to charity on the death of the grantor, but the grantor (or specific beneficiaries) will receive regular profits from the trust during the grantor's lifetime. The IRS will allow a large deduction in the year the funds or assets are donated to the trust, and the tax savings can be used to buy a life insurance policy on the grantor, which will pay his or her children the proceeds upon the grantor's death. Bottom line: the grantor can make a gift to charity, make a return on his or her money and still arrange to make a large gift at death to his or her heirs. The disadvantage is that the assets are permanently tied up or committed.

Child's Trust

A child's trust is a trust that besides helping to protect your assets can also offer you substantial tax savings. For example, let's say you want to send one of your children to a private high school and the tuition is $6,000 per annum. For most people, the $6,000 tuition cannot be deducted from their income tax and thus this expense is paid with after-tax dollars. This means the parents would have to earn about $10,000 (before taxes) in order to leave them $6,000 (after taxes are paid) to pay the tuition. What if you could deduct the $6,000 tuition? The good news is there is a little-known way where you can deduct the entire $6,000 tuition. And best of all, it's completely legal! It only requires the use of a child's trust and some self-employment income. If you don't have any self-employment income, then you should definitely try to find a work-at-home job or else you can set up a home business. These things are relatively easy to do. If you run a business out of your home, then you're entitled to a tax deduction for your home office and certain business-related expenses. In order to qualify for these tax deductions, it's important to strictly perform only work-related activity in your home office; otherwise, it won't qualify for a tax deduction. If you rent a home or an apartment, then you won't qualify for a home-office deduction regardless of whether you run a business out of your residence. The home-office deduction only works for home owners. Regardless of whether you own a home or not, you can still set up a child's trust and this will save you thousands of dollars in taxes. But you must have some form of self-employment income.

Here's how you go about setting up a child's trust. First, you need a trust deed that names you as the grantor (the person who forms the trust) of the trust and describes the assets to be placed into the trust. It also names the trustee (the person who manages the trust) and the beneficiary or beneficiaries (one or more of your children) of the trust. It's also important to indicate that this is an irrevocable trust. This simply means that the trust assets can't be returned to you. Now in order to activate the child's trust, you have to transfer some assets to the trust; and the best assets to transfer to the trust are business assets. For self-employed people, the following is a list of the most common business assets to be considered for transfer to the trust: computer and monitor, printer, scanner, fax machine, copier, business desk, business chair, file cabinets, business telephone, business supplies, etc. Once these business assets have been transferred to the trust, the trustee will then lease these assets back to your business. This is similar to a sale-leaseback agreement. Also, it's important to make sure you have a genuine lease agreement with the trustee. So be sure to have it reviewed by a qualified attorney. For example, the lease agreement can require you to make $500 monthly payments for leasing business equipment from the trust. In one year alone, the lease payments will amount to $6,000, which you get to deduct from your income taxes on schedule C under the category "equipment leasing." A $6,000 tax deduction can easily save you a couple thousand dollars in taxes. The $6,000 you pay will go into the child's trust where it can subsequently be used to pay your child's educational expenses. While the money is accumulating in the trust, the trustee can invest it in bank CDs, treasury bills, stocks, stock index funds, bonds, etc. My recommendation is for the trustee to invest the money conservatively and to shun any risky investments. Remember, it's your child's education money, so don't squander it.

Discretionary Trusts

Discretionary trusts serve a useful function by protecting improvident beneficiaries against creditors as the beneficiary has no claim to any specific part of the trust fund, none of the trust fund is vulnerable to attachment by any creditor or by the trustee in bankruptcy of any beneficiary. Discretionary trusts generally offer greater protection than a spendthrift trust. (See below.) Moreover, discretionary trusts even offer protection against tax claims, alimony, and child support because the trustee is under no obligation to honor the claims of any beneficiary of the trust. Discretionary trusts typically have more than one beneficiary.

A discretionary trust is a trust where the beneficiaries and/or their entitlements to the trust fund are not fixed but are determined by the instructions set out in the trust agreement by the grantor. Discretionary trusts can only arise as express trusts, and therefore, it is not possible for a constructive trust or a resulting trust to arise from a discretionary trust.

Discretionary trusts can be discretionary in two respects. First, the trustees usually have the power to determine which beneficiaries (from within the class) will receive payments from the trust. And second, trustees can select the amount of trust property that the beneficiary receives. Characteristically, discretionary trusts provide for the discretionary distribution of income only, but in some cases, the trustees also have power to distribute capital in the trust, i.e. the corpus.

Spendthrift Trusts

A spendthrift trust is a trust that is created for the benefit of a person (often unable to control his spending) that gives an independent trustee full authority to make decisions as to how the trust funds may be spent for the benefit of the beneficiary. Creditors of the beneficiary cannot reach the funds in the trust, and the funds are not actually under the control of the beneficiary. Bottom line: A spendthrift trust is out of the reach of creditors.

A trust generally will not be treated as a spendthrift trust unless the trust agreement contains language showing that the grantor intended the trust to qualify as spendthrift. This is what is known as a spendthrift clause or spendthrift provision.

A spendthrift provision creates an irrevocable trust preventing creditors from attaching the interest of the beneficiary in the trust before that interest (cash or property) is actually distributed to him or her. Most well-drafted irrevocable trusts contain spendthrift provisions even though the beneficiaries are not known to be spendthrifts. This is because such a provision protects the trust and the beneficiary in the event a beneficiary is sued and a judgment creditor attempts to attach the beneficiary's interest in the trust.

The protection of the spendthrift trust extends solely to the property that is in the trust. Once the property has been distributed to the beneficiary that property can be reached by a creditor, except to the extent the distributed property is used to support the beneficiary. If a trust calls for a distribution to the beneficiary, but the beneficiary refuses such distribution and elects to retain property in the trust, the spendthrift protection of the trust ceases with respect to that distribution and the beneficiary's creditors can now reach trust assets.

TRUSTEES— HOW TO PICK THEM?

My strong suggestion is to use a large well-established bank with a trust department for your trustee. That's because most banks, including the offshore banks, are strongly regulated by their own country's laws and thus there are built-in protections, which make it unlikely for you to go wrong. On the other hand, individual trustees who are not part of any organization could easily embezzle or abscond with your money. Think of Bernie Madoff! In addition, bonding of your trustee could prove helpful and don't forget to perform your due diligence before retaining a trustee. Any outside opinions you get should be seriously weighed as there is no conflict of interest. On the other hand, if you discuss any of these matters with the person you're attempting to evaluate, you might be swayed by his or her argument rather than a more objective view by an outside opinion. Furthermore, an individual trustee is more likely to have a conflict of interest. And please remember, trust departments of major banks tend to be more objective and less likely to have any significant conflicts of interest. The downside with a financial institution's trust department is bureaucracy; your requests most likely will be reviewed by house counsel, and they will probably take longer to implement. But at least, your trust assets should be a lot safer. You don't need a "Bernie Madoff" experience! There are just so many horror stories of individual trustees absconding with people's life savings. A trust department is far safer than an individual trustee. The classic example is Bernie Madoff who bilked billions of dollars from his investors. It's just too tempting for a sole trustee to embezzle or abscond with your money. On the other hand, this rarely happens in a large trust department of a well-established bank. And in the remote chance that it did, the bank has liability insurance to make good on your stolen funds. What would happen in the event your sole trustee dies, disappears, or worse yet, is imprisoned? Folks, you need to carefully consider these possibilities. I would therefore strongly suggest that you stick with a large trust department of a well-established offshore bank. It's really your best bet. On a similar note, when it comes to investing, stick with an investment fund as opposed to using an individual for your investments. An investment fund made up of a large number of directors is not likely to run off with your money whereas an individual who operates as his own investment company can easily embezzle your money (think Bernie Madoff).

Never trust just one person (especially a foreign trustee) with your money. All asset protection plans should be structured so that you never are vulnerable to any one person dealing with your money without your consent. You're much better off dealing with a large, reputable organization with your money. For offshore trusts, large banks (e.g., Barclay's Bank) have large trust departments that won't run off with your money and will uphold the law to ensure your offshore trust will be safeguarded.

OFFSHORE BANKING AND INVESTING[268]

Barclays bank is larger than Bank of America or any other United States bank. In the final analysis, you should not be worried about offshore banking when using large well-known banks.

The best offshore banks:[269]

- AIB International Savings
- Lloyds TSB International
- Nationwide International
- Alliance & Leicester International
- Britannia International
- Skipton International
- Investec Bank (Channel Islands)

Some of the best countries for your offshore trust:[270]

- Antigua and Barbuda
- Austria
- Bahamas
- Belize
- Bermuda
- British Virgin Islands
- Cayman Islands
- Cook Islands
- Dominica
- Gibraltar
- Grenadines
- Luxembourg
- Nevis
- Panama
- Saint Vincent

- Turks and Caicos

If you have more than $50,000 in your bank account, it might be a good idea to have an offshore bank account. A couple of points to consider is whether the foreign country taxes income or assets from the trust and whether the standard of proof for determining a fraudulent conveyance is beyond a reasonable doubt.

There are many salesmen encouraging US citizens and permanent residents to set up secret offshore bank accounts because of enhanced privacy and the fact that most foreign countries don't cooperate with US authorities. Federal law is crystal clear: if you have more than $10,000 offshore, then you must report this information on your income tax return. Failure to do so could possibly result in severe criminal penalties.[271]

I hate to break the myth, but your secret foreign bank account is not really a secret. That's because a creditor can often subpoena your income tax returns as well as your other financial statements and easily discover your foreign bank account(s). So long as you have an ownership interest in a foreign bank account, you must report it to the US government (assuming there's at least $10,000 or more in the account). If you truly want a secret foreign bank account, you'll need the services of a foreign national to help you. There are no reporting requirements for foreign nationals with foreign bank accounts. Moreover, as long as you reside on US soil, you are under the jurisdiction of US Courts. And if you violate a court order, you can be jailed for contempt of court. In some instances, you might have to leave the United States for full protection.

An offshore (asset protection) trust that is structured correctly will not have the grantor of the trust treated as the legal owner of the foreign bank account. It's best for the foreign trustee to establish an IBC (International Business Corporation) and open the foreign bank account under the IBC's name, never the grantor's name. However, there would still be a reporting requirement for the grantor on IRS Form 9-22.1 because the IRS continues to consider him or her the owner of the foreign bank account for tax purposes. Interestingly, on the other hand, the law does not consider the grantor a debtor and thus the creditor cannot get at these funds. Bottom line: Legally, the grantor is not the owner of the foreign bank account, but for tax purposes only, he or she is the owner. Confused? You're not the only one.

Some European and many Caribbean jurisdictions offer highly confidential bank accounts. Always select large and financially sound foreign banks for your offshore bank account. Due diligence is necessary for your protection.[272]

In order to open a secret bank account, the bank will have to check you out[273] in order to make certain you are not laundering money and that you have paid all of your US taxes. The foreign bank is not looking for any problems with the US government. There are two types of secret foreign bank accounts: numbered accounts and bearer accounts.

The numbered account usually requires at least $50,000 or more and the account holder must travel to Europe to open the bank account. The foreign bank will tax the income from your account. There are no reporting requirements, except for criminal investigations.

The bearer account requires at least $7,000 or more to open. Funds can only be deposited or withdrawn upon presentation of both a password and a bearer-bank-account passbook. You can also open this type of account from your home. There's no name on this account, but a password is needed to transact business. It is also necessary to use a local law firm as an intermediary to transact business on this account. This type of bank account is really a short-term holding account to park money, similar to a US bank CD. Additionally, the interest rate on this account is low, and you'll be taxed on the interest. However, like the numbered account, there are no tax reporting requirements. The password is known only to the bank, the attorney and the client. The bearer-bank-account passbook can be retained either by the attorney or by the client.

The bottom line: while a secret bank account is an excellent way to hide assets from creditors, it should never be utilized to hide money from the IRS. Hiding money from the IRS is a very serious criminal offense.

Offshore banks and International Business Companies are not subject to United States capital gains taxes on profits from their publicly traded stocks, bonds, and commodity trades.[274] The United States has never taxed the capital gains of nonresident aliens (NRA), offshore companies, offshore trusts, and offshore banks unless the foreigner was doing business within the United States.[275] Foreign investors receive preferential tax treatment by utilizing tax exemptions.[276] This benefit is not available to a "US person."

Foreign banks and foreign financial institutions have become "qualified intermediaries" or "Qis" with the Internal Revenue Service[277] with myriad possible tax consequences.[278]

A US citizen with $1,000,000 or more may want to consider forming a foreign private bank, which is a corporation, licensed to do banking. When properly capitalized, approved, and implemented, a foreign bank has no accountability as to the types of financial transactions it may enter.

If your money is offshore, it should be in an irrevocable trust that you don't control.[279]

Courts have the power to use "repatriation orders" to force the debtor to return offshore money to the United States and to hand that money over to the creditors. If the debtor refuses to comply with a repatriation order, the debtor may be held in contempt of court and could be jailed. The all-time incarceration record for refusing to comply with a repatriation order is a remarkable fourteen years in jail for former corporate lawyer H. Beatty Chadwick who refused to repatriate offshore money to pay alimony to his ex-wife.

If you have control, even the slightest amount of control in your offshore trust, then you're looking for trouble. The following is a case where the debtors had control over their offshore trust: "Based upon Daniel Allen's testimony and a review of the respective trust documents as to the Shingle Oak Trust and the Southern Breeze Trust, Daniel and David Allen *retain control over the Assets*, respectively, in the Shingle Oak Trust and the Southern Breeze Trust.

Each has the power and ability to repatriate Assets held in their respective trusts."[280]

PERSONAL EXEMPT PROPERTY

What is "exempt property"? It is property that a creditor cannot take to satisfy a judgment against you. If the property is to be taken directly from you, the procedure is termed "execution" or "attachment." If your property is to be taken from another person or bank that is holding it for you, the procedure is termed "garnishment." Personal exempt property of yours includes $5,000 worth of business tools (property). Even in the midst of litigation, you're legally allowed to transfer your exempt property without triggering a fraudulent conveyance! This is good news for you because you can lawfully set up a child's trust during a lawsuit and transfer business property (tools) to your child's trust. Then the child's trust can lease the property back to your business, and you can start to make lease payments on the property in the child's trust. As stated previously, this can be done during a lawsuit without violating any of the fraudulent conveyance laws! This is a wonderful way of spreading income away from your business (thereby diminishing your business assets which in turn could help you to settle the lawsuit or make the plaintiffs drop their lawsuit) and to go directly to your child's trust (not a named defendant in the lawsuit where it would be safe). But to make certain this works, only transfer your exempt property (tools of the trade), which is limited to $5,000 in California. On the other hand, before you are sued or have existing creditors, you can legally transfer any amount of your business property to the child's trust. If you record your child's trust at the recorder's office, you'll then be able to use California's four-year statute of limitations for a fraudulent conveyance action rather than the seven-year statute of limitations. In my opinion, it's worth recording the transfer in order to obtain the shorter statute of limitations.

Below are the Enforcement of Judgment Law (EJL) exemptions and the most commonly claimed federal law exemptions:[281]

1. Motor vehicles—$2,300 is exempt only if a timely exemption claim is filed.
2. Household furnishings and personal effects are exempt only if a timely exemption claim is filed. There is no specific dollar exemption for household furnishings, appliances, provisions, wearing apparel and other personal effects. Furnishings and personal effects located at the judgment debtor's residence are exempt if they are (a) "Ordinarily and reasonably necessary to" the judgment debtor and members of the judgment debtor's family at the judgment debtor's principal place of residence; and (b) Personally used, or procured for use, by the judgment debtor and family at the debtor's principal residence.[282]
3. Jewelry, heirlooms and works of art are exempt only if a timely exemption claim is filed, and up to $6,075.[283]
4. "Tools of trade" are exempt only if a timely exemption claim is filed, and are personal property items reasonably necessary to and actually used by the judgment debtor (or spouse) in exercising the trade, business or profession by which he or she earns a living. These items include but are not limited to: materials, uniforms, furnishings, books, one commercial motor vehicle, and one vessel.[284]
5. Traceable paid earnings are exempt only if a timely exemption claim is filed, and are earnings paid to the judgment debtor within 30 days before a writ of execution is levied or other enforcement method is employed, and that can be traced to deposit accounts or are in the form of cash or its equivalent, are wholly or partly exempt.[285] If the judgment debtor's earnings are not subject to an earnings withholding order or earnings assignment order for child, spousal or family support, 75 percent of any paid earnings levied upon (or otherwise sought to be subjected to enforcement of a money judgment) are exempt.[286]

6. Excess social security/supplemental security income benefits and public benefits are exempt only if a timely exemption claim is filed, and are payments made by the Social Security Administration (e.g., social security and supplemental security income benefits) directly deposited by the government (or its agent) into deposit accounts are exempt in the amount of $2,425 or $3,650 without filing a claim. Any amounts in these accounts in excess of $2,425 or $3,650 (whichever is applicable) are exempt if they consist of authorized payments by the Social Security Administration. However, the creditor may assert that excess amounts are not exempt under California law.[287]
7. Property of debtor in military service—Although not technically an exemption from enforcement, federal law effectively stays certain enforcement activities against a debtor in military service. For example, a person holding a lien on a debtor's property or effects ordinarily may not, during the debtor's military service and for ninety days thereafter, enforce the lien without a prior court order. In proceedings to enforce a lien, the court may on its own motion, or must if requested by a debtor whose ability to comply with the obligation is materially affected by military service, (a) stay the proceedings "for a period of time as justice and equity require" or (b) "adjust the obligation to preserve the interests of all parties."[288]
8. Life insurance policies (including endowments and annuities) are exempt only if a timely exemption claim is filed, and the extent of exemptions for life insurance policies depends on whether the policy has matured. (Policies mature when the beneficiary has an enforceable right to receive payments and there are no conditions to the issuer's obligation to make payments.) The cash surrender value of a life insurance policy is exempt without making a claim. However, the exemption for the aggregate loan value of life insurance policies (including endowment and annuity policies) is more

limited. Benefits from matured life insurance policies are exempt to the extent "reasonably necessary" for the support of the debtor and his or her spouse and dependents.[289]

9. Private retirement plans, Keoghs[290], IRAs; profit-sharing plans are exempt only if a timely exemption claim is filed, and are benefits derived from "private retirement plans" and profit-sharing plans designed and used for retirement purposes are exempt whether payable or already paid.[291]
10. Health aids (including prosthetic and orthopedic appliances) are exempt only if a timely exemption claim is filed, and that are reasonably necessary to enable the judgment debtor (or the debtor's spouse or dependent) to work or sustain health are exempt regardless of value.[292]
11. Personal injury awards or settlements arising out of a personal injury generally are exempt only if a timely exemption claim is filed, and to the extent necessary for the support of the judgment debtor and his or her spouse and dependents.[293] However, if the award or settlement is payable periodically, the creditor may reach the same amount as could be withheld from a like amount of earnings under the Wage Garnishment Law.[294]
12. Wrongful death awards or settlements arising out of the wrongful death of the judgment debtor's spouse, or a person upon whom the judgment debtor or his or her spouse was dependent (e.g., a judgment debtor who was dependent upon a parent for support before the parent was wrongfully killed), are exempt only if a timely exemption claim is filed, and to the extent reasonably necessary for the support of the judgment debtor and his or her spouse and dependents.[295]

The following property is exempt without making a claim and is not subject to enforcement of a money judgment:[296]

1. Proceeds from sale of sole motor vehicle—If the judgment debtor has only one motor vehicle and it is sold at execution sale, as of 2007, $2,300 of the proceeds are exempt without making a claim.[297] However, preferred labor claims and state tax liens, if any, must generally be paid from this $2,300.
2. Deposit account containing social security benefits—A deposit account into which social security benefits are directly deposited by the government or its agent is exempt without making a claim in the following amount as of 2007: $2,425 if the benefits are payable to only one depositor; or $3,650 if payable to two or more depositors who are the designated payees, unless the payments represent a benefit to only one of the depositors, in which case $2,425 is exempt.[298]
3. Deposit account containing public benefits—A deposit account into which public benefits (welfare) (Cal. Welfare & Institutions Code § 11450(a) aid payments) are directly deposited by the government or its agent is exempt without making a claim in the following amount as of 2007: $1,225 if the benefits are payable to only one depositor; or $1,825 if payable to two or more depositors who are the designated payees, unless the payments represent a benefit to only one of the depositors, in which case $1,225 is exempt.[299]
4. Ownership interest (including cash surrender value) in life insurance, endowment and annuity policies is exempt without making a claim.[300] But note: judgment debtors may claim only a limited exemption for the loan value of such policies.
5. Pensions or annuities, or retirement, disability, death or other benefits payable to any person by a public retirement system are exempt without making a claim.[301] However, these benefits may be applied to satisfy a judgment for child, family or spousal support. Other specific rules apply, so please be sure to check the applicable law.
6. Contributions by workers to the Unemployment Compensation Disability Fund and by employers to the

Unemployment Fund are exempt without making a claim.[302] Payable unemployment benefits are also exempt without making a claim.[303] However, payable unemployment benefits may be reached to satisfy support judgments.

7. Payable private disability and health insurance payments: Disability or health insurance payments are exempt before payment without making a claim. After payment, they are exempt (but only if a timely exemption claim is filed and the payments are traceable as proceeds).[304]
8. Personal injury and wrongful death causes of action are exempt without making a claim.[305]
9. The following benefits are also exempt without making a claim if they are payable but have not yet been received by the judgment debtor. After payment, they are exempt only if a timely claim is filed and they are traceable as exempt proceeds: (i) payable workers' compensation benefits, (ii) payable welfare benefits, (iii) relocation benefits, (iv) payable student financial aid while attending school is exempt.
10. Prisoner's funds are exempt in the amount of $1,225 as of 1997 without making a claim. Double that amount if the prisoner is married.
11. A "family plot" is exempt without making a claim.
12. "Homestead" exemption is an automatic "dwelling exemption" against the forced judicial sale of the dwelling occupied by the judgment debtor or the debtor's spouse. The judgment debtor or other exemption claimant need not file a claim of exemption after a real property dwelling is levied upon. Rather, the judgment creditor is required to obtain a court order for sale of the real property homestead. The court must determine at a hearing the amount of the "dwelling exemption" and the fair market value of the property. On the other hand, if the homestead is personal property (e.g., a boat or mobile home not affixed to land) or a real property leasehold with an unexpired term of less than two years at the time of levy, the judgment debtor must file a claim of

exemption within 10 days after the notice of levy is served (at least 15 days if the notice was served by mail).[306]

13. Wage garnishment uses the procedures of the Wage Garnishment Law[307] in which a judgment creditor may compel a judgment debtor's employer to withhold the non-exempt portion (generally 25 percent) of the debtor's wages for payment directly to the levying officer, to be applied to satisfy the judgment. Wage garnishment may be the only means available to enforce a judgment where other property of the debtor is exempt. By means of a debtor's exam, the creditor can learn the name and address of the debtor's employer. An effective earnings withholding order creates a lien on the employee's earnings and generally on all property of the employer. However, this lien is limited to the amount required to be withheld. The garnishment process is easy; however, the downside for the creditor is that, at least 75 percent of a debtor's earnings are automatically exempt from garnishment, except as to judgments for support. Therefore, unless the debtor earns a large salary, the creditor will receive very little from a wage garnishment. It could take years to satisfy a judgment by garnishing the debtor's wages and if the debtor quits or is fired, there will be no wages to garnish. Furthermore, a wage garnishment might prompt the debtor to file a bankruptcy petition. If the debtor receives a discharge in bankruptcy, the wage garnishment will not attach to the debtor's post-petition wages. *However, a court order is required to garnish the wages of a non-debtor spouse.* An earnings withholding order may not issue against earnings of the judgment debtor's spouse unless a court order is obtained upon noticed motion. Reason: Despite the general rule that community property is liable for the debts of a spouse, community property earnings are unique and may not be liable in some situations.[308]

Exempt Income

Under federal law, the following types of income are completely exempt from garnishment or any type of creditor collection efforts except for spousal or child support:[309]

- Social Security income
- Social Security disability income
- Health insurance benefits
- Unemployment compensation
- State welfare benefits
- Workers' compensation benefits
- Veteran's benefits

Convert Non-exempt Property Into Exempt Property

Any competent attorney should aid their clients in exempting as much property as possible before filing bankruptcy. The more property that is exempted, the more property the honest debtor gets to keep. The Seventh Circuit has ruled that "conversions of assets from nonexempt to exempt forms within the year preceding a petition for bankruptcy are not necessarily fraudulent to creditors."[310] Moreover, debtors are allowed to make full use of their entitled exemptions. However, a debtor may not convert nonexempt assets to exempt assets if the conversion was made with the intent to defraud creditors. In order to recover a transfer as fraudulent, the bankruptcy trustee must establish each of the following elements:[311]

1. That an interest of the debtor in property was transferred.
2. That the transfer of that interest occurred within one year before the date of filing of the bankruptcy petition.
3. That the debtor received less than "reasonably equivalent value" in exchange for the transfer at issue.
4. That the debtor was insolvent on the date of the transfer or became insolvent because of the transfer.

When a person is spiraling into financial trouble, a common planning technique is to try to maximize the amount of property that can be held exempt from creditors if bankruptcy is filed. It should be noted that property exemptions can be waived, but this is seldom done. Typically, the largest and most important property exemption is the homestead. Other property exemptions exist for business tools and retirement accounts. Debtors are sometimes tempted to convert nonexempt property (e.g., cash) into exempt assets (e.g., business tools) before filing bankruptcy. There is no general prohibition on such conversions, but courts closely scrutinize the conversions to determine the adequacy of the purchase price and to see if the primary purpose of the conversion is an attempt to hinder, delay, or defraud creditors. If so, the conversion can be challenged. The new bankruptcy rules for the homestead exemption use a ten-year (look-back) period before the bankruptcy filing to evaluate for any fraudulent activity. The homestead exemption is reduced by the amount attributable to the fraud.

Bottom line—non-exempt assets can be converted into exempt assets, but there better be a good reason to do so and it is helpful if it is part of the debtor's overall estate, business, and financial plan.[312]

Summary

Personal property exemptions will not protect your assets against: (1) Collection for child support debts, alimony, or family support payments; (2) tax debts, (3) or subrogation (type of insurance) claims.

The main property exemptions [313] are the following:

1. Cash welfare benefits, Social Security benefits, unemployment compensation, student loans, grant payments, work payments, most pension and retirement benefits.
2. Clothing and jewelry up to $3,500.
3. Books and digital media up to $3,500.
4. Health aids for you and your family, e.g. wheelchairs and motorized scooters.

5. Furniture, appliances, household goods and fuel up to $6,500 ($13,000 for married couple).
6. One automobile up to $3,250 in equity [314]($6,500 for married couple).
7. Tools and instruments for your business/trade up to $10,000.
8. Other property up to $3,000 including no more than $1,500 cash.
9. If creditor is the state, no more than $200 in bank account(s); in all other cases, no more than $500 in bank account(s).
10. Money you have for child support is completely exempt.
11. Money you have for bodily injuries for yourself or your family up to $20,000 (does not include pain and suffering).
12. Money you have for lost future earnings that is reasonably necessary for yourself and your family.
13. 75 percent of your wages or thirty times the federal minimum wage, whichever is greater, is exempt.[315]

The value of your property is the "fair market value." You will need to file an exemption claim with the court that has the judgment. The creditor may object to your claim. In that case, a court hearing will be scheduled for a determination. If the creditor does not comply with a court order, you can sue the creditor. On the other hand, if the judge denies your exemption claim, you will have to pay the creditor's costs. In order to protect your rights, you are advised to seek the advice of an attorney in matters where a creditor is attempting to collect on the judgment.

ONE-PERSON COMPANIES

Can you have a one-person limited partnership? Yes, you can. The same person can be both a general and limited partner simultaneously. For example, in the 2006 New York Code—One Person Both General and Limited Partner. § 101.[316] One person both general and limited partner: (1) A person may be a general partner and a limited partner in the same partnership at the same time. (2) A person who is a general partner, and also at the same time a limited partner, shall have all the rights and powers and be subject to all the restrictions of a general partner; except that, in respect to his contributions, he shall have the rights against the other members which he would have had if he were not also a general partner.

One-shareholder corporations and one-member limited liability companies are business entities that you should not form. These entities no longer provide adequate limited liability protection and are no longer good for asset protection. These entities are a "house of cards." Please see chapter 23.

OFFSHORE TRUST AND INTERNATIONAL BUSINESS COMPANIES ARE NO LONGER "BULLETPROOF"!

The latest court decisions regarding offshore trusts could find you in contempt of court. It all depends on timing. For many years, salesmen have declared the irrevocable trust to be "bulletproof." That is simply not true. Recently, a number of debtors have been jailed on contempt charges for not repatriating their offshore assets by order of the court. They claim the "impossibility defense" to the court, claiming that they neither have the means nor the power to compel the trustee to return the offshore assets to them. Well, folks, the courts are not buying this argument. What the courts have said lately is that many of these debtors are being intentionally deceptive and that they have enough control over their offshore trusts to effectuate a repatriation of their assets. Even the slightest bit of control over your so-called irrevocable offshore trust is likely to spell trouble for you. Courts have said that if the grantor of an offshore trust has any of the following attributes, then he indeed has enough control over the trust to effectuate a return of his assets. The following can cause problems for the grantor of an offshore trust: (1) A trust that is not irrevocable, (2) a trust in which the grantor is also the trustee, (3) a trust that allows the grantor to appoint new trustees, (4) a trust that does not prohibit the grantor from becoming a trustee himself, (5) a trust that does not use a disinterested neutral protector, (6) a trust that does not use a disinterested neutral trustee, (7) a trust in which the grantor is also a beneficiary, (8) a trust without a duress (flee) clause, (9) a trust without a spendthrift clause, (10) a trust formed in violation of the fraudulent conveyance laws. Even if you have no control over your offshore trust and you formed your offshore trust in violation of the fraudulent conveyance laws, the courts will hold you accountable. And you could very well be headed for jail, especially if you are found to be in contempt of a court order.

Folks, a self-created "impossibility defense" will simply no longer work. You can't use the "impossibility defense," meaning "I can't comply with the court order, because I have no control over the offshore trust" if it was fraudulently set up in the first place. The court will hold you in contempt. The only solution is to leave the United States and head for a foreign country where the US courts have no jurisdiction.[317]

The "impossibility defense" simply states to the court that it is impossible for you to comply with the terms and conditions of the court order for one or more reasons. The "impossibility defense" has to be proven by "clear and convincing" evidence. If the court orders you to repatriate (return) your assets from the offshore trust, and you disobey the court order, then you must show the court that you have "no control and no ability to influence" the trust. Furthermore, "impossibility may not be a defense if the inability to comply is self-induced." Moreover, the "impossibility defense is invalid where [the] party created [the] Trust in an obvious attempt to shelter funds from an expected adverse arbitration award."[318]

Where impossibility of compliance is self-created, the defense [of] impossibility is unavailable to the defendant.[319]

If you want to set up an offshore trust,[320] do so before you're threatened with a lawsuit, before there's any pending litigation against you, and before you have any creditors. Also, be sure your trust deed—that is, your trust contract that instructs your trustee—has all the legal terms and conditions that prevents you from exercising any control whatsoever over the trust. Moreover, make sure you use an expert attorney to set up your offshore trust. This is not inexpensive, but the money spent to do it right is well worth it. It could keep you out of jail. One final note: some asset-protection experts are now advocating offshore limited liability companies and offshore annuity companies in lieu of offshore trusts for increased protection. In my opinion, a self-created impossibility defense also applies to these entities as well.

The bottom line: If you set up an offshore trust, or for that matter an offshore company such as a foreign LLC or annuity company, in violation of the fraudulent conveyance laws, then regardless of any excuses you make to the court regarding an inability to repatriate your assets, the court is going to find you in contempt of court. To avoid this potential problem, you will have to physically leave the United States along with your assets.

When it comes to trusts, nothing beats the irrevocable offshore trust—but it's no longer "bulletproof." If you fraudulently convey assets to your offshore trust, your creditors can complain to the US court about it. And lately, US courts are taking a dim view of the "impossibility defense" and are holding the debtors in contempt of court for failing to repatriate their trust assets back to the United States.

In the past, creditors would have needed to file a fraudulent conveyance lawsuit in the foreign country where your trust was located. This was very expensive because attorneys in foreign countries would not take legal cases on a contingency-fee basis. Foreign attorneys require an upfront fee retainer before they begin to work on your case. If your creditor did file a fraudulent conveyance lawsuit in the foreign country where your trust was located (called in rem jurisdiction), then another problem arose. The trust deed required that the trust be relocated once a lawsuit was filed against it! This was called a flee or duress clause. The trustee was then duty-bound to relocate the trust immediately to a new foreign country. Then the creditor had to begin another lawsuit in the new foreign country. As you can see, this became a veritable cat and mouse game. Eventually, the creditor would give up. However, the rules of the "game" have recently changed. US courts are now jailing debtors who don't repatriate their trust assets. As a result, your remaining option is to leave the jurisdiction of the United States and relocate to a foreign country.

If you transfer real property such as your home, to an offshore trust, then you must record the transfer at your local recorder's office. This would also include filing the offshore trust deed itself in the local recorder's office. Otherwise, the transfer won't be effective against third parties. Furthermore, if you transfer assets to an offshore trust in violation of a court order or restraining order (injunction), you could be held in contempt of court and even jailed.

US judgments are not recognized outside of the United States. To register and enforce a US judgment overseas, the case must first be relitigated in the foreign country.[321] This is an important reason for foreign asset protection trusts.

For your offshore trust to easily conduct business, it will need to establish an IBC (international business company). There are countless activities for your offshore trust/IBC: For example, you can buy an offshore annuity, invest in foreign stocks that US citizens are not allowed to invest in, and even invest in US stocks that exempt your IBC from any capital gains taxes! As the grantor, you even get pass-through income tax treatment with your offshore trust.

Your IBC's bank account should be in a different country from the country of your trust. Moreover, your IBC can issue bearer shares of stock. You can even be the president of your IBC without being its owner (the trustee is owner) and have signatory on the IBC's bank account. You can also be a trading advisor and have access to your IBC's stock account. You can even have an import/export company. There are so many unlimited possibilities. You can even partake in investments that US citizens are not allowed to invest in.

Your offshore (irrevocable) trust or even a domestic irrevocable trust can legally own your home, but make certain that you record the trust deed in your local recorder's office so that it becomes effective as to third parties. This is extremely important and can't be stressed strongly enough. Always record a property transfer of your home! Instead of your home being owned directly by the trust, your home could be held by a limited liability company that in turn is owned by your trust.

An offshore trustee, when signing a US deed in a foreign jurisdiction, must file strict procedures. Otherwise, the US deed is invalid. In California, a fraudulent deed can only be challenged for up to three years after it is recorded.

If the trustee of an offshore trust returns trust assets to the grantor, then the trust loses its irrevocable status and thus no longer provides asset protection.

The jurisdictions providing for favorable treatment of asset protection trusts are the Bahamas, Barbados, Belize, Bermuda, British Virgin Islands, Cayman Islands, Cook Islands, Cyprus, Gibraltar, Guernsey, Isle of Mann, Jersey, Labuan, Liechtenstein, Madeira, Mauritius, the Turks and Caicos Islands, and Western Samoa.

Less than 3 percent of US creditors pursue their claims in foreign jurisdictions.[322]

Ordinarily, the offshore trust vests the trustee with absolute discretion over distribution of trust income or principal among the designated beneficiaries. The settlor, however, often provides the foreign trustee with a nonbinding "letter of wishes" describing the settlor's preferences regarding distributions of trust property. Moreover, the settlor typically reserves some authority over the trust either through participation in a "committee of advisors" or as a "protector" of the trust with authority to replace the trustee.

A properly drafted asset protection trust should always be structured so that the foreign trustee does not have any access to the protected assets. It is important, if possible, that you never enter into any contract (and a trust agreement is just a contract) which forces you to trust anybody else (especially a foreign trust company) with your assets. In addition, if a creditor attack comes, the trust will likely be migrated to a different jurisdiction utilizing the Cuba (duress or flee) clause. However, this is not always possible, so therefore, try to use a large trust department at a well-known major offshore bank.

The annual fees for your offshore trust shouldn't cost you more than $2,000 per year, including trustee management costs. Please remember to use an expert with experience setting up foreign asset protection trusts so that protective clauses are included. For example, your offshore trust should provide for the marital deduction or an A-B trust, which may eliminate or reduce gift and estate taxes.

The domicile of your offshore trust determines the legal enforceable rights to manage and control the trust possessions under local laws. If the jurisdiction is within the United States, it's a domestic trust. If the jurisdiction is outside the United States, then it's an offshore trust or foreign trust where the local laws apply. The problem here is that the grantor of the offshore trust typically resides in the United States; and US courts have *in personam* jurisdiction over the grantor, and thus they can influence the grantor as to how they want the trust to operate. Most asset protection salesmen hide this fact. They preach till they're blue in the face how the trust is governed by local (foreign) laws. While that is true, what these salesmen neglect to state is that US courts have considerable influence over the grantor. If the grantor truly wants his offshore trust to be governed by local law and not influenced by a US court, the debtor would literally have to leave the United States. The salesmen will never disclose this to you!

The Offshore Trust/Domestic LLC Combination

If set up correctly, an offshore trust and domestic LLC can be a powerful combination. The LLC would be 100 percent owned by the offshore trust. This combination is typically used for your home. Your home would be correctly and legitimately transferred to a domestic LLC, which in turn would be owned by the offshore trust. According to the IRS, your offshore trust is a foreign grantor-type trust, which allows pass-through tax treatment. Also, the LLC is afforded pass-through tax treatment as well. By placing your home in the LLC/trust combination, you would be taking advantage of lessening your estate taxes and bequeathing your home most likely to your children. There's another favorable upside here with regard to the $500,000 marital capital gains exemption—you get to maintain it with this type of plan provided you elect to be treated as a disregarded entity for tax purposes.[323] One further reminder: *never* be a protector of your offshore trust. Exercising the least bit of control over your offshore trust could wreak havoc with any protection you might have. Another problem is the fact that your home is located in the United States. With real property, most states exercise *in rem* jurisdiction, which means that the court will apply the laws of the real property's actual location despite the fact that it may be owned by an offshore trust. This could pose a problem. The bottom line is that the offshore trust/LLC combination is a very sophisticated type of estate and asset protection tool, which definitely requires the services of an expert tax attorney or similar professional.

Offshore Banking

Offshore banking is associated with the stigma of money laundering, tax evasion, and other fraudulent schemes. However, the vast majority of people utilize offshore banking legitimately, and I encourage everyone to use offshore banking for legitimate and legal purposes only. US citizens have the legal right to utilize offshore banking. In fact, offshore banks have strong advantages and services that US banks do not provide. For instance: (1) Privacy—These banks are not subject to US subpoenas, and therefore, they will not release any information regarding your bank account to the US government and to creditors. (2). No US court jurisdiction—US court orders such as a writ of execution (per creditor) cannot levy money in your bank account, and US courts have absolutely no authority or power in foreign jurisdictions. As a result, the money in your offshore bank account can't be subject to a bank levy by a US court order. (3) Stronger banking laws than in the United States. If a US bank employee illegally discloses confidential information, the employee would probably get reprimanded and maybe lose his job. On the other hand, if an employee at an offshore bank illegally discloses confidential information, the employee would likely lose his job and also be criminally prosecuted.

Once your offshore bank account is set up, it's easy to transfer money to and from your account. If you want to secretly and legally transfer money to your offshore bank, you can use (the little-known) international postal money orders. Any amounts under $3,000 are not recorded by the post office and therefore there's no personal information as to who made the purchase. Money sent overseas in amounts under $10,000 per day does not have to be reported to any federal agency. Therefore, you can easily and anonymously send money (even on a daily basis) directly to your offshore bank account. Need to send more than $3,000? No problem. Just use another person to obtain an international postal money order, or you can simply visit another post office, but be sure to keep the money orders under $3,000. Individual international postal money orders can be purchased in any amount up to $700. Also, if at all possible, use small money orders so it won't attract any attention. After you've purchased your money orders, you'll need to properly endorse them. On the back of the money order, write with an indelible black or blue ink pen the following restrictive endorsement: "For deposit only to (the name of your bank), account number (your bank account number)." Be sure to sign your name under this restrictive endorsement. In case your money order gets lost, this will protect you. If you lose your money order, you can get a refund by promptly reporting it and presenting a receipt to the post office.

Nevis Limited Liability Companies

Compared to offshore trusts, a Nevis LLC is generally cheaper to maintain. Nevis limited liability companies have charging-order remedies similar to those seen in the United States. Even with a charging order, a Nevis LLC can still pay a member in the form of a salary or a loan, both of which are not affected by the charging order. The manager of your Nevis LLC may be under the directive of a duress clause, which prohibits him or her from distributing funds to you if he or she knows that your request is forced by the court. The Nevis LLC even has a provision, which allows you to transfer funds to your LLC when you have creditors and not be guilty of a fraudulent conveyance.[324] It's highly likely that US courts will view your transfer as a fraudulent conveyance despite Nevis's position that it wasn't a fraudulent transfer. In the final analysis however, the problem is with the US courts. No matter what the "experts" tell you, if a US court believes that you have transferred assets to a Nevis limited liability company in violation of *state or federal* fraudulent conveyance laws, you will then be held accountable. Make no mistake, if you're here in the United States, a local court has jurisdiction over you. If you try to pull a fast one over the court by maintaining a self-created "impossibility defense," it isn't going to work. The court will hold you in contempt, and you could be jailed. I'm afraid options are running out as the tide is turning. One of the last remaining options for you is to head to the airport with your passport in hand and leave the United States for a very long time.

The bottom line: It doesn't matter how strong the Nevis limited liability company is because that strength is worthless here in the United States so long as the debtor who transferred assets (in violation of the Fraudulent Conveyance laws) remains here in the United States. This also applies to all other foreign limited liability companies (FLLCs) and international business companies (IBCs) as well.

If you decide to leave United States, then perhaps you have the upper hand over your creditors. That's because creditors cannot seize or investigate bank records in foreign (tax haven) jurisdictions due to strong bank secrecy laws. Also, offshore banks have to go through the local courts, and US judgments are not enforceable in offshore jurisdictions. US attorneys have a significant jurisdictional problem since only citizens of the tax haven jurisdiction can practice law. Therefore, the creditor will have to hire a local law firm and pay upfront legal fees, post bonds, pay court costs, and prepay other expenses to pursue their claims. This deters all but the most determined (and perhaps foolish) and affluent creditors.

HOW TO PROTECT YOUR INHERITANCE

You're the beneficiary of a will, and there's a judgment against you; what should you do? As a beneficiary of a will, you'll eventually inherit future assets that could be seized by your creditors. So you must take immediate steps to avert that possibility. There are three options available to you. The first is to immediately contact the maker of the will to request a change of beneficiary so that the creditors won't be able to seize the assets. The second option is to have the maker of the will stipulate that the transfer of the assets is to be made to your irrevocable offshore trust. And a third option is a restrictive clause in the will with instructions not to transfer any assets to you (the beneficiary) so long as you have existing creditors.

A person with creditor problems or a money judgment against him may feel "lucky" if a relative dies and leaves him an inheritance. Yet the inheritance is an asset as soon as a court determines, or pursuant to a living trust, that you (the debtor) are a beneficiary of the inheritance. If money is distributed from the inheritance to you (the beneficiary), the money is even more accessible to the creditors. If you accept the inheritance and then transfer the money to another (nondebtor) family member or to a protected asset such as an annuity, that transfer will be attacked as a fraudulent conveyance subject to avoidance. The best situation would be for the decedent to make a bequest to his heirs or beneficiaries in a trust for their benefit rather than outright distributions, assuming the trust deed had a proper "spendthrift clause" to provide protection from creditors.

Unfortunately, when preparing a will, most people don't think their heirs have creditor problems; this is something you definitely must remember when preparing a will. One of the most important tools of asset protection planning is involving parents or grandparents in your asset protection plan by encouraging them to leave your inheritance in a protective trust. The heir with asset protection concerns must take responsibility for this part of family planning. For the heir or beneficiary, a bequest in trust with liberal distribution instructions provides nearly unrestricted use of the inheritance yet does *not* protect inheritances from judgments. If you are a judgment debtor who is faced with the prospect of an inheritance in the form of an outright bequest, you may consider a "disclaimer" whereby you waive your right to the inheritance, and the inheritance automatically passes to your lineal decedents. In such a case, a creditor could argue that the disclaimer was a form of a fraudulent conveyance.[325]

If you inherit money from a person who dies within 180 days of the date you filed for bankruptcy, you must tell the court. The money becomes part of your bankruptcy estate and is distributed among your creditors. You can always disclaim an inheritance if you don't want it to go to your bankruptcy estate. You never have to accept an inheritance. Trying to hide an inheritance would be illegal, and you could face penalties for doing so. However, you have no responsibility if you are written out of a will or if a spendthrift trust is set up.

Pour-over Wills

A pour-over will is part of a testamentary will wherein the writer of a will creates a trust and decrees in the will that the property in his or her estate at the time of his or her death shall be distributed to the trustee of the trust. The testator's property is subject to probate until such time as the pour-over clause is applied, and the estate assets "pour" into the trust. The trust instrument must be either in existence at the time when the will with the pour-over clause is executed or executed concurrently with the will to be a valid pour-over gift. However, the trust need not be funded inter vivos (during life). The pour-over clause protects property not previously placed in a trust by pouring it into the previously established trust through the vehicle of the will. A living revocable trust with a pour-over will keeps all of your assets out of probate.

HOW TO HANDLE YOUR CREDITORS

What judgment creditors don't know about can't be taken. In other words, stealth works. Never volunteer anything.

It's true that judgment creditors can only take what you own, but there are different types of ownership—legal and equitable. Also, a court can sometimes unwind transfers under the fraudulent conveyance laws. But generally, if it is not yours, they can't take it.

It's important to note that a judgment will adversely affect your credit score so that you may not be able to obtain credit. What can you do? This could be a favorable time for you to negotiate a possible settlement with the creditors. My suggestion for a possible settlement is pay no more than 10 percent of the judgment or $25,000, whichever is less. Your first settlement offer to the creditors might be 5 percent of the judgment or $10,000 whichever is less. Subsequent settlement offers will raise the stakes but in my opinion shouldn't exceed 10 percent of the judgment or $25,000, whichever is less. Don't forget, as a "judgment-protected" or "judgment-proof" debtor, you ultimately have the upper hand. You really shouldn't give in too easily to the creditors. It's quite possible that your creditors will repeatedly reject your settlement offers out right. Okay, don't worry. Just give them time. Eventually, their frustration will yield to the reality of the situation—the impossibility of ever substantially collecting on a judgment against you. They will be faced with your offer or nothing at all. In many cases, your creditors will "throw in the towel" and reluctantly accept your offer. Just give them time.

Leased equipment, leased furniture, and leased cars, etc., cannot be seized by your creditors. Therefore, you may want to consider leasing to reduce your exposure to assets, which could be seized by a creditor. A creditor can seize checks that come in the mail to you, so therefore I recommend you use a PO Box or have your mail sent to a secret location, e.g., a friend or relative's address.

By nature, most collections attorneys are very aggressive. Some are also dishonest. The FDPCA (Fair Debt Practices Collections Act) can protect you in some instances. Certain judgments related to consumer debts fall under the auspices of the FDCPA and go a long way to protect you. For instance, by law, you can tell a debt-collection agency and collections attorneys to leave you alone. Also, if you are represented by an attorney, a collections attorney cannot contact you but must contact your attorney. On the other hand, debtors who are not represented by an attorney and whose judgment is a nonconsumer debt such as a business debt or a judgment related to a tort (a wrongful act) can be contacted directly by a collections attorney. Never forget that a licensed collections attorney is an officer of the court and must treat you with respect and a modicum of decency. Collections attorneys can paper you to death to annoy, harass, and intimidate; and some collections attorneys are unscrupulous and commit fraud and are deceitful. If that's the case, then the FDCPA may be able to help. Alternatively, if you believe that the collections attorney is harassing you, then you should seek a protective order from the court.

In California, a judgment debtor can be subpoenaed to court for a debtor's exam no more than once every six months. A debtor's exam requires a judgment debtor to answer questions under oath to assist the creditors in satisfying their judgment and sometimes to produce available documents. This information is used solely to enable the creditors to satisfy their judgment against you. Creditors can use many procedures to enable them to collect on their judgment. These ways have been discussed in chapter 4.

A major disadvantage to having creditors is that it could interfere with your ability to launch a lawsuit on your own as a plaintiff. That's because if you win a lawsuit, your judgment could be subject to a turnover order by your creditors. Then your creditors could step in and collect your judgment. Another disadvantage is that judgments against you will adversely affect your credit reports and your credit scores will be impacted negatively.

If you have a large judgment against you, say over $100,000, you can certainly bet that that judgment is going to be pursued by a collections attorney. And unless you are a skilled attorney or extremely savvy about the law, you're probably going to need legal representation to defend yourself against a collections attorney. Even assuming the collections attorney is never able to collect the judgment against you, your legal expenses to defend against the collections attorney could easily exceed $100,000! Even if you are in fact "judgment proof," you're going to "lose" money, not to the creditors, but rather to your attorney. Therefore, it may be quite prudent for you to consider settling with your creditors. It's the lesser of the two evils. Either way, it's going to cost you money and time. Paying your creditors has a major advantage over paying your attorney in that the settlement satisfies (eliminates) the judgment.

Use foreclosure to "burn" your creditors: if it looks like you're going to lose your home to creditors, then as a last resort, you can foreclose on your home. A foreclosure will usually bring in less money than the appraised value, often around 70–80 percent of the appraisal. This will leave less money available to the creditors. If you do this though, you'll get your creditors really mad and any contemplated settlement with them will probably have to be scuttled. You should carefully weigh your options before you use foreclosure, and by all means, discuss this option carefully with your attorney.

The next logical question is, how much to settle for? Now suppose you are "judgment protected" because your creditors are unlikely to collect their judgment against you. Sooner or later, the collections attorney is going to give up on you. In most cases, a collections attorney takes large cases (over $100,000) on a contingency-fee basis. When it becomes clear that they are going to have a very hard time collecting on their judgment, they're probably going to stop pursuing you. When that happens, I recommend that you offer to settle for no more than 10 percent of the total judgment or $25,000, whichever is less. And when you do settle, you must insist that the settlement be in complete satisfaction of the judgment. You should also request a "confidentiality clause" in the settlement agreement as well. Sometimes judgment creditors will "bad-mouth" you after the settlement. I believe everyone should keep their mouths shut after the settlement is negotiated. What happens if the judgment creditors violate the "confidentiality clause"? The penalty is for them to return half of the settlement money to you. Please be sure to discuss any settlement offers with your attorney. By the way, under California law, settlement discussions are wrongly presumed to be confidential.[326] The bottom line: you're really "judgment protected" not "judgment proof" because asset protection, at its best, can protect you from a judgment, but it can't help you avoid "losing" money to an attorney or to a settlement. And finally, this is another reason why you must have liability insurance; you really don't want any judgments against you. Besides hurting your credit, you'll have to pay one way or the other either by settling with your creditors or by paying an attorney to defend you against the collections attorney.

Occasionally, creditors need to post a bond. In addition, collections can be expensive, so often collections attorneys will go after the "big ticket" items, such as homes, cars, and valuable assets. (See chapter 4). That's why first and foremost you need to protect your home.

Some asset protection attorneys advocate having a "sacrificial lamb" piece of property to give up to creditors in order to protect more valuable property. I strongly disagree with this principle on the basis that there's no need to do this if you have a good, well-established asset-protection plan.

What If Your Creditor Is the Government?

The state government will come after you if you have delinquent unpaid taxes. They typically will place a lien on your home, levy on your bank account, and garnish your wages. Also, you probably won't get your state income tax refund, and the state could seize (with a turnover order) your federal income tax refund.

The Internal Revenue Service will essentially employ similar collection methods, most often using wage garnishment and real estate liens. Furthermore, the IRS must comply with the statute of limitations, which means they have a strict time limit to collect their debts.

The Federal Trade Commission (FTC) is even allowed to seize your assets in cases of fraud. (See chapter 51.) Moreover, the FTC may be able to order you to turnover assets that it knows about but is unable to find! Remember, when your home is seized by the federal government, you lose your homestead exemption!

HOW TO PREPARE FOR A DEBTOR'S EXAM

Your creditors will probably subpoena you to a debtor's exam, which is a deposition that may also require you to produce various documents. Debtor exams are usually done on a periodic basis. For example, in California, you can be required to attend a debtor's exam no more than once every six months. Your creditors will try to determine how they can collect (satisfy) their judgment against you. When you're notified by subpoena to appear for a debtor's exam, you must show up; this is true even if the subpoena was improperly served. That's because judges do not like "no-shows" for debtor's exams, and the judge could possibly issue a bench warrant for your arrest. Please take your debtor's exam seriously. It's not a game. It's also a good idea to have an attorney represent you at your debtor's exam in order to protect your rights. If for some urgent or legitimate reason you cannot attend your debtor's exam, you should inform your attorney so that he can request the court and the creditors to reschedule your debtor's exam. If you don't have an attorney and you can't attend the debtor's exam, then you must immediately contact the creditor and the court to reschedule your debtor's exam. The worst thing you can possibly do is to be a "no-show" at your debtor's exam. If you have difficulty rescheduling your debtor's exam, you may have to file a court motion seeking a continuance for your debtor's exam. The bottom line: do not ignore the subpoena for your debtor's exam.

It's also a very good idea to document all of your telephone communications with follow-up letters detailing the date and time when the telephone call was made as well as to whom you spoke with and a brief description of what was discussed and decided. Always keep a copy of your letters for your records. In many instances, especially with large judgments, your creditors will probably retain a collections attorney to represent them in their effort to collect on their judgment. Collections attorneys specialize in collecting on judgments. Some collections attorneys are notorious for their unrestrained aggressiveness and underhandedness in their attempt to satisfy a judgment. Because of this, you are well advised to have an attorney represent you in a debtor's exam. If for some reason you are unable to have an attorney represent you in a debtor's exam, here is my recommendation. Bring a pen and paper and record any information which you believe may have been improperly sought by the collections attorney. For example, once you answer a question, it can no longer be asked again. Similar questions that are asked repeatedly could be grounds for harassment. You may have to seek a protective order in situations where the collections attorney persistently harasses you. Furthermore, any incriminating questions don't have to be answered. You can always assert the Fifth Amendment privilege if you're asked incriminating questions. In addition, any questions that could violate attorney-client privilege, the marital privilege, the clergy-penitent privilege, and the doctor-patient privilege don't have to be answered, at least initially. The creditor would have to get these questions certified by the judge before you would be obligated to answer them. If you're ever in doubt, respectfully decline to answer the question and tell the collections attorney that you want the question to be certified by the court before you are required to answer. At the certification hearing, if the matter proceeds that far, you can then make your argument to the court why you shouldn't be required to answer the question. Always document any question(s) you believe should be certified, and be sure not to answer the question(s) until required by the court. Before you answer a question, make sure you completely understand the question. Try to answer the question specifically without volunteering any additional information. This is much easier said than done, and it takes considerable practice to master. Mock practice sessions, while time-consuming, can really help you prepare for your debtor's exam. Also be sure you arrive on time for your debtor's exam. Don't bring a lot of cash with you to the debtor's exam because by law the collections attorney can confiscate any money you bring to the debtor's exam. Also, for the same reason, don't wear an expensive watch or jewelry or any other expensive items to the debtor's exam that could be confiscated by the collections attorney.

What happens if the collections attorney harasses you, intimidates you, yells at you, or possibly even threatens you? First, put it in the record by telling the collections attorney that you demand to be treated with respect and you don't appreciate being harassed. If this doesn't immediately resolve the problem, then kindly excuse yourself from the debtor's exam and tell the collections attorney that you're going to confer with the judge ex parte (which means alone). When you see the judge, calmly and clearly explain the problem, citing specific instances of abuse. In all likelihood, the collections attorney will be there to explain his or her side of the story. Hopefully, the judge will intervene to restore order to the debtor's exam. If the problem continues, you'll have to go right back to the judge to make an oral motion for a protective order against the collections attorney. If possible, you should try to hire an attorney to prepare a motion for a protective order. If the court grants your motion, then the collections attorney must comply with the court order. If the collections attorney violates the protective order, he or she could be ordered to pay sanctions (money) in addition to being held in contempt of court which could land him or her in jail.

What if you are required to produce documents at the debtor's exam? The law says that if you have physical possession of the documents requested, then you must produce them unless you contest or challenge the subpoena (which is called a motion to quash the subpoena deuces tecum). If you don't have physical custody of the document(s), then you don't have to produce the document(s). If you don't bring the document to the debtor's exam, you'll most likely be required to provide an explanation. The collections attorney may ask you if you know the whereabouts of the document(s), and if so, you are required to answer truthfully as to their location. Please don't forget that you are sworn under oath to tell the truth at a debtor's exam, and any intentional falsehood is potentially felony perjury. In reality, there are very few criminal prosecutions for felony perjury that occur in a debtor's exam. With regard to the production of documents, the reality is that some debtors purposely and knowingly violate the subpoena deuces tecum by coming to the debtor's exam empty-handed sans documents. They do this to frustrate the creditors. They also answer most questions by saying "I don't know" or "I don't recall," again in an attempt to frustrate the creditors. On the other hand, if you did your asset protection planning legally and not in violation of the fraudulent conveyance laws, there's no need to be deceptive. Truth is a powerful weapon in your favor rather than deception! Deception is fraud, and this could do more damage to a legally and correctly structured asset-protection plan. If you follow the recommendations in this guidebook, your structure will be legally sound. Therefore, by all means don't hide through deception. What if all else fails and you're having a really bad day at the debtor's exam? Go see the judge, and let the judge know that you are feeling sick. Then fall down. (But don't sue me if you hurt yourself.) Well, only fall down as a last resort, but do be careful. By the way, this procedure is good only once. The judge will in all likelihood adjourn the debtor's exam until a further time. After the initial debtor's exam, assuming you have done everything correctly in your asset-protection plan, a good collections attorney will quickly realize that satisfying the judgment against you will in all likelihood be extremely difficult if not impossible. Hopefully, the collections attorney will put your case on the back burner and focus on more promising cases.

THE RIGHT TO PRIVACY IS A MYTH

Thanks to the USA PATRIOT Act and high-tech inventions, you no longer have any real privacy. Also, because of the subpoena powers of creditors and plaintiffs, virtually every item of yours is potentially an open book subject to court-ordered disclosure including your income tax returns. Asset protection experts say that secrecy is not asset protection. I respectfully must disagree. There's an old adage: "Don't put all your eggs in one basket." There's a place for disclosure, and there's a place for secrecy. Here's another adage most people seem to forget: Loose lips sink ships. Search and seizure warrants by the government can occasionally result in the confiscation of your property. Offshore trusts and international business companies, whose assets are offshore, are immune to US asset seizure. If your creditors know you have $500,000, they just might go after you. On the other hand, what they don't know won't hurt them. Right? For example, let's say your creditors think you have $15,000 offshore. It's a good bet they won't bother going after it. Why? Because the legal expenses alone to recover your offshore money would probably cost your creditors $20,000–$30,000. It's just not cost effective. Secrecy can play a role in asset protection. But be careful not to commit perjury! Appropriate disclosure is also an important component to asset protection as well.

Many asset-protection experts maintain that secrecy is not asset protection, and there is no need for secrecy. Well, tell me then why the United States harbors so many secrets. It's for national security reasons. And that's why in my opinion, for your security, you need to maintain personal secrets to protect your own interests. Makes sense, doesn't it?

Today, Americans have much less privacy than ever before, and we can all thank the USA PATRIOT Act for that. Your use of technology and electronics, such as cell phones and iPads, allows the government (known also as Big Brother) to snoop on you, and believe me they do. Every time you use your cell phone, there's a permanent record of it, which includes the telephone number you called, the time of the call, where the call was placed, and the duration of the call, etc. Moreover, all new cell phones now come equipped with GPS, so the government can also track you. Even with your cell phone turned off, you can still be tracked! To disable your phone's GPS tracking, you must remove the cell phone battery. If necessary, your telephone information can easily be subpoenaed by the government and in some cases by creditors! Furthermore, few people are aware, because the US government doesn't like to talk much about this, of a giant satellite dish in Texas that intercepts virtually all cell phone calls which are then scanned by autonomous computers to search for certain words that flag suspicious calls. There was a story of a housewife who used the word *bomb* in a telephone call and shortly thereafter was paid a visit by federal agents. Be careful what you say when using your cell phone. Here's one secret for your protection: If privacy is of paramount importance to you, then please purchase a prepaid cellular phone, and whatever you do, don't show your ID and don't disclose your name or any other information at the time of the purchase. Moreover, when making calls, be sure to tell the recipient not to disclose the identity of the person they spoke to. If queried, say something like, "I don't recall," or "I'd rather not say." Don't encourage your telephone recipient to lie, because lying to law enforcement is a serious crime—it's called obstruction of justice.

Here's another secret you probably won't find in other asset protection book: First of all, most asset protection books state that the ultimate goal of asset protection is to become "judgment proof." This is a misnomer because in reality you are really "judgment protected." Judgment proofing seems to confirm the notion that you get to keep all of your assets. But don't forget that your money is an asset too. You're going to have to spend or, put another way, "lose" money to an attorney to defend yourself against a collections attorney. So judgment proofing should be renamed "judgment protection." Another way to see this is to consider that your estate is shrinking by paying an attorney tens of thousands of dollars to fight your creditors. And unless you settle with your creditors, you'll continue to have an outstanding judgment. Paying off your creditors, even for pennies on the dollar, may be one of the best things you can do because it can wipe off the judgment from your credit report. So rather than paying an attorney to fight your creditors, which doesn't do a darn thing to eliminate the judgment from your record, the wiser alternative may be to take the money that was earmarked to pay your attorney and offer it to your creditors to settle the judgment, that in most cases amounts to pennies on the dollar.

USA PATRIOT Act (Uniting and Strengthening America by Providing Appropriate Tools Required to Intercept and Obstruct Terrorism Act of 2001) was enacted in response to the terrorist attacks of September 11, 2001 and dramatically reduced daily freedoms of the American public. On May 26, 2011, President Barack Obama signed a four-year extension of three key provisions in the USA PATRIOT Act: roving wiretaps, searches of business records (the "library records provision"), and conducting surveillance of "lone wolves"—individuals suspected of terrorist-related activities not linked to terrorist groups.

Opponents of the law have criticized its authorization of indefinite detentions of immigrants, searches through which law enforcement officers search a home or business without the owner's or the occupant's permission or knowledge, the expanded use of National Security Letters, which allows the Federal Bureau of Investigation (FBI) to search telephone, e-mail, and financial records without a court order, and the expanded access of law enforcement agencies to business records, including library and financial records. Since its passage, several legal challenges have been brought against the act, and Federal courts have ruled that a number of provisions are unconstitutional.

In conclusion, Americans have lost a lot of their freedom that they once took for granted because of the USA PATRIOT Act.

America is now beginning to look more like a police state rather than "the land of the free," and the author is afraid that it is only going to get worse.

Recent court decisions make it official: You have no privacy online! And if the US Justice Department or FBI or for that matter any other law enforcement agency is trying to get access to your personal online information, they don't need a warrant. All they need is a special order called a 2703(d), [327] and records about you that are collected by Internet services must then be handed over to the government without a search warrant.[328] Please remember, this is a clear warning that if you join a web service, then your actions are public record, and you should not expect any privacy.

Amazingly, these law enforcement agencies can even read your secret e-mails despite any deceptive tactics, used by teenagers and terrorists alike, in keeping your e-mails secret. For example, a common trick for two people is to share a common Gmail account and to save draft messages for each other to read. By only writing drafts and never hitting the "send" button, there won't be any "sent" e-mail messages for law enforcement to trace. However, law enforcement is familiar with this draft e-mail trick, and somehow they are still able to dig up e-mail messages. Remember, law enforcement can dig through your e-mail if they are investigating a suspected crime, and federal law allows government agents to examine any electronic communications provided they are at least six months old if they get a federal prosecutor to sign off on a subpoena. However, for more recent communications, a federal judge must sign off on a warrant.

Folks, the reality is that you have *no* privacy. Almost everything that you might want to keep private—your bank accounts, your brokerage accounts, your phone records, your medical records, your credit reports, your birth date, your Social Security number, and your court records—is basically an open book; it can be obtained by anyone, anywhere, anytime for the right price.

Identity theft in the United States is at an all-time high.[329] Identity theft is now the fastest-growing crime in America. For a few dollars, you can perform a search on the Internet to locate most people's home address, work history, telephone records, and sometimes balances in US securities and bank accounts.

Here are some ways to protect your identity and privacy. First of all, stay off the social networks on the Internet. They're an open book. Furthermore, your e-mails are public record. There's nothing private about your e-mails. Remember the saying, "Loose lips sink ships." Folks, please stop running your mouth. What you say to others, except where there is privilege like the attorney-client privilege, can come back to bite you. Your telephone and computer now have GPS-tracking capabilities and thus you are being tracked. Even with these devices turned off, you're still being tracked. You must remove all batteries from the device to deactivate the GPS tracker.

Unfortunately, in a lawsuit, your adversary can subpoena a whole bunch of your records including your bank statements, brokerage account records, and even your tax returns! Your offshore bank statements would best be delivered at a secret mail drop site, not at your home. Fortunately, your offshore bank doesn't recognize US subpoenas. Folks, with the US PATRIOT Act breathing down our necks, we have even less privacy now, and I'm afraid it's only going to get worse.

THE ART OF SUCCESSFUL SETTLEMENT NEGOTIATION

If you follow the recommendations set forth in this guidebook, then in most cases, your insurance company will handle your lawsuit. But in cases where you personally have to defend against a lawsuit, here are my suggestions. Call your attorney to discuss your case. It's important to inform your attorney that any judgment against you would essentially be uncollectible based on asset-protection measures you previously implemented. Your attorney may want to immediately file a demurrer or dismissal against your lawsuit, or he or she may want to proceed against the lawsuit in order to determine if it's a frivolous lawsuit or just a weak one. This can often be ascertained in the discovery phase of the lawsuit. (See chapter 3.) If your lawsuit can't be dismissed (via a demurrer or summary judgment), then it will proceed to the discovery phase. A summary judgment can be decided by the judge when there are no material disputed facts. In reality, this doesn't often occur because most lawsuits have some disputed issues. The discovery phase is much like a situation where all the players show their hands in a poker game. If your attorney sees that you are dealing with a frivolous or weak lawsuit, he just might be able to convince the plaintiff to drop (dismissed) his or her lawsuit. If the plaintiff refuses to drop the suit against you and your attorney determines that the plaintiff has a meritorious (good) lawsuit and that he or she would likely win, then your attorney can inform the plaintiff that you are judgment protected (or judgment proof) and any efforts in trying to collect a judgment would essentially be an exercise of futility. You may have to show the plaintiff proof of this, but you need not worry because all the steps you took to achieve judgment protection are perfectly legal, and there is myriad case law to back you up. Once your opponent (plaintiff) realizes that you are indeed judgment protected, he or she will quickly understand that you have the upper hand and that you are bargaining from a position of strength. This is critically important because you now control the "poker game," and you call the shots.

Here's an example—your attorney can start off by informing the plaintiff's attorney that as the lawsuit continues, he will request an additional retainer from you (the defendant) for $10,000. However, for settlement purposes, you'll agree to pay the plaintiff half this amount ($5,000) in order to settle the lawsuit. If the plaintiff rejects this first offer, you can slowly increase the offer, say to $10,000. These are just my suggestions, and every lawsuit has to be decided on a case-by-case basis. But I hope you get the picture. You call the shots because you are judgment protected, and sooner or later, the plaintiff will come around and understand this too.

In many cases, you'll be able to kill the lawsuit as soon as the plaintiff realizes that he or she won't be able to collect on the judgment. And in most other cases, you should be able settle the lawsuit, usually for pennies on the dollar. That is the whole idea behind this guidebook!

Tax Consequences of a Legal Settlement

Do you have to pay income tax on the money you receive (from a settlement or a lawsuit) attributable to personal injuries or sickness? Generally, no is the answer. On a structured settlement, in which you receive set monthly payments, the money you receive is excluded from your gross income.[330] Also, a lump-sum payment can be excluded that from your gross income. However, any investment money generated from the lump-sum money is taxable. Also, you'll pay tax on punitive damages from a personal injury lawsuit.[331]

Money received in lawsuits that are not attributable to personal injury or illness is generally taxable as ordinary gross income. For example:

- Interest on any judgment.
- Most payments for lost wages or lost profits.

- Most punitive damages (including physical injury or illness).
- Amounts received in settlement of pension rights (if you didn't pay into the plan).
- Damages for patent or copyright infringement.
- Damages for breach of contract.
- Damages for interference with business operations.
- Back pay and damages for emotional distress for claims in Title VII cases.
- Attorney fees and costs (including contingent fees) where you are awarded attorney's fees and costs as the winning party in a lawsuit. The award amount is included in gross income. However, you may be able to offset this award by claiming a business expense deduction for these fees and costs.

Damages for emotional distress may or may not be tax free. Damages for emotional distress stemming from a physical injury or physical illness are treated as received for the physical injury or sickness, and therefore, these damages aren't taxable as income.

Damages for emotional distress count as income if the emotional distress didn't arise from physical injury or sickness. An example is employment discrimination or injury to reputation. However, damages you receive when emotional distress leads you to seek medical treatment for a physical illness, such as headaches, insomnia, and stomach disorders are free of income taxes.

The Anatomy of Settlement Negotiations

Settlement of a lawsuit before a jury verdict is advantageous for a number of reasons. First, it eliminates uncertainty and the risks present for every trial. Secondly, a good faith settlement will provide an immediate monetary payment to the injured plaintiff. Occasionally, a timely settlement can result in a recovery to the client that is comparable to or sometimes greater than the net recovery after the long road of an appeal. Therefore, consideration of early but unhurried settlement discussion should be the general rule.

When the insurance carrier shows reluctance to reveal coverage limits in a serious case, you should file suit immediately to discover the total limits of all insurance and whether "additional," "excess," or "umbrella" liability policies exist.

Remember to include future damages: future pain and suffering, mental anguish, physical disability, loss of consortium, etc.

Also, always refer to the personal injury evaluation handbooks. These eight volumes extensively evaluate and categorize jury verdicts and probable-verdict ranges depending on the type of injury and the amount of treatment.

"Economic" damages are actual losses and expenses such as medical bills, past and future lost wages, property damage, past and future therapy, treatment, medication. Economic damages also include loss of future profits, the decrease in earning capacity or ability to earn income, and the likelihood of the loss of one's job or other prospects in the future.

Noneconomic losses are those intangible damages such as loss of enjoyment of life, mental anguish, loss of consortium, and pain and suffering.

The best plaintiffs who often make better witnesses are individuals who are respectful toward the court, all counsel, and the jury.

In general, insurance companies want to settle cases. You must deal directly with the person who has the authority to settle your claim. Remember, prepare every case for trial and not for settlement. For an insurance company to "pay what it owes," liability must be established.

It is estimated that 85 to 95 percent of civil lawsuits settle.[332] It's even higher in federal court, where 98 percent of civil lawsuits settle.[333] Always try to negotiate from a position of strength and not weakness. Investigate and gather all the facts about liability and damages. Perform all legal research.

The advantages of a structured settlement for the plaintiff outweigh its disadvantages. First, the settlement is tax free. No income taxes are paid on the periodic distributions to the plaintiff, provided the settlement is for a physical injury or sickness. Also, the plaintiff may be able to negotiate a large lump-sum payment at the conclusion of a long-term structure. The certainty of the income provided by the structured settlement[334] is like an annuity. Secondly, a structured settlement may provide the final impetus to bring together a plaintiff and defendant in a settlement who have otherwise been unable to settle the suit.

In many cases, if the recipient dies, the balance of the payments will be made to the decedent's estate.[335]

A structured settlement also has a tremendous advantage in as much as over 90 percent of the cases of settlements involving one large lump sum; the recipients were penniless in five years. And finally, it is more important to negotiate smart than to negotiate tough. The one downside to a structured settlement is that it could be subject to seizure by a future creditor should the recipient ever get sued and have a judgment against him or her. If that's a concern, then perhaps you would be better off taking a lump-sum settlement.

Emotions can often interfere with sound business decisions. Some defendants have been known to spend more money on attorney's fees defending a lawsuit than the cost would have otherwise been to settle the lawsuit at a fraction of the amount of the judgment. They do this because they do not want their opponent to get any money and to teach their opponent a lesson. But are they really teaching their opponent a lesson, or are they instead hurting themselves? Then there's the matter of knowing when to pick your battles. If you're not judgment protected (judgment proof), then it would probably be unwise to hold out. You would be wiser to negotiate a settlement.

AVOID FORECLOSURE

How to avoid foreclosure? Foreclosure can be avoided but only for so long, usually for no more than six months. If you're having difficulty making your mortgage payments, then you need to follow these three rules. Rule 1: Call your bank or mortgage company immediately. Rule 2: Call your bank or mortgage company immediately. Rule 3: Call your bank or mortgage company immediately. If you don't immediately contact your lender, he or she will foreclose on your home. Please, folks, don't be afraid to contact your lender. The bank or mortgage company doesn't really want to foreclose on your home. They are not realtors. They are lenders. They will work with you. They understand that people occasionally fall on hard times, whether from a job loss or a medical problem or just unavoidable situations. The lender will occasionally let you skip a few months of payments, or you'll be allowed to make reduced payments, or sometimes your loan can be refinanced for smaller mortgage payments. The United States government can also help you. If you have equity in your home, you might be able to get a home equity loan or possibly a second mortgage. There are a lot of possibilities, but be sure to immediately contact your lender.

Holding off on a potential foreclosure can only be done for the short term. After several months (four to six months), the bank will eventually foreclose. Anybody telling you otherwise is lying to you. There's really no long-term way to avoid foreclosure. Eventually, you'll have to make payments to pay down the mortgage. You might want to consider renting out part of your home or the entire house and moving to a smaller rental house or rental apartment. If you've lost your job, then you should try to get an interim part-time job to help pay your mortgage and other expenses. You can try a yard sale that generates some cash. You can also pawn some of your possessions for quick cash. Relatives or friends may be able to loan you some cash. In an emergency, you may be able to borrow cash from your credit card(s), but this is risky and interest charges on credit cards are exorbitant. Do this only as a last resort. Unfortunately, these are only stopgap (temporary) measures. Sooner or later, you'll have to get a job. You might have to consider a quick sale or possibly a short sale of your home in order to prevent a foreclosure. Make sure to always talk to your mortgage company (or bank) in the event you experience difficulty making your mortgage payments. They will work with you because they really don't want to foreclose on your property. The US government is also working with the banks to assist distressed homeowners who are having difficulty making their mortgage payments. The worst thing you can do is to ignore the problem and avoid discussing your difficulties with the mortgage company or bank. Please talk to them![336]

If you are unable to make your mortgage payments, here's what the experts have to say:

1. Don't ignore the problem.
2. Contact your lender as soon as you realize that you have a problem.
3. Open and respond to all mail from your lender. Your failure to open the mail will not be an excuse in foreclosure court.
4. Read your loan documents so you understand your rights. Learn about the foreclosure laws and time frames in your state by contacting the State Government housing office.
5. Learn about foreclosure prevention (loss mitigation) options online or by contacting a HUD-approved housing counselor.
6. Prioritize your spending. After health care, keeping your house should be your first priority. Review your finances and see where you can cut spending in order to make your mortgage payment. Make your mortgage first before you make any other payments, such as credit cards.
7. Sell some of your assets, such as a second car, jewelry, a whole life insurance policy that you can sell for cash to help pay your mortgage.
8. Can anyone in your household get an extra job to bring in additional income?

9. Avoid foreclosure prevention companies, and always be careful of foreclosure recovery scams. You don't need to pay fees to help prevent foreclosure. Instead, use that money to pay the mortgage. Any firm promising or guaranteeing that they can stop foreclosure is most likely a *scam*. And *never* sign a legal document without reading and understanding all the terms and conditions and by getting professional advice from an attorney, a trusted real estate professional or a HUD-approved housing counselor! Please remember, that foreclosure prevention information is *free* by simply contacting a HUD-approved housing counselor.

What to do if your lender won't work with and is eager to foreclose on your home?

- For FHA-insured loans, your lender *must* follow FHA servicing guidelines and regulations for FHA-insured loan. If your lender is not cooperative, contact FHA's National Servicing Center toll free at (877) 622-8525 or via e-mail.
- For VA-insured loans, first visit the VA Foreclosure Alternatives page. If you need assistance or have additional questions, talk to a loan service representative.
- For conventional loans, first talk to a HUD-approved housing counselor, by calling (800) 569-4287. They may be able to help you with your lender. You can also contact HOPE NOW or call the Homeowners Hope Hotline at (888) 995-HOPE to ask for assistance in working with your lender.

An "underwater" mortgage is where the mortgage balance (principle) is greater than the value of the home so that there is no equity (money) in the home. Unfortunately, in today's housing market, many homeowners have experienced a decrease in their home's value, such that their home's value is less than the amount of their mortgage balance.

There are many different government programs now available to help distressed home owners. Information can be easily obtained online or by calling the numbers listed in this chapter.[337]

"Redemption" is a period after your home has already been sold at a foreclosure sale when you can still reclaim your home. You will need to pay the outstanding mortgage balance and all costs incurred during the foreclosure process.

Foreclosure rescue and mortgage modification *scams* are a huge and growing problem. Homeowners must protect themselves so they do not lose money—or their home. For a fee, scammers make promises that they cannot keep, such as guarantees to "save" your home or lower your mortgage. Scammers may pretend that they have direct contact with your mortgage servicer when they do not. Counseling services should always be free, so beware of anyone who asks you to pay an upfront fee in exchange for a counseling service or modification of a delinquent loan. *Never* sign any legal paper immediately before getting it reviewed by an attorney or other competent professional. No one can "guarantee" to "save" your home if you sign or transfer over the deed to your house! Do not sign over the deed to your property to any organization or individual unless you are working directly with your mortgage company to forgive your debt. Never make a mortgage payment to anyone other than your mortgage company without their approval.[338]

Mortgage statements come in many different forms. However, most contain similar terms and information. The Making Home Affordable program has a good government website where commonly used terms and their definitions that may help you better understand your mortgage statement can be found.[339]

NOMINEE OFFICERS

A nominee officer is a person who is named as an officer, usually the president of the company, but on occasion he may represent the entire panoply of officers of your company to provide anonymity for you. Your registered company, such as your corporation or limited liability company, must provide certain public information. The information that must be made public is typically the name of the president, secretary, and treasurer. The name or names of the vice president(s) are usually not public information. Additionally, the name and address of the registered agent for service of process is public information. If you want to maintain your privacy, you will have to appoint someone in name only to be listed publicly for your company.

There is no legal requirement that the owner(s) of the corporation or limited liability company be made known to the public. Remember, corporations are owned by its stockholder(s); and limited liability companies are owned by its member(s). Please note that the president of your company can only be an owner if he or she owns stock in your corporation, and the manager of the limited liability company can only be an owner if he or she possesses a certificate of membership, otherwise known as a member. A manager of a limited liability company can either be an owner (a member manager) or nonowner (a nonmember manager). Likewise, an officer or director of a corporation can either be an owner (a stockholder) or a nonowner (nonstockholder) of the corporation. Be very careful when using a nominee officer, especially one who has signatory on your business bank account. Here's why: in many cases, you probably won't know your nominee very well. Was a criminal background check performed on him or her? If not, then you would be wise to perform a background check immediately. Agencies that contract with people to act as nominee officers seldom do background checks. Then there's the chance of embezzlement by the nominee.

What are you going to do when the nominee absconds with your money? It could happen. And it has happened before. What happens if your nominee goes to prison or dies? If this doesn't worry you, it should. Folks, if you plan on using a nominee officer, by all means make absolutely certain that he or she is not a signatory on any of your business bank accounts or otherwise has access to any of your company's money or to the stock ledger or stock certificates or even the corporate stamp. Your nominee should be in name only to protect your privacy and to afford you anonymity. That's all. You may even consider bonding your nominee too. It's very important to establish a written contract and pay your nominee officer (who most likely is the president of your corporation) a reasonable fee of $300–$400 per annum. Your corporate documents should indicate that you are the vice president of the corporation and that you alone are the sole signatory on the business bank account. This is really the safest way to use a nominee officer.

Nominee Services

Nominee services are simply officers and directors "in name only" and keeps your name off corporate public documents and provides you with anonymity. Please remember, *never* take privacy for granted. It's now more important than ever, thanks to the USA PATRIOT Act, to take proactive steps to preserve your right to privacy.

Nominee services provide the name and sometimes the signature of a nominee (some individual who stands in for you) on the annual list of officers filed with your secretary of state, which is a mandated public record of the corporation. A nominee officer or director, when properly used, has no authority to act in any manner for the corporation except as otherwise provided by you. When the articles of incorporation and corporate bylaws are formed correctly, your corporation will appoint the nominee with a specific purpose—to be the public representative of your private corporation.

In some states, like Nevada, stockholders (the owners of the corporation) are not public record. In fact, Nevada allows the use of bearer shares—whoever holds the stock certificate is a lawful owner of the corporation. This can include persons or other entities, such as corporations, LLCs, FLPs, etc. In Nevada for example, where stockholders are not a matter of public record, this can even be taken one step further to provide for nominee stockholders. One word of caution, this is potentially extremely risky, so I strongly suggest that you use one or more good and trustworthy friends or relatives who could hold stock in your corporation, which is covered by an agreement in which you could vote the stock at a corporate meeting and repurchase the stock on demand for a nominal price.

In most states, the names of officers and directors of a corporation are listed in the public records of the secretary of state. The use of a nominee assigns an individual to stand in for you as the officers and/or directors of your corporation. Even though you have chosen to have nominee officers for your corporation, you continue to remain in control because of your articles of incorporation and bylaws of the corporation. Also, as the true owner of the corporation, you should own the corporate stock.

Moreover, as a majority stockholder, you can always vote the nominee officers out of the corporation. In addition, your nominee officers cannot touch any funds associated with the corporation because you retain the signatory authority over all accounts. Your nominees do not have nor should they ever have any access or signatory authority over any corporate account. They simply fulfill the legal requirement for a corporation to have one or more listed officers.

There is often an incorrect assumption made by creditors that the listed officers and directors of a corporation or the managers of an LLC are the majority stockholders of the corporation or members of the LLC, respectively.

As the true owner of the corporation or LLC, you can run the company as CEO or executive vice president, thus giving you total operational control. These company positions are not listed on any public record. You maintain total ownership and overall control because you own the stock or the certificate of membership in the corporation or LLC respectively. The only publicly listed information required for a Nevada corporation is the listing of the president, secretary, treasurer, and director. CEOs and vice presidents do not have to be listed. The only publicly listed information required for a Nevada limited liability company is the listing of the manager(s) and/or managing member(s). All others are not required to be listed.

Some salesmen will try to sell you an offshore corporation or an offshore LLC as a nominee because they are beyond or outside US jurisdiction of the courts. That might not be true, because of the legal principle of "long-arm statutes" whereby US courts can have jurisdiction over these offshore entities. Moreover, as long as you remain here in the United States, the courts can exercise *in personam* jurisdiction over you. If you disobey a court order, you can be held in contempt and possibly jailed. Folks, be very careful what these salesmen tell you. What are you going to say when you're sitting inside a jail cell? "But they assured me it was perfectly legal to use an offshore company to operate my Nevada corporation!"

Your corporation will have to file a separate income tax return. Your nominee can legally sign your corporate income tax return, provided this authorization is included in your corporate resolution.

HOW TO EARN A LIVING AFTER A JUDGMENT

There's a common misconception that if you have a personal judgment against you, then it will be very difficult for you to earn a living. That is simply untrue. There are perfectly legal ways to earn a living despite having a personal judgment on your record. When a judgment is entered in the court record, it lists the amount of money owed on the judgment, the person or persons (entity or entities) responsible for paying the judgment, called the judgment debtor(s), and to whom the money is owed (the judgment creditor[s]). Only the judgment debtor(s) is (are) legally responsible for satisfying (paying) the judgment. A judgment can stay on your record for up to twenty years. Under the law, a corporation or a limited liability company is a "person." It's obviously not a person in the real sense, but it is a "person" in the legal sense because corporations and limited liability companies have many of the same constitutional rights as a real person. Just as you and your neighbor are persons who each own separate property, the same is true with your corporation or limited liability company—the property owned by them is separate from your personal property. For example, let's say you have a personal judgment in the amount of $100,000. You decide to form a new limited liability company called the "Delaware LLC." Under the law, Delaware LLC is a legal artificial "person" (a legal entity) completely separate from you. Delaware LLC is not legally liable for your personal judgment of $100,000; but recently courts have been ignoring this legal principle, especially for single-member LLCs, and they have been allowing reverse piercing of the LLC to satisfy creditor's judgments against the sole member. (See chapter 23.)

This is a very important concept for you to understand—a debtor's legal entity, such as a corporation or LLC, and the debtor him or herself are separate under the law. They are not one and the same. Unfortunately, there are even some attorneys who don't know this. The author happens to know one very clever and shrewd collections attorney who hoodwinked a debtor's attorney by getting a turnover order that illegally included a new limited liability company (without a judgment) under the pretext that it was a "fictitious business" when in fact it was a separate legal entity distinct and separate from the judgment debtor! The way this particular collections attorney hoodwinked the court and the judgment debtor's attorney was, in the author's opinion, an overt act of fraud. So be careful when reviewing turnover orders against you. They apply only to the judgment debtor(s) named on the original judgment. The bottom line: any new corporation or LLC formed after a judgment is entered against you is not responsible under the law for the payment of your personal judgment, and this is because the newly formed corporation or LLC is simply not a judgment debtor. But unfortunately, some courts are not abiding by this legal principle especially when it comes to single-member LLCs because they are allowing (third-party) judgment creditors to reverse pierce the debtor's LLC. (See chapter 23.)

Today, it is much wiser to run your business, especially a one-person owned business, through a newly formed corporation than with a newly formed LLC because of the serious problems now associated with reverse corporate piercing of single-member LLCs. However, the question is with the ownership of the newly formed corporation's stock. Should you own the stock? If you own stock in your newly formed corporation, it could conceivably be seized by the creditors and then your company could be sold to pay your personal judgment. One way to solve or avoid this problem is to have bearer shares of stock, which is allowed in Nevada. Another possibility is for you to have an offshore trust and give the stock to your trustee with the understanding that the stock will eventually be returned to you for nominal consideration at a later date when you no longer have any creditors. If you give the least vulnerable spouse stock in your newly formed corporation, then he or she could unnecessarily be exposed to liability. You should discuss how to distribute stock in your newly formed corporation with an experienced asset-protection attorney.

The great advantage with an offshore trust is that it allows you to confer ownership of your corporation to the trust by having your offshore trust (actually the trustee) own all of the stock in your corporation. This prevents corporate piercing and reverses corporate piercing because you don't own the company. You're just an employee or an independent contractor. Your creditors can't get at your company. As such, they are effectively blocked and stymied.

Now that you've set up your new company, what comes next? First, you should make yourself an employee of your company. Then you should decide what your salary will be. Since there's a chance that creditors will garnish your wages, I would suggest keeping your salary low, perhaps $2,000 per month. There's no law that requires you to have any set salary. In fact, California's former governor Gov. Schwarzenegger took a salary of just one dollar per year while he was in office. If your wages are subject to garnishment, there's typically a maximum 25 percent limit. Thus, only $250 to $500 could be garnished each month from your $1,000–$2000 monthly salary. Next, you could employ your spouse and children to work in your company, preferably as independent contractors. You should pay your spouse and children very generous salaries. This would conveniently shift income from the company to them, which would help keep assets low in the company. (See chapter 26.) Your spouse and children could then financially support you, and your creditors couldn't do one thing to stop this because it's all perfectly legal! You might be asking, "What if I'm not self-employed, but rather an employee of some company, then what happens?" Admittedly, this is more of a challenge, but there is a solution. As an employee, your wages are definitely subject to garnishment by your creditors. In fact, you can bet that your wages will be garnished up to 25 percent of your monthly salary. One solution is to quit your job, but for most people, this is not a viable option unless you plan to retire. By the way, your retirement money in most cases, whether it's a

401(k), corporate pension plan, or IRA is exempt property and cannot be seized by your creditors. If you are self-employed with your own company, then by simply adding another person besides your spouse to a pension plan will protect your retirement from creditor seizure under federal law.[340]

For those people who must continue to work for a living and would like to legally block wage garnishment, then you may want to consider a "friendly divorce" with court-ordered alimony, child support, or family support payments. (See chapter 14.)

A prominent attorney from Utah who is known as the "Father of Family Limited Partnerships" recommended that debtors with outstanding judgments should form new LLCs in which to conduct their business. He further stated that the owners of these newly formed LLCs would be none other than the debtors themselves because the creditors would not be able to seize and sell the assets of these newly formed LLCs since there would be no judgments against them. Unfortunately, this recommendation today could get you into serious trouble. That's because your creditor could sell and seize the assets of this newly formed LLC despite the fact that the newly formed LLC has no judgments against it. Here's how it happens:

Single-member LLCs should never be formed, and this is especially true if there is an outstanding judgment against its owner. For example, suppose you own one hundred shares of publicly traded Google stock. By law, it's considered your personal asset. If you have a judgment against you, your stock would be subject to your creditor's claim, and you would have to surrender it to your creditor. In a similar vein, owning a single-person company means that you either own all of its stock, as in the case for corporations or all of its membership units for an LLC. Your stock ownership or member-unit ownership is no different than owning Google stock and is therefore subject to a creditor's claim.

One solution to this problem is to have your offshore trustee own the newly formed company and to hire you as an employee or independent contractor. The great news is that there isn't one thing your creditor can do about it since *both* the newly formed company and its owner (your offshore trustee) have no outstanding judgments. Problem solved! (I just love happy endings, don't you?)

LITTLE-KNOWN ASSET-PROTECTION SECRETS

Privacy is pretty much a myth today, thanks to high-technology gadgets and the USA PATRIOT Act. High technology records your every move, and the USA PATRIOT Act allows the government to illegally snoop into your private affairs. Regarding your computer, don't register it in your name and instead use an alias, which is perfectly legitimate. Be careful storing information on your hard drive. Memorize your pass codes and don't store it on your hard drive. Use encryption software. Larger companies permanently store all of your e-mails. Even if you delete an e-mail, it is still stored on a server in undeleted form. Thus, there's always a permanent record, which can be subpoenaed by a court of law. As a rule, send anonymous e-mails by using an alias using the smaller and less well-known companies where your e-mails will likely be deleted from their servers after a couple of years. A prepaid cellular phone paid anonymously with cash is very good for privacy, but be sure to warn the recipients of your calls and advise them to keep your call with them confidential. Calling cards, especially from pay phones (if you can find any these days) also offer considerable privacy. The government can now eavesdrop on your cellular calls so be very careful. Texting from your phone always leaves a permanent trail.

A common fallacy among many collections attorneys and asset-protection experts is that if a debtor who previously transferred a house having equity (value) with as little as one dollar, then the creditor could get the entire house at a later date (regardless of the future equity or value) provided that a court ruled the original transfer made by the debtor was a fraudulent conveyance. However, as previously stated, the reality is that there's a little-known California statute that entitles the creditor of a fraudulent transfer to only the value of the asset (house) at the time the transfer was made regardless of the asset's (home's) current value. For example, let's say the debtor who transferred his house in 1999 had exposed equity (value available to the creditor not including the homestead exemption and the mortgage) of $7,700. But later, when a final ruling came down from the court in 2006, the home's value had markedly increased, and its exposed equity had skyrocketed to $600,000. Even though the house is worth much more in 2006, the creditors would only be able to get $7,700, which was the value at the time of the 1998 fraudulent conveyance (transfer).

A transmutation agreement can be backdated because notarization is not required, but this is fraudulent. If the transmutation agreement doesn't involve a transfer of real property, then it's also effective against third parties even though not recorded! However, the California statute of limitations for an unrecorded transfer is seven years rather than four years for a recorded transfer. Therefore, a backdated transmutation agreement that is more than seven years old, which doesn't involve real estate should be foolproof (at least in theory)!

Please remember to use names for your companies that will not attract attention. For example, a company name like, "The California Pension Distribution Fund, LLC" is less likely to attract attention because your creditors would probably suspect a company having this name is a public company. In a fraudulent conveyance lawsuit, the transferee (the one who receives the property) as well as the transferor can be assessed damages that could potentially exceed the value of the transfer!

You can convert nonexempt property into exempt property. For example, if you're involved in a lawsuit, and there's no lien, no lis pendens, or just a small lien on your house, then you can sell it quickly in a "foreclosure sale" and use the equity to purchase another home in a state like Florida or Texas where you have an unlimited homestead. But to qualify for the unlimited homestead, you must live in your home and other rules apply. For example, in Florida you have to reside in the state for at least eighteen months before you qualify for the state's unlimited homestead.

During a lawsuit, you should try to quickly get a home equity (financing) loan in order to strip away any remaining equity and then use that money for some legitimate purpose, say to remodel your home. Perhaps some of you would consider taking that money and squirreling it away where it would be safe from creditors. You certainly could do this too. And after the exposed equity has been stripped away, you can safely transfer your home to the least vulnerable spouse using a quitclaim deed or a transmutation agreement or you can even quitclaim your house to a family limited partnership. You can do all of this legally because there's no exposed equity in your home and your transfer under the law is not a fraudulent conveyance! (See the *Mehrtash* decision).[341]

How do you quietly and legally get money out of the United States? Just visit your friendly neighborhood post office and request an international postal money order to the country where your money is to be sent. The maximum limit is $700 per postal money order.[342] No ID is required, and no questions are asked. All of this is done privately and anonymously. Just be sure not to mail any more than $10,000 out of the United States per day; otherwise, you'll be required to fill out a US customs declaration form. And always be sure to include a restrictive endorsement on the back of your money order: All of this is perfectly legal and a great way to quickly and secretly get your money offshore.

Talking about offshore, (and based on precedent), your offshore trust deed can also be backdated, usually for an extra fee. And when discussing extra fees, some of our upstanding attorneys will provide you with backdated legal documents, but as always, you must pay a hefty fee, usually about $25,000 –$50,000. I guess as they say, everybody and everything has his racket and his price. I'm neither condoning nor encouraging anyone to commit fraud or any other criminal act, but I do know that desperate people do desperate things when the going gets tough. My strongest recommendation is to begin your asset-protection planning well before you get desperate.

Besides, you'll save a lot of money too, and you won't get yourself into any trouble. Start your plans well before you are threatened with a lawsuit, before you're actually involved in a lawsuit, and before you have any existing creditors. Based on a true incident, for example, you can convert cash into diamonds by hiding the diamonds in a tube of toothpaste, and then travel to Amsterdam where you can quickly convert your loose diamonds right back into hard cash.

Here's an amazing piece of trivia that most people don't know. The US government gives foreign companies and foreign citizens special tax-favored treatment for all of their stock profits (otherwise known as capital gains); it's called no taxes! Folks, that's right, if you're a foreign company or a foreign citizen, then you don't have to pay any capital gains taxes on your stock profits! But here's another secret the US government doesn't want you to know: you too can get into this act. You just have to establish an offshore trust. Your offshore trustee can buy stocks for you through the trust's IBC, and you never have to pay any capital gains taxes on your profits! Conversely though, your trust can't deduct any capital losses (until you close down your trust), so you better pick winning stocks or perhaps just stick with shares of an index fund.

For extra privacy, set up two offshore banks, one of which receives money by wire from the United States, and then use this bank to secretly wire money to your second offshore bank (super-secret bank). No one will ever know about your second offshore bank account since it never transacts any business with any bank in the United States. Therefore, there will never be any paper trail in the United States linking you to this second offshore bank.

Bearer shares of stock can help keep the ownership of your company private. Nevada allows you to use bearer shares for your Nevada corporation. Also, the state of Nevada doesn't share information with the IRS, and this gives you additional privacy.

Remember: what you say to a friend or stranger is not privileged (protected) and can be used against you; and if that person is subpoenaed to court, the information you told your friend or stranger will almost certainly be used against you unless that person is your friend. Bottom line: Be careful what you say because it can literally come back to haunt you.

A financial planner can be hired under your attorney's umbrella, for up to two years, to protect you under the attorney's work-product, a part of the attorney-client privilege.

Today, the good news is that high-technology gadgets, such as electronics and computers, make life easier and more efficient. The bad news is that it also leaves a permanent record of your activities, which can be used against you in a court of law. It's really so much fun to text messages until you realize that law enforcement agencies can subpoena your text messages, which could then form the basis of a criminal complaint and arrest. Even your creditors can sometimes subpoena your text messages as well. Personally, I no longer text because of this risk. (I'll explain later how to get around this.)

A prepaid cell phone that you purchase without disclosing your identity is the best way to remain anonymous. Please remember not to use a credit card for the purchase. Pay by cash only! Don't show any ID when making the purchase. If the merchant requires a name, address, and phone, you are not required to give them your personal information. With your prepaid phone, you can call and/or text anonymously but be sure to always tell the recipient of your calls and/or text messages to never disclose your identity. If anyone, including law enforcement, calls to inquire about your identity, people have been known to say "I don't recall."

What should you do if you're on the verge of losing your home to a judgment (but the judgment has yet to be filed with the clerk)? If you have the misfortune to find yourself in this anxiety-provoking situation, then I suggest you must act immediately. You must quickly file a motion with the court for reconsideration; and if you still believe that you'll end up losing your home, then I suggest you go immediately to the bank and prepare for a very quick foreclosure. If there's no lien or lis pendens on your home, then you'll probably be able to receive the home's equity from the escrow company; otherwise, the escrow company will have to hold the funds (equity).

If you file for bankruptcy, you should list every piece of property you believe belongs to you in order to potentially qualify for any property exemptions. How should you handle disputed property? For example, let's suppose you previously transferred your home and you firmly believe the home no longer belongs to you. However, on the other hand, your creditors maintain you have an ownership interest in your home. The best advice I can give you is to list the home with the bankruptcy court as possible exempt property with an explanation that the ownership of the home is in dispute but is simply listed to claim the homestead exemption just in case the court determines that the home belongs to you, the debtor.

Please remember that liens pass through bankruptcy and can't be discharged. Sorry.

Transmutation agreements don't require consideration, which means property transfers are just like gifts. This means that if you wish, you can transfer the entire community property to just one spouse without any payment from you!

There's a tricky way to transfer a home in the midst of bankruptcy that may be the only way you can save your home from creditors. An expert bankruptcy attorney should be used for this very specific transfer.[343]

There's an old saying: a creditor steps into the shoes of the debtor. But if the debtor doesn't own anything, then the creditor is left holding an empty bag, or is it an empty shoe?

A transmutation agreement that involves *no* real property can be backdated. While this is illegal and actually constitutes fraud, it is very nearly impossible to discover. That's because there is no legal requirement that a transmutation agreement needs to be notarized or recorded. The only exception is a real property transfer, which needs to be recorded in order to be binding on third parties (including creditors). If you want to correctly execute a transmutation agreement, then I suggest you do the following three things: (1) both spouses should get their own lawyers to review the transmutation agreement and to receive a written approval letter, (2) notarize the transmutation agreement, and (3) record the transmutation agreement in your county recorder's office.

If your business has been dissolved and there is a judgment against it, then the creditors can go after the owners of the defunct business for up to two years. How should you handle this situation? My suggestion is to keep the original business active as an "empty shell" with no assets in it and to form a new company performing the same activity as the original company.

What should you do if you're threatened with a lawsuit? You might want to consider quickly taking out a second mortgage or equity loan from a lender, or alternatively, you can quickly transfer or sell the home, or you can quickly foreclose on the home well before a lien or lis pendens attaches to it.

Is it possible to secretly smuggle money quickly out of the United States? Yes. One way was previously explained using international postal money orders. Another way, would be to convert your cash to precious gemstones. Then hide your gemstones, for example, in the lining of your jacket. And finally travel overseas with your hidden gemstones to a place where there is a strong market, where you can quickly convert your gemstones right back to cash.

Here's a little-known secret in legal circles. Most people think that they can do no worse if they appeal a conviction or judgment. But in a small percentage of cases (about 3 percent), you can have a worse outcome or result when you appeal a judgment, conviction, or even a nonbinding arbitration award. This is true in both criminal and civil matters. For example, in the author's case, a nonbinding $20,000 arbitration award that went to trial turned into a $1,010,000 judgment on appeal. Most people don't know that the infamous Birdman of Alcatraz who killed a prison guard was originally sentenced to life in prison for the guard's murder, but then on appeal he got the death penalty. There's an old saying, "Quit while you are ahead." Then the Birdman's mother interceded, and she was able to get the president of the United States to commute her son's death penalty to life imprisonment—back to his original sentence.

The moral of the story is to think twice about appealing because you might do worse!

In a civil lawsuit that goes to arbitration, you can vacate the arbitration award by requesting a trial de novo (new trial). But beware, the outcome could be worse.

Turn a promise into an agreement. If you promise to pay someone in the hope that you won't be sued, then you need to turn that promise into a legal agreement. Under the law, your promises are considered an offer and are neither binding on you nor the recipient unless and until your offer (promise) is accepted by the recipient (also known as the offeree). Additionally, the recipient has to exchange some sort of value to you, which is called consideration. Consideration can be money, jewelry, or even not suing you. For example, let's say you promise to give a recipient $2,500 in the hope that he won't sue you. Turn that promise into a legal agreement by sending a letter stating that your $2,500 payment is in exchange for not being sued and releasing you of any and all claims related to the incident. The point here is that a promise is not the same thing as a legal agreement and thus is not legally binding on the promisor (the one who made the promise).

Fraud alert: Recently, a number of unqualified salesmen are marketing themselves as asset-protection experts. You should always check references and perform due diligence of the purported expert. Anyone claiming expertise in asset protection should have impeccable credentials as well as substantial tax and corporate law training, including offshore business practices.

Asset protection planning is not for saving taxes. Any salesman emphasizing tax savings should be viewed with suspicion. Asset protection planning is foremost for protecting your assets. And tax planning is for saving on your taxes. However, if you have an offshore trust with an IBC, may be able to save you on capital gains taxes if your offshore company invests in stocks and those stocks turn a profit. Additionally, your offshore trust and IBC could help you save estate taxes. But stay clear of salesmen who emphasize tax savings over asset protection.

Never forget to be very careful of your foreign trustee. Your best bet is to use a large trust department at a prominent offshore bank to be the foreign trustee of your offshore trust. Stay clear of the individual foreign trustee who could literally disappear tomorrow with all of your money.

Recently, some asset-protection salesmen are using a popular scam that encourages you to fully encumber various assets and entities with bogus loans. Folks, this is a "house of cards" that will get you into serious trouble. If you want to encumber your assets and other legal entities with loans, make sure your loans are legitimate loans from bona fide third parties such as financial institutions.

If you are a citizen or permanent resident of the United States, then you have to pay taxes on all your income worldwide regardless of its origin. For example, if you own a company in Europe, then you have to pay income taxes in the United States for money generated in your European company. So long as you have an ownership interest in a foreign company, then you are required to pay taxes on that foreign company's income. Therefore, if an asset-protection salesman suggests that you don't have to pay any tax on your offshore company, watch out. That dangerous and misleading advice could result in criminal charges filed against you by the US government.

While it's true that Nevada does not have any state income tax, and that, generally speaking, it does not share information with the IRS, beware of salesmen who stress that Nevada is a great place to hide assets and a place where you pay no taxes. Also, Nevada corporations may raise more suspicions from the IRS compared to Delaware corporations. Moreover, more corporate information is divulged online with Nevada corporations compared to Delaware corporations. Therefore, my recent opinion is that it might be slightly better to use a Delaware corporation rather than a Nevada corporation.

When threatened with a lawsuit, facing an actual lawsuit, or when existing creditors are present, you can no longer transfer assets or simply give them away. That's a fraudulent conveyance. If a salesman suggests that you can transfer or give away your assets at this time, watch out. You're getting terrible advice that can get you into a lot of trouble.

If an asset-protection salesman suggests you use deception, or to lie, or to otherwise engage in any illegal activity, watch out. You risk extremely serious repercussions. You could even go to prison. Asset protection is based on abiding by the law and should be done when you haven't been threatened with a lawsuit, when you are not facing a lawsuit, and when you don't have any existing creditors. If done correctly, it will work!

THE NEW BANKRUPTCY—SHOULD YOU USE IT?

Should you declare bankruptcy under the new bankruptcy act, and if so, when should you file for bankruptcy? Bankruptcy stays on your credit report for ten years. Judgments adversely affect credit reports and credit scores. Nowadays, in order to completely eliminate your debts and judgments under the new chapter 7 bankruptcy laws, you need an income that's below the median level for your area. If you qualify, you can get a discharge under chapter 7. Since so many people today are doing bankruptcies, there's less of a stigma associated with bankruptcies than before. If you need to do a bankruptcy, then by all means go for it. I definitely recommend you have an attorney represent you, especially if your bankruptcy is being challenged by creditors. Bankruptcy laws are complicated, and most general attorneys know very little about bankruptcy law. You need an attorney who specializes in bankruptcy. Check the Internet or the Yellow Pages to find a local bankruptcy attorney to represent you.

The New Bankruptcy Act provides less protection now than before. Here are the new property exemptions:

- Homestead exemption for your residence (includes mobile homes) in California varies from $75,000 to $175,000 depending on whether you are single or married, disabled, or older than sixty-five, and even on your income.
- Motor vehicle exemption is limited to $2,725.
- Jewelry, heirlooms, and art limited to $7,175.
- Building materials to repair or improve home limited to $2,875.
- Business assets and equipment ("tools of the trade") limited to $7,175 total ($14,350 total if used by both spouses in same occupation).

- Business (commercial) motor vehicle not to exceed $4,850 ($9,700 if used by debtor and spouse in same trade).

In bankruptcy, you get to keep some of your property. Each state has its own laws that designate specific property you get to keep so that you can continue to live a reasonable life. In Texas and Florida, the bankruptcy court cannot sell your home even if your home is a multi million-dollar mansion.[344] The new bankruptcy law[345] now makes filing bankruptcy somewhat more complicated. Chapter 7 and chapter 13 bankruptcy protects some of your property through the use of "exemptions" or "exempt property." When you file a chapter 7 bankruptcy, the trustee takes all of your "nonexempt" property and sells it for the benefit of your unsecured creditors. The trustee cannot take your exempt property, and you are allowed to keep all of your exempt property. What property is "exempt" and what property is "nonexempt" depends on each state's applicable laws. Each state has its own laws about what assets are exempt and nonexempt for purposes of bankruptcy. Florida and Texas have unlimited homestead exemptions. Only Florida residents (who meet residency requirements) are eligible for Florida exemptions. You have to reside in Florida for two years before you qualify for residency status under the new bankruptcy law. If less than two years, then your former state of residence determines the amount of your homestead exemption.

Here's the difference between *unsecured* and *secured* debts: If you owe $11,000 on your Visa credit card, that debt is "unsecured" because there's no collateral or any property attached or associated to it. Your medical bills, utility bills, telephone bills, student loans, and lawsuit judgments are also "unsecured" debts. No matter what, the credit card company, the medical center, the utility company, telephone company, and the student loan facility can't take away any of your exempt property. These unsecured entities (creditors) have several options. First, they can send you dunning (demand) letters demanding that you pay your unpaid bill. They can also contact credit-reporting agencies, which will hurt your credit score. Moreover, your unsecured creditors can contract with third-party collections agencies. However, if all else fails, they can sue you in court; and after they get a judgment against you, they can get the court to attach a "judgment lien" to your property. In bankruptcy, if any of your exempt property has a "judgment lien," then you must request the bankruptcy court to remove the judgment lien from your exempt property. The bankruptcy court will not automatically do it for you.

Debt consolidation agencies will help get you a "secured" loan, which utilizes your home equity or other property as collateral to "secure" the loan. As a general rule, if you sign a contract that pledges your exempt property as security for a loan, the property exemption laws no longer protect your exempt property. And if you don't repay your loan, then the creditor can repossess your exempt property.

In bankruptcy, you must fully disclose your asset-protection plan. Anything less than a full disclosure usually results in a denial of discharge, and the failure to make a truthful disclosure could result in charges of perjury and bankruptcy fraud—serious federal felonies.

Any property that is collateral for a (purchase-money) secured loan such as your car, which secures your car loan or your home and which secures your mortgage, is not protected by exemptions from repossession actions by that lender. Any equity you own in that property is protected. Property exemption laws don't protect you from losing your secured property if you don't make the payments. Don't forget about the "repo man" for taking your car away when you don't make your car payments and "foreclosure" when the bank or mortgage lender sells your home because you failed to make your mortgage payments.

There are several different types of bankruptcy—chapter 7, chapter 11, chapter 13, etc. Chapter 11 and 13 bankruptcies require payment plans over three to five years. Businesses can also apply for bankruptcy protection, and your company can declare its own bankruptcy in addition to your personal bankruptcy. However, in most cases, it's just easier to shut your company down and transform it into an empty shell. Commencement of a bankruptcy operates as an immediate stay, which means your creditors must immediately cease and desist in any and all of their collections efforts.

Can you safely transfer your property before you file for bankruptcy? It all depends on when you make the transfers. Timing is everything. Some debtors transfer their property shortly before they declare bankruptcy. They might give their property to one of their relatives for less than the fair market value of the property. For example, they might sell their $250,000 home to one of their siblings for $150,000. With most debtors, their total debts exceed their total assets. Let's say, for example, the debtor has $50,000 in the bank and equity in his or her home of $150,000. This means that the value of his or her total assets (estate) is $200,000 ($50,000 + $150,000). Now let's suppose the debtor has a judgment in the amount of $250,000. By legal definition, the debtor is insolvent. Now if the *insolvent* debtor transfers his or her property for less than the fair market value at any time within two years of his or her bankruptcy, then the law considers this to be a fraudulent transfer, and the bankruptcy trustee can undo (avoid) the transfer.

There's a second way your transfer can be considered a fraudulent transfer. This way is direct—it actually hinders, delays, or defrauds either a present or future creditor. You may wonder what a "future creditor" has to do with this. Most commonly, this would be a plaintiff who is now suing you and who later becomes a creditor after winning a judgment against you.

In a bankruptcy trial, the court has a choice of using either federal law or state law to challenge your property transfers as a fraudulent transfer.

In bankruptcy, [346] a fraudulent transfer is any transfer of any asset or any interest in any asset (such as part ownership in a home) that is made within two years prior to filing the bankruptcy case and in which either of the following are true:[347]

1. The transfer was made with *actual* intent to hinder, delay, or defraud any entity to which the debtor was or later became indebted to.

2. The debtor received *less* than reasonably equivalent value for the exchange *and* was *insolvent* on the date the transfer was made (or became insolvent as a result of the transfer).

Here's something else to consider that you probably never suspected. You're probably thinking that the transfers we're talking about are all voluntary, such that in order to be a fraudulent transfer you have to proactively make the transfer yourself. The amazing thing with fraudulent transfers is that an *involuntary* transfer can also represent a fraudulent transfer!

Almost all states have their own versions of the fraudulent transfer law. For example, in California, the fraudulent transfer law is very similar to the bankruptcy fraudulent transfer law.[348] The statute of limitations for California's fraudulent transfer law is similar to federal law, except that it is seven years for an unrecorded transfer and four years for a recorded transfer. Thus, if you file for bankruptcy in California, the bankruptcy trustee can sue the transferee (the person or entity who received the property) for any transfer that took place within seven years or four years prior to the filing of the bankruptcy case, depending on whether the transfer was recorded or not. And under California's general fraud statute,[349] the statute of limitations is three years from the date the affected party discovers the fraud.

What happens if the bankruptcy court determines that a fraudulent transfer was made? A creditor (in state court) or the bankruptcy trustee (in federal court) can sue the recipient of the transfer (the transferee) for the value received on the date the transfer was made in order to avoid (unwind) the transfer (recover title to the property). Moreover, in addition to recovering the property, if your transfer was intentionally done to hinder, delay, or defraud your creditors, then your entire bankruptcy discharge can be denied.

Bottom line: be very careful about transferring your assets, especially two years before you declare bankruptcy. If you do transfer any assets, make sure the transfer is for consideration (money) at the fair market value of the property. For example, if your home is worth $350,000, then sell it for $350,000. Furthermore, be very careful when transferring your assets to family members. The courts often view these transfers with a great deal of suspicion. Remember, you could end up in jail for bankruptcy fraud.

What about credit card transfers? Any credit card transfers made ninety days prior to a bankruptcy will be avoided (dissolved) by the bankruptcy court. Bankruptcy takes place under federal jurisdiction. Fraud and perjury can be prosecuted as federal felonies, so I recommend that you do not commit any of these crimes. There's also a filing fee that you must pay[350] except in limited circumstances under chapter 7 bankruptcy.[351] You can only do one chapter 7 bankruptcy every six years.

The main purpose of bankruptcy is to give debtors a fresh start while also addressing the issues of their creditors as fairly as possible. When you file for bankruptcy protection, all collection activities must stop immediately and the bankruptcy court tries to settle the entire affair as a single case. The only real limitations against who can file for bankruptcy are rules governing the frequency of filing. Chapter 7 protection is only available to a debtor no more than once every six years, and chapter 13 limits filing to once every two years, assuming there hasn't been a chapter 7 filing during the past four years.

There are two main types of bankruptcy: (1) liquidation and (2) reorganization. Liquidation occurs under chapter 7 where a court-appointed trustee collects the debtor's assets and sells what isn't exempt property. The proceeds from the liquidation that the bankruptcy trustee collects are then paid to the creditors to the fullest extent possible. Any remaining debt is quashed. Reorganization is a simpler process, which results in a payment plan to the creditors based on the future earnings of the debtor. The chapter for reorganization depends on the type of entity seeking bankruptcy protection. In general, reorganization occurs when the debtor is behind on payments of secured debt or has insufficient income to make ongoing payments. Liquidation usually occurs when the debtor has few, if any, assets or earning potential.

Bankruptcy restructuring is an attempt to lower interest rates or monthly payments and, occasionally the principal, to allow a debtor to make good on his or her obligations. Restructuring is done under chapter 11 for corporations and chapter 13 for individuals.[352] Creditors often benefit from reorganization bankruptcy because it can provide a greater level of repayment than might have otherwise been realized. Chapter 7 liquidation does not restructure the debtor's obligation(s) but rather gives the debtor a fresh start by wiping out his prior debts.

The new bankruptcy law[353] modified eligibility for chapter 7 liquidation by requiring a means test for anyone earning above the median income in his state. Debtors (petitioners) are disqualified from chapter 7 if their monthly income is $166 over the median income for their state after subtracting certain expenses, such as clothing, transportation, food, and payments on mortgages, cars, child support, and alimony or back taxes. Filing for bankruptcy is a complicated process and failing to fill out the correct paperwork, or doing so incorrectly, could result in lost property, dismissal of the bankruptcy proceedings, or even criminal charges. Therefore, I highly recommend you retain the services of a competent bankruptcy attorney.

Bankruptcy is often very helpful for individuals with a lot of debt (including judgments) and insolvent businesses, but there are important consequences to consider. Bankruptcy appears on credit reports for ten years, during which time loans and credit will be more difficult to obtain. Even when loans and credit are available, higher interest rates will apply. Potential landlords, insurance companies, and some employers may also deny applicants on the basis of a bankruptcy.

Property transfers can be contested and challenged by your creditors by bringing a fraudulent conveyance lawsuit against you in either state or federal court. Disputed bankruptcies can linger for many years in the court system. A bankruptcy court judgment can be appealed to the US District Court or to the Bankruptcy Appellate Panel (BAP) and then that decision can be further appealed to the

Circuit Court of Appeals and finally that decision can be petitioned for review in the United States Supreme Court. However, less than 1 percent of all cases are reviewed by the US Supreme Court. So you can see how a bankruptcy judgment can be appealed for many years as it works its way through the federal court system. There's no right to a jury trial in a bankruptcy so the judge decides your case. A bankruptcy transfers all of the debtor's property to the bankruptcy trustee, except for trust property in which the debtor is not a beneficiary (or equal equitable owner). All property (legal and equitable), which belongs to the debtor (petitioner), is transferred to the bankruptcy trustee. Occasionally, a bankruptcy can be converted from one chapter into another.

Few people know that your creditors can occasionally force you into bankruptcy. This is called an *involuntary* bankruptcy.[354] What is *involuntary* bankruptcy?

When a person or business owes money to creditors, those creditors can occasionally force the debtor to file bankruptcy. This is called an involuntary bankruptcy. The creditors requesting involuntary bankruptcy believe this is the only way they will ever collect on what they are owed. In order to begin the process of an involuntary bankruptcy one or more creditors file a petition in the bankruptcy court, and if the petition is approved, then the debtor is forced into bankruptcy. This is not without risk to the creditors because the debtor can challenge involuntary bankruptcy. Should the debtor win, he or she is eligible to collect attorney's fees and all other costs associated with the hearing and the defense process. He or she may also be able to sue the creditors for damages. The recoveries on these claims could be quite large! These damages include both compensatory and punitive damages. Furthermore, creditors cannot simply force any debtor into involuntary bankruptcy. There are certain minimum amounts of debt that must be met in order for an involuntary bankruptcy petition to be filed, which depends on whether the debtor is an individual or a company.

Involuntary bankruptcy can be filed under a chapter 7 bankruptcy against an individual debtor but cannot be filed under a chapter 13 business debtor. This means that a debtor who is forced into involuntary bankruptcy and approved by the court will have his or her assets liquidated as a part of the bankruptcy, and the money generated from the liquidation of assets will be distributed among the creditors based on formulas set by bankruptcy law that establish priority of creditors. Any remaining debts will then be forgiven.

Federal courts look on bankruptcy as a last resort whether the bankruptcy is voluntary or involuntary. Any creditor (even only one) may initiate an involuntary bankruptcy against an individual or business. Typically, however, there will be a group of creditors working together to file a bankruptcy against the individual or business. As long as they make a showing that they are in jeopardy of not being paid by the debtor, their involuntary bankruptcy petitions are seldom turned down by the courts. Federal courts understand the need to protect creditors just as much as the need to protect debtors forced into bankruptcy. Individuals are seldom forced into involuntary bankruptcy; and if they are, then they usually choose either chapter 13 reorganization or a chapter 7 full liquidation. Most often though, it's corporations who are forced into involuntary bankruptcy because corporations have significantly more creditors who stand to lose significantly more money and fear they may not get paid.

The Bankruptcy Reform Act (the new bankruptcy law) deprives Florida debtors of their unlimited homestead exemption. Outside of bankruptcy, Florida debtors retain their unlimited homestead protection and as well as other Florida property exemptions from creditors. The new federal bankruptcy system is much more creditor oriented. Because of creditor's advantages created in the new Bankruptcy Reform Act, many debtors are concerned about their creditors forcing them into an involuntary bankruptcy. The good news is that involuntary bankruptcies are rarely filed against individuals but are filed mostly against insolvent companies. The reason why individuals are rarely forced into an involuntary bankruptcy is because involuntary bankruptcy petitions are very complicated. Most bankruptcy attorneys lack the knowledge and experience to file an involuntary petition, and the creditor has to find a very sophisticated bankruptcy firm. As a result, involuntary petitions are risky and expensive. A bankruptcy court can deny a creditor's petition for any number or reasons. If the creditor's attorney makes even one small mistake, the court will probably sanction the creditor. This is good news for debtors. It means that the prospect of a creditor filing an involuntary petition to deprive a wealthy debtor of homestead protection is exceedingly remote. Asset protection is not foolproof and nothing is guaranteed in a courtroom. Most people can minimize the already unlikely prospect of an involuntary bankruptcy by making sure they don't have more than twelve unsecured creditors (e.g. credit card companies). Either a single creditor with a claim over $12,000 or at least three of twelve or more unsecured creditors must join together to file a petition for involuntary bankruptcy.[355]

Bankruptcy property exemptions are an important part of the bankruptcy system. In a chapter 7 bankruptcy, property exemptions determine what property you get to keep. If your property is exempt, the bankruptcy trustee is not entitled to sell it, and you may keep it. On the other hand, if your property is nonexempt, the trustee is entitled to sell it to pay your unsecured creditors. In a chapter 13 bankruptcy, property exemptions determine how much you'll have to pay some of your creditors through your chapter 13 reorganization plan.

Property Exemptions

Each state has a set of property exemptions that apply in bankruptcy. Most states require you to use the state exemptions even though bankruptcy is a federal procedure. However, seventeen states allow debtors to choose between the state property exemptions or the federal bankruptcy exemptions. California is unique in that it has two sets of state exemptions that debtors may choose from.

If you have a choice of exemption systems, you must choose one system or the other. You are not allowed to mix and match. If you choose to use your state exemption system, you may also use a short list of additional exemptions prescribed by federal law called the federal nonbankruptcy exemptions.

The Federal bankruptcy exemptions:

If you own property with a certain value and that value is no greater than the exemption amount available in your state, you get to keep the property. For example, let's say you own a car worth $3,000 and your state has a vehicle exemption of $5,000. If you file for chapter 7 bankruptcy, you will get to keep your car. In the same example, if your car is worth $15,000, the bankruptcy trustee will likely sell your car, pay off your car loan with the proceeds, pay you $5,000 for the exemption, and pay the rest to your unsecured creditors.

Keep in mind that the trustee will incur costs in selling your property. So if your equity in the property is not significantly more than the exemption, the trustee is unlikely to sell the property. For example, if you own a piano worth $2,500 and your state has an exemption for musical instruments in the amount of $2,250, the trustee is unlikely to sell the piano. This is because the costs of moving and selling the piano would probably be greater than $250—so the trustee would end up with nothing to pay your unsecured creditors.

Which state exemption system you may use depends on where you have lived for the past two years. Here are the rules:

If your domicile (location of your permanent home) has been in your current state for at least two years, use that state's exemptions (or the federal exemptions if allowed in your state). The homestead exemption applies to your home or other real property (the exact definition depends on your state). The domicile rules for the homestead exemption are different. If you acquired your home in the state where you currently live within forty months prior to filing for bankruptcy, your homestead exemption is capped at $146,450.[356]

The following states allow debtors to choose either the state exemption system or the federal system: [357]

Arkansas, Connecticut, District of Columbia, Hawaii, Kentucky, Massachusetts, Michigan, Minnesota, New Hampshire, New

Jersey, New Mexico, New York, Pennsylvania, Rhode Island, Texas, Vermont, Washington, and Wisconsin.

To determine which set of exemptions is best for you—state or federal—make a list of your property and its value. Then compare what property you can keep under each system.

The federal bankruptcy exemptions (last adjusted in 2010) are the following:

- Homestead:[358] Real property, including mobile homes and co-ops or burial plots up to $21,625. Unused portion of homestead, up to $10,825, may be used for other property. (Married filing jointly is $43,250).
- Personal Property:[359] Motor vehicle up to $3,450.
- Animals, crops, clothing, appliances and furnishings, books, household goods, and musical instruments[360] up to $550 per item and up to $11,525 total.
- Jewelry[361] up to $1,450.
- Health aids[362]—entire value of the property is exempt.
- Wrongful death[363] recovery for person you depended upon—entire value of the property is exempt.
- Personal injury[364] recovery up to $21,625 except for pain and suffering or for pecuniary loss.
- Lost earnings payments[365]—entire value of the property is exempt.
- Pensions and tax exempt retirement accounts[366] (including 401(k)s, 403(b)s, profit-sharing and money purchase plans, SEP and SIMPLE IRAs, and defined benefit plans)—entire value of the property is exempt.
- IRAs and Roth IRAs[367] to $1,171,650.
- Public assistance, Social Security, Veteran's benefits, unemployment compensation[368]—entire value of the property is exempt.
- Crime victim's compensation[369]—entire value of the property is exempt.
- Tools of trade[370] including implements, books, and tools of trade up to $2,175.

- Alimony and child support needed for support[371]—entire value of the property is exempt.
- Unmatured life insurance policy except credit insurance[372]—entire value of the property is exempt.
- Life insurance[373] policy with loan value up to $11,525.
- Disability, unemployment, or illness benefits[374]—entire value of the property is exempt.
- Life insurance payments for a person you depended on, which you need for support[375]—entire value of the property is exempt.
- Wildcard[376]—$1,150 of any property and unused portion of homestead up to $10,825.

Property exemptions—Isn't the government nice? They occasionally let us choose which exemptions we want to declare in a bankruptcy. In a bankruptcy, you can occasionally choose either the federal or state property exemptions. My choice is to keep all my property and not have to worry about exemptions. This can be done if you plan carefully before you're hit with a lawsuit. The property exemptions set by the government essentially allow your creditors to almost completely wipe you out. Obviously, the government doesn't want you to be walking around in the nude because your creditors took away all your clothing, so they allow you only the bare essentials. Isn't this nice of our government?

There were a total of 1,467,221 bankruptcies filed in the federal courts for the 2011 fiscal year ending September 30, 2011.[377] Here are some additional facts regarding bankruptcy:

Bankruptcy will not permanently ruin your credit. In fact, many people's credit scores actually rise in the years following their bankruptcy because they change their spending habits. Also, your credit is not ruined for the ten years following bankruptcy. Even with a bankruptcy on your credit reports, you can still get a job. You can even get a loan although it may be more difficult.

To get a free copy of your credit report, visit annualcreditreport.com or call (877) 322-8228. The three major credit bureaus are Equifax, Experian, and TransUnion. Consumers are entitled to receive free copies of their credit reports from all credit bureaus every twelve months. You also don't need to order all three reports at once; by staggering your requests, you can order one from each credit reporting agency every four months. Bankruptcy will appear on your credit report for ten years. Obtaining a secured credit card may be easier than obtaining an unsecured credit card. Make sure you pay your bills on time as well as your credit cards. In that way, when you're ready to take out a car loan or mortgage, you want your good payment history to help you.

Most people[378] believe what the US government tells them about bankruptcy—it gives the debtor a "fresh start."[379] While that may be true, there's another important purpose to bankruptcy. It's to protect the creditors by using a bankruptcy trustee to gather the debtor's nonexempt assets for liquidation in order to pay most or all of the creditors' claims. As stated previously, a minimum of three creditors are needed to force the debtor into an involuntary bankruptcy. However, in the legal system, there always seems to be an exception, and that is true as well with bankruptcy. If a bankruptcy court finds "special circumstances," it may allow fewer than three creditors to file an involuntary bankruptcy petition. Debtor fraud allows a "special circumstances" exception to the three creditor requirement of Bankruptcy Code § 303(b).[380]

Summary of Chapter 7 Bankruptcy

In a chapter 7 bankruptcy (liquidation case), the debtor has to turn certain property over to the bankruptcy trustee so that the property can be sold and the proceeds used to pay off debts and to pay creditors' claims. Debtors, whether they are businesses or individuals, are often justifiably concerned about what property they will be allowed to keep and what they must give up. Below are examples of property that a chapter 7 debtor will usually have to give up ("nonexempt" property), and property that the debtor may usually keep ("exempt" property):

1. *Nonexempt Property*—Items that the debtor usually has to give up include:

- Expensive musical instruments, unless the debtor is a professional musician.
- Collections of stamps, coins, and other valuable items.
- Family heirlooms.
- Cash, bank accounts, stocks, bonds, and other investments.
- A second car or truck.
- A second or vacation home.

2. *Exempt Property*—(items that a debtor may usually keep) can include:

- Motor vehicles, up to a certain value.
- Reasonably necessary clothing.
- Reasonably necessary household goods and furnishings.
- Household appliances.
- Jewelry, up to a certain value.
- Pensions.
- A portion of equity in the debtor's home (Homestead allowance)
- Tools of the debtor's trade or profession, up to a certain value.
- A portion of unpaid but earned wages.
- Public benefits, including public assistance (welfare), social security, and unemployment compensation accumulated in a bank account.
- Damages awarded for personal injury.

It's best not to receive any cash right after you file bankruptcy, otherwise the creditors might be able to recover the money. The bankruptcy court cannot take gifts made after the bankruptcy is final.

Cars and heirlooms are treated the same as cash in a bankruptcy and are subject to the administration of the bankruptcy estate. A debtor can claim an exemption of an asset in a bankruptcy estate and the bankruptcy trustee has a certain amount of discretion in choosing what to liquidate. Planning to avoid the long arm of bankruptcy courts is not illegal or immoral. Think of it the same way you would consider tax planning. Tax planning is fine; tax evasion is not. The difference is whether you play by the rules and are honest.

TAX CONSEQUENCES OF ASSET PROTECTION

There are pros and cons with regard to your taxes when transfers are made for asset-protection planning purposes and for estate planning purposes. The asset-protection planning strategies discussed in this guidebook have great importance, especially during the years you are working and, most importantly, when you are self-employed and operating your own business. That's because of the high risk associated with a lawsuit. Once you retire, however, the risk of a lawsuit declines appreciably, and essentially each spouse becomes the "least vulnerable spouse." When this occurs in a community property state like California, you can then use a transmutation agreement to convert separate property back into community property. In noncommunity property states, you can use a quitclaim deed to convert your separate property into tenants in common, joint tenants with right of survivorship, or in some states, tenants by the entirety. One reason to do this would be for tax-planning purposes. In many situations, asset planning may not be good tax planning and vice versa. When the risk of lawsuits is highest, asset-protection planning is more important than tax planning. When the risk of lawsuits diminishes, often in the retirement years, tax planning becomes more advantageous than asset-protection planning.

The tax advantage of owning a home in the form of community property in a community property state like California is that when the first spouse dies, the tax basis of the home typically increases.[381] And when the second spouse dies, fewer estate taxes are paid.

Even if just one of the spouses owns the home, both spouses are entitled to the full homestead exemption. However, if your home is owned by a family limited partnership or limited liability company, you may not qualify for the homestead exemption, and in some states like California, you may pay a little more in property taxes.

A family limited partnership that owns your home and/or other assets is entitled to some nice tax deductions where you can probably deduct about 20 percent of the partnership value. Since this gets somewhat complicated, it is definitely best to seek competent professional tax advice for a professional opinion.

Your offshore trust can invest in the US stock market and all profits are exempt from the capital gains tax! On the flip side, your trust or IBC can't deduct any capital losses until these entities are dissolved, which could many years later, and the money repatriated to the United States. Consequently, you need to be very careful and invest conservatively, perhaps by diversifying in several mutual funds or investing in multiple index funds, which long term, has been shown to produce 10 percent annualized returns.

You can deduct payments made for your leased business equipment as well as business payments that you make to your child's trust. You can even hire your children as paid independent contractors, and though they'll have to pay income taxes, possibly even at your income tax rate, this is an excellent way for your company to spread its income. Also, by law, your company has to pay its workers first before creditors can be paid. In addition, employing your family helps to minimize company assets.

Income spreading, while in some cases, may not help with your taxes, will help to reduce company assets that creditors could potentially seize. Here's an example: you and your spouse each can gift tax free $13,000 per person per year. Obviously, your children for the most part are not going to get sued and so my suggestion would be for you and your spouse to annually gift cash to each and every one of your children. Each child can receive up to a maximum of $26,000 ($13,000 by each spouse) annually. This is what is known as spreading your assets. If you wish, you can set up multiple children's trusts and gift money every year to each of the children's trusts.

Here's a great way to use a Nevada corporation to lower your income taxes provided you live in a state where there is a state income tax (which is the case for most of the states), and this is especially helpful for states with high state income taxes like California (highest in the country). It's called income shifting, and this is how it works: suppose you have a California business and you have a Nevada corporation. Let's say your California business orders merchandise from a supplier. Have your Nevada corporation place the order for the merchandise/supplies and make sure the invoice is in the name of your Nevada corporation. Your Nevada corporation will inform the manufacturer/supplier to drop ship the merchandise /supplies directly to your California business address. The manufacturer/supplier will then invoice your Nevada corporation who then pays the manufacturer/supplier from the original invoice. Afterwards, your Nevada corporation prepares a *new* invoice of its own which inflates the price it paid (the "wholesale" price) and sends this new invoice (the "retail" price) to your California business for payment straight back to your Nevada corporation. This is like the left hand paying the right hand and has the effect of shifting income from a high income tax state (California) to a no income tax state (Nevada). Since your California business will be able to deduct the higher-priced invoice from its income taxes, this will save you significant money that would have otherwise been paid to the state of California were it not for your Nevada corporation. This is all perfectly legal and will save you a lot of money on your income tax. Every little bit helps, and I hope this information will help you too.

The Omnibus Budget Reconciliation Act provided that the highest individual marginal tax rate of 39.6 percent would govern trust income over $7,500. A grantor trust utilizes pass through tax treatment for the grantor.[382]

LIVING (REVOCABLE) TRUSTS, ADVANCED MEDICAL DIRECTIVES, FINANCIAL DIRECTIVES, DURABLE POWER OF ATTORNEY

A living revocable trust (LRT) is used primarily to avoid probate. It keeps your estate private, and it saves your estate a lot of money by not having to use the legal services of a probate attorney and administrator or executor[383] of the estate. Some asset-protection experts recommend putting your entire asset-protection plan under the "umbrella" of an LRT.

Many financial planners sell boilerplate living trusts to the gullible public for exorbitant fees, which in my opinion, is little more than a gimmick for making a killing (no pun intended) off the public.[384] Before you prepare a living trust, I recommend you first discuss this matter with an attorney or financial planner to determine whether a living trust is best for your situation. A living trust has absolutely no asset-protection features because it is by its very nature a *revocable* trust.[385] Another potential downside, depending on your state and with bankruptcy, is that you lose your homestead exemption when you transfer your home to an LRT.

Living trusts can avoid probate and reduce or eliminate federal estate taxes for your estate. In most cases, a living trust will avoid probate for all assets that have been transferred to the trust. Probate is a costly, time-consuming process that many estates should avoid.

A living trust can also avoid a conservatorship, which is a court proceeding that is expensive, time-consuming, and restrictive.

Conservatorships are needed when an individual can no longer manage his or her financial affairs. A conservator[386] is appointed by a court and given the power to manage and make decisions regarding the individual's (conservatee's) financial affairs and living arrangements. A properly prepared living trust can provide a successor trustee who will manage the trust for the benefit of the grantor, sometimes avoiding the need for a conservatorship.

For married couples with estates subject to the federal estate tax, a living trust can reduce or eliminate federal estate taxes by setting up an exemption trust and bypass trusts.

A living trust is prepared that typically names the grantor as the trustee of the living trust. The trustee is responsible for managing the trust and its assets. The living trust usually nominates other persons, banks, or trust companies as successor trustees. The successor trustee(s) will take over management of the living trust after the death, resignation, or incompetency of the original grantor (trustee).

The living trust also provides for distribution of the grantors' (married couple) estates after the deaths of both spouses (grantors). These provisions can be the same as those found in a will and might include trusts for younger beneficiaries, gifts to charities, etc.

Depending on the size of your estate, the living trust might also include provisions that will reduce or eliminate federal estate taxes.

After the living trust is signed, the grantor *must* transfer his or her assets to the living trust. If this is not done properly, the living trust would be defective, and the assets could be subject to expensive and time-consuming probate after the grantor's death. Assets held by a valid living trust will not need to be probated. Legal fees for probating an estate are typically much higher than the fees for administering a living trust. Probates can also take a year or longer to complete, but a living trust administration can often be completed in a couple of months. Please remember, the living trust is revocable during the lifetime of the grantor and therefore provides *no* asset protection whatsoever.

Refinancing real property that is owned through a living trust may require transferring the property out of the trust before the refinancing and then putting it back into the trust. A few lenders do not require that property be taken out of the trust when it is refinanced.

If the grantor becomes mentally incompetent, a successor trustee can take control of the living trust and, in most cases, avoid the cost of a conservatorship.[387]

By using a disclaimer trust, Federal estate taxes can be reduced or avoided with a proper living trust. If an exemption trust is used, part of the living trust will become irrevocable after the death of the grantor (first spouse). Administration of an exemption trust (typically used to reduce or eliminate estate taxes) can involve additional effort for the surviving spouse. Transferring assets to the living trust involves more costs and paperwork than just having a will. If you have a living trust, you should also have a pour-over will. (See chapter 38.)

A pour-over will is like any other will, except that it has only one primary beneficiary, which is the grantor's living trust. The pour-over will transfers assets to the living trust to ensure that these assets will be subject to the distribution plan in the living trust and will also receive the benefit of the living trust's tax reduction provisions. It is called a pour-over will because it "pours" assets into the living trust. The pour-over will controls only probate assets—assets that are not in any trust, not in joint tenancy, not being inherited by a surviving spouse, and not in an IRA or 401(k). Probate assets are usually titled in the name of the decedent only. However, probate assets can also be found in situations in which a mistake has been made, such as failing to name beneficiaries for an IRA or 401(k). Probate assets covered by a pour-over will whose total value exceeds \$100,000 will have to have to go through probate. If the amount does not exceed \$100,000, the assets can be transferred to the living trust by using declarations as authorized by California Probate Code section 13100.

Besides transferring assets to a living trust, a pour-over will can distribute tangible personal property, such as furniture, jewelry, clothing, etc., to the grantor's beneficiaries; it can nominate executors and guardians for the grantor's minor children; it can revoke prior wills; and it can also include other provisions, such as tax allocation clauses.

Probate

Probate is a legal proceeding after a person's death that is used to wind up the decedent's legal and financial affairs. In California, probate proceedings take place in the Superior Court in the county where the decedent lived. The proceedings can last anywhere from eight months to several years. Please remember, assets owned through a living trust do not need to be probated!

The person who is named in the will as executor files a petition with the Superior Court requesting official appointment as executor. If there is no will, the Probate Code provides a list of persons who can become an administrator. The probate petition is filed along with the will, and notices are sent to the heirs and/or relatives to let them know when the probate hearing will be held. If there are objections to the probate petition, or if the validity of the will is contested, the probate hearing will be used to resolve any problems that have arisen. In some cases, the validity of the will is not upheld or some person other than the original petitioner is chosen to administer the estate. However, in most cases, there is no objection, and the probate petition is granted. The executor then makes an inventory of the estate's assets, locates creditors, pays bills, files tax returns, and manages the estate assets. When all of the duties of the executor are completed, another petition is filed with the court asking that the estate be distributed to the heirs. If this petition is granted, the administrated estate is completed by distributing the assets to the heirs and filing final tax returns.

Probate is advantageous because a judge can resolve disputes and creditors are required to submit their claims against the estate within a four-month period, provided they have been notified of the probate. On the other hand, probate is disadvantageous because probate is more expensive than a living trust, and it takes longer to probate an estate than to administer a trust. Also, living trusts don't need the supervision of a court unless disputes occur.

Many estates don't need to be probated. If there is a surviving spouse and there is no will, or if the will gives the estate to the surviving spouse, then a spousal property petition may be used. Also, for small estates, the small estate law may be used.

If the decedent is survived by a spouse, the spouse can file a spousal property petition with the court in order to change the titles of the assets to the surviving spouse's ownership. The petition is a simplified form of probate and takes much less time than a full probate. Legal fees are typically much lower for this type of petition than a full probate. Spousal property petitions can be used when the decedent did not have a will and the couple owned community property, or when there was a will and the spouse is the main beneficiary.

The California Probate Code provides that probate estates of less than $150,000 do not need to be probated. In some cases, the total estate may be considerably larger than $150,000, but the small estate law can still be used. The reason is that many assets are not defined as probate assets, such as life insurance (unless it was payable to the estate), IRAs, 401(k)s, assets held by a living trust, and joint tenancy assets. The $150,000 amount is calculated by totaling all of the probate assets owned by the decedent.

Living Trusts without Pour-Over Wills

A living trust without a pour-over will could result in two distribution plans, one for the assets in the living trust and another distribution plan for the probate assets (assets not in the living trust, which could be subject to probate). In some cases where the beneficiaries of the two distribution plans are the same, there would be no problem because the same people would inherit the assets in both plans.

However, if the beneficiaries are not the same as the heirs of the decedent, the assets would be distributed to two different groups of people. For example, if the living trust left all of its assets to charitable organizations and the decedent did not have a pour-over will, any probate assets would not go to the charities but instead would be distributed to the decedent's nearest relatives.

Defective Living Trusts

Occasionally, grantors fail to transfer their assets to the living trust, due to negligence, mistake, excusable neglect, or procrastination. Sometimes lack of understanding about how a living trust works contributes to this problem. Confusion might also be a factor, particularly when real property is refinanced. The lender often requires that the real property be taken out of the living trust when it is refinanced, but the lender probably will not inform the owner of the real property to transfer it back to the living trust after the refinancing. In these circumstances, California courts have allowed exceptions to these problems that can avoid probate.[388]

The Federal Estate Tax

Any transfer of assets from a deceased person's estate to his or her heirs, except for transfers to spouses, is subject to the Federal estate tax. An asset is defined as all property owned by the decedent including property in joint tenancy, living trusts, IRAs, and life insurance (if the insurance was owned or controlled by the decedent). Each estate has an estate tax exclusion, which for 2012 is $5,120,000. Assets that are subject to the estate tax (an estate greater than $5.12 million for a single person and $10.24 million for a married couple) are taxed at a top rate of 35 percent.[389] Assets that are transferred from one spouse to the other spouse at death are not taxed. This is called the "marital deduction," and there is no limit on how much can be transferred. If a spouse does not use his or her exclusion amount by funding an exemption trust or making bequests to anyone other than his or her spouse, the surviving spouse can use the unused exclusion amount of the first spouse to die. Portability doubles the amount available to the surviving spouse in many cases, and up to $10 million of assets can be excluded from the estate tax.

The Federal Gift Tax

The Federal gift tax is simply a tax imposed on gifts you make to any person other than your spouse. There is an annual exclusion of $13,000 that can be made by a single person and $26,000 that can be made by a married couple. This means you can give up to $13,000 ($26,000 by a married couple) to any person without having to pay any gift taxes. Additionally, there is a lifetime gift exemption of $5.12 million per donor, but any gifts made during one's lifetime will be deducted from the donor's exclusion amount.[390]

Inheritance Disclaimers

An inheritance disclaimer is a beneficiary's refusal to inherit all or part of an asset or of an entire estate. The reason for doing this is that the beneficiary who is entitled to receive a bequest either doesn't need or doesn't want the bequest. In most cases, the bequest would only make a sizable estate larger and increase the amount of federal estate taxes that will eventually be collected from that estate. The disclaimer operates as though the disclaimant died before the decedent, and the decedent's estate plan specifies a contingent beneficiary, who is often the disclaimant's children. If that is the case, the effect is that the bequest goes to the disclaimant's children and is never taxed in the disclaimant's estate. Occasionally, the beneficiary will disclaim an inheritance because he or she has creditors who could seize the inheritance.

Exemption Trusts

Exemption trusts (also known as a bypass trust, credit shelter trust, or B trust) reduce or eliminate federal estate taxes for a married couple's estate. This type of estate plan sets up an irrevocable trust that will hold the assets of the first spouse to die. The amount transferred to the irrevocable trust usually will not be taxed for federal estate tax purposes when the second spouse dies.

Disclaimer Trusts

Disclaimer trusts minimize or eliminate federal estate taxes for a married couple. After the death of the first spouse, the surviving spouse has the option of disclaiming all or part of the estate of the first spouse to die. The assets that are disclaimed are transferred to the disclaimer trust and are not included in the estate of the surviving spouse when he or she dies. The disclaimer trust will probably have the same distribution plan as the living trust, but the couple can also specify a different distribution plan for the disclaimer trust. The main disadvantage of the disclaimer trust is that the decision to disclaim must be made within nine months of the date of death, and the person making the disclaimer cannot have received any benefits from the asset being disclaimed. If the surviving spouse does not remember this deadline, or does not understand it, the disclaimer trust won't work, and depending on the circumstances, the estate could face heavy taxes. The main advantage of a disclaimer trust is that it is easier to set up than an A-B Trust.

Portability of the Estate Tax Exclusion [391]

Portability of the estate tax exclusion is used to minimize or eliminate federal estate taxes for a married couple. Portability allows the surviving spouse to use the exclusion ($5.25 million in 2013) that the first spouse to die did not use. If the first spouse to die gave all of his or her estate to the surviving spouse, the surviving spouse will wind up with double the estate tax exclusion. In order to qualify, the surviving spouse must elect to use portability by filing an estate tax return for the estate of the first spouse to die within nine months. However, failing to file the return will cancel portability for the first spouse to die. Estate tax returns are complicated, and you are encouraged to seek the professional services of a CPA or tax attorney.

Living Wills

A living will is a type of advance directive that outlines your medical treatment wishes should you become terminally ill or enter a persistent vegetative state. It is highly recommended that your living will be in written form in case you are unable to communicate your wishes. A living will directs health-care professionals as to which services you want or don't want. For example, you can specify that you don't want cardiopulmonary resuscitation, or a ventilator, but you do want feeding tubes to provide you with necessary nutrition and you want to die at home. Living wills are often written in vague terms because you are trying to cover a variety of circumstances, which are unknown to you when the living will is drafted. You may choose to sign a more restrictive living will, known as "do not resuscitate," which prohibits the use of cardiopulmonary techniques to keep you alive during cardiac arrest.

It should be noted that unless you are wearing a special identifier such as a bracelet, your living will does not apply to the efforts of an Emergency Medical Team (EMT).

A living will is a legal document and must be signed in the presence of witnesses and notarized.

In the absence of a living will, most states will elect someone close to you (usually a family member) to make decisions for you. This person (a surrogate) may have no idea what your personal beliefs are regarding artificial nutrition and resuscitation. The problem is that if you are unable to communicate, this individual must act in what he or she believes is in your best interest, and that could be contrary to your wishes. In some states the appointment of this surrogate will only occur when you are determined terminally ill, and all treatments leading up to this diagnosis are up to your doctor who has taken an oath to preserve life. If you have a living will, you can alleviate indecision in your family by outlining the terms of your treatment.

The disadvantages to a living will are that it typically is written in vague terms that could cause confusion with the medical personnel who treat you. Further, a living will may not "kick in" until you are deemed terminally ill. (But doctors may disagree when your condition becomes "terminal.") Moreover, a more specific living will could increase the chance of excluding a wide range of scenarios in which you would want your living will applied. And finally, you need to make your living will accessible to your health-care provider. Some people choose to keep their living will locked up in a safe deposit box or another secretive location in their home. If you fail to provide your doctor with a copy of your living will, and you become unable to communicate, they will treat you as if you never had a living will drafted.

Living will forms can be found on the Internet for free. Also, your health-care provider has access to free living will forms, which are state specific. However, it is always wise to check with an attorney when using these forms or if you move to a different state to ensure your living will is in accordance with state laws.

A living will is revocable, and you can change your mind at any time. Once you have completed your living will, it is important to provide a copy to your doctor, a potential surrogate, and other family members so there is no doubt what your final wishes are in the event of a terminal illness or vegetative state.

The Advanced Medical (Healthcare) Directive[392]

By law, you can legally authorize anyone as your agent, whether your spouse or anyone else, with written instructions in an advanced medical directive involving any health-care decision including end-of-life decisions. Your agent is your legal spokesperson.

The advanced health care directive along with a financial directive (see below) should be a part of everyone's estate planning tools. These directives provide precise instructions involving your health care and financial decisions.

An advanced health care directive is legally binding in most states and becomes effective when the all of the following occurs:

1. You cannot communicate your own wishes for your medical care, either orally, in writing, or through gestures.
2. You are diagnosed to be close to death (from a terminal condition), *or* you are permanently comatose.

3. The medical personnel attending to your care are notified of your written advanced health-care directive.

An advanced medical directive is a legal written instrument (document) providing instructions for your health care signed by both you and your agent before a notary public. An advanced health-care directive can make legal, life-saving decisions for you when you cannot. Your written instrument should contain the following:

1. Your legal identity including name, address, date of birth, and social security number.
2. Your agent's legal appointment and identity including his or her name, address, date of birth, and social security number.
3. Legal identity of an alternative agent, in case your agent cannot or will not fulfill his or her role.
4. Provide a copy of your advanced healthcare directive to medical personnel.
5. Authorizations from your agent should be in writing.
6. Pursuant to your advanced healthcare directive, your agent is authorized to consent or refuse to any form of health care that is not in violation of the law.
7. Your agent is authorized to request and to receive your medical information.
8. Your agent is authorized to make end-of-life decisions regarding orders not to resuscitate and decisions to withhold or to withdraw artificial nutrition and hydration and all other forms of health care to keep you alive.
9. Your agent is authorized to select and discharge health care providers and medical institutions and to make and change health-care choices and options relating to plans, services, and benefits.
10. Your agent is authorized to apply for public or private health-care programs, including Medicare and Medicaid without your agent incurring any personal financial liability.

11. If your wishes are unknown, your agent is authorized to make all health-care decisions in accordance with your best interests.
12. When and where appropriate, your agent can be appointed to become your legal guardian.
13. [Optional] You can refuse to being placed in a mental health treatment facility, or receiving electric convulsive treatment (ECT), or psychosurgery, sterilization, or an abortion.
14. [Optional] You can refuse to donate your bodily organs and body parts for purposes of transplant, therapy, research, or for other educational purposes.
15. A severability clause not to void the agreement or any provisions of the agreement if any part or parts are considered nonessential to the primary purpose and essential to the principal objective.
16. A modification clause allowing the agreement to be modified or revoked at any time for any reason by the principal (the maker of the advanced healthcare directive).
17. A provision for the final disposition of your body and any funeral arrangements.

The bottom line: a medical directive is an essential estate planning tool.

Financial Directives [393]

A financial directive is a legal financial instrument (document) that authorizes an individual of your choosing to be your agent in order to control and manage all of your financial matters and to exercise or perform any act recognized under the legal principal/agent relationship.

In order for your financial directive to be legally binding on all third parties, your financial directive must be in writing and notarized with power to indemnify all those who accept it in good faith. Moreover, your financial directive should be recorded in the local recorder's office in order to put all third parties on notice and to legally bind all third parties.

Your financial directive should grant your agent full power and authority to do everything necessary in exercising any of the powers as fully as you might or you could do if you were personally present, with full power of substitution or revocation, ratifying and confirming all that your agent may lawfully do or cause to be done by virtue of your financial directive.

A financial directive is an essential estate tax planning tool. Your financial directive should address the following general powers and prohibitions assigned to your agent, which *briefly* stated include the following:

1. Your agent is authorized to do whatever is necessary in matters regarding money or value to the principal (i.e., the maker of the financial directive).
2. Your agent is authorized to enter into any contract made by or on behalf of the principal.
3. Your agent is authorized to transact any real estate matter.
4. Your agent is authorized to prosecute or defend any claim in favor of or against the principal or intervene in litigation relating to the claim.
5. Your agent is authorized to seek the assistance of a court on behalf of the principal to carry out an act authorized by your financial directive. Moreover, your agent is authorized to engage, compensate, and discharge an attorney, accountant, expert witness, or other assistant as it becomes necessary or relevant to established objectives.
6. Your agent is authorized to keep appropriate records of all transactions.
7. Your agent is authorized to safeguard or promote the principal's interest under a government statute or regulation.
8. Your agent is allowed to be reimbursed for expenditures properly made by the agent in exercising the powers granted by the financial directive.
9. In general, your agent is authorized to do any other lawful act with respect to the financial directive.

10. Your agent is not permitted to execute a will or codicil on your behalf.
11. Your agent is not permitted to execute any trust on your behalf; however, your agent can enter into a custodial agreement with a trustee.
12. Your agent is not permitted to divert your assets to him or herself, his or her creditors, or his or her estate. Your agent must at all times maintain a fiduciary relationship to the principal.
13. Your agent is not permitted to own any life insurance policies on the principal's life and shall have no power and no authority over life insurance policies you may own on your agent's life.
14. Your agent shall have no power to void or modify any portion of your financial directive in any way whatsoever. Only the principal may revoke or amend by written notice to all parties and only by certified mail with return receipt.

Your financial directive becomes effective when you are considered disabled or incapacitated. For purposes of your financial directive, "disabled or incapacitated" means when a physician certifies in writing at a date subsequent to the date when your financial directive was executed that, based on your physician's medical examination of you, he or she declares you mentally incapable of managing your financial affairs. Your financial directive should have a paragraph to "legally authorize any physician" who examines you to disclose your physical and/or mental condition to another person for validation. Subsequent to this verification and disclosure of your incapacitated condition, a third party that accepts your financial directive is fully protected from any action taken.

When one is temporarily incapacitated, a financial directive is stronger than a general power of attorney. A power of attorney gives your agent general powers whereas a financial directive gives your agent specific powers as follows (but not all inclusive):

1. Collection powers.

2. Real estate (property) powers.
3. Personal property powers.
4. Banking powers.
5. Tax return powers.
6. Personal and family maintenance powers.
7. Powers of business interests.
8. Social Security and government benefits powers.

Durable Power of Attorney (DPOA)

You should know ahead of time where this document is before an emergency arises to ensure that your parent's and/or grandparent's wishes are followed. Having a durable power of attorney allows someone your parents and/or grandparents trust to act on their behalf and make legal and financial decisions for them, including the transfer of valuable assets, if they become incapacitated.

THE POWER OF POVERTY

Homeless people and many criminals are very rarely, if ever, sued. That's because these people generally don't own any assets, so no one wants to sue them. For example, suppose an aggressive, homeless pan handler assaults you and knocks you to the ground, which breaks your arm. The police and an ambulance are summoned. The assailant is arrested for assault and battery. The paramedics splint your arm and transport you to the emergency room of a local hospital. You're hospitalized for two weeks. You've lost two weeks of your wages, and you have experienced severe pain. After being released from the hospital, you meet with an attorney to discuss filing a lawsuit against the assailant. The attorney explains that he can't take your case on a contingency-fee basis because there's no realistic prospect of ever collecting on a future judgment. The attorney will further state that while the good news is that you have a strong case because of clear liability and damages and eye witnesses, the bad news is that you will never be able to collect on any future judgment because the assailant/defendant is a homeless man without any assets. The attorney should also disclose that in good conscience he could not even accept your case on a retainer because there would be no way to ever satisfy a future judgment. The assailant has no assets and is not working and thus there's no prospect that he can ever pay any future judgment. Even with punitive damages, which are nondischargeable in bankruptcy, there would be no way to collect on the judgment. Moreover, the attorney recommends that you simply drop the idea of ever suing the assailant because you would be throwing away good money after bad. The winner in this situation is the homeless man because he has successfully "killed" a potential lawsuit. That's the power of poverty!

The bottom line: When you neither own nor control anything, you have the greatest protection.

When it comes to judgments, poverty is power. This at once appears to be a paradox until you understand the reasoning here. A judgment is worthless when applied to an indigent (poor) person or an empty shell corporation. There's an old adage: "You can't squeeze blood from a stone." If you're a worker just making ends meet or you have a corporation with little or no assets, then there's absolutely no way a judgment can be satisfied. It's just not possible. Therefore, the fewer the assets you have including your business assets, the less likely it is that you could ever satisfy (pay) a judgment. When the plaintiff is informed of this, he or she just may get cold feet and drop the lawsuit. That's how you kill a lawsuit.

ASSET FORFEITURE LAWS

Certain crimes can expose your assets to forfeiture. Often in criminal matters, your property will be seized for evidence and will be returned to you when the case is over. Occasionally, some evidence is returned before the case is over. If the seized property is contraband, such as drugs, guns, or other illegal items, it will be destroyed when the case is over. Sometimes your property will be forfeited under state or federal forfeiture laws. In order to get your property back under the forfeiture laws, you'll have to win your case. The law doesn't allow you to sue the federal government to get your property back, including money damages. Instead, you'll have to fight a forfeiture action after being notified by the government of a "notice of forfeiture" action.

There are over three hundred federal offenses that allow the government to permanently confiscate your property without paying you for it—this is termed asset forfeiture—and occurs if the property and/or the owner is involved in one or more of over three hundred federal offenses. There is no restriction on the kind of property that can be seized. All makes and types of automobiles, yachts and boats, airplanes, all sorts of houses, and real estate have been seized and sold at auction. Cash and bank accounts are routinely seized. Even businesses are occasionally seized.

Contrary to popular belief, even if you are exonerated in a criminal case, your property won't necessarily be returned to you. If the government decides to keep your property under the forfeiture laws, then you'll have to fight the government in court to get it back. I strongly recommend hiring a lawyer with experience in forfeiture cases to give you the best chance of getting your property back. This is a very specialized area of law that few attorneys have any knowledge of.

Sometimes the state will turn your property over to the feds in order to get a kickback of up to 80 percent of the property's value under the "equitable sharing" program.

There are both state and federal forfeiture laws. In federal cases, there will either be (1) a *civil* forfeiture which will start with a notice of forfeiture or a civil (judicial) forfeiture complaint, or there will be (2) a *criminal* forfeiture when there is a criminal prosecution of the property owner. The government may pursue a "criminal forfeiture" in the same case by adding a "forfeiture count" to the indictment. Unfortunately, you will have to wait for the government's notice of forfeiture before you can expect to ever get your property returned. It's really best to have an experienced attorney represent you in this situation. The government will attempt to trick you by suggesting you file a "petition for remission." But a much better alternative is for you to file a claim in order to have the right to a hearing in court to defend your property. There is no court hearing in the petition for remission process—everything is decided by the agency that seized your property, and most of the time, not surprisingly, they choose to keep it.

In customs cases and cases under the USA PATRIOT Act, you may have to post a 10 percent bond to file a claim to recover your property—the bond is to cover the government's legal costs in case you lose. On the other hand, in civil cases, you usually won't have to post a bond as the Civil Asset Forfeiture Reform Act (CAFRA) abolished bonds in most types of civil forfeiture cases. Once again, and it's worth repeating, you should immediately seek the services of a competent attorney with experience in forfeiture cases when your property has been confiscated by the government and you want it returned.

The procedures with state forfeiture and the District of Columbia are different from the federal procedures. Your attorney should be able to handle this for you.

The following defenses will usually get your property returned to you: (1) The innocent owner defense states that you didn't know of or consent to the illegal use of your property; [394] (2) the unreasonable delay defense states that the government waited too long to file the forfeiture case or bringing it to trial, and the delay harmed your ability to put on a defense; (3) the illegal search and seizure defense may be able to suppress evidence illegally seized, and therefore the government may be unable to prove its case; (4) the disproportionality defense states that forfeitures of property that are grossly disproportionate to the severity of the offense committed are unconstitutional;[395] and (5) statutory defenses contain additional defenses, which may help you get your property back.

In some cases, you may be able to get a court-appointed attorney to represent you. In a federal criminal case, your public defender may be able to represent you in a forfeiture proceeding; and in some cases (except Customs cases) where your residence has been seized and you are indigent, you may be able to get a court-appointed attorney to represent you. If you win your case, you are entitled to have your attorney's fees reimbursed. In some instances, you may be able to retain an attorney on a contingency-fee basis.

In most cases, the government will not forcibly evict you from your home pending a forfeiture case of your home. However, movable assets such as cars, boats, airplanes, and money will be immediately seized by law enforcement. If you stop making your mortgage payments, you'll almost certainly lose your property to foreclosure and any remaining equity in the property will go to the government, provided they win their case against you. Forfeiture cases can sometimes take years to resolve. The forfeiture statutes have been held to be constitutional.[396]

DEEDS AND MORTGAGES

Grant Deeds

A grant deed is used in some states and jurisdictions for the sale or other transfer of real property from one person or entity to another person or entity. Each party transferring an interest in the property, or "grantor," is required to sign it. Then the document must be acknowledged before a notary public (notarized) or other official authorized by law to administer oaths. The notary public or other official then places a seal and marks the document accordingly to show that it was properly signed and acknowledged. The reason the document must be notarized is to provide evidence that the signature of the grantor is genuine as transaction documents are sometimes forged. Some jurisdictions use the warranty deed to transfer real property instead of the grant deed. The quitclaim deed is also sometimes used; although this document is most often used to disclaim any interest in a property rather than selling a property that one owns.

Quitclaim Deeds[397]

A quitclaim deed is a legal instrument by which the purported owner of a piece of real property, called the grantor, transfers his or her interest, if any, to a recipient, called the grantee. The owner/grantor terminates ("quits") his or her right of any claim to the property, thereby allowing the claim to transfer to the recipient/grantee. Unlike most other property deeds, a quitclaim deed offers the grantee no warranty (guarantee) as to the status of the property title; the grantee (recipient) is entitled only to whatever interest the grantor actually possesses at the time the transfer occurs. This means that the grantor does not guarantee that he or she actually owns the property at the time of the transfer; or if he or she does own it, that the title is free and clear. It is therefore possible for a grantee to receive no actual interest and—because a quitclaim deed offers no warranty—have no legal recourse to recover their losses. In contrast, other deeds often used for real estate sales (called grant deeds or warranty deeds, depending on the jurisdiction) contain warranties from the grantor to the grantee that the title is clear and/or that the grantor has not placed any encumbrance against the title. Because of this lack of warranty, quitclaim deeds are most often used to transfer property between family members as gifts, placing personal property into a business entity (and vice versa) or in other special or unique circumstances. Quitclaim deeds are rarely used to transfer property from seller to buyer in a traditional property sale. Another common use for a quitclaim deed is in divorce whereby one spouse terminates any interest in the jointly owned marital home, thereby granting the receiving spouse full rights to the property. For example, the husband could quitclaim his interest in the marital home to the wife pursuant to a divorce settlement.

In some jurisdictions, quitclaim deeds may also be used in tax deed sales where a property is sold in a public auction to recover the original homeowner's outstanding tax debt. The auctioning body is usually the local government, which claims no interest to the property whatsoever, but is selling only to recover the unpaid taxes without extending any warranty for the property title. The purchaser then may need to initiate a quiet title action to remove any clouds to the title.

Most jurisdictions restrict or prohibit the use of a quitclaim deed as collateral for a bail bond.

Joint Tenants with Right of Survivorship (JTWROS)

A concurrent estate or cotenancy is a concept in property law that describes the various ways in which property is owned by more than one person at a time. If more than one person owns the same property, they are referred to as co-owners, cotenants or joint tenants. Most common law jurisdictions recognize tenancies in common, joint tenancies, and some also recognize tenancies by the entirety. Many jurisdictions refer to a joint tenancy as a joint tenancy with right of survivorship, and a few US States treat the phrase joint tenancy as synonymous with a tenancy in common. The type of ownership determines the rights of the parties to sell their interest in the property or to will the property or to sever their joint ownership of the property.

Assets that are owned by two or more people as joint tenants or joint tenants with right of survivorship (JTWROS) will usually not be probated. When a joint tenant dies, the other joint tenant takes 100 percent ownership of the asset, regardless of any provisions of a will or living trust of the deceased joint tenant.[398] Joint tenancy is not recommended for assets that can increase in value, such as a residence, because the surviving joint tenant will not receive a "stepped-up cost basis" to fair market value at the date of death of the other joint tenant.

Cost basis is used to determine capital gains. For many homeowners, the cost basis is the price they paid for their home, plus any capital improvements that have been made. The cost basis is subtracted from the selling price to determine the capital gains. When a married couple owns an appreciated asset as community property, the surviving spouse will get a step up in the cost basis to the fair market value at the date of death of the other spouse. In other words, if the surviving spouse has to sell the residence, he or she is unlikely to have to pay any capital gains. But if the residence is held in joint tenancy, it is more likely that some capital gains tax may be due. Federal law allows the surviving spouse a capital gains exclusion of $250,000, but for some California residents, even this amount may not be enough to prevent payment of capital gains tax when a residence is sold.

Tenants by the Entirety[399]

A tenancy by the entirety (sometimes called a tenancy by the entireties) for real property is typically available only to married couples in a few states. Like a JTWROS, the tenancy by the entirety also includes a right of survivorship, so if one spouse dies, the entire interest in the property passes to the surviving spouse without going through probate.

Also, besides sharing the four unities necessary to create a joint tenancy with right of survivorship—time, title, interest, and possession—there must also be the fifth unity of marriage. However, unlike a JTWROS, neither party in a tenancy by the entirety has a unilateral right to sever the tenancy. The termination of the tenancy or any dealing with any part of the property requires the consent of both spouses. A divorce breaks the unity of marriage, leaving the default tenancy, which may be a tenancy in common in equal shares. Many US jurisdictions no longer recognize tenancies by the entirety. Where it is recognized, benefits can include the ability to shield the property from creditors of only one spouse as well as the ability to partially shield the property where only one spouse is filing a petition for bankruptcy relief. If a nondebtor spouse in a tenancy by the entirety survives a deceased debtor spouse, the creditor's lien can *never* be enforced against the property. On the other hand, if a debtor spouse survives a deceased nondebtor spouse, the creditor's lien may be enforced against the whole property, not merely the debtor spouse's original half interest.

In many states, tenancy by the entireties is recognized as a valid form of ownership for bank accounts and financial assets. One must be careful to ensure that the tenancy by the entireties designation is chosen as opposed to other forms of joint ownership such as joint tenancy with rights of survivorship so that the benefits of tenancy by the entireties status is not lost.

Tenants in Common (TIC)

Tenancy in Common is the default form of concurrent estate (ownership), in which each owner, referred to as a tenant in common, is regarded by law as owning separate and distinct shares of the same property. By default, all co-owners own equal shares, but their interests may differ in size. This is the most common form of shared property.

TIC owners own percentages in an undivided property rather than particular units or apartments, and their deeds show only their ownership percentages. The right of a particular TIC owner to use a particular dwelling comes from a written contract signed by all co-owners (often called a "tenancy in common agreement"), not from a deed, map, or other document recorded in county records.[400] This form of ownership is most common where the co-owners are not married or have contributed different amounts to the purchase of the property. The assets of a joint commercial partnership might be held as a tenancy in common.

Tenants in common have no right of survivorship, meaning that if one tenant in common dies, that tenant's interest in the property will be part of his or her estate and pass by inheritance to that owner's devisees or heirs, either by will or by intestate succession. Also, as each tenant in common has an interest in the property, they may, in the absence of any restriction agreed to between all the tenants in common, sell or otherwise deal with the interest in the property (e.g. mortgage it) during their lifetime, like any other property interest. There is no asset protection with tenants in common, except that your home cannot be seized if only one spouse has a judgment, but rather, the other spouse retains his or her interest in the house and the creditor steps into the debtor spouse's shoes with unpredictable consequences.

Mortgage Loans

A mortgage loan is a loan secured by real property through the use of a mortgage note, which evidences the existence of the loan and the encumbrance of that realty through the granting of a mortgage, which secures the loan. However, the word *mortgage* alone, in everyday usage, is most often used to mean mortgage loan.

A home buyer or builder can obtain financing (a loan) either to purchase or secure against the property from a financial institution, such as a bank or credit union, or other lender either directly or indirectly through intermediaries. Features of mortgage loans such as the size of the loan, maturity of the loan, interest rate, method of paying off the loan, and other characteristics can vary considerably.

Fixed Rate Mortgages (FRMs)

Few individuals have enough savings or liquid funds to enable them to purchase real property outright. The most popular home financing option is the traditional fixed rate mortgage (FRM). Approximately 70 percent of all mortgages are FRMs. Fixed rate mortgages have fixed interest rates that remain the same throughout the term of the loan, regardless of changes in the prevailing market rate. This allows the consumer to rely upon a stable monthly payment on the principle and interest throughout the term of the loan, whether it spans thirty years or fifteen.

With FRMs, there are no surprises because the interest rate stays the same over the entire term, usually thirty years. However, if interest rates fall, you'll be stuck paying a higher rate. With amortization over thirty years, a $300,000 mortgage will cost you about $1,200,000.

Balloon mortgages are similar to that of a fixed rate loan, except that the term of the balloon loan is much shorter, often only five to seven years. At the end of the short loan term, the outstanding balance must be paid in one lump sum, either out of pocket or by refinancing the home. This loan could be risky for some homeowners.

Adjustable Rate Mortgages (ARMs)

Adjustable rate mortgages (ARMs), are another option in real estate transactions. However, when FRMs are low, ARMs. are less popular. These loans have an interest rate that is tied to an index, which changes depending on prevailing market rates. The interest rate fluctuates and is adjusted periodically. Also, most ARMs. have an interest rate, which is capped.

With ARMs, you'll usually have a lower initial interest rate than fixed-rate loans. However, after a short initial period, your interest rate will fluctuate over the life of the loan; and when interest rates rise, so will your loan payments.

Option ARMs (Adjustable Rate Mortgages)

Option ARMs, also referred to as flexible payment ARMs, have an interest rate that adjusts every month with no adjustment caps. These loans allow borrowers to make very low mortgage payments initially, but these monthly payments will rise steeply over time, so generally they are not advisable.

Option ARM loans were once popular during the housing boom as they allowed you to buy a home with a large loan, yet you were able to pick which payment you wanted to send in monthly. In good times, you may have chosen the lowest payment, which would accrue negative amortization, or you may have wanted to bump it up to an interest only or even a fully amortized payment. These loans may be beneficial to someone starting out in a career who needs a lower loan payment option, but as you progress in life, you can pay the higher amount, thus combating or making up for the early negative amortization.

Additionally, there are myriad hybrid variations of the two main categories of home loans: fixed rate and adjustable.

Government-Guaranteed Mortgage Loans

- *FHA Loans*

Government-guaranteed mortgage loans such as FHA loans are fixed rate mortgages designed especially for the first time home buyer of moderate or low income. Guaranteed by the Federal Housing Administration (FHA), these loans are easier to qualify for than a traditional fixed rate mortgage and allow a smaller down payment than most other home loans, usually about 3 percent. Also, interest rates are usually lower than standard fixed rate loans.

A FHA (Federal Housing Administration) loan allows buyers who may not otherwise qualify for a home loan to obtain one with a low down payment. However, the size of your loan may be limited.

- *VA Loans*

VA loans are another government-guaranteed mortgage. To be eligible for a VA loan, you must have a history of active military service or be the surviving spouse of an active service member. Often, a veteran can obtain a VA loan with little or no down payment but must demonstrate the ability to make monthly payments.

A VA loan is a guaranteed loan for eligible veterans, active duty personnel, and surviving spouses. It offers competitive rates, low or no down payments. However, the size of your loan may be limited.

- *USDA Rural Development Guaranteed Housing Loans*

The USDA Rural Development Guaranteed Housing Loan is another government-guaranteed home loan option. This type of home mortgage loan is provided to low and moderate income individuals who are purchasing a home in an area designated as a rural development eligible area. No down payment or mortgage insurance is required with this loan program, and qualification can be much easier than your average home loan, allowing consumers with less than perfect credit to obtain financing for home purchases.

Interest-Only Mortgages

Interest-only mortgages are loans that allow the borrower to pay only the interest on the loan for a predetermined period of time. The principle of the loan is not paid down during this period at all, leaving the homeowner a lower monthly payment to meet over the short term. However, after this initial interest-only period expires, the payments increase to include repayment of the principle and are steeper than a standard loan as the principle must be paid over a shorter time period.

Biweekly Mortgages

Biweekly mortgages are loans in which the borrower makes payments every two weeks instead of the typical monthly payment arrangement. This result in a slightly shorter repayment term because paying biweekly results in twenty-six payments a year, which is equivalent to thirteen monthly payments, rather than the twelve payments made with a standard monthly mortgage payment.

Semimonthly Mortgages

Semimonthly mortgages do not require any extra payments but save slightly on interest by advancing the payment by half the month. On average, these types of arrangements only shorten the loan term by approximately one month on a thirty-year mortgage!

Reverse Mortgages

A reverse mortgage allows seniors to convert equity in their homes to cash, and you don't have to pay back the loan and interest as long as you live in the house. These loans are plagued by aggressive lending practices and false advertising promises, particularly by lenders that prey on seniors. Always check to make sure the loan is federally insured.

Negative Amortization Mortgages

Negative amortization is a mortgage loan in which the payments do not cover the principle and the interest payments do not fully cover the amount of interest due. Consequently, the unpaid interest builds up and is then added to the principal of the loan, resulting in you owing more on the loan balance each year instead of chipping away at the principal balance.

Graduated Payment Loans

Graduated payment loans are a type of negative amortization that allows you to buy a home with a larger loan and a smaller payment up front. However, the payments go up at predetermined times throughout the loan and keep accelerating into larger payments toward the end of the loan in order to catch up for the earlier lower payments. During this time, especially the early years, these loans are building up negative amortization, thus you owe more each year on your loan balance than you started with.

Mortgage Lenders Are Secured Creditors

As secured creditors, banks, mortgage companies, and other lenders can foreclose on your home or other real estate if you fail to repay your loan. No asset protection tools can completely protect you against a foreclosure. Most US mortgages are nonrecourse loans in which the lender's remedies are limited solely to the liquidation of your home, even if that results in an outstanding balance on your loan. In other words, the lender normally can't sue you to collect on any remaining loan balance. Contrary to a well-known asset-protection book, an unsecured creditor who obtains a judgment against you can liquidate your mortgaged home. One example would be a judgment creditor who places a judgment lien on your home; he or she can eventually execute a lien sale on your home to satisfy his or her judgment. Another example would be an individual who works on your home and doesn't get paid; he or she can place a mechanics lien on your home and then apply to the court for a lien sale.

ESTATES AND TAXES

An estate (inheritance) patrimonio (possession) is a term in common law used to denote the sum total of all the possessions owned by a person at the time of his or her death. An estate tax is a tax on your possessions on the date of your death, which includes, but is not limited to the following: cash, bank accounts, CDs, stocks, mutual funds, bonds, treasuries, jewelry, cars, stamps, boats, paintings, coins, and other collectibles, real estate, your business, limited partnerships, general partnerships, mortgages and notes receivable you hold, retirement plan benefits, IRAs, and inheritance from others, etc.

Your federal death (estate) tax, up to 35 percent [401] is based on the "fair market value" of your property on the date of your death, not what you originally paid. State probate and death taxes are based on the "location" of your property. Thus, if you own property in different states, each state has to be probated and each state will want its fair share.

The only real alternative to a will is to set up a trust during your lifetime which, with careful planning, can operate to eradicate estate taxes as well as giving a large number of additional benefits. For these reasons, the use of trusts is increasing dramatically.

The major problem is that many Americans have no plan. They incorrectly assume that joint ownership takes care of things, or they believe that their property is not worth enough to be concerned. Such practices can be shortsighted, cost money, and raise unnecessary and unexpected problems, long time delays, and high administration costs.

For one thing, most people have a larger estate than they may realize. For another, joint ownership will not necessarily beat probate or estate taxes.

A will is not a substitute for a trust. A will does not avoid probate.

Certain types of property have special rules for estate taxes. Property that spouses jointly own, half the value is included in the estate of the first spouse to die, no matter whose funds bought it or that survivor automatically inherits it. And the full value is counted in the survivor's estate, which could result in a bigger estate tax at that time.

Insurance agents often won't tell you that your life insurance is taxed in your estate if you had any incidental ownership at death. This means that if you can name new beneficiaries or can borrow against the insurance policy or take out the cash value, then it's included in your estate. The bottom line is that life insurance—whether individual or group—that you own is part of your estate and subject to estate taxes.

What Assets and Liabilities Are Counted to Determine If an Estate Is Taxable?

Every asset of yours at death, anywhere in the world, is counted. The IRS calculates your gross estate at the time of your death, which includes your probate assets as well as your nonprobate assets. The types of property included in your estate are your home, personal property, business interests, life insurance death benefits, deferred compensation, stock options, IRAs, retirement plans, pensions[402], 401(k)s and profit-sharing plans, investments, real estate, bank accounts, jewelry, artwork, jointly owned assets, promissory notes, 50 percent of your community property, mortgages, and cash. Your gross estate also includes any taxable gifts[403] given away before your death. Also, property partly given away, where you retain the right to use it, is included in your estate. For example: A house that you give to your children but still use rent free. (Incidentally, giving your house to your children creates a problem for them, and for you, if they get sued, or they die before you.) And stock you give away, but keep voting rights, if in a company that you control. Or the property of others over which you have certain rights such as the power under another's will to name who will get part of that estate. If you could name yourself, your estate, or creditors, it's taxable in your estate, including assets you give a child and keep the right to control.

Next, the IRS subtracts your liabilities, such as loans, funeral expenses, debts owed at the time of death, legal, and other estate administration costs and any charitable contributions made. Also subtracted are those assets transferred outright to a surviving spouse (marital deduction) because of the rule which permits an unlimited amount to pass to a spouse with no estate tax burden.

The balance, if any, will roughly estimate your taxable estate. Finally, estate tax laws do change, and it behooves you to stay informed.

Gift Taxes

If you transfer an asset,[404] say your home, for less than fair market value, then you (the transferor) owe the IRS a gift tax. Moreover, if the transfer is done when you've been threatened with a lawsuit or when there is pending litigation against you or if you have present creditors, then this would also be considered a fraudulent conveyance as well.

Summary of Estate Planning

A basic estate plan has several elements:

- A will
- A power of attorney
- A living will or health-care proxy (medical power of attorney)
- A trust for some people may also make sense

Your assets include your investments, retirement savings, insurance policies, real estate, business interests, etc. Here are three questions:

1. Who do you want to inherit your assets?
2. Who do you want handling your financial affairs if you're ever incapacitated?

3. Who do you want making medical decisions for you if you become unable to make them for yourself?

Everybody including you, the reader, needs a will. A will clearly informs others exactly to whom you want your assets distributed when you die. It's also a good way to name guardians for your children. Dying without a will—the legal term is dying "intestate"—can be costly to your heirs and lets the state decide who gets your assets. Even if you have a trust, you still need a will[405] to take care of any assets outside of that trust when you die.

Trusts are legal contracts that let you put conditions on how and when your assets will be distributed upon your death. They also allow you to reduce your estate and gift taxes and to distribute assets to your heirs without the cost, delay, and publicity of probate court where wills are administered. In addition, irrevocable trusts also offer greater protection of your assets from creditors and lawsuits.

Discussing your estate plans with your heirs may prevent disputes or confusion. The federal estate tax exemption—the amount you may leave to heirs free of federal tax—changes regularly. In 2013, estates under $5.25 million are exempt from the tax. Amounts above that are taxed up to a top rate of 35 percent.

You may leave an unlimited amount of money to your spouse tax free, and by utilizing portability, you're able to use your estate tax exemption.

There are two easy ways to give gifts tax free and reduce your estate. You may give up to $13,000 a year to an individual (or $26,000 if you're married and giving the gift with your spouse). You may also pay an unlimited amount of medical and education bills for someone if you pay the expenses directly to the institutions where they were incurred. If you donate to a charitable gift fund or community foundation, your investment grows tax free, and you can select the charities to which contributions are given both before and after you die.

WILLS AND SUCCESSION PLANNING

Wills

Seventy percent of Americans die without a will.[406] A will is a listing of your wishes to be executed on the date of your death. A will cannot take the place of a trust, and a will does not avoid probate. A will is a legal document outlining a person's final wishes for distributing his or her property postmortem. A will contest is a type of litigation stating there is a disagreement with the current will and must go through probate court to be resolved.

In order to file a contest, you must have "standing" to make an objection. You can file a will contest if, for example, you have been left out of the will by an angry parent; if your sibling received a higher percentage of the inheritance; if your parent left all their inheritance to charity because they felt the money would be better spent; or if you feel entitled to receive a portion of your relative's estate. Once it is determined you have "standing," you must also have a valid objection to the will. Simply being unhappy about the outcome is not sufficient to warrant a will contest.

Some typical and valid objections for pursuing a will contest are the following:

1. The person making the will (testator) never signed the will. Even if an attorney prepared the will, the will is invalid if the testator did not also sign it.
2. The will did not meet statutory requirements. For example, some states require a specific number of witnesses to sign the will in addition to the testator and the attorney.
3. The testator was influenced when drafting the will. This means that a third party, often a child or spouse, convinced

the testator to leave a disproportionate amount of the estate to him or her.

4. The testator lacked the mental capacity to understand the will he or she drafted. A common example of this would be an elderly parent with a condition affecting his or her memory (Alzheimer's disease, senility, etc.).

If the probate judge determines you have a valid case, then you'll win the will contest. The court then has several options:

1. The court can throw out the entire will. In this case, property will be distributed as if no will existed.
2. The court can disallow only the part or parts of the will that were contested.
3. Depending on individual state law, the court may use a previous will if the testator drafted one.

To protect a will, there are several provisions you can follow to deter a will contest. The first step is to use an experienced attorney to help draft your will. A knowledgeable attorney will use language when drafting your will, which minimizes ambiguity and helps minimize (or avoid completely) the taxes your beneficiaries will pay when it comes time for probate. If you are worried that a beneficiary may contest your will, then your attorney may contact a physician to evaluate your mental state and serve as a witness to the will signing.

A second step is for your attorney to include a noncontest provision, or forfeiture clause, to your will. This provision states that a beneficiary who chooses to contest your will loses any right to the inheritance that they might have otherwise received. In other words, if someone disagrees with your will, they will be awarded nothing from your estate if they pursue a will contest.

It is important to note that you cannot stop a beneficiary from taking the case to court, and this provision only serves to strip that individual from their inheritance if the case goes that far.[407] It's important to have a will and inform others of its location. A will should be reassessed by an attorney every few years to make sure all the people listed as beneficiaries are still alive and that you still want them to receive a portion of your estate. Also, you should have an irrevocable trust as part of your estate planning eldercare needs, which will avoid the high expenses of probate and reduce estate taxes.

Be careful of free Internet wills. These free wills may be fine if you have a simple estate with very few items. You should use an attorney to prepare your will if you have a moderate to large estate. Assets in joint tenancy can't be simply given away. The other tenant has survivorship rights, so you just can't simply give it away. Life insurance policies may be taxed as part of your estate. Also, a trust may be more beneficial than a will, especially if you have young children and you don't want to bequeath your assets to them and also if you and your spouse should both die, then you would want a guardian to take care of them, and a trust would be a better legal instrument than a will for this purpose.

Succession Planning

The first step in determining your financial plan will be to obtain an accurate valuation of your business. You may need to hire a professional appraiser to determine the fair market value of your tangible and intangible assets in a manner that conforms to IRS standards and will prevent an audit of your estate once it passes out of your control.

Once you have determined the value of your business, you have several options on how you may transfer control to your successor:

1. Gifting: This is an option that allows you to transfer ownership of your business over a set number of years without taxes, assuming you follow the current annual IRS gift limits. Gifting your business is also an excellent way to protect the financial security of your family and successors by removing the gifted amounts from your overall estate value. Staying within IRS limitations will help your family avoid gift and estate taxes.

2. Buy/Sell Agreements: These agreements are usually made between multiple shareholders in a company. A typical agreement might stipulate that if one shareholder decides to leave the company, the other shareholders are obligated to buy back his or her shares to keep the company from being sold to an outside party. Some agreements allow for all shares to be sold back to the business at the fair market price, which means that employees other than the principals would have the opportunity to own part of the business.

Even if you do not have business partners, you should consider purchasing a business life insurance policy. If something were to tragically happen to you, a properly funded life insurance policy will provide your family and successors with the financial stability to continue business operations and pay off any necessary estate taxes. To protect the future of your business, it is important to have an accurate valuation performed by a genuine appraiser and to discuss changing tax laws with your financial advisor.

HOW AMERICA IS TURNING ITS SENIOR CITIZENS INTO CRIMINALS

The new Medicaid provisions for nursing home assistance are very restrictive. In order to qualify for nursing home assistance, you have to be poor, literally with few assets. If you have too many assets or too much net worth, you don't qualify. So what do so many of our senior citizens do in a valiant attempt to qualify for a nursing home? They break the law and give away their assets. Now you're probably saying, "Just wait a minute, there's nothing wrong with giving your assets away, they're yours." However, if you give away or otherwise transfer assets in the five-year period[408] before you go into a nursing home under Medicaid, you won't qualify. And if you lie about any of the transfers in the five-year look-back period, that's perjury. And if you intentionally transfer assets and lie about in order to get into a nursing home, then you're guilty of a fraudulent conveyance and perjury. Unfortunately, quite a few of our senior citizens are committing criminal acts in order to qualify for nursing home care under Medicaid. The intention is for you (a senior citizen) to become a welfare and food stamp recipient before you qualify for nursing home assistance.

Not many insurance companies are willing to pay for long-term care. It's important to check the details of your insurance policy and read the fine print for restrictions. For example, Medicare will not pay for long-term care, but it will pay a very short-term benefit. However, Medicaid will pay for long-term care but only if the care is received in a Medicaid facility.

America is telling our senior citizens that you have to become a welfare and food stamp recipient in order to qualify for a nursing home. This is extremely humiliating for most senior citizens. So what are some senior citizens doing these days? They're trying to hide their assets.

It's unfortunate to see a senior citizen wrongly transfer his or her assets. He or she incorrectly believes that giving away assets, usually to the children, is a good away to dispose of the problem of having too many assets to qualify for nursing home assistance under Medicaid. This is not a good way to hide assets. For instance, giving a home to the children requires a deed, usually a quitclaim deed, which must be recorded in order to be effective against any third party. As one can see, a paper trail has been established. Furthermore, this transfer is dated, and if it was made within the five-year look-back period, the senior citizen won't qualify for nursing home assistance.

One of the best ways to hide your assets is by using an "irrevocable trust." You legally no longer own the assets. However, depending on the circumstances, you could be committing a fraudulent conveyance. This involves the actual transfer of assets to a trustee who will manage and legally own the assets in the trust for the benefit of the beneficiaries.

An irrevocable special needs trust or Medicaid trust is truly the best asset-protection device for avoiding the Medicaid spend-down provisions. The primary purpose of this trust is to reduce your assets to a level where you can qualify for Medicaid. It must be funded at least five years prior to applying for Medicaid. Since it is often difficult to predict when you will need Medicaid and the fact that once you place your assets in the irrevocable trust, they will no longer be accessible; this then becomes a difficult situation.

Bottom line: Senior citizens must use up all of their funds first before they can qualify for the nursing home. It's clear that these new rules are designed to impose an additional hardship on our senior citizens, the generation who made America strong and respected.

After retirement, the threat of lawsuits diminishes, especially after you close your business. As a result, it is often advantageous to rearrange assets. Separate property can be converted into community property via a transmutation agreement so that there is a step up in the basis of property when the first spouse dies. In fact, tax considerations often outweigh asset-protection considerations during retirement when the threat of a lawsuit markedly diminishes. However, the look-back period for an asset transfer is five years with Medicaid. This could present a potential problem and is something to take into consideration when contemplating a rearrangement of assets during retirement. A long-term care insurance policy is an excellent solution to the potential Medicaid problem that many seniors face.

ANNUITIES

Annuities have been available to the public since the early twentieth century. An annuity is an agreement between you and your insurance company that you will pay a certain sum of money to the insurer (either a lump sum or series of payments), and they will make scheduled payments to you, sometimes immediately but more commonly they will delay payments until after a certain period of time. An annuity can only be sold to you by a licensed and registered insurance agent. Even if your insurance company goes bankrupt, other licensed insurance companies in the state are required to step in and honor your annuity. Annuities grow tax deferred, and you will not have to pay any taxes to the Internal Revenue Service (IRS) until you begin receiving payments from your annuity; and those taxes are based only on the final accumulation of your annuity at the time you begin receiving payments from the annuity.

There are basically two types of annuities: *fixed* and *variable* annuities. In addition to deciding when you will receive annuity payments, you can also choose between a fixed and a variable annuity. A fixed annuity guarantees the interest rate and the payment amounts of your annuity. There won't be any surprises here. On the other hand, a variable annuity cannot guarantee the amount of your payments but does allow for different investment options that could result in a larger payment to you compared to a fixed annuity.

Annuities can be further categorized either as a *deferred* or *immediate* annuity. A deferred annuity is ideal for a long-term goal such as retirement. It is important to remember that if you choose this type of annuity there are penalties for early withdrawal. The IRS imposes a standard 10 percent penalty, in addition to income tax on accrued funds, if you withdraw money before the age of fifty-nine and a half. Your insurer may also charge you surrender fees for an early withdrawal.

If you wait until retirement to withdraw money, there are three methods for requesting payment from a deferred annuity. You can

1. request a lump-sum payment,
2. take out money only when you need it, or
3. annuitize and receive a set dollar amount every month for as long as you live.

Many people choose to annuitize because it also spreads out the required income tax payments. If you die before withdrawing all the money from the annuity, your beneficiaries are entitled to receive the balance of your annuity by these methods as well; although if they choose a lump sum, they will be immediately charged all the tax on the accrued interest.

Most people close to retirement, or already retired, choose an immediate annuity. Immediate annuities must be purchased with a lump sum since payments will usually begin within one month of purchase. When you purchase an immediate annuity, you are guaranteeing a steady income either for the rest of your life or for a predetermined time period. When you receive payments from an immediate annuity, you are only taxed on the earnings from your initial investment; none of the principal is taxable.

You have three main options to choose from when receiving an annuity payment:

1. Income for life—which guarantees you a set income for the duration of your life, but payments will cease upon your death. This option is risky. If you should die before your annuity has been completely paid out, the insurance company, and not your beneficiaries, will receive the remainder of the annuity funds.
2. Income for life with a guaranteed period—which guarantees you a set income for the duration of your life, but if you die before the predetermined guarantee period expires, your beneficiaries will continue to receive payments until the guarantee period ends.

3. Joint and survivor option—which guarantees payment to you and another person, usually your spouse, until both of you die.

Annuities may also be used to fund your 401(k), 403(b), and Individual Retirement Account (IRA); although this is generally not advised. Additionally, once you have used your annuity to finance your 401(k), barring a few exceptions, you will incur a 10 percent penalty for early withdrawal if you withdraw money before you reach age fifty-nine and a half.

The downsides of an annuity are a contribution limitation; the federal government requirement for you to begin receiving minimum payments by age seventy and a half; and, once you begin receiving annuity payments you cannot make any changes, you cannot stop payments, and you will continue to receive payments for the predetermined time frame established during the accumulation phase.

A private annuity trust use assets other than money to fund this type of annuity. For example, you can transfer ownership of a home or land with high value to a trust. The trust then makes lifetime payments to you and can sell the asset you gave them and use the money to fund this annuity agreement through investments. You cannot use retirement funds such as a 401(k) to fund a private annuity trust. The withdrawal period from a private annuity trust must begin by no later than age seventy and a half. By law, the annuitant is not allowed to have any direct control over the investments of their annuity. Your transfer of ownership to the private annuity trust is irrevocable.

It is fairly easy to estimate what your annuity payments will be for the asset transferred into a private annuity trust. The IRS uses the following factors to determine your payment:

1. Your life expectancy.
2. The selling price of your asset.

3. The Annual Federal Midterm Rate (AFMR) effective when your property was transferred. (This rate will be the rate used for the duration of your annuity.)
4. The length of time you defer payments.

These factors will determine the fixed amount you will receive from the annuity, and once the withdrawal period begins, you will continue to receive payments for life.

Owning a joint spouse private annuity trust will allow your spouse to continue receiving annuity payments should you die first. After your spouse dies, payments will cease and your beneficiaries will inherit any surplus money remaining in your private annuity trust created by the trust's investments. By law, there must be enough money set aside for the trust to fulfill its annuity agreement with you, and there will usually be a reserve account established of 5–10 percent of your asset's value as a safety precaution. Remember, your annuity payment is fixed and will not increase regardless of any profit your assets create via the private annuity trust.

There is no estate tax, income tax, or gift tax on a private annuity trust transfer because the transfer of ownership of an asset to a trust is "paid for" by the annuity agreement. The IRS cannot accurately determine your life expectancy and therefore cannot determine how many payments you will actually receive. Taxes will be deferred on the transfer until you start receiving payments, and a portion of your payment will be taxed based on your income amount. The transfer of ownership involving your assets is not considered a gift to the trust because the trust is agreeing to pay you for the asset (which makes this a sale, not a gift) at a later date, and as a result, you will not have to pay a gift tax. Once your asset is transferred to the trust, it is removed from your taxable estate. This is of particular benefit to your beneficiaries who will not be held responsible for paying estate taxes when they receive excess funds from your annuity. After your death it is the responsibility of the trust to cover any unpaid taxes due on the assets.

The Allstate Insurance Company has developed something similar to the private annuity trust called the Ensured Installment Sale..

Are Annuities Protected from Creditors?

Under federal bankruptcy, most annuities are protected (exempt) from creditors "to the extent reasonably necessary for the support of the debtor and any dependent of the debtor."[409] There are certain exceptions.[410]

Also, many states provide some protection to annuities. In fact, Florida has an unlimited exemption for annuities.[411]

Charitable Gift Annuities

A charitable gift annuity (CGA) is very similar to an insurance annuity, except that your annuity payment will come directly from the charity or organization. Here's how it works: you donate money to a charity or an organization of your choice and then you receive payments either immediately or at a future date. There are four different types of charitable gift annuities: immediate annuity, deferred annuity, college annuity and flexible annuity. A charitable gift annuity (CGA) is a great way to donate funds to an educational, religious, or other charitable organization, and in return you get a tax deduction and annuity payments. Here are the different types of charitable gift annuities:

1. Immediate gift annuity—Payments will begin in the payment period immediately following the final contribution date.
2. Deferred gift annuity—Payments are made at least one year or more from the contribution date as predetermined by the donor.
3. College annuity—A parent or grandparent may want to establish a college fund for a child (annuitant) by donating money for a college annuity, which will begin payments when the child is old enough to attend college. Payments are made directly to the child (annuitant).
4. Flexible annuity—Allows the annuitant to decide when the payments start. Most choose retirement to begin receiving

payments. One factor for the size of the annuity payment is age: the older you are, the larger the payment.

IS YOUR RETIREMENT PLAN SAFE FROM CREDITORS?

Participants of tax-qualified retirement plans generally are protected from creditors' claims and their plans are insulated from claims in bankruptcy.[412] Under the revised bankruptcy laws,[413] 403(b) accounts, IRAs, and other retirement accounts are, in general, protected from creditors in bankruptcy. Retirement plans that cover only the business owner and/or the owner's spouse and section 403(b) tax-sheltered annuity plans whose assets are held in custodial accounts rather than in trusts are not protected from creditors' claims.

Retirement plans are marital assets subject to division in divorce or attachment for child support by a qualified domestic relations order (QDRO). Furthermore, retirement plans are subject to attachment by federal tax levies, judgments, and fines imposed in federal criminal actions. Treasury regulations provide that plan benefits are subject to attachment by the IRS.

Between 1975 and 1999, the total value of pensions, 401(k) plans, and IRAs increased from $400 billion to more than $12 trillion.[414]

The bottom line: A businessperson can qualify as a participant in an Employee Retirement Income Security Act (ERISA) plan as long as the plan covers one or more employees other than the business owner and/or his or her spouse.[415]

Antialienation Provisions

The antialienation provisions of the Employee Retirement Income Security Act of 1974 (ERISA)[416] protect (tax-qualified) retirement plans from creditors' claims of plan participants and their beneficiaries with four major exceptions:

1. Divorce action. Qualified Domestic Relations Orders (QDROs) are exempted.[417] Thus, retirement plan assets are considered a marital asset subject to division in divorce and attachment for child support. Moreover, pension plans awarded under a QDRO before a bankruptcy are not protected by bankruptcy and must be paid to the former spouse.[418]
2. Federal tax lien. The IRS can stake a claim to assets held in retirement plans. Federal tax levies and judgments are exempted from ERISA protection.[419]
3. Fiduciary violation. Criminal or civil judgments, consent decrees and settlement agreements offset retirement benefits when the plan participants commit fiduciary violations or crimes against the plan. [420]
4. Criminal fine. The general antialienation rule[421] does not preclude a court's garnishing the account balance of a fined participant in a qualified pension plan in order to collect a fine imposed in a federal criminal action." The IRS cited favorably three recent federal district court cases[422] that concluded that ERISA plans were subject to garnishment to satisfy criminal fines under the Federal Debt Collection Procedures Act of 1977 (FDCPA).

What Individual Retirement Accounts (IRAs) Are Protected from Creditors' Claims Under ERISA?

IRA protection depends on a number of factors. There is a lot of confusion here because the laws vary considerably from state to state, and even the federal law doesn't provide full protection.[423] Generally speaking, if you have filed for bankruptcy protection, then your IRA is more fully protected. However, most states afford some IRA protection but not as much as bankruptcy. In a few states, IRA protection is quite limited.[424] Another important factor to consider is the type of IRA you have. All ERISA-protected IRAs have limited federal protection because the antialienation provision does not apply. And the amazing thing to remember, which even some of the experts have mistaken, is that once the IRA funds have been disbursed to you, they are no longer protected!

An Individual Retirement Account (IRA)[425] is a retirement plan that provides tax advantages for retirement savings. There are several types of IRAs:

- SEP IRA—Typically a small business or self-employed individual makes contributions into a traditional IRA established in the employee's name, instead of to a pension fund in the company's name. [*Protected* under ERISA].
- SIMPLE IRA—A savings incentive match plan for employees that requires employer matching contributions to the plan whenever an employee makes a contribution. The plan is similar to a 401(k) plan but with lower contribution limits and simpler (and thus less costly) administration. [*Protected* under ERISA].
- Traditional IRA—Most contributions are tax deductible and withdrawals at retirement are taxed as income. [*Not* protected under ERISA].
- Roth IRA—Contributions are made with after-tax dollars. [*Not* protected under ERISA].

The new bankruptcy law protects tax-qualified retirement plans—pensions, profit-sharing, and 401(k) plans—from creditors in bankruptcy. SEP and SIMPLE IRAs are excluded from bankruptcy estates under the new law because they qualify as ERISA pension plans. Traditional and Roth IRAs that are created and funded by an individual are subject to a maximum bankruptcy exclusion of $1 million.

However, in a state action (outside of bankruptcy), SEP and SIMPLE IRAs, being ERISA plans, but not enjoying ERISA antialienation protections, could be subject to attack in a state action since any *protecting* state law may be preempted or overridden by ERISA and thus *no* antialienation protection. In other words, a SEP and SIMPLE IRA could be vulnerable to creditor attack in state court.[426]

On the other hand, traditional and roth IRAs are *not* ERISA pension plans. Thus, they are *protected* in state (nonbankruptcy) proceedings by any state laws specifically protecting IRAs since such state laws are not preempted or overridden by ERISA.

Retirement Funds Are Protected in Bankruptcy

The new bankruptcy law protects retirement funds by excluding them from federal bankruptcy estates. It applies to any fund or account as follows:

1. Tax exempt under IRC section 401(a)—Tax-qualified retirement plans like pensions, annuities,[427] profit-sharing, and IRC section 401(k) plans.
2. IRC section 403(b)—Tax-sheltered annuity plans generally available to individuals working for IRC section 501(c) (3) employers.
3. IRC section 457(b)—Deferred compensation plans for employees of tax exempt and state and local government employers.

In bankruptcy, a debtor can exempt his or her IRA up to the amount necessary for retirement from the bankruptcy estate.[428] Many states already have laws effectively allowing an individual to exempt an IRA in bankruptcy, but the Supreme Court now allows federal protection for IRAs. The New Bankruptcy Law (BAPCPA) expanded the protection for IRAs. Certain IRAs (rollovers from SEP or Simple IRAs, Roth IRAs, individual IRAs) are exempt up to at least $1,000,000 (adjusted periodically for inflation) without having to show necessity for retirement. The law provides that "such amount may be increased if the interests of justice so require." Other IRAs (rollovers from most employer sponsored retirement plans 401(k)s, etc. and nonrollover SEP and SIMPLE IRAs) are entirely exempt.[429]

Please note that if an IRA engages in a "prohibited transaction," the assets in the IRA will no longer qualify for bankruptcy protection.[430]

For protection from creditors there are several options of protecting an IRA:

1. Roll it over into a qualified plan like a 401(k).
2. Take a distribution, pay the tax, and protect the proceeds. Rely on the state law exemption for IRAs.
3. File for bankruptcy protection.

IRAs do not receive protection in cases of divorce, failure to pay taxes, deeds of trust, and fraud.

Owner-Only Retirement Plans Are Not Protected From Creditors

Retirement plans must ensure that they include nonowner employees as well as owners and their spouses so that the retirement plans of business owners and their spouses are protected from creditors in case of bankruptcy. Remember, a retirement plan that covers only the owners of a business may be attached by the bankruptcy creditors of the owner/plan participant.

Department of Labor regulations also provide that a husband and wife, who solely own a corporation, are not employees for retirement plan purposes and that a plan that covers only partners or sole proprietors is not protected under ERISA. However, a plan that includes one or more (common-law) employees (in addition to the owners) is protected, making ERISA protections applicable to all participants.

The US Ninth Circuit Court of Appeals[431] held that an ERISA-qualified employee pension benefit plan could lose its ERISA status for bankruptcy purposes if nonowner participants left, and it covered only the owner-employee at the time of the bankruptcy filing. The court also said section 541(c) of the Bankruptcy Code invalidated certain nonbankruptcy state law protections for retirement benefits.

Assets Held in a Trust Are Excluded from Bankruptcy

All assets held "in a trust" are excluded from bankruptcy and thus protected from creditors.[432]

Some 403(b) Pension Plans May Not Be Protected from Creditors

The difference between 401(k) plans and 403(b) plans is that 401(k) plans are nearly always protected under ERISA while 403(b) plans are now gaining more protection under ERISA through the new bankruptcy law—Bankruptcy Abuse Prevention and Consumer Protection Act of 2005 (BAPCPA).

403(b) Plans with Trust Accounts Are Safe from Creditors

Consider transferring assets of public school employees and tax-exempt organizations to 403(b) plans with trust accounts.

Distributed Retirement Funds Are Not Safe from Creditors

The antialienation provisions of ERISA and the Internal Revenue Code don't protect pension benefits that already have been removed from retirement plans and distributed to plan participants or beneficiaries.[433] Therefore, please remember when facing creditors or possible bankruptcy to withdraw only the minimum required annual distributions from the retirement plan to shield the balance from creditors.

Inheritance Rules of Retirement Plans

The rules regarding the inheritance of retirement plans is complicated, and you're strongly encouraged to seek the services of an experienced tax attorney as soon as you receive or about to receive an inherited retirement plan.

Summary—The Law Is Constantly Changing

ERISA's antialienation protections are extensive. However, some changes have occurred under recent rulings by the courts and the IRS. By federal law, no creditor can get your money that's due you under an employer-provided pension plan. The antialienation rule is applicable to qualified plans subject to ERISA which include the 403(b) plan, savings incentive match plans for employees (SIMPLEs), profit-sharing plans and defined benefit plans. ERISA features an "antialienation" provision that bars employers from allowing creditors to garnish or seize employees' retirement funds while the employer still possesses them. If the employer violates the rule, its retirement plan will permanently lose its tax advantages. However, once the funds are distributed as retirement benefits, they're no longer in the employer's possession and therefore don't enjoy the same protection from creditors. Also bear in mind that there are four exceptions to ERISA's antialienation provision:

1. Divorce action
2. Federal tax lien
3. Fiduciary violation
4. Criminal fine

ADVANCED TECHNIQUES

Beneficiary Defective Discretionary Spendthrift Trusts

A beneficiary defective discretionary spendthrift trust (BDDST) is a new type of trust that combines the powerful asset-protection attributes of intentionally defective trusts, discretionary trusts, and spendthrift trusts into an all-powerful trust. The trust can be structured to have the income taxed either to the grantor or the beneficiary. To add to the awesome power of this trust, you can elect to have a third party, such as your attorney, set up the trust for you. This type of trust rivals offshore trusts in terms of asset protection and is thus a viable alternative to an offshore trust. This is a complicated trust that's best left to the experts.

Charitable Remainder Unitrusts

Charitable planning will lower your taxes while reducing your assets and is useful for asset and lawsuit protection. A charitable remainder unitrust[434] is an irrevocable trust that can be very useful. This special, irrevocable trust (known as a "CRUT") has two primary characteristics: (1) Once established, the CRUT distributes a fixed percentage of the value of its assets (on an annual or more frequent basis) to a noncharitable beneficiary (typically the grantor of the trust) and (2) at the expiration of a specified time (usually the death of the grantor), the remaining balance of the CRUT's assets are distributed to charity. The trustee determines the fair market value of the CRUT's assets at the time of contribution and thereafter on the applicable valuation date. The fixed annuity percentage must be at least 5 percent and no more than 50 percent of the fair market value of the assets in the trust. The remainder (the amount expected to go to charity) must be at least 10 percent of the fair market value of the assets contributed to the CRUT.

For example, suppose you have $500,000 of publicly traded stock and would like to establish a CRUT. Assume the CRUT is set up to pay an annuity to you over your lifetime. You select a 10 percent CRUT. The CRUT will pay you 10 percent of its assets (initially $50,000) per year until you pass away. At that time, any remaining balance in the CRUT will be distributed to charity. The term *unitrust* means the annuity percentage is fixed; the CRUT will distribute 10 percent of the value of the CRUT's assets each year, which may increase or decrease over time.

Closely Held Insurance Companies

Closely held insurance companies (CHIC) are often set up in foreign jurisdictions and allow you to transfer up to $1.2 million (pre-tax) annually. A closely held insurance company (CHIC) can be used as a captive insurance company (CIC) for wealth transfer and for providing insurance against perils. A significant amount of commercial insurance is written offshore with premiums estimated to be around $60 billion each year.[435] In order to form these structures properly, you should utilize a skilled tax attorney.

Domestic Asset-Protection Trusts

Domestic asset-protection trusts (DAPT) are a special type of trust that was first developed in Alaska allowing protection for self-settled trusts (in 1997) and was shortly followed by Delaware, Nevada, South Dakota, and a few others. Usually, a DAPT must comply with the following requirements:

- The trust must be irrevocable and spendthrift.
- At least one resident trustee must be appointed.
- Some administration of the trust must be conducted in the respective state.
- The grantor cannot act as a trustee.

There are a number of problems with the DAPT:

1. Conflict of laws can occur because each state has its own set of unique laws. If the state you live in doesn't recognize DAPTs, then it's unlikely your DAPT will be recognized.
2. Full faith and credit clause means that every state must recognize and give deference to another state's judgment. But if your state doesn't allow DAPTs because it would be against public policy, then how can this be reconciled with the full faith and credit clause?
3. Statutory exceptions could result in further confusion even if the conflict of laws and the full faith and credit issues are resolved.
4. Legal standards vary by jurisdiction and create further problems.
5. DAPTs are governed by US law and are therefore vulnerable to the US court system; a problem that does not plague offshore trusts.
6. Bankruptcy may or may not protect a DAPT from creditors. Interestingly, with regard to transfers, state law must be followed by a bankruptcy court.[436]

In conclusion, DAPTs are the newcomer on the block, and there is a dearth of case law, which is sorely needed to guide asset-protection professionals. Therefore, offshore trusts are clearly superior to DAPTs in terms of asset protection.

Foreign-Based Tax-Exempt Entities

A very strong asset-protection structure is based on the formation of a tax-exempt entity in a foreign jurisdiction, which is a holding company for the protected assets. The stock in this tax-exempt entity is held by an asset-protection trust. Consequently, the stock and any income generated from the protected assets will not show up on the client's tax return or on any other financial statement. This is the ultimate cloaking device. Moreover, the tax-exempt entity will not pay any tax and should be invisible to the creditors.

It's also possible for your trustee to set up secret stock trading accounts with a major financial institution and appoint the client as the trading advisor who will make stock trades on behalf of the trust. And best of all, there are no capital gains taxes on any profits generated from the client's offshore trust.

Foreign (Offshore) Limited Liability Companies

One advantage of using a foreign (offshore) limited liability company or limited partnership is that it is easier to file tax forms than with a foreign asset protection trust (FAPT). Also, with regard to the IRS, you obtain more privacy with foreign limited liability companies than you do with FAPTs. And finally, a creditor may be left with only one viable remedy, which is to seek a charging order in the jurisdiction of your offshore limited partnership or LLC.

Experts now suggest combining a foreign limited partnership or LLC with an FAPT. This would indeed make a formidable asset-protection structure. Please seek a professional advisor who is familiar with this arcane area of asset protection.

Freeze Partnerships/Preferred Partnerships

Freeze partnerships[437] are a type of preferred partnership. This is a complicated estate planning technique that's best left to an expert tax attorney. A freeze partnership is a partnership in which there are two classes of interests, a preferred interest and a common interest. When properly structured, the freeze partnership can help you obtain up to a 90 percent discount on an FLP interest whereas a traditional FLP provides a 20 percent discount depending on the assets held.

Intentionally Defective Grantor Trusts

An intentionally defective grantor trust (IDGT) is an advanced technique that uses a trust that is "defective" solely for income tax purposes. IDGTs provide asset protection for assets transferred to them. Although the grantor is treated as the trust owner for income tax purposes, he is not the owner for legal or equitable ownership purposes. Unless the grantor retains control, IDGT assets are not available to his creditors. The IDGT should be drafted by an expert tax attorney with a spendthrift clause, and it should be discretionary.

Section 79 of the Internal Revenue Code

Section 79 of the Internal Revenue Code lets corporations install a group-term life insurance plan, thereby allowing them a tax deduction, and a way to reduce the corporations' assets.

Series LLCs

A series limited liability company, commonly known as a series LLC and sometimes abbreviated as SLLC, is a specialized form of a limited liability company that provides liability protection across a number of separate underlying ("series") LLCs, each of which is theoretically protected from liabilities arising from the other series. Presently, only ten states have approved the Series LLC.[438] In overall structure, the series LLC has been described as a master LLC that has separate divisions, which is similar to an S corporation with Q-subs.

However, as opposed to a Series LLC (which is a newcomer with a dearth of case law), conventional LLCs have the advantage that additional liability protection may be gained by properly forming and maintaining a separate LLC to hold each property or business entity. By forming a separate LLC to own and hold each legally titled separate property or business entity, theoretically only the assets owned by a specific LLC would be subject to claims or lawsuits arising against that LLC. However, there are costs and administrative burdens associated with properly forming, qualifying and maintaining each separate LLC. A Series LLC should only be used in the ten states where they statutorily approved. California has taken the position that it will only tax income from those series conducting business in California but that each such "sub-series" will owe the annual franchise fee, making this a very expensive entity for California residents.

Summary

The realty of lawsuit and asset protection is that the trial courts are biased in favor of creditors against debtors. Appellate courts are somewhat fairer and less biased. However, most of the time, trial court judges rule in favor of creditors over debtors. Moreover, recent court decisions are slowly eroding the remaining protections that the debtors have and thus are procreditor. And finally, be very careful of the road shows associated with the asset protection salesmen who try so very hard to sell you a bill of goods—basically a "house of cards." Their asset-protection schemes don't work and won't work. It only makes the salesmen very rich. Since the law is constantly changing, you must make sure your asset protection is up to date.

The asset-protection paradox is that complicated asset-protection plans will often confuse the court, and consequently, judges often make mistakes in favor of the creditors. Furthermore, complicated plans arouse suspicion of debtor fraud. You're much better off keeping your lawsuit and asset-protection plan simple and easy to understand. Moreover, if your plan is predicated on sound legal principles, you stand a much better chance of a favorable debtor ruling. And simple plans cost a lot less than complicated ones.

If you engage in criminal activity, besides possibly facing criminal charges, you could also face civil litigation and possible asset forfeiture. (See chapter 51.)

CONCLUSION

Now that you are judgment protected, what should you do if you're ever sued? You certainly could ignore the lawsuit and get a default judgment entered against you. Then the creditor could haul you into court every six months for debtor's exam that could possibly extend to more than one business day (although this seldom occurs). Or the creditor could hire a collections attorney who really could make your life miserable. The collections attorney could compel you to hire an attorney to defend against various legal filings initiated by the collections attorney. What if the lawsuit had been frivolous, but now the plaintiff has a free windfall judgment against you because you defaulted. And then your credit will be adversely affected too. In my opinion, you need to take every lawsuit seriously even if you are judgment protected. Hopefully, in most cases, your insurance company will defend you. If that's not the case, then your lawsuit may go away when the plaintiffs' attorney is convinced that it would be virtually impossible to collect a judgment against you. Believe me, most attorneys, assuming they're smart, are going to "pack it up" and move on to bigger and better cases when they realize they have little or no chance to ever collect on their judgment against you. Only rarely will you ever have to contend with the stubborn (or stupid) plaintiff who refuses to quit even when they see that they're going to lose. In those instances, you just might want to pay them off so they go away.

Winning in life and doing well in life are no accidents. It first takes preparation. With proper preparation, you'll feel confident of success. That will instill a feeling of power and strength. Negotiating life's obstacles from a position of power and strength accomplishes three remarkable things. First of all, it gives you the confidence you need to succeed. Secondly, that strong confidence of yours will compel you to act successfully. And thirdly, your power and strength will give your morale a boost. Also, remember to think smart, act smart, and do the right thing!

Military generals will tell you the same thing. They inspire their troops in order to boost morale, and they do so from a position of power and strength. So how can you be in a position of power and strength when you get sued? The answer is simple. All that is required is proper preparation before you get sued, and your judgment-protected status will intimidate and undermine your adversaries, which gives you an added advantage.

Lawsuit protection is closely tied to asset protection, which seeks to make the satisfaction of judgments against the debtor extremely difficult if not virtually impossible and additionally allows the judgment debtor some limited control over his protected assets.

There are nearly one million practicing lawyers in the United States today, and they are always looking to represent clients to sue someone. Thus, it's imperative that you fully prepare for a future lawsuit, which sooner or later, is bound to happen. A good asset-protection plan will discourage litigation and promote settlements in your favor. Your offshore trust and its IBC along with the foreign bank account will keep the ownership of your assets confidential. Before you can potentially lose any of your assets, the plaintiffs will first have to win their lawsuit against you. Remember, begin to transfer your assets long *before* you are threatened with a lawsuit, engaged in active litigation, or have existing creditors. Once you are threatened with a lawsuit, engaged in active litigation, or have existing creditors, then it's already too late. Any transfers would be deemed a fraudulent conveyance. Once your assets have been legitimately transferred, they're no longer yours. Spread your transfers around so that they're not all in one place. What your creditors don't know won't hurt them, so never volunteer any information. U.S. judgments are not honored nor are they enforced in foreign countries. Your creditor will have to relitigate his or her case in the foreign country with a paid attorney as there are no contingency-fee attorneys outside the United States. (The United States is the only place in the world that permits contingency-fee attorneys.)

Also, your creditor must put up a bond, pay court costs, and must prepay attorney fees. Moreover, if your creditor loses his case, he must pay your attorney's fees!

In the United States, there's a greater chance that you will be sued than you will have a hospital stay! While wealth may be the American dream, lawsuits are the American nightmare! I wish you the *best* and *thank you*!

Now You Know How to Kill a Lawsuit and Stop It Dead in Its Tracks!

APPENDIX A

What Should I Do First?

Purchase plenty of liability insurance. This is absolutely the very first thing you must do. If you do nothing else, just get lots of liability insurance! Your first priority is making sure you have plenty of liability insurance. Call your insurance agent to make sure that you are adequately covered with liability insurance.

Once your insurance coverage is up to date, the next important consideration is to make sure that you separate your assets appropriately through legal transfers. Before you can legally transfer your assets, three conditions must be met: (1) you haven't been threatened with a lawsuit, (2) you don't have any pending lawsuits against you, and (3) you don't have any present creditors. Assuming all three conditions are met, you can then freely transfer your safe and expensive assets to the least vulnerable spouse, a family limited partnership (FLP), a limited liability company (LLC), a corporation, or even a trust. You can even legally have an offshore trust. If you're running a business, you need to operate it through a corporation or limited liability company. Please remember that when you transfer assets to an FLP, LLC, or a corporation, it should be for a business purpose. Otherwise, you will probably be better off transferring your assets to an irrevocable trust.

Summary

Here's my suggestion on how to proceed with your lawsuit and asset-protection plan. First, it's important to make sure you have plenty of liability insurance. (Did you know that statistically you'll be sued more times than you will ever have a hospital stay?) Call your insurance agent, or go online to find an insurance agent or insurance company that can assist you in providing you with adequate liability insurance. This can be accomplished very quickly often in just one day.

Afterwards, the next task is to protect your home. This will most likely require transferring your home via a transmutation agreement or setting up a family limited partnership. In some instances, you may want to transfer your home to an offshore trust. This process can take up to a month to complete.

If you're interested in maximum protection, then you'll definitely want to set up an offshore trust. On an urgent basis, you can probably get an offshore trust set up in as little as twenty-four to seventy-two hours. But more often, it can take up to thirty days to set up your offshore trust. If you own automobiles, then you'll probably want to transfer them to the least vulnerable spouse. Or you just might want to consider selling them and then begin leasing your cars.

Most people are not self-employed, but for those who are, it would be worthwhile to consider incorporating or possibly forming a limited liability company.

A child's trust should be set up so you can deduct taxes (siphon money from your company) and divert money to places where you normally cannot achieve favorable tax benefits.

A friendly divorce with large family support payments can effectively kill garnishments.

You'll need to form a new company if your original company becomes a judgment debtor.

Establishing a foreign bank account makes a lot of sense. And remember to always password-protect your offshore bank account.

APPENDIX B

The Top US Insurance Companies

According to TopRatedInsuranceCompanies.com, here the top ten insurance companies in the United States:

1. Allstate Insurance Company
2. State Farm Insurance Company
3. Prudential Insurance Company
4. Travelers Insurance Company
5. Fidelity Insurance Company
6. MetLife Insurance Company
7. Farmers Insurance Company
8. AIG Insurance Company
9. MassMutual Insurance Company
10. The Hartford Insurance Company

Finally, it's unbelievably hard to find the five "best" insurance companies. But here they are based upon fifty years' experience in personal injury and wrongful death litigation:

1. Chubb Corporation
2. Wausau
3. Amica Mutual
4. Travelers
5. USAA

APPENDIX C

Supplemental Insurance Companies

- Aflac
- Allstate
- American Fidelity Assurance
- Colonial Life & Accident Insurance Company
- Conseco
- Family Heritage
- Liberty National Life Insurance Company
- MEGA Life and Health Insurance
- Mutual of Omaha
- State Farm Insurance

BIBLIOGRAPHY[439]

- Asset Protection : Concepts and Strategies for Protecting Your Wealth 1st (first) edition by Jay Adkisson (2005)
- Asset Protection 1st (first) edition Text Only by Jay Adkisson (2004)
- http://www.assetprotectionbook.com/

INDEX

A

B

C

D

E

F

G

H

I

M

N

O

P

T

U

V

W

ABOUT THE AUTHOR

Brian Turner is a former businessman who for more than twenty years was the CEO and president of several companies that provided services for the life insurance industry. He's been involved in numerous lawsuits both as a plaintiff and as a defendant. He explains how a $20,000 nonbinding arbitration award against him and his company unexpectedly and shockingly exploded into a $2 million judgment! He studied and researched the law extensively for the past twenty years. His conclusion is that everybody living in the United States today is highly vulnerable to a lawsuit that could easily wipe them out because of unpredictable jury verdicts and corruption in our legal system. His recommendation is that everyone must take proactive steps to protect themselves against lawsuits and to protect all of their assets. All of this information is clearly explained in a simple step-by-step approach in this guidebook. Brian Turner is an alumnus of the University of Illinois, and he now lives in California.

THE AUTHOR'S PHILOSOPHY

1. Think smart—You must think about protecting yourself because America is the most litigious (lawsuit-prone) society in the world.
2. Act smart—You must act now to implement a protection plan that will protect you.
3. Do the right thing—Setting up a protection plan is doing the right thing.

THE TWELVE LAWSUIT PROTECTION LAWS

If you follow these twelve laws, you'll have *maximum* protection against lawsuits!

1. Always have plenty of liability insurance.
2. Always use multiple layers of protection.
3. Always separate and protect your dangerous assets from your safe assets.
4. Transfer your home and other expensive assets for protection.
5. Never commit a fraudulent conveyance and always record your transfers.
6. Use irrevocable offshore trusts for maximum protection.
7. Never run a business as a sole proprietorship or general partnership.
8. Always use corporations and limited liability companies to run your business.
9. Always keep few assets in your business.
10. Never commingle your personal assets with your business assets.
11. Hold valuable assets in an irrevocable trust.
12. Always adequately capitalize your business.

Use the twelve lawsuit protection laws and never lose a lawsuit again!

ENDNOTES

1 *Grupo Mexicano de Desarrolo S.V. v. Alliance Bond Fund, Inc.* (1999) 119 S.Ct. 1961.

2 U.S. Census Bureau estimate at www.census.gov/main/www/popclock.html.

3 According to Towers Watson at http://www.forbes.com/sites/mattkibbe/2012/01/19/americas-ongoing-tort-litigation-nightmare/.

4 See Asset Protection for Business Owners and High-Income Earners by Alan Northcott.

5 Volunteer Protection Act of 1997: In 1997, President Clinton signed into law the Volunteer Protection Act of 1997 (Act) that, generally speaking, provides immunity from tort claims that might be filed against the volunteers of nonprofit organizations.

6 For additional information, see Wikipedia–http://en.wikipedia.org/wiki/Liebeck_v._McDonald's_Restaurants.

7 Source: Wikipedia–http://en.wikipedia.org/wiki/Pearson_v._Chung.

8 Source: Jehovah's Witnesses Forum at http://jwforum.net/portal/index.php?option=com_content&view=article&id=824:state-supreme-court-dismisses-jehovahs-witnesses-blood-transfusion-lawsuit&catid=48:news#.UZsRlcpMtMw.

9 For additional information, see Food Libel Laws at Wikipedia–http://en.wikipedia.org/wiki/Food_libel_laws.

10 See America's Best Companies at http://www.americasbestcompanies.com/magazine/articles/frivolous-lawsuits.aspx.

11 Id.

12 Id.

13 Id.
14 Id.
15 Id.
16 See Chicago Tribune's article, Juries' Huge Penalties In Lawsuits Seen As Message To Business, at http://articles.chicagotribune.com/1999-01-08/news/9901080372_1_largest-verdict-million-verdict-lawyers-weekly-usa.
17 Id.
18 Id.
19 Id.
20 See the article, 10 Outrageous Lawsuits, at http://www.howstuffworks.com/8-outrageous-lawsuits.htm.
21 Id.
22 Id.
23 Id.
24 Id.
25 Id.
26 Id.
27 Id.
28 See http://billshapcott.com/Target_for_Litigation.html.
29 See www.LegalMatch.com; www.WhoCanISue.com; and www.SueEasy.com.
30 See www.LawsuitFunding.com.
31 See www.Probono.com.
32 *Turner v. Rogers,* 2012, U.S. Supreme Court.
33 *Federal Trade Commission v. Affordable Media, LLC*, 179 F.3d 1228 (9th Cir. 1999). This case is also known as the Anderson case. The defendants, Denyse and Michael Anderson, were the trustees of a trust in the Cook Islands. The United States District Court issued a temporary restraining order to have the funds transferred to the United States for the purpose of a trial where the defendants were charged with fraud. The defendants were jailed when they failed to comply with the court order.
34 According to the American Bar Association.

35 According to Wiki Answers:

In United States: Total Lawyers = 1,143,358; Total Pop. = 303 Million; 1 lawyer for every 265 people.

In Brazil: Total Lawyers = 571,360; Total Pop. = 186 Million; 1 lawyer for every 326 people.

In New Zealand: Total Lawyers = 10,523; Total Pop. = 4 Million; 1 lawyer for every 391 people.

In Spain: Total Lawyers = 114,143; Total Pop. = 45 Million; 1 lawyer for every 395 people.

In Italy: Total Lawyers = 121,380; Total Pop. = 59 Million; 1 lawyer for every 488 people.

In UK: Total Lawyers = 151,043; Total Pop. = 61 Million; 1 lawyer for every 401 people.

In Germany: Total Lawyers = 138,679; Total Pop. = 82 Million; 1 lawyer for every 593 people.

In France: Total Lawyers = 45,686; Total Pop. = 64 Million; 1 lawyer for every 1,403 people.

In India: Total lawyers = around 1 million; Total Pop. = 1,241,491,960; 1 lawyer for every 1,241 people.

36 One such accounting firm was Arthur Anderson.

37 The Fair Debt Collection Practices Act (FDCPA), 15 U.S.C. § 1692 et seq., is a United States statute enacted by congress in 1978. Its primary purposes are to (1) eliminate abusive practices in the collection of consumer debts, (2) to promote fair debt collection, and (3) to provide consumers with an accurate debt information and an avenue for disputing erroneous debt information.

38 All officers and employees of the US Government are exempted from the FDCPA, but they are covered by 15 U.S.C. § 6304, the Fair Tax Collection Practices Act.

39 The Enforcement of Judgments Law ("EJL") is codified under California Civil Procedure §§ 694.010–724.260. It is a comprehensive statutory scheme governing the enforcement of virtually all civil judgments in California. It includes: (1). money judgments; (2). bonds [Cal. CCP

§ 996.495]; (3). taxes [Cal. CCP § 688.110]; (4). fines [Cal. Penal Code §§ 1214, 1214.2 & 1397]; (5). restitution orders [Cal Penal Code §§ 1202.4(a),(f), (h),(i), 1203(j), 1203.1(a) & 1214(c)]; (6). probation costs [Cal. Penal Code § 1203.1(b)]; (7). monetary sanctions [See *Newland v. Superior Court (Sugasawara)* (1995) 40 Cal.App.4th 608, 615; *Jones v. Otero* (1984) 156 Cal.App.3d 754, 759; (8). support orders [Cal. Family § 17522; Cal. CCP § 689.020(a)]; (9). sister state (foreign) money judgment [Cal. CCP § 1710.10 et seq.; Cal. CCP § 1710.35]; (10). employer to enforce payment of its lien on an employee's recovery against a third-party tortfeasor (workers' compensation cases) [Cal. Labor § 3862]; (11). public defender costs [Cal. Penal Code § 987.8(e),(f); see also Cal. Penal Code § 987.8(a)]; (12). bail bond [Cal. Penal Code § 1306(e)(2)]; (13). hazardous waste administrative penalty [Cal Health & S § 25184.1]; (14). costs entered against a complainant in a criminal case [Cal. Penal Code §§ 1447 & 1448]; (15). arbitration award [Cal. CCP § 1287.4]; (16). Judgments are enforceable upon "entry." [Cal. CCP § 683.010; see also Cal. CCP § 664].

40 A money judgment is the original amount of the judgment, plus court costs and accrued interest on the judgment, minus any payments or amounts no longer enforceable. [Cal. CCP §§ 695.210, 680.300, 685.010(a)] The interest on a money judgment is 10 percent per annum. [Cal. CCP § 685.010(a)] The 10 percent annual interest rate also applies to sister-state judgments from and after the date they are entered as California judgments (Cal. CCP § 1710.25(b)). Interest accrued prior to the date of such entry is computed at the interest rate as provided under the law of the state where the judgment was rendered. [Cal. CCP §§ 1710.15, 1710.25]. Interest accrues from the date the judgment is entered. [Cal. CCP § 685.020(a)] Where the judgment is payable in installments (e.g., spousal support judgments),

interest accrues from the date each installment becomes due unless the judgment provides otherwise. [Cal. CCP § 685.020(b); Cal. Fam. § 155]. Interest on the judgment is not compounded (i.e., interest is not paid on the accrued interest) except when the judgment is renewed. When a judgment is renewed, whatever interest has accrued on the original judgment is added to and becomes part of the principal amount of the judgment. [Cal. CCP § 683.110].

41 Judgments are final determinations in an action [Cal. CCP §§ 577, 1064]. In addition, dismissal orders by courts constitute judgments. [Cal. CCP § 581d]. All other court directives that are not part of a judgment constitute a court order. [Cal. CCP § 1003].

42 If the judgment is collected completely in one lump sum, interest ceases on the date of levy. [Cal. CCP § 685.030(a)(1)]. If the judgment is satisfied pursuant to an earnings withholding order, then interest ceases either (i) on the date the full amount required to satisfy the order is withheld from the judgment debtor's earnings or (ii) on the date a (Cal. CCP § 706.028) final order for costs and interest is issued. [Cal. CCP § 685.030(a)(2)]. In all other cases, interest ceases on the date the proceeds of sale or collection are actually received by the levying officer. [Cal. CCP § 685.030(a)(3)]. A money judgment is deemed wholly satisfied when the judgment amount specified in the writ is fully collected even though a minimal amount of interest remains uncollected due to the continual daily interest accrual calculation. [Cal. CCP § 685.030(e) the court enters the writ in Register of Actions as "returned wholly satisfied"]. Interest ceases to accrue as to the part of the judgment satisfied. [Cal. CCP § 685.030(c),(d)]. Partial payments must be applied first to the accrued interest on the judgment. Partial payments reduce the principal judgment only after all accrued interest is paid. In levying a writ of execution, the levying officer must add interest at

the daily interest rate shown on the writ from the date it was issued until interest ceases to accrue. In cases of partial satisfaction, the amount of daily interest accruing on the money judgment is recomputed. [Cal. CCP § 685.050(b)(2)].

43 Superior court judgments are enforceable immediately upon entry. [Cal. CCP §§ 683.010] However, if the debtor files a timely appeal from the judgment, enforcement is stayed pending appeal under the provisions of Cal. CCP § 916 et seq. Money judgments are stayed on appeal only by posting a bond. [Cal. CCP § 917.1]. Enforcement of a small claims judgment (including issuance or recording of any abstract of judgment) is automatically stayed (suspended) without defendant's filing a bond pending expiration of the time for appeal, and if a timely appeal is taken, until the appeal is dismissed or the judgment affirmed. [Cal. CCP §§ 116.730, 116.740, 116.810].

44 In California, a judgment is valid for ten years and can be renewed for an additional ten years, for a grand total of twenty years. [Cal. CCP §§ 683.120(b), 683.150(a), 683.120(a); see also Cal. Fam. § 291]. For judgments not previously renewed, application to renew may be filed any time prior to expiration of the ten-year enforcement period. [Cal. CCP § 683.130(a)] However, as to judgments previously renewed, no new application for renewal can be filed for five years. (This is to prevent judgment creditors from frequently renewing judgments merely to compound interest, below.) [Cal. CCP § 683.110(b); Cal. Fam. § 4502(b)(2)]. Filing the renewal application (and paying the appropriate filing fee) results in automatic renewal of the judgment. No court order or new judgment is required. The court clerk simply enters the renewal of judgment in the court records. [Cal. CCP § 683.150]. Upon expiration of the judgment, all enforcement procedures must cease; any liens based upon the judgment are automatically extinguished. [Cal.

CCP §§ 683.020, 683.030]. When installment judgments (e.g., family support payments) are renewed, the renewed amount of the judgment is treated as a lump-sum money judgment entered on the date the renewal application was filed, and is enforceable for ten years from that date. [Cal. CCP § 683.120 (c)].

45 A judgment lien on real property establishes and preserves the judgment creditor's priority over later claimants. It is a general lien, attaching to practically all of the judgment debtor's real property interests in the county where an abstract or certified copy of the judgment, or a 42 USCA § 652(a)(11) interstate lien form, is recorded. Moreover, the lien reaches any future real property interests that the judgment debtor may acquire, thus assuring the judgment creditor priority as to after-acquired interests. [Cal. CCP § 697.340(b)].

46 See Cal. CCP §§ 704.950(a), 697.340.

47 See Cal. CCP; § 697.310(a). Alternatively, a certified copy of the judgment, a notice of support judgment, or a 42 USCA § 652(a)(11) interstate lien form may be recorded to create a judgment lien or installment orders for child, spousal or family support. [Cal. CCP § 697.320(a)].

48 Unless the judgment creditor files proof of service of notice of the lien to the judgment debtor, the county recorder is required to notify the judgment debtor (or his attorney of record) of the creation of a judgment lien within ten days after the recordation of an abstract (or certified copy) of judgment. [Cal. Govt. §§ 27297.5(a), (b)].

49 See Cal. CCP § 697.380(c),(d).

50 A judgment lien on real property is enforced by levy and sale of the real property interest under writ of execution. As long as the writ of execution is levied while the judgment lien is in effect, priority under the execution lien "relates back" to creation of the judgment lien. [Cal. CCP § 697.020(b)]. A judgment creditor may release all or part of

any real property that is subject to a judgment lien; or may subordinate the judgment lien to another lien or encumbrance. [Cal. CCP § 697.370(a)] A real property judgment lien is also extinguished upon recordation of either an acknowledgment of satisfaction [Cal. CCP § 724.060] or a clerk's certificate of satisfaction [Cal. CCP § 724.100].

51 The EJL provides for a lien on certain types of business personal property by filing a prescribed notice with the secretary of state. The procedure is similar to that required to perfect a security interest in such property under the Commercial Code. The filing constitutes constructive notice to potential transferees and lenders and gives the judgment creditor priority over later liens. However, the EJL does not provide any means of foreclosing on the lien; other enforcement procedures must be used to forcibly apply the judgment debtor's money or property to reduce a money judgment.

52 The judgment lien on personal property does not protect against transfers to certain types of persons [Cal. CCP §§ 697.740, 697.910, 697.920]. The judgment lien on personal property continues after the property is transferred, unless inventory is transferred in the ordinary course of business [Cal. Commercial § 9320] or the transfer is to a person under Cal. CCP § 697.610.

A judgment lien on personal property reaches only the following types of personal property in which a security interest could be perfected by filing a financing statement with the secretary of state under the Commercial Code: (1) accounts receivable, (2) chattel paper, (3) equipment, (4) farm products, (5) inventory (not including retail inventory items with a unit retail value of less than $500), and (6) negotiable documents of title. [Cal. CCP § 697.530(a)].

Personal property in which a security interest cannot be perfected by filing a financing statement with the secretary of state is not subject to a judgment lien on personal property: (1) deposit bank account, (2) letter-of-credit rights, and (3) insurance policy [Cal. Commercial §§ 9310(a) & (b), 9311(a), 9312(b); cf. Cal. CCP § 697.530(a)].

A judgment lien on personal property cannot attach to a vehicle or vessel required to be registered with the Department of Motor Vehicles, or a mobile home or commercial coach required to be registered under the Health & Safety Code. [Cal. CCP § 697.530(d)(1)], nor does it attach to inventory of a retail merchant with a unit retail value of less than $500. [Cal. CCP § 697.530(d)(2)].

If personal property subject to a judgment lien (e.g., equipment) is affixed to real property in such a manner that it becomes a "fixture" [Cal. Commercial §§ 9102(a)(41), 9334], the judgment lien thereon is automatically extinguished. [Cal. CCP § 697.530(e)]. A judgment lien on personal property is created by filing a Notice of Judgment Lien in the office of the secretary of state. [Cal. CCP §§ 697.510(a), 697.670(b)]. A judgment lien on personal property is a lien for the total amount of thc judgmcnt. [Cal. CCP § 697.540(a)] and cannot be created for most installment judgments, including spousal support judgments. [Cal. CCP § 697.510]. There are some exceptions to these rules, so be sure to check the law.

Unless the judgment is satisfied or the judgment lien is terminated or released, a judgment lien on personal property continues for five years from the filing date [Cal. CCP § 697.510(b)] The five-year period cannot be renewed [Cal. CCP § 697.510(c)] and therefore since the lien period cannot be extended, the only way to preserve the priority established is to enforce the judgment by a writ of execution. [Cal. CCP § 697.020].

A "first in time" rule ordinarily applies: A judgment lien on personal property generally has priority over a subsequently filed one's or other security interests. [Cal. CCP

§ 697.590] There are some exceptions to these rules, so be sure to check the law.

Interestingly, a state tax withholding order trumps a judgment lien on personal property.

The Franchise Tax Board need only serve those persons or entities having possession or control of the taxpayer's personal property with a withholding order to obtain priority over the judgment lien. [Cal. Rev. & Tax § 18817].

A judgment lien on personal property continues even after the sale, exchange or other disposition of property subject to the lien. [Cal. CCP § 697.610] Exceptions:

A judgment lien on personal property (including a negotiable document of title or chattel paper [Cal. Commercial § 7501; Cal. CCP § 697.610(c),(d)]) is completely terminated where the purchaser or lessee who gives "new value" and takes possession of the property in the "ordinary course of business" [Cal. Commercial §§ 1201, 10103(a)(1),(15)]. Such a buyer or lessee takes the property free of any security interest and/or free of any judgment lien in the goods [Cal. Commercial §§ 9320, 10307(c), 697.610(a) & (b)].

Filing with the secretary of state either an acknowledgment of satisfaction of judgment executed by the judgment creditor [Cal. CCP § 724.060] or a clerk's certificate of satisfaction [Cal. CCP § 724.100] generally extinguishes the judgment lien "as a matter of record." [Cal. CCP § 697.640(a)].

53 See Cal. CCP §§ 680.230, 699.010, 699.510(a).

54 See Cal. Rev & Tax § 2191.4.

55 See Cal Corp §§ 16504, 16111, 16112.

56 Does not apply to single-member LLCs.

57 See Cal Bus. & Prof. § 22443.1(j).

58 See Cal. CCP § 699.720(a).

59 See Cal. CCP §§ 712.010, 712.020.

Regarding Writs of Execution:

The clerk of the court where the judgment was entered issues a writ of execution upon the judgment creditor's request and payment of the appropriate fee. [Cal. CCP § 699.510(a); Cal Govt. § 70626(a)(1)] No court order is required for issuance of a writ of execution (except for certain Family Code judgments). The clerk "issues" the writ by signing and dating the completed writ form and affixing the court's seal thereto. [Cal. CCP § 153] Any additional names by which the judgment debtor is known (other than the name listed on the judgment), requires court approval ("affidavit of identity") before a writ can issue. [Cal. CCP § 699.510(c)(1)].

A separate writ of execution must be issued for each county in which a levy is to be made because writs of execution are directed to the levying officer of a particular county. [Cal. CCP § 699.510(a)] However, and this is important, since each writ issued is for the full amount necessary to satisfy the judgment, there is a risk of excessive levies where writs are issued for several counties. Excessive levies could expose the judgment creditor to liability for abuse of process, and a potential lawsuit against the creditor. A successive writ cannot be issued for levies in the same county unless the original writ has been returned or at least 180 days have expired since its issuance. [Cal. CCP § 699.510(a)].

A court order is required to obtain a writ of execution to enforce a Family Code judgment that is not for child, spousal, or family support. [Cal. Fam. § 290]. Prior court approval is not required to enforce a child, spousal, or family support order or judgment.

If the judgment creditor applies for a writ of execution on a judgment that is more than ten years old (other than for support), the application must be accompanied by a declaration showing why the writ should issue. [Cal. CCP § 683.040].

60 See Cal. CCP § 699.040.

61 See Cal. CCP § 714.030(a).
62 See Cal. CCP § 699.030.
63 See Cal. CCP § 699.070.
64 The levying officer then "levies" upon specified property of the judgment debtor by taking it into custody or otherwise subjecting it to a lien in favor of the judgment creditor in the manner described below. The property levied upon is usually sold at an execution sale to satisfy the judgment. The "levying officer" is the sheriff or marshal of the county to which the writ is directed [Cal. CCP § 680.260]. The judgment creditor must deposit with the levying officer amounts sufficient to cover the costs of carrying out the instructions. Otherwise, the levying officer has no liability to take or hold property. [Cal. CCP § 685.100(a)(1)] The fee for levying a writ varies, but for large ticket items can be several hundred dollars or more. The levying officer's authority commences upon receipt of the writ and continues for 180 days after the date of its issuance. Thereafter, no further levies may be made thereunder (although a successive writ may issue). Any number of levies may be made during the 180-day period. [Cal. CCP § 699.530(b)].
65 See Cal. CCP § 700.010.
66 See Cal. CCP § 697.710.
67 See Cal. CCP §§ 683.020 & 699.030.
68 See Cal. CCP §§ 697.020 (b), 688.200, 697.030 & Comment to § 683.190.
69 See Cal. CCP § 699.060(a).
70 See Cal. CCP § 918.
71 See 16 Cal. Law Review. Commission Reports 1165 (1982).
72 See Cal. CCP § 917.1 (a)(1).
73 See Cal. CCP § 917.1(a)(2).
74 See Cal. CCP § 917.1(a)(3).
75 See Cal. CCP § 917.2.
76 See Cal. CCP § 917.4.
77 See Cal. CCP§ 917.5.

78 See Cal Const. Art. XX, § 1.5.
79 See Cal. CCP § 703.020(a).
80 See Cal. CCP § 703.030(a).
81 See Cal. CCP § 703.030(b).
82 See Cal. CCP § 684.120.
83 See Cal. CCP § 703.550.
84 See Cal. CCP § 703.020(b)(1).
85 See Cal. CCP § 703.020(b)(2).
86 See Cal. CCP § 703.520(a); The claim is deemed filed when actually received by the levying officer. [Cal. CCP § 681.040].
87 The hearing on the exemption claim must be held no later than twenty days from the date the notice of motion is filed with the court unless the court continues the hearing for good cause. [Cal. CCP § 703.570(a)].
88 See Cal. CCP § 703.550.
89 See 15 USC § 1673–Restriction on garnishment.
90 See Cal. Fam. § 5200 et seq.
91 See Cal. CCP §§ 706.031, 706.020, 706.031; Cal. Fam. § 5200 et seq. (governing earnings assignment orders for support).
92 See Cal. CCP §§ 706.020, 708.720(b).
93 5 USC § 5520 a.
94 After the wage garnishment begins (ten days after service of earnings withholding order), the employer pays the levying officer by the fifteenth of the month all money withheld (nonexempt pay) from the preceding month. [Cal. CCP §§ 706.022(b), 706.025(a)]. The wage garnishment (earnings withholding order) continues until the earliest of the following: (1) the date the employer withholds the full amount required to satisfy the order, (2) the date the court order is terminated and served on the employer, (3) when a termination notice is served on the employer by the levying officer, (4) the date the withholding order falls dormant or is suspended and thus automatically terminates

as determined under Cal. CCP § 706.032 (debtor leaves employment or earnings are subject to order/assignment with higher priority). [Cal. CCP § 706.022(a)].

95 See Cal. CCP § 706.072(b).

96 See Cal. CCP § 706.030(a).

97 See Cal. CCP § 706.030(c)(1).

98 See Cal. Civil Procedure § 706.052(a).

99 See Cal. CCP § 706.052(b).

100 See Cal. CCP § 706.052(c).

101 See Cal. CCP § 706.051(a),(b).

102 See Cal. CCP § 706.105(a). An earnings withholding order is effective ten calendar days after service. An exemption is claimed by filing with the levying officer (not the court) an original and one copy of the official Claim of Exemption form and a Financial Statement. [CCP § 706.105(b)] After the exemption claim is filed, the levying officer must promptly send it to the judgment creditor [CCP § 706.105(c)].

103 See Cal. CCP § 706.105(d). In addition, the judgment creditor must file with the court within ten days after the levying officer mailed the Notice of Claim of Exemption, a Notice of Motion for an Order Determining the Claim of Exemption. [CCP § 706.105(e)] The judgment creditor must also complete and file with the court the official form Notice of Hearing on Claim of Exemption. [CCP § 706.105(e)] The judgment creditor must give written notice of the hearing to the levying officer at least sixteen court days before the hearing. [CCP §§ 706.105(e), 1005(b)] At least sixteen court days before the hearing, the judgment debtor must receive notice of the hearing. [CCP §§ 706.105(e), 1005(b)]. If the notice of opposition and notice of motion are timely filed, the court hearing on the claim of exemption must be held no more than thirty days after the notice of motion is filed (unless continued by the court for good cause). If the court grants the exemption claim, it

may direct that the earnings withholding order be modified or terminated. The effective date of termination can precede the date of the hearing. The court may also order that any exempt earnings previously withheld be repaid to the judgment debtor. [CCP § 706.105(g),(i)] The levying officer must then promptly serve on the judgment debtor's employer either a copy of the modified earnings withholding order or a notice that the withholding order has been terminated. [CCP§ 706.105(g)].

104 See Cal. CCP § 706.102(a).

105 See Cal. CCP § 706.050; 15 USCA § 1673(a); 29 CFR § 870.1 et seq.

106 See 15 USCA § 1672(b).

107 See 15 USCA § 1673(b); Cal. Civil Procedure § 706.074(b).

108 See Tex. Prop. Code Ann. § 42.001 (b)(1): "current wages [are exempt from garnishment] for personal services, except for the enforcement of court-ordered child support payments."

109 See Fla. Stat. Ann. 222.11 (2)(a).

110 See Cal. CCP § 708.110(a).

111 See Cal. CCP § 708.120.

112 See Cal. CCP §§ 708.130, 708.140.

113 See Cal. CCP § 708.170(a)(1).

114 See Cal. CCP § 708.170(a)(2).

115 See Cal. CCP § 708.205(a).

116 See Cal. CCP §§ 1209-1222; CCP § 708.205.

117 See Cal. CCP §§ 708.010(a), 708.020(a).

118 See Cal. CCP § 708.030(a).

119 See Cal. CCP § 708.210.

120 See Cal. CCP § 708.620.

121 See Cal. CCP §§ 699.720(a)(2), 708.310.

122 See Cal. CCP §§ 699.720(a)(5), 708.720(a).

123 See Cal. Cal. Civil Code § 954.

124 See Cal. CCP § 187.

125 See Cal. CCP § 699.720(a)(8).

126 See Cal. CCP § 709.010(a); Cal. Probate § 82.
127 See Cal. CCP § 699.720(a)(9).
128 See Cal. CCP § 709.020.
129 See Cal. CCP § 709.030; Cal Probate § 2404.
130 See Cal. CCP § 686.010.
131 See Cal. CCP § 720.110(a); Cal. CCP § 514.050.
132 See Cal. CCP §§ 720.110(b), 720.210.
133 See Cal. CCP § 720.310.
134 See *Commercial Credit Plan, Inc. v. Gomez* (1969) 276 Cal. App.2d Supp. 831.
135 See Cal. CCP §§ 720.260, 720.270.
136 See Cal. CCP § 720.380(a).
137 See *Cassel v. Kolb* (1999) 72 Cal.App.4th 568, 579-580; CCP § 720.410]. The third-party claimant has the burden of proof. [Cal. CCP § 720.360] However, if the creditor contends the property was fraudulently transferred to the third-party claimant and the third-party claimant introduces evidence showing he or she owns the property, the burden shifts back to the creditor to prove the property was fraudulently transferred. The judgment may be appealed. [Cal. CCP §§ 720.390, 720.420].
138 See Cal. CCP § 712.060.
139 See Cal. CCP § 712.060.
140 See Cal. CCP § 714.020(a).
141 See Cal. CCP § 699.030.
142 See Cal. CCP §§ 714.020(a), 700.080.
143 See Cal. CCP §§ 716.010, 712.060.
144 See Cal. CCP § 712.040(a),(c).
145 See Cal. CCP §§ 1710.10–1710.65.
146 See Cal. CCP § 1913.
147 See Cal. CCP § 1710.10 et seq.
148 See Cal. CCP § 1710.10(c).
149 See Cal. CCP § 1710.25(a).
150 See Cal. CCP § 1710.45(a).
151 See Cal. CCP § 1710.10(c).

152 See Cal. Fam. § 4900 et seq. Nonmoney judgments are all outside the scope of the Act. [CCP § 1710.10].

153 See Cal. CCP § 724.010(a).

154 See Cal. CCP § 724.110(a).

155 Debt collection agencies with $10 million or more in receipts.

156 The Consumer Financial Protection Bureau.

157 The creditor in this case is a judgment creditor.

158 This can be expensive, so a cost-benefit analysis should be undertaken before a creditor decides to administer a debtor's estate.

159 In some instances, service must comply with the Hague Service Convention, if the country is a signatory; and in other cases, especially South American countries, the letter rogatory process must be used. Where a defendant's whereabouts are unknown, the Court may permit service by newspaper publication.

160 Service by mail is not available if the foreign country has filed objections to service by mail pursuant to the multina tional Hague Service Convention. International service of process is generally governed by the 1965 Hague Service Convention, where member countries designate a central authority for service of process and requests go directly there. In addition, many countries allow some type of service directly by mail or personal service.

161 *State Farm Mutual Automobile Insurance Co. v. Campbell*, 538 U.S. 408 (2003), was a case in which the United States Supreme Court held that the due process clause usually limits punitive damage awards to less than ten times the size of the compensatory damages awarded.

162 According to The Economist.

163 Source: The 2010 Update on U.S. Tort Cost Trends, Towers Watson, 2010.

164 Source: Citizens Against Lawsuit Abuse (CALA).

165 Source: 1995 Department of Justice study.

166 Source: Insurance Information Institute.
167 See 42 U.S.C. § 1983.
168 See 65 F.Supp.2d 353 (D. Md. 1999).
169 See 207 F.3d 1303, (11th Cir. 2000).
170 See Appendix A for the best-rated insurance companies. All of the insurance companies listed in this guidebook are amongst the highest-rated insurance companies in the industry. They fulfill the criteria I have previously listed. My suggestion is to use one of the insurance companies listed in this guidebook.
171 Source: Bizstats.com.
172 PC's function in much the same way as a limited liability partnership (LLP) but under the rules of incorporation rather than a partnership. The ability to form a PC and the type of professional who may form a PC is determined by the individual states.
173 See 11 U.S.C. §§ 522 (d)(7) and (8).
174 See Me. Rev. Stat. Ann. tit. 14, § 4422 (11).
175 See Haw. Rev. Stat. § 431:10-232(a); Fla. Stat. Title XV Chapter 222.13.
176 See *Crummey v. Commissioner of Internal Revenue*, 397 F.2d 82 (9th Circuit 1968).
177 See I.R.C. §§ 672-679.
178 If your neighbor is a joint tenant of your house, the house could be sold to pay the creditors, but your neighbor would be entitled his share of the equity in the house.
179 California Family Code § 2550.
180 *In re Marriage of Eastis,* 47 Cal. App. 3d 459 (1975).
181 Internal Revenue Service Publication 555.
182 Bill Shaikin, "Frank and Jamie McCourt reach settlement involving Dodgers," Los Angeles Times, 17 October 2011.
183 California Family Code Section 125; *Addison v. Addison* (1965) 62 Cal.2d 558.
184 California Family Code Section 721.
185 California Family Code Section 1500.

186 California Family Code Sections 850-853.

187 California Probate Sections 140-147.

188 California Family Code Section 851; Civil Code Section 3439-3439.12: "Uniform Fraudulent Transfer Act."

189 The Uniform Fraudulent Transfer Act (UFTA) gives creditors the right to avoid (rescind) property transfers in order to satisfy their claims when the transfer was made with actual fraudulent intent ("actual intent to hinder, delay, or defraud" a creditor) or the transfer was made without receiving a "reasonably equivalent value in exchange" and the debtor either (1) was engaged in (or about to engage in) a business or transaction "for which the remaining assets of the debtor were unreasonably small in relation to the business or transaction" or (2) intended to incur (or reasonably believed he or she would incur) debts "beyond his or her ability to pay as they become due" or the transfer was made without receiving a "reasonably equivalent value in exchange" and the debtor was insolvent at the time of the transfer or became insolvent as a result of the transfer. (See Civil Code Section 3439 et seq.)

190 Director Steven Spielberg failed to have a formal written prenuptial agreement. Instead, his prenuptial agreement was scribbled on a napkin; and his ex-wife, Amy Irving, got half of what he earned during their four years of marriage—$100 million!

191 Arizona, California, Idaho, Louisiana, Nevada, New Mexico, Texas, Washington, and Wisconsin.

192 See 11 USC § 522(p). Also, you must have lived in your home for at least two years and acquired your home during the preceding forty months prior to bankruptcy.

193 See *Finalco, Inc. v. Roosevelt* (1991) 235 Cal. App. 3d 1301.

194 You should not be making the mortgage payments directly unless it is a gift.

195 If you insist on continuing to make the mortgage payments on behalf of the new legal entity, then you must notate that it's a gift.

196 Using statutory exclusions to avoid property tax reassessment in California. Using the legal entity exclusion to avoid reassessment section 64(a)(c) and (d) using the proportional interest exclusion to avoid reassessment section 62(a)2, using the original transferor rule to delay reassessment section 65 and amended Rule 462.040, using the domestic partner exclusions to avoid reassessment property tax rule 462.240(k) and section 62(p), using the parent-child exclusion to avoid reassessment section 63.1.

197 See *Olmstead v. FTC*, No. SC08-1009 (Fla. June 24, 2010).

198 See *In re: Ashley Albright,* 291 B.R. 538 (Bkr. D Colo. 2003).

199 The factors a court considers in equitable distribution states for divorce assets are the following:

1. The difference in income and property from when the marriage began to the date divorce was filed.
2. The age of both individuals and how long they were married.
3. The needs of a parent who has won full custody of children involved.
4. Any loss of pension or inheritance.
5. What contributions the parties made to acquire the property.
6. Future earning potential of both parties.
7. Tax consequences.

200 Technically speaking, there is no legal term, "family limited partnership." This term is actually a misnomer used by salesmen referring to a limited partnership that holds or invests business property managed by the spouses and belonging to the limited partnership. Moreover, the parents often gift limited partnership shares to the children, and those shares are essentially illiquid, and thus qualify for

steep tax discounts. Substantial gift and estate tax savings can often be realized.

201 Phantom income is partnership income that is not distributed to the partners but rather is retained by the partnership.

202 Another similar clause: "Notwithstanding any other provision of this agreement, no Partner shall have the right to demand or to receive the return of all or any portion of such partner's capital account, partnership interest, or of such partner's capital contribution. Earnings shall be distributed at least annually, except those funds which, at the sole discretion of the general partners, are reasonably reserved for the conduct of the FLP business."

203 Your Nevada FLP is registered as a "foreign" entity in California even though technically it's an out-of-state entity rather than an out-of-country (foreign) entity. Confused? You're not alone.

204 A reverse piercing claim will allow a creditor to seize assets in a company belonging to an individual judgment debtor provided the judgment debtor has an ownership interest in the company.

205 This is outlined by the Uniform Limited Partnership Act (ULPA), which provides a judgment creditor with a charging order. See ULPA section 703.

206 See ULPA section 702.

207 The charging order has the effect of a making the creditor a lienholder or an assignee of the debtor's right to receive distributions from the partnership or LLC. In most cases, the court grants the creditor a charging order, which then perfects the lien; in other words, it makes the lien permanent until the judgment has been fully paid or satisfied. The creditor is actually a limited assignee, in so much as he is not allowed to vote or otherwise be involved in administrative decisions. His assignment is only for distribution of income from the entity.

208 See IRS § 721(a)—Nonrecognition of gain or loss on contribution.

209 See instructions for IRS Form 2553 regarding who may elect to be an S corporation.

210 A child's trust should not be used because typically the parents manage the FLP.

211 Use an LLC as the general partner to prevent any partner from having personal liability.

212 Domestic Corporations as General Partners could pose a problem because a creditor of a shareholder who gains control of 51 percent of the corporate stock would control the corporation and through the corporation would control the FLP. However, an IBC (foreign corporation) owned by an offshore trust would make a good general partner.

213 A limited partner may donate his or her interest to an irrevocable protective trust established for the benefit of family members.

214 A limited partner is not dissociated from the FLP upon bankruptcy.

215 See IRS General Counsel Memorandum 36960 (1977) and (IRS) Revenue Ruling 77-137.

216 See *Evans v. Commissioner*, 447 F.2d 547 (7th Cir. 1971); Revenue Ruling 77-137, 1977-1 C.B. 178,

Section 761—Partnership Definitions, IRS Headnote: "Limited partnership; assignment of interest. An assignee acquiring substantially all of the dominion and control over the interest of a limited partner is treated as a substituted limited partner for Federal income tax purposes."

217 See IRC §708(b)(1)(A).

218 See *In re Turner,* 335 B.R. 140, 147-48 (Bankr. N.D. Cal. 2005) (stating that an entity may not be created with no business purpose and personal assets transferred to them with no relationship to any business purpose, simply as a means of shielding them from creditors).

219 A charging order is an order obtained from a court or judge by a judgment creditor, by which the property of the judgment debtor in any stocks or funds or land stands charged with the payment of the amount for which judgment shall have been recovered, with interest and costs. The rationale behind the charging order applied initially only to general partnerships, where every partner was involved in carrying on the business of the partnership; it did not apply to corporations because of their centralized management structure. However, over the years the charging order protection was extended to limited partners and LLC members.

220 Most asset-protection experts charge their clients thousands of dollars to set up an FLP based in part on the hype of the charging order protection. Please be careful of this trap.

221 *In re Albright,* 291 B. R. 538 (Bankr. D. Colo. 2003). To date, with the exception of the Albright case, there are no cases analyzing the efficacy of charging orders in the single-member LLC context.

222 See *Kellis v. Ring,* 92 Cal. App. 3d 854, 859-860, (1979) (assignee cannot bring an action for breach of fiduciary duty).

223 See *In re Ashley Albright*, 291 B.R. 538 (2003).

224 *Hellman v. Anderson*, 233 Cal. App. 3d 840 (1991). In *Hellman,* the court concluded that foreclosure would not be allowed if it would cause a partner with essential managerial skills to abandon the partnership. However, it would be allowed if it would have no appreciable effect on the conduct of partnership business. The effect of foreclosure on the partnership needs be evaluated on a case-by-case basis.

225 Corporations Code Section 17302 (b) states: (b) A charging order constitutes a lien on the judgment debtor's transferable interest. The court may order a foreclosure upon the interest subject to the charging order at any time. The purchaser at the foreclosure sale has the rights of a transferee. See also

Hellman v. Anderson, 233 Cal. App. 3d 840 (Foreclosure of partnership interests); Section 17302 (Foreclosure of LLC interests); *In Re: Ashley Albright,* U.S. Bankruptcy Court for the District of Colorado (decided April 4, 2003); *Olmstead, et. al., vs. The Federal Trade Commission*, Supreme Court of Florida. Case No. SC 08-1009 June 24, 2010).

226 It may be advisable to create one FLP that owns several limited liability companies (LLCs). Each LLC can own one dangerous asset to avoid the domino effect that an FLP generated judgment could cause to all the assets held within that one vehicle to be forfeited.

227 A due on sales clause in the mortgage agreement may allow the bank to call the mortgage loan. If the partner continues to pay the mortgage, a resulting trust will form. Other areas of special concern deserving caution in transferring real property to an FLP is contaminated property, and in California, Proposition 13 tax advantages.

228 *The Estate of Albert Strangi,* 293 F.3d 279 (5th Circuit 2002). This frequently cited case involves the $10 million estate of Albert Strangi, a Texan who made his money in manufacturing and was in declining health when his son-in-law moved nearly all his assets into an FLP. After seven years of litigation, the federal courts ruled that the partnership had been set up solely to avoid estate taxes.

229 See *In re Marriage of Eastis* (Endnote 180) where money was taken from the FLP to make nursing home payments. Don't put all of your assets in the FLP.

230 Experts suggest a minimum of thirty days.

231 Parental liability refers to the parents' obligation to pay for damage done by negligent, intentional, or criminal acts of their children. In 47 states, parents are responsible for all malicious or willful property damage done by their children; in thirty states, parents are liable for all malicious or willful personal injuries inflicted by their children. Eight states obligate parents only when their children have

acted illegally. Hawaii, Louisiana, and Oregon hold parents responsible for all torts committed by their children. Only Washington, D.C. does not hold parents liable at all. All parental liability laws limit the amount of liability to between $300 and $15,000, depending on the state. Parental liability usually ends when the child reaches the age of majority, and does not begin until the child reaches somewhere between eight and ten. The age of majority is the age at which a minor, in the eyes of the law, becomes an adult. This age is eighteen in most states. In a few other states, the age of majority is nineteen or twenty-one. A minor is considered to be a resident of the same state as her custodial parent or guardian. (No one is liable for damage done by a child younger than eight or so unless the parent was grossly negligent, for example, giving the child a loaded gun.) Source:www.lectlaw.com/files/fam17.htm.

232 See California Penal Code § 531—Fraudulent Conveyances.

233 California Civil Code § 3439.08 provides that if the judgment creditor prevails in a fraudulent conveyance action, the creditor may recover judgment for "the value of the asset transferred" or" the amount necessary to satisfy the creditor's claim, whichever is less."

234 Asset Protection for Business Owners and High-Income Earners by Alan Northcott, page 57.

235 While UFTA applies clearly to present creditors, the distinction between a future creditor and a future potential creditor is not as clear. The UFTA is commonly held to apply only to future creditors and not to future potential creditors (those whose claim arises after the transfer, but there was no foreseeable connection between the creditor and the debtor at the time of the transfer).

236 A stockholders' derivative lawsuit usually results.

237 See *Cortez v. Vogt*, 52 Cal.App.4th 917 (4th Dist. 1997); "*Macedo v. Bosio* (2001) 86 Cal.App. 4th 1044."

238 The statute of limitations also includes "one year from when the transaction could reasonably have been discovered by the creditor." This provision could potentially extend the statute of limitations for an incredibly long time. However, on the bright side, "The Act recognizes that laches and estoppel may operate to preclude a particular creditor from pursuing a remedy against a fraudulent transfer or obligation even though the statutory period of limitations has not run."

239 It helps if the transfer was made for "reasonably equivalent value."

240 *Merhtash v. Mehrtash,* 93 Cal.App.4th 75 (Appellate 2d Dist. 2001).

241 *A/S Kreditt – Finans v. Cia Venetico De Navegacion S.A. of Panama,* 560 F.Supp. 705 (D.C. PA. 1983).

242 *In re Valente,* 360 F.3d 256 C.A. 1 (R.I.) 2004; *Travelers Ins. Co. v. 633 Third Associates,* 14 F.3d 114 C.A. 2 (N.Y.) 1994; *Hobthaus v. Parsons,* 238 Neb. 223 (1991); *In re Weaver,* 128 B.R. 224 (1991) Bkrtcy W.D. Ark.; *Matter of O'Brien,* 94 B.R. 583, W.D. Mo. 1988.

243 *Grupo Mexicano de Desarrolo S.V. v. Alliance Bond Fund, Inc.* (1999) 119 S.Ct. 1961.

244 If there's a personal judgment against you, a court can "reverse pierce" your LLC and collect its assets to pay your personal judgment.

245 See Cal. CCP § 410.70.

246 Do away with.

247 See *In re Ashley Albright,* 291 B.R. 538 (2003).

248 Corporations can last forever whereas LLCs typically terminate (around thirty years or so after formation). However, corporations can be liquidated if necessary.

249 Most punitive damages can't be discharged in bankruptcy.

250 This could result in a gift tax. Also, this raises suspicion of a fraudulent conveyance even though it may be legitimate.

251 The following states have no state income taxes: Alaska, Florida, Nevada, South Dakota, Texas, Washington, and Wyoming. The following states tax only interest and dividends: New Hampshire and Tennessee.

252 See *International Harvester Co. v. Department of Taxation*, 322 U.S. 435 (1944).

253 Subchapter S of the internal revenue code.

254 Some salesmen create sham, one-person, non-profit religious corporations that will get you into serious trouble.

255 See *Bogosian v. All American Concessions*, 2011 WL 4460362 (E.D.N.Y., Slip Copy, Sept. 26, 2011).

256 A recent bankruptcy opinion from Iowa demonstrates how little liability protection a single-member LLC can afford its sole owner. *In re Advanced Custom Builders LLC*, 2011 WL 3608004 (Bkrtcy.N.D.Iowa, Aug. 16, 2011).

257 At-will employment defines an employment relationship in which either party can break the relationship with no liability, provided there was no express contract for a definite term governing the employment relationship and that the employer does not belong to a collective bargaining group (i.e., has not recognized a union). Under this legal doctrine: "any hiring is presumed to be "at will"; that is, the employer is free to discharge individuals "for good cause, or bad cause, or no cause at all," and the employee is equally free to quit, strike, or otherwise cease work. At-will employment disclaimers are a staple of employee handbooks in the United States.

258 The owners of corporations and LLCs are corporate shareholders and LLC members, respectively.

259 Closely held corporations are corporations that are owned by one or just a few people.

260 See Cal. CCP § 187.

261 See *Carr v. Barnabey's Hotel Corp.* (1994) 23 Cal.App.4th 14, 20-21; *In re Levander* (9th Cir. 1999) 180 F.3d 1114, 1122 (applying Calif. law).

262 A transfer for no consideration could also subject the transferor to gift taxes.

263 An appellate court recently affirmed a $1,000,000 judgment against U.S. Bank National Association (the Trustee) for failure to adequately diversify a portfolio. In an opinion released September 1, 2006, an Ohio Court of Appeals affirmed the lower court finding that US Bank breached its fiduciary duty to diversify by not diversifying quickly enough. The Grantor had established a $2,000,000 charitable remainder Unitrust funded with Procter and Gamble stock. The investment officer began to reduce the concentration in P&G stock by selling shares of the stock each month. He postponed sales when the price of the stock dropped and resumed diversification when prices began to go up. By the end of the year, the value of the trust had dropped in half. The successor trustee brought an action for breach of fiduciary duty and a jury returned an award of $1,040,222.

Source: *Fifth Third Bank v. Firstar Bank, N.A. n.k.a. U.S. Bank National Association* (2006-Ohio-4506).

264 See Cal. Probate § 18200.

265 Pursuant to Cal. Probate § 19400 et seq. [Cal. Probate §§ 19300(a) & 19003(a)].

266 This is a complicated area of law, so please check with a professional tax advisor.

267 See Uniform Trust Code § 505; Restatement (Second) Of Trusts § 156(2) and Restatement (Third) Of Trusts § 58(2). This principle has been adopted in hundreds of cases throughout the country and many states have enacted statutes with this identical language. See, e.g., Alabama Code § 19-3B-505, Florida Trust Code § 736.0505(b), Michigan Code § 7506(c)(2), Ohio Code § 5805.06, Utah Code § 75-7-505(b), Virginia Code § 55-545.05.

268 US Income Tax Reporting Requirements for Offshore Banking: if at any time during the taxable year you had an

interest or a signature or other authority over a financial account in a foreign country, such as a bank account, securities account, or other financial account, then you must answer yes on 1040 income tax return schedule B, Line 7a. You also have to file an additional form "TD F 90-22-1." Additionally question 8 of form 1040 Schedule B, asks if you received a distribution from, or were the grantor of, or a transferor to, a foreign trust. Answer the question truthfully. It's perfectly legal for a US citizen to have a Foreign Asset Protection Trust. It is unlawful to answer IRS questions falsely.

269 The banks are ranked by the number of times their savings accounts appeared in the 'best buy' tables printed in the eleven issues of Nexus Expatriate News magazine during 2011 and at www.expatnetwork.com.

270 Always perform due diligence before deciding on the country where you desire to do offshore banking.

271 There is also IRS Form 90-22.1 which you are required to file as well.

272 Switzerland is no longer the haven for secret bank accounts as it has come under attack for contributing to money-laundering and is now sharing information with the US government.

273 An official letter from an attorney or CPA vouching for you is sufficient.

274 Section §871(a)(2) of the Internal Revenue Code (IRC); also see IRC §881 and IRC §897(c)3 together with Treasury Regulations §864-2(C)1 & (2).

275 "Doing business within the United States" generally means operating through a US office or permanent establishment from within/inside the United States.

276 Internal Revenue Code (IRC) §881; §897(c)(3); §936; U.S. Treasury Regulations §864-(C)(1) and §864-(C)(2).

277 Treasury Regulations §§1.144-1 through 1.114-7 and CFC rules under the provisions of the Internal Revenue Code §§951-964.

278
- Withholding tax of 30 percent.
- Capital losses from investments by the "US person" are not tax deductible until the foreign entity is liquidated.
- Capital gains normally taxed at 20 percent are converted to ordinary taxable income, taxed at 39.6 percent.
- The "US person" may be double taxed on dividend distributions from United States sourced income, i.e., dividends from US companies.
- Sale of the foreign entity is taxed as ordinary income taxes (39.6 percent), *not* capital gains tax rate of 20 percent.
- The basis in the foreign entity does not get the "stepped-up" basis for estate tax valuation.
- Foreign inheritance taxes may apply if a "US person" purchases foreign-based securities.
- Passive investment income may be subject to CFC (Foreign Corporation Classification) and PFIC (Passive Foreign Investment Company) complex rules and a 30 percent withholding tax.
- Twenty-five percent of Americans investing offshore have an annual income over $100,000 (source: The US Department of Commerce)
- Fifty percent of the world's wealth is found in offshore financial centers. (source: The Tax Haven Guidebook)
- The Cayman Islands has the fifth largest banking in the world, and nearly six hundred commercial banks exceeding an estimated $600 billion in deposits. The Bahamas has more than four hundred banks and trust companies with an unconfirmed estimate of $300 billion in deposits.
- There are *no* capital gains taxes on securities purchased in the United States and sold by foreign investors. A US

citizen utilizing an IBC with an offshore trust can get the same benefit as a foreign investor. His IBC won't have to pay any capital gains taxes on stock profits! According to US tax code section 871(a)(2), nonresident aliens (NRA) who invest in stocks and commodity securities in the USA are not subject to tax on any gain from such investments by the USA if the gains are not "effectively connected" with a US trade or business and if the NRA is not present in the US for more than 182 days in the taxable year. Gains on the disposition of debt securities such as bonds may be exempt from tax if there is no original issue discount on the bonds.

279 IRS 5.21.3.6 (02-17-2009)

Suit to Repatriate Property—Repatriation Orders:

1. A repatriation order is an order issued by a federal judge after a hearing, requiring a taxpayer who has transferred the assets to a foreign country back into the United States. If the taxpayer refuses or neglects to return the assets, the taxpayer is subject to contempt proceedings.
2. A repatriation order must show the following:
   A. An outstanding tax liability.
   B. A reasonable basis that the taxpayer has assets outside the United States.
   C. Levy on domestic assets is not sufficient to satisfy the tax liability.
   D. United States is able to get personal jurisdiction over the taxpayer. The revenue officer must show that the taxpayer is either in the United States or US territory of the likelihood that the taxpayer will be returning to or passing through the United States.
3. Consider a repatriation order in concert with all other possible actions that fit the facts of the case such as appointment of a receivership, a suit to reduce the tax to a judgment, and a Writ Ne Exeat Republica.

4. Develop a request for a repatriation order as applicable.
5. Consult with area counsel prior to considering a repatriation order. Area counsel will coordinate as necessary with the Office of Associate Chief Counsel (International).

280 See *In re Advanced Telecommunication Network, Inc.*, Chapter 11, Debtor. *Advanced Telecommunication Network, Inc.*, Plaintiff, v. *Daniel W. Allen, David D. Allen*, Defendants. Case No. 6:03-bk-00299-KSJ, Adversary No. 6:03-ap-122. United States Bankruptcy Court, M.D, Florida, Orlando Division. July 28, 2011.

281 For a complete list of all the state and federal exemptions, see the Judicial Council list of exemptions (EJ-155) The judicial council publishes a list of the current CCP § 704.010 et seq. exemption dollar amounts (as well as the § 703.140(b) exemption dollar amounts, along with the effective date. (Cal. CCP § 703.150(d)).

282 See Cal. CCP § 704.020(a)(1).

283 See Cal. CCP § 704.040.

284 See Cal. CCP § 704.060(a).

285 See Cal. CCP § 704.070.

286 See Cal. CCP § 704.070(b)(2).

287 See Cal. CCP § 704.080(c).

288 See 50 USCA App. § 537(a),(b).

289 See Cal. CCP § 704.100(c).

290 Keogh Plans with multiple participants are protected under ERISA.

291 See Cal. CCP § 704.115(a),(b),(d).

292 See Cal. CCP § 704.050.

293 See Cal. CCP § 704.140(b).

294 See Cal. CCP § 704.140(d).

295 See Cal. CCP § 704.150(b).

296 See Cal. CCP § 703.030(b).

297 See Cal. CCP § 704.010(d).

298 See Cal. CCP § 704.080(b)(2),(4).

299 See Cal. CCP § 704.080(b)(1),(3).
300 See Cal. CCP § 704.100(a).
301 See Cal. CCP § 704.110(b).
302 See Cal. CCP § 704.120(a).
303 See Cal. CCP § 704.120(b).
304 See Cal. CCP § 704.130(a).
305 See Cal. CCP §§ 704.140(a), 704.150(a).
306 See Cal. CCP §§ 703.520, 704.740(b).
307 See Cal. CCP § 706.020.
308 See Cal. CCP § 706.109 and Comment thereto.
309 See 42 U.S.C. § 407–Assignment of benefits:

> (a) In general, the right of any person to any future payment under this subchapter shall not be transferable or assignable, at law or in equity, and none of the moneys paid or payable or rights existing under this subchapter shall be subject to execution, levy, attachment, garnishment, or other legal process, or to the operation of any bankruptcy or insolvency law.

Also, see 11 U.S.C. § 522 –Exemptions:

(d)(10): The debtor's right to receive—

- (A) a social security benefit, unemployment compensation, or a local public assistance benefit;
- (B) a veterans' benefit;
- (C) a disability, illness, or unemployment benefit.

310 See *Matter of Smiley,* 864 F.2d 562, 567 (7th Cir. 1989).
311 See *Matter of Smiley,* 864 F.2d 562 (7th Cir. 1989).
312 See *Addison v. Seaver,* No. 06-6060MN, 2007 Bankr. LEXIS 972 (BAP 8th Cir. Mar. 30, 2007).
313 Where amounts are not listed, there is no limit on the asset's value.
314 Equity is the value of an asset you own minus what's owed on it, including any debts listed as collateral.
315 For most people, it will be 75 percent of their wages which will be exempt.

316 See http://law.justia.com/codes/new-york/2006/partnership/ptr0101_101.html.

317 *Lawrence v. Goldberg* (*In re Lawrence*), 279 F.3d 1294, 1300 (11th Cir. 2002); *Oliner v. Kontribecki*, 305 B.R. 510 (2004, N.D. Cal.); *Securities and Exchange Commission v. Solow*, 682 F. Supp. 2d 1312 (2010); *Hobby v. Georgia Power Company*, Civil Action No. 1:01-cv-1407 (2006); *In re Advanced Telecommunication Network, Inc., Debtor. Advanced Telecommunication Network, Inc. v. Daniel W. Allen*, Case No. 6:03-bk-00299-KSJ, Chapter 11, Adversary No. 6:03-ap-122 (2011).

318 *Oliner v. Kontrabecki*, 305 B.R. 510 (2004).

319 *SEC v. Bilzerian*, 131 F. Supp. 2d 10 (D.C. 01/12/2001).

320 IRS rules require the filing of IRS Form 8886 (Reportable Transaction Disclosure Statement) once funding of a Foreign Asset Protection Trust has occurred.

321 This is not true with respect to certain arbitration awards because of the growing importance of international arbitration as a means of settling international commercial disputes. There is the convention on the recognition and enforcement of Foreign Arbitral Awards.

322 According to Asset Protection for Business Owners and High-Income Owners by Alan Northcott, page 154.

323 See Rev. Proc. 2002-69.

324 Nevis uses a fair value argument to get around the appearance of a fraudulent conveyance.

325 A disclaimer/waiver of an inheritance has never been determined to be a Fraudulent Conveyance.

326 Lawyers routinely send and receive settlement communications marked "Privileged and Confidential Pursuant to California Evidence Code Sections 1152 and 1154." These statutes make settlement communications inadmissible to prove or dispute liability. However, settlement communications can be sought in discovery and later admitted into evidence for purposes other than to attack liability.

327 2703(d) orders are issued under 18 U.S.C. § 2703(d), part of the Stored Communications Act, and they fall somewhere in between a subpoena and a warrant.

328 Only applies to electronic communications at least six months old or older.

329 Identity Theft Victims Hit All-Time High in 2010. Approximately 8.6 million households had at least one person age twelve or older who experienced identity theft victimization in 2010, according to the Bureau of Justice Statistics (BJS). This is a huge increase, as only 6.4 million households were victimized in 2005.

330 See Internal Revenue Code Section 104 (a) (2), which is explained by Revenue Ruling 79-220.

331 Punitive damages received after August 20, 1996, unless pursuant to a written binding agreement, court decree, or mediation award in effect on or issued on or before September 13, 1995, or included in gross income under Section 104(a)(2).

332 See http://wiki.answers.com/Q/How_many_of_the_lawsuits_filed_every_year_are_settled_out_of_court.

333 Source: Wikipedia at http://en.wikipedia.org/wiki/Lawsuit.

334 In order for the structured settlement to be tax free, the claimant must give up the rights of control over the fund. Otherwise, the IRS will deem this a "constructive receipt" and the claimant will lose the tax-free advantages. However, prior to accepting the structured settlement, the claimant has some flexibility in negotiating the terms and conditions of the structured settlement.

335 However, be careful of reversionary annuities because they may be "refundable" if the beneficiary dies, which prevents payment of the benefits to heirs. It is suggested therefore that a guarantee with the insurance company be contracted for, such as "life with twenty years certain." This means that

the insurance company will pay for twenty years whether or not the claimant lives for twenty years.

336 Are you having trouble keeping up with your mortgage payments? Have you received a notice from your lender asking you to contact them? Don't ignore the letters from your lender. Contact your lender immediately, or contact a HUD-approved housing counseling agency at (800) 569-4287 (toll-free).

337 The Federal Housing Administration (FHA), which is a part of the US Department of Housing and Urban Development (HUD), is working aggressively to halt and reverse the losses represented by foreclosure. Through its National Servicing Center (NSC), FHA offers a number of various loss mitigation programs and informational resources to assist FHA-insured homeowners and home equity conversion mortgage (HECM) borrowers facing financial hardship or unemployment and whose mortgage is either in default or at risk of default.

The NSC Loss Mitigation Programs may be able to help you. FHA staff are available to help answer your questions and assist you to better understand your options as an FHA borrower under these loss mitigation programs. There are several ways you can contact FHA for more information, including: Call the NSC at (877) 622-8525 or call the FHA Outreach Center at 1-800-CALL FHA (800-225-5342).

HOPE for Homeowners (H4H): The HOPE for Homeowners Program will refinance mortgages for borrowers who are having difficulty making their payments, but can afford a new FHA-insured loan. Call (800) 225-5342 for more information.

FHA Home Equity Conversion Mortgage Program (HECM) may be able to help.

338 Tips to Avoid Scams: The Federal Trade Commission—Watch the Foreclosure Rescue Scams Video on the FTC's

YouTube Channel. Office of the Comptroller of the Currency—The U.S. Department of the Treasury's Office of the Comptroller of the Currency provides tips and materials to help homeowners avoid mortgage modification and foreclosure rescue scams. The Loan Modification Scam Prevention Network—The Loan Modification Scam Prevention Network is a national coalition of governmental and private organizations created by Fannie Mae, Freddie Mac, Neighbor Works America™ and the Lawyers' Committee for Civil Rights Under Law to provide resources to educate homeowners about the dangers of loan modification scams and support federal, state and local efforts to combat these scams. If you believe you have been the victim of a scam, you should file a complaint with the Federal Trade Commission (FTC). Visit the FTC's online Complaint Assistant or call 1-877-FTC-HELP (1-877-382-4357). Also visit www.StopFraud.gov.

339 See http://www.makinghomeaffordable.gov/pages/default.aspx.

340 Employee Retirement Income Security Act (ERISA).

341 Under some circumstances a creditor may sue to set aside a transfer of property by a debtor, where the transfer defrauds that creditor. (Civ. Code, § 3439 et seq., the Uniform Fraudulent Transfer Act.) A well-established principle of the law of fraudulent transfers is, "A transfer in fraud of creditors may be attacked only by one who is injured by the transfer. Mere intent to delay or defraud is not sufficient; injury to the creditor must be shown affirmatively. In other words, prejudice to the plaintiff is essential. It cannot be said that a creditor has been injured unless the transfer puts beyond [her] reach property [she] otherwise would be able to subject to the payment of [her] debt." (16 Cal.Jur.3d (rev.) Creditors' Rights and Remedies, § 430, p. 540, fns. omitted; *Bennett v. Paulson* (1935) 7 Cal.App.2d 120, 123; *Haskins v. Certified Escrow & Mtge. Co.* (1950)

96 Cal.App.2d 688, 691; 37 Am.Jur.2d (2001) Fraudulent Conveyances and Transfers, § 157, p. 644; 37 C.J.S. (1997) Fraudulent Conveyances, § 46, p. 579.

342 International Postal Money Orders: Always valid—they never expire. Available in values up to $700 each if sending abroad. Cashable in 29 countries. Can also be cashed or negotiated at your bank and other financial institutions. May be replaceable if damaged, lost, or stolen. Just hold on to your purchase receipt.

343 *Finalco, Inc. v. Roosevelt*, 87 F.3d 311 (1996, 9th Circuit).

344 Texas and Florida are the only two states with an unlimited homestead exemption.

345 Effective October 17, 2005.

346 Pursuant to 11 U.S.C. § 548.

347 These are the most common situations for a fraudulent transfer. There are other much less common ways for a fraudulent transfer, but we won't concern ourselves about these transfers.

348 See California Civil Code § 3439.04.

349 See California Code of Civil Procedure § 338.

350 Total Fees Collected at Time of Bankruptcy Filing:
Chapter 7-$306
Chapter 9-$1046
Chapter 11-$1046
Chapter 12-$246
Chapter 13-$281
Chapter 15-$1046

351 Fee waiver provisions set forth in Section 418 of the Bankruptcy Abuse Prevention and Consumer Protection Act of 2005 (Pub. L. No. 109-8, 199 Stat. 23), and codified at 28 U.S.C. § 1930(f)(1-3).

352 Restructuring is done under chapter 9 for municipalities, chapter 12 for farmers, and chapter 15 for international entities.

353 The Bankruptcy Abuse Prevention and Consumer Act of 2005 ("BAPCPA").

354 Bankruptcy Code § 303. Where the debtor has twelve or more creditors, at least three creditors holding unsecured claims totaling at least $13,475 that are not contingent as to liability or the subject of a bona fide dispute as to liability or amount must join in the filing of the involuntary bankruptcy petition. Where the debtor has fewer than twelve otherwise eligible unsecured creditors, excluding any employee or insider and any transferee of a voidable transfer, such as a preference and fraudulent conveyance claim, then one such unsecured creditor with a claim of at least $13,475 that is not subject to a bona fide dispute as to liability or amount, can file an involuntary bankruptcy petition. However, single creditor petitions are very risky and should be the exception rather than the rule.

355 Congress imposed several criteria to compel an involuntary bankruptcy: (1) First, each filing creditor must prove that their claim is not subject to a dispute, e.g. debtor's challenge to liability or the amount of damages, *and* that the debtor must not be paying his nondisputed debts; or (2) the debtor transferred substantially all of his assets to a third party such as a trustee or receiver, e.g., a voluntary assignment of assets for the benefit of creditors in a state court proceeding or in an out-of-court settlement triggers the right to involuntary bankruptcy if filed within 120 days of the debtor's transfer. And finally, the most important requirement for a creditor's involuntary bankruptcy petition is that the petition be filed in good faith. A court will dismiss a petition upon determination that the creditor's motives were in bad faith. The historical purpose of involuntary bankruptcy was to prevent unfairness to creditors as a group caused by ensuring fair and proportionate distribution of a debtor's nonexempt assets. Involuntary bankruptcy properly should be imposed to prevent a debtor from fraudulently convey-

ing assets or from giving preferential payments to favored creditors. Courts will dismiss involuntary bankruptcy petitions filed for improper purpose such as malice, harassment, or other improper use of bankruptcy procedures. Applying this standard, courts have dismissed involuntary bankruptcy petitions which were designed to shut down a debtor corporation's business, to gain settlement leverage, or which were used as a substitute for customary state court collection. Most bankruptcy courts will not allow involuntary bankruptcy to be used as a creditor collection tool employed by an aggressive creditor. The appropriate use of involuntary bankruptcy is preserving assets and enforcement of fairness among a group of creditors. The main reason involuntary bankruptcy petitions are rare is the creditor's liability for filing an unsuccessful petition. In most cases damages and fees may be awarded even the absence of bad faith!

356 This cap does not apply if you bought your home with the proceeds from selling another home in that state.

357 The federal bankruptcy exemptions are a list of exemptions available to bankruptcy filers in certain states.

358 11 USC § 522(d)(1), (5).

359 11 USC § 522(d)(2).

360 11 USC § 522(d)(3).

361 11 USC § 522(d)(4).

362 11 USC § 522(d)(9).

363 11 USC § 522(d)(11)(B).

364 11 USC § 522(d)(11)(D).

365 11 USC § 522(d)(11)I.

366 11 USC § 522(b)(3)(C).

367 11 USC § 522(b)(3)(C)(n).

368 11 USC § 522(d)(10)(A).

369 11 USC § 522(d)(11)(A).

370 11 USC § 522(d)(6).

371 11 USC § 522(d)(10)(D).

372 11 USC § 522(d)(7).

373 11 USC § 522(d)(8).

374 11 USC § 522(d)(10)(C).

375 11 USC § 522(d)(11)(C).

376 11 USC § 522(d)(5).

377 http://www.uscourts.gov/News/NewsView/11-11-07/Bankruptcy_Filings_Down_in_Fiscal_Year_2011.aspx.

378 Even most salesmen who sell asset protection wrongly believe that bankruptcy is designed to help a debtor.

379 To get the "fresh start" discharge, the debtor has to comply with all of the bankruptcy rules. Failure to comply with the bankruptcy rules and/or perpetrating bankruptcy fraud will deny the debtor a discharge. Debtors must continue to pay their debts as they come due. (See Bankruptcy Code § 303(h)).

380 See *In re Smith,* 437 B.R. 817 (Bkrpt.N.D.Tex., Oct. 12, 2010); *In re Moss*, 249 B.R. 411, 424 (Bankr.N.D.Tex.2000) (exception to one of the technical requirements of sec. 303(b) exists when there is fraud, trick, artifice or scam by an alleged debtor); *In re Norriss Bros. Lumber Co., Inc.,* 133 B.R. 599 (Bankr.N.D.Tex.1991).

381 IRS tax law allows you to step up the basis of your home after one of the spouses dies.

382 See IRS §§ 671 – 679.

383 A female executor is termed an executrix.

384 Today, these "boilerplate" living trusts are so ubiquitous that you can easily find them on the Internet, often for free. But you are cautioned to seek professional consultation before preparing and signing this important legal document.

385 However, any protected assets contained inside a living trust will continue to be protected.

386 A female conservator is termed a conservatrix.

387 Conservatorships are often used in situations in which someone can no longer manage his or her own financial affairs or personal care. A conservatorship is a court-supervised proceeding that can involve substantial legal fees.

388 A procedure known as a Heggstad petition, avoids a full probate of the assets that were not transferred to the living trust by changing their titles. It is based on a California case, *Estate of Heggstad*, 16 CA 4th 943 (1993).

389 In 2013, the estate tax rate exclusion is $5.25 million.

390 The lifetime gift exemption in 2013 is $5.25 million.

391 Portability applies only to estates of those who died after Jan. 1, 2011.

392 This also represents a HIPAA authorization.

393 The financial directive includes a durable power of attorney for financial purposes.

394 See *Bennis v. Michigan*, 516 U.S. 442 (1996). Also, if a guest in your home does something illegal during their stay, your property can be seized. And you're not innocent until proven guilty in such cases. Rather, it's up to you to prove your innocence or lose your property.

395 *Austin v. United States*, 509 U.S. 602 (1993); *United States v. Bajakajian*, 524 U.S. 321 (1998).

396 See 18 U.S.C. § 981(a)(1)(C); 18 U.S.C. § 1956(c)(7)(B); 18 U.S.C. § 1961(1); 18 U.S.C. § 982 et seq.; Most criminal offenses allow for asset forfeiture.

397 References:

Lectlaw, s.v. "Quitclaim Deed," retrieved 10 Feb 2011; LexisNexis, s.v. "Property: The Deed," retrieved 14 Feb 2011; Wilken, JD, Sean; Theresa Villiers (February 2003). The Law of Waiver, Variation and Estoppel (2nd ed.). Oxford University Press USA. ISBN 0-19-925321-8; Dukeminier, Jesse; James Krier, Gregory Alexander, Michael Schill (March 2006). Property (7th ed.). Aspen Publishers. ISBN 0-7355-8899-6.

398 To avoid the automatic right of survivorship for the surviving tenant, some other form of ownership should be used, such as tenancy in common.

399 References:

Brickwood v. Young, (1905) 2 CLR 387; 11 ALR 154;

http://www.andysirkin.com/HTMLArticle.cfm?Article=1; Denis Clifford, Plan Your Estate, Nolo, 9th ed. (April 2008), p. 168 Kurtz, Hovenkamp. Cases and Materials on American Property Law, Fifth Edition. Chapter 5: Concurrent Estates.

400 www.andysirkin.com/HTMLArticle.cfm?Article=1

401 The top Estate Tax rate may increase in 2013 to 55%.

402 Except for pensions established before 1985.

403 Gifts exceeding $13,000.

404 The asset has to be valued over $13,000.

405 This is a pour-over will.

406 According to Wealthcare.com.

407 Also, this provision is only valid if the beneficiary has something to lose if they contest the will. The last section of a noncontest provision is called a "gift over" and covers what will happen to the forfeited estate if a beneficiary purses a will contest. Without the "gift over" your noncontest provision is considered invalid.

408 The Deficit Reduction Act of 2005 establishes severe new restrictions on the ability of the elderly to transfer assets before qualifying for nursing home care under Medicaid coverage. The law extends Medicaid's "look-back" period for all asset transfers to five years (it was originally 3 years), and changes the start of the penalty period for transferred assets from the date of the transfer to the date when the individual enters the nursing home. Qualification to enter the nursing home occurs when the individual is out of funds, meaning he or she cannot afford to pay for the nursing home. The effective date for the new federal law is February 8, 2006.

409 See 11 U.S.C. 522 (d)(10)(E).

410 See 11 U.S.C. 522 (d)(10)(E):

(i) such plan or contract was established by or under the auspices of an insider that employed the debtor at the time the debtor's rights under such plan or contract arose;

(ii) such payment is on account of age or length of service; and

(iii) such plan or contract does not qualify under section 401(a), 403(a), 403(b), or 408 of the Internal Revenue Code of 1986.

411 Fla. Stat. Ann. § 222.14: Exemption of cash surrender value of life insurance policies and annuity contracts from legal process. The cash surrender values of life insurance policies issued upon the lives of citizens or residents of the state and the proceeds of annuity contracts issued to citizens or residents of the state, upon whatever form, shall not in any case be liable to attachment, garnishment or legal process in favor of any creditor of the person whose life is so insured or of any creditor of the person who is the beneficiary of such annuity contract, unless the insurance policy or annuity contract was effected for the benefit of such creditor.

412 See *Patterson v. Shumate*, 504 U.S. 753 (1992). (A debtor's interest in an ERISA pension plan is excluded from the bankruptcy estate and not subject to attachment by creditors.)

413 Bankruptcy Abuse Prevention and Consumer Protection Act of 2005 (BAPCPA).

414 Source: National Bureau of Economic Research, www.nber.org, 2004.

415 See *Yates v. Hendon,* 541 US 1 (2004).

416 See section 206(d) and IRC section 401 (a) (13).

417 IRC § 414 (p) and ERISA § 206 (d) (3).

418 *McCaferty v. McCaferty*, 96 F.3d 192 (6th Cir. 1996).

419 Treasury regulations section 1.401 (a) -13 (b).

420 Under IRC § 401 (a) (13) (C) and ERISA § 206 (d) (4).

421 IRC § 401 (a) (13).

422 See *United States v. Tyson*, 265 F. Supp. 2d. 788 (ED. Mich. 2003); *United States v. Clark,* No. 02-X-74872 (E.D. Mich.

June 11, 2003); *United States v. Rice*, 196 F.Supp. 1196 (N.D. Okla. 2002).

423 Please note that IRAs, which are protected under ERISA, do not enjoy antialienation protection!

424 $15,000 in the State of Maine.

425 Individual Retirement Accounts—Tax-deferred savings plans account for roughly one-third of the assets held in retirement savings accounts. Americans have invested nearly $4.8 trillion in IRAs and hold another $10.2 trillion in assets held in employer-sponsored retirement accounts, according to the 2011 Retirement Market Insights published by Spectrem Group.

426 Clients with SEP or SIMPLE IRA assets under $1 million can roll over these assets and avoid the potential problems with SEP and SIMPLE IRAs outside of bankruptcy.

427 Annuities are protected (exempt) with certain exceptions under 11 U.S.C. 522 (d)(10)(E) "to the extent reasonably necessary for the support of the debtor and any dependent of the debtor."

428 See *Rousey v. Jacoway*, 544 U.S. 320 (2005).

429 See 11 U.S.C. § 522 (n).

430 Unpublished decision in *Willis v. Menotte*, 11th Circuit Court of Appeals, 2011.

431 See *Lowenschuss v. Selnick*, 98-1529203/17/99.

432 See *Rhiel v. Adams (In re Adams)*, 302 B.R. 535, 540 (B.A.P. 6th Cir. 2003); Also, see § 541(c)(2) of the Bankruptcy Act.

433 See *Hoult v. Hoult*, 1st Circuit 2004.

434 See Internal Revenue Code § 664.

435 See www.rexwyon.com/captive.htm.

436 See 11 U.S.C. § 541 (c)(2)—A restriction on the transfer of a beneficial interest of the debtor in a trust that is enforceable under applicable nonbankruptcy law is enforceable in a case under this title.

437 See Internal Revenue Code § 2701.

438 Delaware; Illinois; Iowa; Nevada; Oklahoma; Tennessee; Texas; Utah; Wisconsin; Kansas.

439 Note: A number of asset protection books that the author has reviewed contain significant errors and consequently cannot be recommended. On the other hand, however, Jay Adkisson's books on asset protection are amongst the best, and they are very accurate and the author is pleased to recommend them. Moreover, Mr. Adkisson has an excellent website for your review.

440 Bankruptcy Abuse Prevention and Consumer Protection Act (BAPCPA).

Made in United States
North Haven, CT
10 November 2026

22106118R00272